The Anti-Politics Machine in India

Anti-politics rests on antipathy to a particular kind of politics, which is political in itself. Quite simply put, anti-politics is merely another type of politics.

James Ferguson's memorable metaphor of development as an 'Anti-Politics Machine' that serves to entrench state power and depoliticize development continues to appeal to those cynical of the widespread tendency of development discourses to treat various issues apolitically. The book considers this problem in India, a country where post-independence development planners have adopted a scientific stance and claimed to distance themselves from mass politics, yet the groundswell of democratic political mobilization has been considerable in recent decades. The book examines key transformations towards decentralization and participatory development within a technocratic state watershed development programme. Based on an interrogation of the idea of anti-politics and a careful reading of state watershed policy, the book shows that depoliticization is first of all about characterizing politics in particular ways and giving it selected meanings. With extensive primary research in two states, Andhra Pradesh and Madhya Pradesh, it then goes on to show that the adoption of a strategy of depoliticization depends on specific political and institutional configurations of decentralization with a range of different outcomes. This is an account of how 'development as anti-politics machine' actually plays out in practice.

Vasudha Chhotray is a lecturer in Development Studies at the University of East Anglia, UK.

The Anti-Politics Machine in India

State, Decentralization and Participatory Watershed Development

Vasudha Chhotray

ANTHEM PRESS
LONDON · NEW YORK · DELHI

Anthem Press
An imprint of Wimbledon Publishing Company
www.anthempress.com

This edition first published in UK and USA 2011
by ANTHEM PRESS
75-76 Blackfriars Road, London SE1 8HA, UK
or PO Box 9779, London SW19 7ZG, UK
and
244 Madison Ave. #116, New York, NY 10016, USA

Cover design by Devdas Chhotray and Jyoti Ranjan Swain

British Library Cataloguing in Publication Data
A catalogue record for this book is available from the British Library.

Library of Congress Cataloging in Publication Data
A catalog record for this book has been requested.

ISBN-13: 978 0 85728 767 0 (Hbk)
ISBN-10: 0 85728 767 2 (Hbk)

This title is also available as an eBook.

CONTENTS

List of Maps and Tables   vii

Acknowledgements   ix

Introduction
The Anti-Politics Machine in India   xv

Chapter One
The Idea of 'Anti-Politics'   1

Chapter Two
The Indian 'Anti-Politics Machine'   25

Chapter Three
The Anti-Politics Watershed Machine: The Making
of Watershed Development in India   51

Chapter Four
Two Landscapes of Decentralization   85

Chapter Five
Depoliticizing Local Institutions? Panchayats and
Watershed Committees   119

Chapter Six
The Dialectics of Consent in Participatory Practice   155

Conclusion   195

Notes   207

References   219

Index   231

LIST OF MAPS AND TABLES

Maps

1. India showing Andhra Pradesh and Madhya Pradesh   xi

2. Veldurthi Mandal, Kurnool district, Andhra Pradesh   xii

3. Tonk-Khurd and Bagli tehsils, Dewas district, Madhya Pradesh   xiii

Tables

1. Financial performance 1997–2001, Lilapuram watershed project   170

2. Financial performance 1998–2001, Malligundu watershed project   176

3. Physical and financial achievements under Kishangarh watershed project   181

4. Principal changes in land use, Neelpura   186

5. Land area devoted to food and non-food crops, Neelpura   186

ACKNOWLEDGEMENTS

This book draws on my doctoral research which I carried out nearly ten years ago at the School of Oriental and African Studies (SOAS) in London. It has taken ten years, and journeys through two other Universities, at Manchester and now Norwich in East Anglia, for me to write it fully. It bears the imprint of these institutions, especially SOAS, my alma mater, where over formal supervisions and informal conversations I was exposed to the many debates I have pursued in the book. I wish first of all to acknowledge the teachers, colleagues and friends in these institutions who have been endlessly patient with my ideas. I also want to thank the Felix Trust for awarding me a doctoral fellowship at SOAS and the Economic and Social Research Council (ESRC), UK for giving me a postdoctoral fellowship, without which I could not have carried out this research.

I am deeply grateful to my PhD supervisor, guide and confidante Rathin Roy for his inspiration and nurturing, and for critically reading not just the thesis, but also the full draft of the book. Rathin has had a seminal influence on my approach to critical thinking, and his incisive reviews have helped me construct and refine the key elements of this research. I want to thank David Mosse and Maureen Mackintosh, whom I was privileged to have as PhD examiners, and for their extremely constructive and exciting engagement. I was exceptionally lucky to discuss so many of these ideas with Stuart Corbridge, who has been warm and generous in his support in the years since. There are many others who have at different points helped to improve my ideas. They are Sudipta Kaviraj, Subir Sinha, Sangeeta Kamath, David Hulme, Sam Hickey, Phil Woodhouse, Diana Mitlin, Rene Veron and David Owen. I am especially indebted to Gerry Stoker for his encouragement and a post-doctoral opportunity that any young researcher can only dream about. I thank them all for enriching the perspectives contained in this book. I am particularly grateful to Professor John Dunn for his remarks on a paper presented at the University of Southampton in March 2008, where I was treated to his exclusive attention to my ideas. I would like to acknowledge the anonymous referees of Development and Change, the Journal of Development Studies and Contemporary South Asia, where papers relating to this study have appeared in previous years. I want to thank Thomas Sikor for always taking an interest in my ideas, and for reading draft chapters with his graduate students and offering me very high-quality critical feedback. Janet Seeley has been generous with information and support. My own students here at the School of International Development in the University of East Anglia have received and challenged my ideas. Lastly, I am very grateful to the two anonymous reviewers of the manuscript for their generous and insightful comments.

My fieldwork in India spanned fourteen long months, where I received the generous hospitality, assistance and support of many different persons. I want to acknowledge them all with warmth and gratitude. Satyanand and Yashodhara Mishra, Rashmi and Sanjeev Shami, Sunil Chaturvedi, Snehalatha, Satya Mishra, Tirupat Reddy and Srinivas Reddy not only helped me at every step but also opened their homes to me. I want to thank B. N. Yugandhar, Sanjay Gupta, S. P. Tucker, Gauri Singh, Hariranjan Rao, all bureaucrats par excellence, for their frank and valuable insights.

My fieldwork with Samaj Pragati Sahyog in Dewas was a very special part of my fieldwork, and I thank the wonderful members of this organization for their kind hospitality. Dr Mihir Shah and Rangu Rao educated me patiently on so many different issues, Vijayashankar guided me through my fieldwork and gave me his friendship, and Nivedita Rao always made sure that I was comfortable in Bagli. I would like to thank Deven and Rajaram for their camaraderie and motorcycle rides into the villages. I was very lucky to have a wonderful and loyal group of research assistants, and my special thanks to Mukesh and Ram Prakash for their affection and patience. To Sunita and Vani, my interpreters in Kurnool, I owe appreciation for their intelligent and perceptive assistance.

I would like to express my deep affection and gratitude to the people of the villages where I spent precious time learning about India.

In the ten years I have taken to write this book, I have acquired the debt of so many wonderful friendships that have sustained me. My friend Anasuya Mathur has kept me sane by showing a healthy scepticism of academic preoccupations. Atreyee Sen, Priya Das, Farhad Vania, Jonathan Pattenden, Carina Vanrooyen, Rajiv Narayan, Lopamudra Mohanty, Anju Yadav, Adarsh Kumar, Amitabh Behar and Elissaios Papyrakis have each supported me at different stages of my writing and work. Prafulla Mohanty and Derek Moore, and Prodeepta and Kaumudi Das gave me a home in London each time the strains of student life grew too heavy to bear.

Chris gave me his unflinching love and support, and soothed me during my endless ups and downs. Without him, not much would have been possible.

I am grateful to my mother for her love and for trying, even if not always succeeding, to instill in me a sense of balance, and to my brother, for lightening my worries with humour. To my father, I owe my greatest debt, for giving me confidence and courage. It is to him this book is dedicated.

Map 1. India showing Andhra Pradesh and Madhya Pradesh.

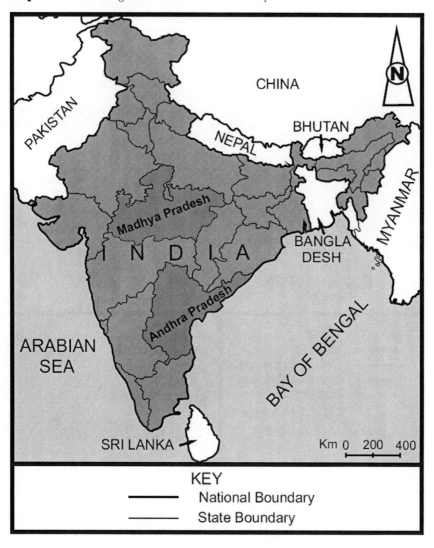

Map 2. Veldurthi Mandal, Kurnool district, Andhra Pradesh.

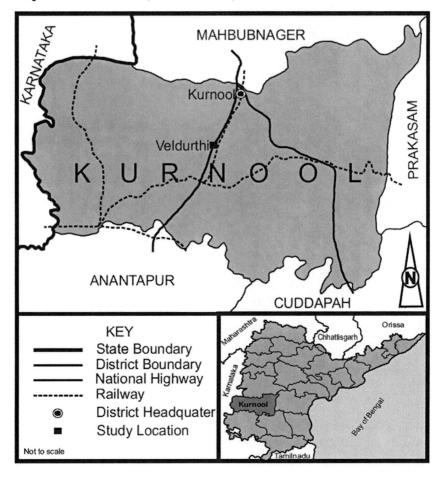

Map 3. Tonk-Khurd and Bagli tehsils, Dewas district, Madhya Pradesh.

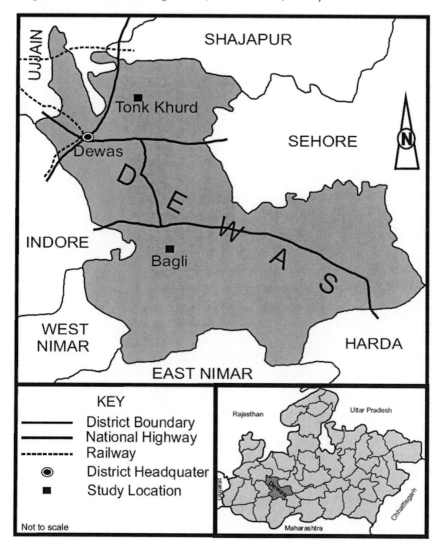

Introduction

THE ANTI-POLITICS MACHINE
IN INDIA

India is often described as a country of paradoxes. There are skyscrapers and slums, free newspapers and moral policing, global achievers and never-schooled children, deserts and flood plains. It is also amongst the world's most vibrant and reliable democracies. The remarkable life history of Indian democracy since its independence from colonial rule in 1947 has brought about the irrevocable expansion of popular politics. Paradoxically, while India is feted for its democratic institutions and processes, the politics that accompanies these institutions and processes has been subject to a great deal of disparagement. Such cynicism seems to affect a generally negative perception of what democratic politics and politicians can deliver: efficient services in cities, proper disbursement of state welfare in villages and security against terror. This irritation with politics and politicians was initially observed as part of an elite urban discourse (Hansen 1999), but researchers documenting talk, gestures and strategic manoeuvring amidst a cross-section of social groups even in rural India have noted the description of politics as 'dirty' and 'morally ambivalent' (Osella and Osella 2001, Ruud 2001).

In this book, I am concerned with such cynicism about politics; but more specifically, I am interested in examining the notion that development is indeed apolitical, or devoid of politics, no matter how trenchant the view of political influences, processes and behaviour. Indeed, my purpose is to question the very belief that implementers of development are wilfully engaged in keeping politics away from development. The idea that politics is messy, constitutive of particularistic agendas and therefore not conducive for development has accompanied development planning in India. Indeed, a discourse of 'rational' and 'neutral' planning for development that could tower over the narrow interests of politics has characterized the 'Indian developmental state' from the outset. That was at a time when it was fashionable to approach development in a top-down manner, through the acknowledged expertise of planners and bureaucrats. It was even acceptable to justify the exclusion of people from decision-making about development.

This is not the case any longer. The expansion of democratic politics together with the now accepted wisdom that people must have a say in decisions that impact upon their lives has meant a near fanatical obsession with participation. Decentralization in different forms has been emulated ostensibly in order to bring about maximum participation in government. Decentralization policies are informed by a mix of influences ranging from making big government smaller and more responsive towards local needs to facilitating robust community-level engagement in its own decision-making. The idea is to promote participation through a variety of imaginative decentralization policies, but somewhat paradoxically, these policies are commonly informed by a strong desire to prescribe and bureaucratize participation, to render it apolitical and generally isolate participatory development from the 'menace' of politics. These tensions have widely resonated in critical academic analyses and there is a rich literature that frowns upon development policies, programmes and practices that portray development apolitically.

I was first confronted with this attitude in the course of my doctoral research when I interviewed government officials responsible for administering watershed development projects in Kurnool district in Andhra Pradesh. Watershed development is a soil and water conservation based rural livelihoods programme that has become the subject of intense attention since the 1990s for its adoption of innovative measures towards decentralized and participatory decision-making. I noticed how these officials commonly said that their projects 'were interested in participation, not politics'. At first, I was not sure of what they meant. As I spent more time in and around the project villages in this part of India, interviewing both government officials and villagers, I realized that a lexicon of politics shared particularly by officials and village elites was in use. Politics was being referred to as shorthand for all manner of distasteful but widely prevalent activities, ranging from corruption to factionalism to violent conflict. These were activities that could easily be described as destructive and distracting especially when contrasted with the constructive and serious business of development. It was also directed against the involvement of elected political representatives in watershed development.

Equally, a few months later when I travelled to another part of India, to Dewas district in Madhya Pradesh, to observe the same development programme in a different location, I found that such antipathy to politics, especially with respect to the involvement of political representatives, was not being openly expressed by government officials. I even encountered a more radical politics being embraced for the purposes of participation by an NGO responsible for implementing a state-funded watershed project. I became gradually interested in how different agencies and actors engaged in the same development programme were both describing and engaging politics. The question that posed itself to me was whether these descriptions and engagements were purely coincidental, down to individual whims and fortuitous coincidences, or as a result of how actors and agencies were being influenced by their larger contexts. I also became concerned with whether such talk about politics was tantamount to empty and insignificant posturing or indeed producing significant effects. The pursuit of these questions is the principal business of this book. In the rest of this chapter I will lay out the analytical terrain within which I will address these questions.

Politics within 'Anti-Politics'

The idea of development as an 'anti-politics machine' was memorably put forward by anthropologist James Ferguson in 1990 in his analysis of a donor-driven development project in the southern African country of Lesotho. Ferguson was gripped by the unintended effects that development was capable of unleashing. He argued that while the project may not have met its stated objectives of agricultural development or livestock keeping, it did nevertheless have the significant effect of consolidating and entrenching bureaucratic state power in Lesotho, especially in the Thaba-Tseka region where the project was based. Moreover, he documented how project officials regularly used a discourse of development that described poverty in apolitical terms warranting a technical solution, and as a strictly national matter that could be resolved by country-based development agencies. He observed that they made little or no reference to the rather more complex and contentious issues that impacted upon poverty, such as the relations of economic subordination and political subjugation with South Africa. Development, he concluded, was an 'anti-politics machine' that entrenched bureaucratic state power (the 'institutional' effect) and 'depoliticized' poverty (the 'ideological' effect). This image of development as a robotic machine expediently flicking off a button called politics has endured ever since. The metaphor is a strong one and finds appeal with a wide range of critical observers who disapprove of development organizations internationally, nationally and locally eschewing explicit and adequate political engagement. Their writings encompass a rich and stimulating literature critiquing the rational models and technical discourses that strip poverty and development of politics as well as history.

While these criticisms are significant, they do not adequately explore why it is that politics becomes the subject of so much distrust within the official and influential narratives of development. As a student of politics, or political science as it is still referred to in many parts of the world, I understood politics to be the gateway to a fascinating world of collective decision-making of which we were inescapably a part. The result of this broad-based focus has been to bring nearly every conceivable aspect of human existence into the fold of the study of politics: rule and resistance, social organization and disintegration, faith and disenchantment, access and exclusion, identity and violence. If politics as a field of study was concerned with such a rich terrain of issues, why had politics as a set of practices become synonymous with a particular kind of individual behaviour, Hobbesian in spirit, that the mere mention of the word was like the invocation of a shared and unquestioned belief that politics was a nasty business, divisive and ultimately futile. Either that, or there was a strategic labelling of politics in these terms, and the crowding out of its more sanguine meanings. Here we should admit upfront that the anti-politics association with development has 'something to do with the failure of politics to deliver' (2008).[1] So at least a part of the anti-politics characterization of development is an accurate assessment of how politics often is, worthy of cynicism. While it may be a good thing to be suspicious of politics, as is implicit in development's anti-politics character, is it at all complete as a concrete strategy? In the words of John Dunn, 'there is never no political dimension and the political dimension is never trivial' (ibid). Taking this pronouncement as a reasonable guide to the presence of politics, it is not difficult to establish that it is in fact never the case that the development apparatus successfully strips development practices of politics. However we are still left with the powerful idea that development discourses have been and often are profoundly apolitical.

Ferguson's critics have pointed to the need for a more nuanced analysis. The perhaps implicit conclusion that depoliticization or other unintended effects of development unfold inevitably in all scenarios has been questioned (as by Tordella 2003). The point is mainly about not reducing development to a homogenous experience, and accepting that not all development projects, programmes and policies seek to depoliticize. The second main criticism is the demotion of agency within Ferguson's conceptual approach. Development anthropologist David Mosse (2004) takes exception to the conclusion that development's unintended effects could apparently occur 'behind the backs or against the wills of even the most powerful actors' (1990, 18). For Mosse, such emphasis on the 'anonymous automaticity' of the machine is plainly misleading, for it obscures the 'complexity of policy as an institutional practice' and disregards the 'diversity of interests behind policy models and the perspectives of actors themselves' (2004, 644). He goes as far as to say 'little wonder that critics such as Ferguson apparently spend so little of their time talking to development workers' (ibid, 644).

So the argument that depoliticization of development is not inevitable has been made, and my enquiry embodies this spirit of uncertainty, that unless proven and empirically demonstrated, we can neither assume the coherent presence of the anti-politics machine nor its successful operation.

Depoliticization relies on the representation of places or processes in particular ways. Even after establishing that a state embodies elements of an anti-politics machine with respect to its development operations, it is worth examining the precise forms or means of representation by which this depoliticization discourse is expressed. Ferguson richly describes the representation of Lesotho as an aboriginal, agricultural, bounded national economy that is amenable to planning and manipulation for development by national development agencies. This account, he argues, underplays the extent of Lesotho's penetration by the capitalist regional economy of southern Africa, its historical role as a labour reserve for South African mining and industry, and the extra-national factors that serve to undermine the effectiveness of national planning. This representation has two sides as Li (2007) correctly identifies in her persuasive thesis on the making and execution of explicit programmes for 'improvement' in Indonesia.

The first is the practice of 'rendering technical' or drawing boundaries around a domain that is to be governed as 'an intelligible field with specifiable limits and particular characteristics' (Li 2007, 7). Here Li is alluding to a well documented phenomenon, the construction of the modern economy, which has been the subject of writings since Karl Polyani in 1944 to Michel Foucault in 1991 (Mitchell 2002). While Polyani focused on the creation of an economy disembedded from wider social networks that had previously shaped it, Foucault argued that the construction of an identifiable and limitable domain called the economy was cardinal to the birth of government in the 18th century. In a similar vein, Ferguson relies heavily on the argument that development experts need to construct an 'intelligible field' that is 'appropriate for intervention' (Li 2007, 7). For Li, the 'will to improve' by trustees responsible for the welfare of people and development experts rests on the translation of concrete and 'calculated' programmes into technical matters, precisely in order to draw firm lines between those who are responsible for detecting the need for improvement and those who are then the subject of this expertise (2007, 7, 12). Boundary creation is essential for sustaining the practice of technical expertise.

But the second equally important dimension to this representation is that issues that are rendered technical are 'simultaneously rendered non-political' (Li 2007, 7). Technical expertise therefore is firmly non-political, thus denying the possibility of forms of expertise that are secured within politics. There are forms of expertise within politics especially in relation to the analysis of situations but this expertise may not necessarily stretch to taking appropriate practical action. For the trustees of welfare and experts of development, this is not necessarily an expertise of a very inspiring kind especially when contrasted to technical authority and epistemic reliability in terms of taking concrete action.[2] In her analysis, Li tries to uncover the content of this anti-politics focus of experts. The exclusion of structural and relational matters from the range of their intervention is predominantly discussed. Such anti-politics is Fergusonian in emphasis: 'they (experts) focus more on the capacities of the poor than on the practices through which one social group impoverishes another' (Li 2007, 7). The other dimension to the programmes of improvement which might be called anti-politics is that these programmes are designed precisely to contain those disgruntled groups, like the poor and marginalized, from challenging the status quo. Li is quick to dismiss conspiracy theorists, maintaining carefully that rather than assuming 'a hidden agenda', the will to improve can be 'taken at its word' (2007, 9).

If the non-political is either the denial of political and economic structures and relationships or the strategic (or guileless, depending on how one views things) deployment of programmes of improvement to preserve configurations of domination, what then is the content of politics? This in my view is a key question since the meanings associated with politics surely play a critical role in the experience and effectiveness of depoliticization. The idea that development is not political must rest on some view of what the political indeed is. Li tackles this question by counter posing politics to government, where governing takes place – in the Foucauldian sense – by containing or bounding specific spheres as technical. Politics on the other hand refers to all those practices that serve to blur these boundaries and demystify government and improvement by throwing up critical challenges. If the purpose of government is to contain and order, the purpose of politics is to rupture and create disorder.

In my understanding, this is a significant characterization of politics and embodies its core purpose, which is surely to foster a wider deliberation of issues that matter and challenge exclusionary and repressive forms of government. It is equally interesting to see how particular meanings of politics are deployed by those charged with the business of development, for these become constitutive of government in a sense as opposed to standing counter to it. How do the various constituents of government – experts, officials, planners and other implementers in tow – actually respond to the imperative of presenting matters as technical and non-political? I am interested in lifting the cloak over depoliticization, in pursuing systematically which meanings of politics predominate in which contexts and why because, as I observed in my research, these were not the same. Moreover, I am keen to expose how the pursuit of such meanings actually produces concrete outcomes for people, by focusing not just on a textual reading of project intentions, but also on the unfolding of such projects into practice. This approach will hopefully allow for well-evidenced critiques of technocratic development that desist from equating development with depoliticization. It could potentially be applied to the international development arena – where issues relating to bureaucratization, technocratic expertise and target driven development (all within a larger umbrella of neoliberalism) prevail – as much as to development initiatives in India as explored in this book.

State policies for decentralized and participatory watershed development India in the 1990s contained a strong thrust towards casting both contentious issues as well as matters to do with collective engagement in technical and non-political terms. They underplayed differentiation and power in local communities, exaggerated the potential of community-based local bodies for participatory decision-making and drew unsustainable dichotomies between these and other more 'political' forms of decentralization that were simultaneously underway. All these rested on a particularly pejorative view of politics and led to the distancing of watershed development from 'politics'. In the villages of Kurnool and Dewas, these ideas were not similarly pursued by the medley of governmental and non-governmental actors who were recruited by the state under its decentralization initiatives. I observed variations in the characterization of politics in two main areas: first, in the way elected local bodies were being contrasted with specially constituted watershed committees; and second, in the use of consent as a proxy for participation. In the first case, the 'political' character of elected bodies was contrasted with the 'apolitical' character of watershed committees, producing a powerful rationale of depoliticization in some cases, but not in others. In the second case, some implementers relied on consent as an indicator of the 'apolitical' business of participation, while others treated consent as a powerful political tool for mobilization and change. These diverse, and often contradictory realities, affirmed the need to take seriously the constraints and contexts of actors and agencies implicated within a larger project of depoliticization.

Actors and Agencies

The question of actors and agencies assumes a special resonance for the problem at hand. Even when the conditions for depoliticization are present, or metaphorically speaking, the development apparatus is in fact an 'anti-politics machine', why is it that the depoliticization project is not always pursued similarly? Li has emphasized her divergence from scholars who believe in the 'effective *achievement* of depoliticization' (2007, 11). If we are to understand why depoliticization is not always an effective project that consolidates state power, we first of all need to know whether the actors and agencies that are a part of the development apparatus are even pursuing the project in the first place. My enquiry is open-ended; it relies on a 'non-instrumental and non-normative research perspective' (Mosse and Lewis 2006, 3) that takes care not to assume, perhaps unlike Ferguson, the automatic complicity of all development workers in the anti-politics machine. It holds regard for the complexity of institutional practices that constitute development policy (Mosse 2004). It thus hopes to go beyond a tradition of critiquing and deconstructing development that has been recognized for its critical prowess but also attacked for going too far. For instance, it has been criticized for offering a larger than life 'diabolical image of development' (de Sardaan 2005 cited in Mosse and Lewis 2006, 4), and turning a blind eye to 'incoherences, uncertainties and contradictions' (ibid) that characterize the daily grind of development work.

The earliest contributions to this line of thinking are clubbed together under the epithet 'actor-oriented approaches' that basically emphasize how the processes and interactions of development can and do hold different implications for the various actors involved (Long and Long 1992, Arce and Long 1990). These approaches generated interest in studying the '"intermediary" actors or brokers operating at the "interfaces" of different world views and knowledge systems' (Mosse and Lewis 2006, 10). While they were applauded for producing methods that allowed rich empirical descriptions of development processes and dynamics, they were also criticized for lack of analytical clarity and reductionism. Key actor-oriented concepts such as 'interface' and 'negotiation' were criticized: the first for leading to a rather unhelpful segmentation of identities, and the second for acting as an ineffective descriptor of far more complex phenomena that include a range of stances between strategic manoeuvring and unwitting compliance. Equally serious was the charge of reductionism. Gledhill (1994 cited in Mosse and Lewis 2006) scathingly argued that actor-oriented approaches may have arisen to escape the 'structuralist-functionalist' strait-jacket, but their own privileging of actor-oriented explanations at the 'expense' of broader casual factors is no less restricting. Defendants of actor-oriented approaches like Oliver de Sardaan have responded to the charge by emphasising that the intention of these new methodologies was never to separate actors from structures (2005 in Mosse and Lewis 2006, 11), but to point the explanation, as Long did, at how actors respond differently to similar structural circumstances.

Actor-oriented approaches can also serve to demonstrate the significance of different structural and institutional contexts more visibly through intimate observations of how actors respond. This dialectic between structures and actors runs through the heart of my study, as I became interested in why particular actors and agencies involved in watershed development in two districts of two states in India approached the issues of participation and politics so differently. As I tried to unravel how the same national watershed guidelines were being interpreted in two different states, I realized that these interpretations were not contingent on the watershed programme framework alone. In fact, I found that these were inextricably tied-in with the larger political and institutional landscapes of decentralization. It became clear to me that it would not be possible to understand the actual practices of decentralized watershed development without also appreciating the dynamics around political decentralization to elected local bodies (panchayats) and administrative decentralization in the general body of the state government. This made sense because bureaucratic, non-governmental and political actors engaged in implementing the watershed development programme were simultaneously locked into other debates, contests and collaborations as well. Decentralization, as I will explain more fully in the next section, is never a neutral and technocratic institutional process but is fundamentally predicated on dynamic relationships between old and new players, and inevitable contestations of power. Equally, the ways in which programme actors responded to these contestations were different with significant effects.

These issues reflected the more general conundrum of how development policies are translated into practice. What I saw concerned the translation of the watershed development guidelines into a variety of practices, but not in an orderly, predictable or indeed 'scripted' way (Mosse and Lewis 2006, 9). Actor-oriented approaches have been extremely influential in directing our attention to the messy and unscripted realities of development. They have highlighted the activities of 'brokers' or social actors who actively constitute their social, economic and political roles instead of blindly following dictated agendas. Brokerage, write Mosse and Lewis (2006), has been cast as an analytical framework to appreciate various sorts of intermediary activities: for example, enlisting patron-client relationships to make a 'weak' state more effective as in India, or utilising unchartered spaces between aid funders and recipients as in Africa. While the empirical worth of this framework is recognized, critics have pointed to the dangers of presuming pre-existing realms within which brokers operate, such as state and peasant society. The presumption of brokers entering the scene from the vantage point of pre-determined social and institutional positions or careers in development is criticized (Mosse and Lewis 2006). They argue that actors do not simply respond to existing arrangements of development through their own interpretations, and that actors play a far more crucial role in the constitution of development projects. Development projects only become real when actors produce interpretations 'recruiting' others into their 'scripts' (ibid). Project realities are composed when actors sign up to particular interpretations because it serves their mutual interests to do so. Translation in this sense leads not to countless different interpretations, but to continuous attempts at producing and protecting 'unified fields of development' (Mosse and Lewis 2006, 14). This is the core of actor-network theory, which advances upon actor-oriented approaches precisely by showing what lies beneath the ostensible coherence of development projects.

I have found these insights especially useful in interrogating the differences in interpretations of the watershed guidelines and resulting approaches to participation and politics in the two states I studied. Actor-oriented approaches explained why and how the multitude of actors involved in programme implementation responded to these guidelines, and how their interpretations varied depending upon the broader structural-institutional contexts that they were embedded within. However they did not fully explain how these interpretations related to one another and whose interpretations were more powerful in the end and why. They did not explain intra-organizational dynamics in a nuanced way. In the end, they did not shed light on the complex interplay of interests, motives and considerations that impact upon the words and actions of a range of actors who found it expedient to go along with the dominant interpretation. Actor-network approaches are useful because they unsettle compositions of order and coherence that often characterize development projects.

In Kurnool for instance, I found important differences in the extent to which senior and junior project officials subscribed to a technocratic format of participation. Senior district officials, faced with the twin imperatives of meeting financial targets and demonstrating conformity with the nationally driven participatory guidelines were extremely keen to push forward a participatory project protocol. Junior officials, who were more immediately confronted with visible social power in the form of local elites and could not risk offending either these elites or their bosses in the project offices, adopted differing degrees of strategic compliance. A vortex of upward representations followed with extremely perverse effects in terms of excluding the poorest from decision-making and securing further the position of elites. In a different sense in Dewas, members of a grassroots NGO refused to sign up to the state script for participatory development at the incipient stages of the government funded watershed project that they were responsible for implementing. Their very explicit recalcitrance was tied into a larger struggle for overturning unequal power relationships in the area. However, in later years as the NGO established itself as a major power holder in this part of Dewas, it became interested in composing its own scripts around decentralized and participatory engagements. Those who shied away from allying with it were left exposed, standing relatively alone. These contrasts showed that not all actors engaged in decentralized watershed development tried to depoliticize it, and even when they did, the consequences were not to entrench state power in a straightforward manner. The picture was a lot more complex than alluded to by Ferguson (1990) in his analysis of development as an anti-politics machine that served to consolidate bureaucratic state power.

The Anti-Politics Machine and the Indian State

The Indian state presents unique dimensions when subjected to the analytical framework of Ferguson's anti-politics machine. The 'Indian anti-politics machine' is characterized in full detail in Chapter 2, but there are four issues that can be highlighted here. The first is related to the state's planning-driven development mission after independence that was steeped in a rationalist and technocratic logic and derived its distinctiveness precisely from its proclaimed ability to steer clear of politics. The planning commission under Nehru was composed of a range of 'experts' of scientific persuasion and received his personal stamp of approval: 'To me the spirit of cooperation of the members of the Planning Committee was particularly soothing and gratifying, for I found a pleasant contrast to the squabbles and conflicts of politics' (Nehru 1946 as cited in Chatterjee 1998, 84). Yet, it was precisely in the early years of independence that India witnessed major political experiments to do with state reorganization for development. There was a tension between Nehruvian ideas around a state-led project of modern development and Gandhian ideas of village self-government, though ultimately the former prevailed. The Community Development Programme (CDP) of 1952 embodied a Gandhian approach in its emphasis on community development and rural extension and was in effect India's first decentralization exercise, but it was largely ineffective. The CDP aimed to provide a substantial increase in agricultural production and an improvement in basic services that would transform the economic and social life of the village. Despite being modelled on the idea of a harmonious and socially undifferentiated village, the CDP did not take local power relationships and inequalities seriously. As a result, it ended up securing further the positions of agrarian elites who already wielded considerable power.

The second follows. The Indian state reflects politics in that the interests of elites have been accommodated within development strategies, resulting in the draining of state resources and the frequent frustration of broader development objectives. The bulk of scholarly writing on the Indian state is devoted to this theme (Bardhan 1984, Chatterjee 1988, Frankel 1978, Kaviraj 1988, Rudolph and Rudolph 1987 and Kohli 1990 among others). Equally, ethnographic research has shown that the poor are aware of the 'regimes of relative scarcity of the state' (Corbridge et al 2005, 38), or simply that the state often does not work for them. The poor know that they need to negotiate both the inefficiencies of India's public sector (both rent seeking behaviour and real capacity constraints) and the 'pressures that are brought to bear on government officials by ethnic and other interest groups and their political representatives and antagonists' (ibid). In other words, it has been patently clear that the Indian state was not doing a very good job of keeping politics out of development, a point that has only been driven home more clearly as the pressures of democratic politics have multiplied. This has meant that the idea of the Indian state as an anti-politics machine has not been a totally credible one.

The third dimension considerably complicates the picture, however. Though the credibility of a discourse of depoliticization has weakened over the years since independence, the same cannot be said for its attractiveness. Simply put, while it is increasingly clear that politics does indeed shape development practices and outcomes, a discourse of politics as a negative activity has become progressively stronger and now occupies a central place in public imagination. Inevitably, both of these phenomena are due to the intensification of democratic politics which has led to the proliferation of popular pressures and crosscutting competition. Social elites, particularly the higher castes, who may have justified politics as a virtuous vocation in the early years after independence, are eager to dismiss politics as full of vulgarity and moral decrepitude (Hansen 1999). Their stance may well be double-faced and strategic, as Hansen persuasively argues, but it is an influential stance nevertheless. Besides, these negative characterizations of politics are no longer restricted to elite discourses, and also occupy a wider place in popular discourse (confirmed by a variety of ethnographic studies in Fuller and Harriss 2001). It is not difficult on this basis to justify an anti-politics association for development, since politics it would seem has nothing by which to redeem itself. This has complemented the strong thrust towards depoliticising development through the promotion of technical discourses in the international arena. The state, therefore, has continued to subscribe to discourses of depoliticization in a variety of senses, as I observed in the making of the watershed development programme in India.

The fourth dimension is to me the most perplexing. It is not just the case that the state finds it attractive to subscribe to a discourse of depoliticization even though such a discourse is not entirely convincing. It is also that we cannot simply assume that the actors and agencies responsible for implementing the state's development initiatives will automatically pursue a project of depoliticization. Apropos actor-network theory discussed in the previous section, I have argued that even when they do, their precise motivations, constraints and considerations need to be regarded if we are to appreciate the fuller implications of their talk, silence and actions. These concerns become magnified in the context of decentralization as an unfolding process of profound political magnitude in India. The reform of watershed development programmes has been one of the premier state initiatives for decentralization in this country since 1994. This has led both to the (downward) transfers of responsibilities and resources (from centre to district and then village) and the (outward) involvement of non-governmental and market actors in implementation. This is an empirical statement whose conceptual implications need to be weighted seriously. The problem as it appears is as follows: in what ways do decentralized actors impact upon the use of state power? And how does such use shape the effectiveness of projects of depoliticization? How are decentralized actors enrolled into larger projects of depoliticization and do they necessarily participate in such projects? The practices of decentralization that I have observed suggest complex, even contradictory, uses of state power. These warrant some careful disentangling, which depend in essence on an interrogation of the theories of state and decentralization, but in the Indian context.

Decentralization and the State

It is by now a familiar story that decentralization the world over has become critical to the theorization and practice of government. The remarkable range of motivating factors prompting the adoption of decentralization as a package of measures for institutional reform contributes to its broad appeal. Decentralization is regarded as an essential state strategy for responding to pressures of democratization, in particular to the political aspirations of a wide range of actors and groups. It is also decidedly at the 'heart of a bundle of measures that is meant to enhance state capabilities' (Veron et al 2006, 1923) by promoting levels of political accountability, participation and more generalized citizen engagement. Presented in this way, advocates of decentralization do appear to be subscribing to a fuller view of the state as compared with the outrightly neoliberal clarion call for 'rolling back the state' (ibid). Nevertheless these frameworks of understanding contain a strong sense that state actors are corrupt and inefficient and need to be subject to the disciplining vigilance of morally upright and enlightened actors within civil society. Critics have long complained about the problems with this approach (see Mackintosh and Roy 1999, Corbridge et al 2005, Hadiz 2004, Mosse 2003, Veron et al 2006), so I will only summarise briefly the key conceptual issues to which they are drawing attention.

There are two powerful normative justifications associated with mainstream arguments for decentralization. The first is a 'communitarian' view of decentralization that celebrates the inherently 'capable local'. The second is a New Political Economy (NPE) view of decentralization that attacks the inherently 'corrupt and sub-optimal state'. The two views are associated with distinctive theoretical traditions. The first draws upon a rich repertoire of thinking around the value of communities both for meaningful social existence and for responding to the challenges of cooperation and collective action. Communitarians like Alasdair MacIntyre and Charles Taylor offered a powerful critique of liberal individualism with the argument that the 'only way to understand human behaviour is to refer to individuals in their social, cultural or historical contexts' or indeed the 'community' of which they are a part (Avineri and De-Shalit 2001, 2–5). Subsequently, new institutionalism took up the intellectual challenge of responding to the question of why individuals cooperate, more famously known in development studies as the 'tragedy of the commons'. Elinor Ostrom (1990) and Michael Taylor (1987, 1989) put forward persuasive arguments in favour of community based solutions to collective action, as opposed to absolute state control or privatization, the solutions in Garrett Hardin's initial framework. The second view is derived from the key axiom of NPE that governments are prone to excesses in the form of rent-seeking behaviour, which not only impinges on individual freedom but also wastes social resources (Nonneman 1996, Srinivasan 1985 and Colclough and Manor 1991). Being rent-seeking, states need to be checked through decentralization, which allows individuals to control the expansionist tendencies of governments. This argument motivates not only the downsizing of central government, with increased transfers of powers to local governments, but also the involvement of non-governmental and market actors.

There is also a third normative justification for decentralization. This is a political as well as constitutional view that is concerned specifically with the level at which the nation state should be calibrated. It embodies an outright concern with the inter-governmental division of powers right down from the centre to the smallest local unit. The village is articulated as a subset of the nation-state, with a share in its sovereignty and a claim to appropriate powers and finances. Arguments for decentralization comprise fundamentally political and constitutional matters regarding the internal reorganization of the state. Unlike the communitarian and NPE viewpoints, these have not been adequately expressed in mainstream arguments, especially those pursued by external agencies like the World Bank, to the same extent. Instead, ideas of community engagement and a reduced state are at the forefront of decentralization discourses, and these are now being expressed in the more reasonable intellectual climate of the Post-Washington Consensus (PWC). This consensus does not attack the state as sharply as the Washington Consensus had done, and presents a more synergetic view of state-market-society relationships (Fine 2001). Decentralization as a policy prescription fits neatly within the PWC's normative chord of good governance, synthesising NGOs, community-based organizations, private corporations within a state-facilitated symphony. In this fervour, the question of what is actually going on within and between the different levels of the state as a consequence of decentralization is obscured away from mainstream discourse.

Besides, there are a number of other problems with the mainstream discourse on decentralization. First, communities and community-based bodies cannot be treated in general terms, and their potential and particular character needs to be carefully appraised. Communitarian arguments for decentralization have been widely criticized both for denying the specificity of local communities and underplaying their complex and multifaceted relationships with the state (Leach et al 1997, Mosse 1997, Sundar 2000). Second, whether decentralization occurs from the public to the private, or from the central to the local has become 'analytically irrelevant' in these formulations (Mackintosh and Roy 1999, 16). The World Bank views that the rationale for decentralization is 'similar' to the rationale for 'liberalisation, privatisation and other market reforms' (1997, 120–121). There is a danger here in attempting to substitute market-based and customer-driven forms of accountability for political citizen oriented accountability. Third, the negative view of state actors as rent-seeking and corrupt is so pervasive still that not enough attention is paid to the growing implication of civil society actors in such activities. Harriss-White and White (1996) have argued that corruption has actually increased during the course of implementing economic liberalization, and that businessmen amongst other civil society actors are more likely to initiate corruption than state actors (discussed in Veron et al 1996, 1923). Similarly, Kumar and Corbridge (2002) have discussed the relationship between local elites, political brokers and forest officials in obstructing forest trade deregulation.

All these criticisms stem from the basic concern that influential advocates of decentralization are disregarding the links between state and society which characterize most developing countries, and promoting a rather unsubstantiated state-society dichotomy. In India, as I will shortly discuss, this issue holds special significance. What is missing in mainstream prescriptions is an interest in uncovering what exactly unfolds when states decentralize. Both the communitarian and the NPE 'routes' to decentralization might suggest that decentralization is 'less of state', especially the central state. The Indian experience in this respect sits extremely uneasily with the proposition that decentralization has diminished the state, either its size or presence, in any significant manner. This can be more usefully explained with a brief discussion of the antecedents of contemporary decentralization policies in India. Starting with the era of colonial rule, it is clear that decentralization has been shaped by the varying constraints of the central state and more latterly, regional configurations of the state as well.

A Brief History of Decentralization in India

At a time when there was no systematic unity called India, the imperial government's strategies to entrench colonial power focused on carving stronger links between the many localities and larger more integrated processes around production, exchange, administration and politics (Frykenberg 1965, Ludden 1992, Washbrook 1973). The British government was content to create a level of locality that was accessible to it through local intermediaries alone. By 1857, however, the British were increasingly concerned about the stability of their rule, and ideas of devising a system of representation crept in (Seal 1973, 12). Major successive reforms included the Indian Councils Act 1861, Morley-Minto Reforms in 1909, Montague Chelmsford reforms in 1919 and the Government of India Act in 1935. Local bodies in British India, especially the village panchayats, were at best 'modest representative bodies', with few financial powers or functions (Seal 1973, Isaac and Frank 2000). Their importance for the British lay in providing an 'elective veneer' to the new councils (Seal 1973, 13), and accordingly, reforms from 1909 onwards concentrated on extending the links between higher and lower councils. Leading Indian politicians were disinterested in such limited and insular local self-government and demanded that local bodies be 'tied more firmly to the structure of rule above' (ibid). These were linked to fast enveloping political demands for the need to organize nationally. From the late 19 century onwards there was a steady rise of Indian associations claiming to represent All-India interests. These eventually gave rise to the Indian National Congress, the Muslim League and the Hindu Mahasabha. By the hour of independence, discourses of nationhood and a strong Indian state had pushed ideas of 'locality' and local government into second place.

After independence, Gandhian ideas around self-sufficient villages gave way to Nehruvian ideas around a strong centralized modern state, and this reflected in the negligible pursuit of decentralization as a state objective. The constitution did mention village self-government but in the non-justiciable Directive Principles of State Policy. The absence of any constitutional requirement meant that there was little state interest in empowering village panchayats or institutionalising their upward links, and local bodies around the country were in a sorry shape. The Community Development Programme of 1952 (CDP) was inspired by Gandhi and emphasized community development and rural extension but also more abstract notions like the development of the human being and social organization (Sinha 1999). CDP performed dismally, suffering from a paucity of resources and effective coordination. Among many other criticisms was the charge that it was no different from the long line of state initiatives for community-management that only allowed the state 'to abdicate serious responsibility without abdicating overall control' (Mosse 1997, Sundar 2000). A review by the state-constituted Balwantrai Mehta Committee in 1957 concluded that the CDP had done badly because it was unsupported by a vigorous system of local government. The committee's recommendations for the adoption of a three tier structure for Panchayat Raj Institutions (PRIs) proved influential in the sense that panchayats properly entered the agenda of the Indian state. However, these institutional reforms would prove to be limited in the absence of any wider structural changes which the state was constrained from undertaking.

The conditions for an uneasy dynamic between centralized state power and ineffective decentralization followed right from independence when the new regime refrained from undertaking any measures that would hurt the interests of the dominant propertied classes. Local power structures systematically ensured the capture of village panchayats and the steady rise of clientelistic politics through the 1960s further ensured that panchayats were also nodes of political mobilization for all political parties. So when the next state constituted body, the Ashok Mehta Committee, made proposals for panchayat reform in 1978, it came as no surprise that these were not linked to structural reform either. Soon it was clear that panchayats were not merely vehicles of electoral mobilization for regional elites, they were also being used as implementers of top-down development programmes. There was no real interest on the part of central or state governments to treat panchayats as units of representative democratic government in their own right (Mathews 1995, Isaac and Frank 2000, Jain 1985). The lack of systematic thinking around decentralization meant that panchayat related initiatives were nearly divorced from any broader attempts at reforming centre-state relations. As panchayats were being routinely treated as implementers of centrally formulated development programmes, financial devolution to panchayats was not seriously pursued. Panchayats were not entrusted with core regulatory functions expected of functioning local government.

While central efforts at decentralization were mostly inadequate for strengthening panchayat bodies, some state level initiatives were more successful. The cases of West Bengal and Kerala reinforce the importance of linking decentralization to local bodies with matching initiatives for structural reform and political mobilization. The ruling Communist Party of India (Marxist) (CPI-M) in West Bengal, late 1970s onwards, launched a definite policy of using panchayat raj bodies as vehicles of structural reorganization of land based relations and held panchayat elections on a direct party basis (Kohli 1987, Webster 1992). The Keralan experience was different because panchayat reform was part of a much broader process of popular mobilization complemented by active initiatives by the Left Democratic Front (LDF) government for financial devolution and decentralized planning. The growing regional basis of political mobilization, as in Andhra Pradesh and Karnataka, besides West Bengal and Kerala, drew panchayats into a more dynamic relationship with party politics at the state level.

This refractory and disparate nature of regionalism together with the continuing centralized form of the state apparatus bore a clear consequence for the possible trajectory that decentralization would take in the next few years.

Regional political articulations have translated into numerous pressures, but no coherent or systematic 'demand', for decentralization. The basic model of centralized economic planning has not been altered, and subsequent attempts to decentralize planning are not related clearly with the overall process of national planning.[3] Decentralized planning in most states has been far from comprehensive, with innovations in Kerala, West Bengal and Karnataka more the exception than the rule (Isaac and Frank 2000). For most parts of India, the 1980s witnessed a stasis in developments related to decentralization. The Sarkaria Commission, 1983–1988, rested on the shibboleths of a Congress Party that desperately tried to achieve a new equilibrium in changed conditions of national and regional 'political universes'.[4] Its recommendations for reforming the nature of Indian federalism lacked both political will and intent. The 64th constitutional amendment bill seeking panchayat reform was defeated in the upper house of the Parliament following staunch opposition from regional political elites who protested the Centre's attempts to bypass state governments altogether.

In this chequered context of uneven, unsystematic and insufficient decentralization initiatives in India, the 1990s were a decade of bold and definitive moves in favour of decentralization. 1993 was a landmark year, as panchayats and urban local bodies were granted constitutional recognition for the first time. The significance of the 73rd and 74th constitutional amendments lies precisely in their attempt to end the vulnerability of panchayat bodies to highly variable regional political conditions. Prima facie, it was an unequivocal statement that panchayats could not be neglected or ignored by state governments, which now had a mandatory responsibility of enacting basic provisions laid down by these amendments. The most important provision is the creation of a uniform three-tier system for PRIs for a standard five-year term throughout the country. Moreover, re-elections are mandatory within six months, in the event of dissolution.[5] However, despite the strong nod from the centre that panchayats could no longer be ignored, Article 243 G of the constitution accorded vital discretionary powers to state legislatures to decide the extent to which panchayats were to be strengthened as institutions of self-government. The 11 constitutional schedule contains a list of 29 subjects that may be transferred to panchayats by state legislatures at their discretion.

Perhaps unsurprisingly, therefore, different states have pursued a political agenda of panchayat reform with differing degrees of seriousness. Panchayats all over the country had suffered at the hands of bureaucrats and political elites unwilling to transfer powers backed by resources. Consequently, their fate post the 1993 amendment depended greatly on the entrenched political stakes at the state-level that either favoured panchayat reform or obstructed it, but also on the particular orientation of state-level political leadership. It is these contrasts that have made for extremely interesting variations in the quality of panchayat reform in different states. This book pursues two such cases: Madhya Pradesh where the Congress-led government of Digvijay Singh privileged panchayat reform within the state's decentralization agenda and Andhra Pradesh where the Telugu Desam Party's Chandrababu Naidu pursued a more overtly technocratic programme of decentralization underpinned by a host of heavily bureaucratized participatory development programmes. Following on from the time at which the primary research for this book was conducted, state-level investigation broadly coincides with their time in power (until 2003 for Singh and 2004 for Naidu).

Contemporary decentralization policies in India stretch beyond panchayat reform alone. The Indian state has responded to a wide range of international influences favouring participatory decision-making through community-based bodies accommodated within a larger framework of administrative decentralization. Besides watershed development, a whole host of programme innovations in areas ranging from joint forestry management to community-based disaster management have mimicked these patterns. The intellectual climate of the PWC with its normative anchoring in good governance has played no insignificant part. At the same time, there is no one explanation for why the Indian state has gradually moved towards decentralization as state policy in the 1990s. The diversity of specific forms that decentralization policies have taken is a testimony to the medley of foreign and home-grown influences. Gandhian social action groups, NGOs and popular social movements (like Chipko) view that it would be misleading to regard decentralization in India purely as a state-initiated project. They argue that important strides have been made towards empowering local bodies because of their sustained critiques against decades of centralized state interventions. The proliferation of actors with articulated interests in the decentralization process has inevitably meant that particular policies have not been free of contention.

The watershed development programme is a crucible containing several of the tensions characterising debates around decentralization in India. Policy makers have been vehemently criticized for attempting to disregard panchayats, as these were not originally given principal charge of implementation. Subsequent reforms since 1994 (in 2001, 2003 and 2008) have favoured panchayats and watershed committees on a near alternate basis. The panchayat-watershed committee debate has become the great mascot of intellectual rivalry over decentralization in India in our times – political decentralization versus community based development; however, there is a real danger in this obscuring various levels of power play implicit amongst the actors involved. Observed struggles encompass both governmental and non-governmental actors. Secondly, the antecedents of contemporary watershed development lie in soil and water conservation programmes, which have been a key arena of state control and intervention in India since colonial times as a technocratic and top-down discourse has accompanied conservation in India (Hinchcliffe et al 1999, Farrington et al 1999, Sivaramakrishnan 2000). Decentralization in this particular programme has followed the shift to micro-watershed based planning upon evidence that comprehensive treatment of land, water and forest resources in an interrelated manner was urgent if further degradation had to be arrested (Dharia Committee, Government of India, 1995). A large number of participatory experiments in micro-watershed development undertaken by non-governmental organizations in India have proved to be influential (Kerr 2002).

While these influences have combined to produce a remarkable transformation in state policy for watershed development from 1994 onwards, it is also clear that the new policies have pursued a heavily bureaucratized and prescriptive approach towards participation and decentralization. Exposing the level of detail regarding the state script for participation and decentralization is among the foremost tasks of this book. Equally, these policies rely on familiar assumptions about highly coherent and cooperative communities and a state-community dichotomy that is untenable in India. Policy discourse is also heavily concentrated on the workings of newly formed project bodies, i.e., watershed committees, but in a way that obscures the specific role of the state (and its multitude of extended actors) in bringing this policy into operation. This leads to the final point in this chapter. We cannot truly investigate how decentralized actors manipulate or respond to state power, unless we are informed by a grounded view of how state power interacts with social power in India.

State-Society Relationships in India

State-society relationships have been the subject of state theory in general (Mitchell 1991, Hansen and Stepputat 2001) but they hold a special resonance for scholars conceptualising the state in India. The British brought the concept of state to India, a country that had extremely dispersed forms of social and political power. The state, while 'ceremonially eminent', had very limited powers to interfere with or shape social organization (Kaviraj 1994). There is a rich literature that captures the making sense of India by the British filtered through notions of modernity and statehood (see Chatterjee 1994, Kaviraj 1994, Khilnani 1998). A centralized state apparatus emerged exercising a high level of disciplinary power over shaping the economy but there remained a pervasive disjuncture between state endorsed 'modern rationalist' norms and wider socialized sensibilities that did not quite fully internalize these. The extent and nature of this disjuncture has been greatly debated generating attention to the broader issue of how people negotiate the forces of the state. Conversely, there is interest in understanding the workings of the state not as a homogenous bloc but as a complex and extremely differentiated organization that is continuously 'buffeted by contending social forces' (Corbridge et al 2005, 36).

Scholarship on the Indian state in recent years has echoed the broader trend to study the state not as a received unitary and monolithic entity, but empirically as an 'ethnographic site' (Hansen and Stepputat 2001, 3) characterized by contestations and contradictions and whose historical trajectory of formation is vital to understand. This has been inspired as much by Gramscian ideas around the articulation of the power of the dominant class through uncertain and impermanent hegemonies, as by Foucauldian notions of governance through the diffusion of governmentalities within society at large (ibid). Scholars of post-Marxist persuasions have gone beyond Poulantzas' (1973) analysis of the capitalist state as a set of structures that acts to preserve the long-term interests of the dominant class. Phil Abrams (1988) paved the way for a line of research that focused attention on the very idea of the state as an 'illusion' that serves to conceal the political disunity of capitalist societies. A few years later, Timothy Mitchell (1991) influentially endorsed Abrams' thesis through the argument that the state ought to be understood not as a structure but as a 'structural effect' that rendered the appearance of structures. However, Mitchell was cautious to emphasize that the 'real' interacts with the 'ideological' as opposed to not existing at all, and modified his previous essay by viewing that 'the state-idea and the state-system are better seen as two aspects of the same process' (1999, 77). This crucial modification has granted explanatory significance to Abrams' and Mitchell's views in the Indian context, for it would have been impossible to make the case that the Indian state was illusory! Fuller and Harris have rightly pointed out that the 'idea of the state is a form of symbolic capital that enters into the material power of the state-system and is reciprocally upheld by it' (2001, 5).

This issue is particularly interesting in India because of the ostensible divide in the way elites and subalterns understand the state and what it stands for. Kaviraj (1988) and Chatterjee (1998) have highlighted the incorporation of pre-capitalist structures (rich peasantry) in capital's 'passive revolution' owing to the weakness and inability of the bourgeoisie to challenge existing dominant classes. Development planning was mobilized as a vehicle of rationalist transformation but the very project was crippled because, as Kaviraj memorably put it, the state 'had feet of vernacular clay' (1984, 227). In this view, the Indian public as well as lower level government officials do not appreciate the modernist discourses of the upper echelons of the state. This alleged discontinuity, not simply in language but in normative frameworks too, meant that most Indians did not even expect the state to 'behave in this "modern" fashion' (Corbridge et al 2005, 36). Corbridge et al argue that to the extent that such 'life-worlds' depart, research ought to pay close attention to the 'language and staging of state-society interactions' (ibid). Others have warned against extreme interpretations of so-called incompatibility between the modern state and its 'indigenous demotic values' on the basis that the public regularly displays a close understanding of the state and its 'administrative procedures' (Fuller and Harris 2001, 24). When citizens display deferential behaviour, like feet-touching for example, in a government office, they are in a stroke 'blurring' the boundaries between impersonal and personal norms or between state and society, but this does not mean that they do not 'grasp the logic of impersonal norms' (Ibid). In this sense, the staging of state-society interactions may also refer to performance and enactment both by officials and citizens in order to make sense of the state, despite the ever present, though shifting, blurred boundaries.

Ethnographic research on the Indian state has provided evidence of local state officials collapsing the distinctions between their roles as public servants and private citizens (Gupta 1995) or furthering their interests by populating the state with their kin (Harriss-White n.d. cited in Fuller and Harris 2002). It has just as importantly shown that citizens construct discourses around the state and devise pragmatic strategies to deal with it. Research by Ruud (2001) and the Osellas (2001) reiterates that the general public expect the business of politics and government to be thoroughly infected by corruption and cheating, but they also pragmatically recognize that they have to deal with politicians and officials. The widow who goes to the block headquarters to collect her pension sees the state working through her own eyes and necessarily participates in its procedures, perhaps through signing a form or making petty payments to gatekeepers. She learns to employ an effortless mix of two different discourses: her own entrenched understanding as a mere recipient of the state's largesse to be accorded arbitrarily, but also a more assertive one arising from her citizen's entitlement to those benefits (Corbridge et al 2005, 19–20). The 'seeing the state' argument has enduring relevance therefore for it allows us to appreciate the often forgotten but never insignificant 'sightings' of state authority by India's citizens (ibid).

Such sightings are profoundly important in the context of decentralization in India that is now no longer new. In their in-depth analysis of decentralized anti-poverty programmes in India, Corbridge et al have rightly argued that the nature of the decentralization agenda is such that its 'precise meanings' will 'vary sharply from place to place' (2005, 44). It is beyond question that the extent and levels of decentralized decision-making that are observed in Kerala are nowhere close to being duplicated in other states, even West Bengal which has similarly experienced Communist Party rule. Despite this sobering realization, it is also the case that decentralized discourses are 'intent on changing the conditions in which different groups of poorer people are coming to see the state' (Corbridge et al 2005, 44). Moreover, contrary to mainstream good governance driven scenarios, decentralization disaggregates the state in two important ways. First, though state-led decentralization allows for the creation of all kinds of new local institutions and bodies, ranging from watershed committees to other user bodies, there is equally a high component of integration of community-based decision-making with state procedures. This imbues the former with claims to state authority. Second, decentralized state programmes, like watershed development, depend on all manner of collaborations between local people and government and non-governmental project officials. The sheer multiplicity of actors involved in the production of a project has implications given that different actors position themselves in relation to the state (its resources, rules and regimented procedures) in very different ways. Disaggregation of the state is a function of the sheer multiplication of perceptions of it. Even as the 'co-production' of decentralized development by state and society ostensibly blurs their boundaries, it simultaneously unleashes processes that seek to define and sustain all that the state stands for.

These aspects shaped the contours of what was observed in the four research sites. As a doctoral researcher confronted with the need to inject some methodological rationale into my project design, I had decided to select two project villages in each district, Kurnool and Dewas. The distinction between the two villages had to do with the institutional nature of the Project Implementing Agency (PIA): it was a government official team in one village and an NGO in the other. This followed from my interest in the diversity of actors and agencies interpreting and implementing the same set of watershed policy guidelines issued by the central government in 1994. What I observed, however, went far beyond these rather staid distinctions between institutional types. Above all, these different actors did not equally or straightforwardly pursue the state script for participatory watershed development which attempted to depoliticize participation, community-based decision-making and decentralized institutional engagement. Three different factors played a part in this variation: firstly, the regional political context which set the stage for the dominant narratives of decentralization that actors throughout a project hierarchy would be expected to sustain; secondly, the intra-institutional dynamics within the project structure that either intensified or defused the need for upward representations of depoliticization; and ultimately, the local and regional configurations of domination and subordination that enveloped the relationships between project officials at different levels and people.

Towards a Nested Approach

This book is devoted to exposing the interactions between these different factors. In Kurnool, both the government and NGO project actors were harnessed within an extremely tight bureaucratic protocol for participation, which in itself was a response to the technocratic procedures favoured by Chief

Minister Naidu. Even when an NGO was responsible for implementation, projects centred on strong vertical reporting structures, where all lower level project staff were required to meticulously report to senior government officials. The interaction between local elites and project actors played a significant part in these reporting structures, and therefore in the effective pursuit of projects of depoliticization. In Lilapuram, a village where a handful of high caste Reddys are also the biggest landholders and occupiers of key positions of official authority including the panchayat, project officials quickly learnt that any attempts to form watershed committees that did not see the Reddys at the helm would fail. The Reddys for their part found the prospect of exercising their traditional domination in a yet new forum very attractive, especially as it allowed proximity to state officials and a new claim to prominence and authority without compromising their symbolic and material interests. Local politics and political relations coloured the watershed project from the start, even though the panchayat was kept separate in theory.

In Malligundu, the second Kurnool village, local power relations differed in that village politics was dominated by an 'ascendant' Backward Caste group, the Boyas, whose leader was a man with a criminal record of violence and murder. The rich Reddys here were timid in comparison to their counterparts in Lilapuram. Naidu was panchayat sarpanch, and so officially disqualified to lead a watershed committee, and so his supporters were in charge. As a result, village-level power relations shaped the actual procedures of participation in very different ways. In Lilapuram, the Reddys' continuous subversion of project procedures through practices like the manipulation of signatures and thumbprints greatly interfered with the substantiation of project participatory procedures. The Boya leader in Malligundu was content for the project to distract attention from other harsh aspects of his power and did not interfere with project attempts to substantiate consent in a variety of ways. In neither case was consent an instrument of depoliticization as it was intended to be by the project protocol, but state authority and social power interacted in tangibly different ways.

The situation in Dewas was significantly different from that in Kurnool, especially because there was no comparable attempt to crystallize bureaucratic power for managing watershed development at the district level. Digvijay Singh's government pursued serious political and administrative reform for greater panchayat involvement that sought to widen the interface between elite bureaucrats and regional political leaders. This contributed to the diffusion of authority for watershed related decision-making at the district level. Research here also captured the very different types of dominant politics that prevailed in the two main parts of the district: the ghaat-upar or fertile Malwa plateau which has been the site of entrenched high caste power extending both to political and economic domination, and the ghaat-neeche that has pockets of tribal populations interspersed with high caste majorities. The selection of watershed projects openly mirrored political considerations, unlike Kurnool, where a stringent discourse of depoliticized selection was in place. The first watershed project of the state went to Kishangarh, a large and prosperous ghaat-neeche village, where the local configuration of power produced a remarkable disinterest in the symbolic and material resources of the watershed project. Unlike the Kurnool villages, the two principal castes here comprised the Rajputs and the Khatis (a Backward Caste group) that were economically prosperous and considered the project to be an unnecessary distraction. The government PIA was not required to sustain upward representations of 'apolitical participation' to his bosses unlike his counterparts in Kurnool, but he was driven by considerations of building large, expensive and permanent watershed structures to impress district and state watershed officials.

The second Dewas village was Neelpura in the ghaat-neeche part of the district. Its very selection for watershed development was mired in the radical confrontations between a grassroots NGO and local stakeholders of power that constituted an exploitative anti-tribal coalition. The case study reveals the pursuit of simultaneously contradictory relationships between different levels of the state. While the NGO was locked in hostile confrontation with lower level revenue bureaucrats, it earned the stated support of senior district and state level government officials. Their support for the NGO's pro-tribal stance broke the twin myths that state actors necessarily depoliticize development and that depoliticization actually entrenches state power. For the poor tribals of ghaat-neeche and Neelpura village in particular, the state was a venal entity, and the NGO from the outset adopted a winning strategy of emphasising the rights and responsibilities of the state that were being contravened by local power-holders. When confronted with revelations over the violation of key state laws, senior state officials found it more appropriate for preserving overall state legitimacy to take a clear stand in favour of progressive politics than turning a 'technocratically' blind eye. Following on from this dramatic beginning, the NGO as the project's PIA adopted an explicitly political stance towards local leadership and mobilization. It enjoyed enthusiastic local support and involvement, but the underbelly of these interactions revealed discontent and alienation on the part of a few. The later part of the NGO's trajectory in the ghaat-neeche area has seen a remarkable strengthening of its position, and the makings of a new power. The NGO, while continuing to pursue a progressive social agenda, has closely allied itself with the idea of the Indian state. Indeed, framing its role as a key partner of the state in the region has been an important ingredient of its power and effectiveness.

These different case studies confirmed that there was no one set of imperatives driving the strategies of decentralized actors or the nature of their representations to others. Even though there were powerful thrusts towards depoliticization, too many factors prevented any 'shared' pursuit of the same. The state played a key role in shaping the practices of decentralized actors, but their respective considerations and constraints in upholding state scripts for decentralization or participation were noticeably different. All these had direct implications for the real and observed functioning of the so-called anti-politics machine in India. This book has tried to explore these factors through nested comparisons: between state political strategies and contexts; between implementing arrangements illustrating different relationships among government bureaucracy, elected representatives and NGOs; and between villages with contrasting power structures and forms of social differentiation.

I pursued this multi-sited fieldwork over fourteen months primarily through the lens of a political scientist trained to study the structures and processes of government, i.e., the formal arenas of policy-making and implementation, mainstream politics and political contexts, and the new dynamics of governing that have accompanied the proliferation of non-governmental organizations in development. At the same time, my preoccupation with the state meant that I was looking beyond visible structures and processes alone and was interested in the 'idea' of the state following Abrams (1988) and Mitchell (1991, 1999). Moreover, given the centrality of the local in my research, I was equally concerned with village level social and political relations, but not in isolated terms, more as a part of regional configurations of power instead. I combined my training in the study of politics with an extended engagement with the anthropology of development to understand how and why actors interpret policies in the ways they do and to examine the frequent representations of positions that accompany the realities of policy implementation. It was here that an interdisciplinary approach proved to be most valuable.

Reflecting the multi-sited nature of this study, I conducted fieldwork in capital cities (New Delhi, Bhopal and Hyderabad), district headquarters (Dewas and Kurnool), block offices (Tonk-Khurd, Bagli and Veldurthi), and the four case study villages (Kishangarh, Neelpura, Malligundu and Lilapuram). I examined documentary records obtained from government and NGOs, archival information including old police records and newspaper reports, but mainly I acquired primary insights through an extensive range of unstructured and exploratory, as well as semi-structured, interviews with officials, politicians, NGO workers and other local and regional key informants, besides several individuals and groups in each village. As I spent nearly two months in each village, I was also able to participate in and observe to some extent the daily lives of people. The names of the case study villages have been changed to afford some anonymity to key actors, though I am deeply aware of the limits to such measures for those familiar with these places will easily see through such pseudonyms. The names of the organizations observed in this research either from government or NGOs have been left unchanged, though as a rule I have refrained from naming individuals who trusted me with information, only mentioning names where explicit permission had been received and where naming the respondent was appropriate.

The organization of this book reflects my concern with depoliticization and the anti-politics machine at different levels. Chapters 1–3 explore the meanings of development as an anti-politics machine in theory, then specifically in the context of development in India, leading up to its particular manifestation in the state watershed development programme. In Chapter 1, I attempt to develop an intellectual explanation for the idea of anti-politics in development and argue that this idea rests on particular constructions of the economy as well as of politics. While one side of the coin is the (much explored) intimate association of the economy with development and a view of economic behaviour as rational and suitable for this purpose, the other side of the coin is necessarily a characterization of politics in negative terms, as the fount of base human behaviour that is dominated by conflict. In Chapter 2, I ask whether there is in any sense an anti-politics machine in India and respond to this question by examining the history of the state, development and democracy in India. Although state planners since independence have claimed that development has been approached apolitically, above and away from the narrow conflicts of politics, the realities of development have abundantly demonstrated otherwise. The intensification of democratic mobilization has expanded the arena of politics, multiplied political competition and lent many more possibilities to politics across the country but also increased disdain of electoral politics within popular discourse. In Chapter 3, I chart the making of the watershed development programme in India from soil and water conservation with restricted objectives in a small proportion of lands to a comprehensive rural livelihoods programme across the country, and show how this has contributed to an enormous expansion of the scope and scale of state intervention in rural development. I also trace the contours of a specifically anti-politics 'watershed' machine which creates the conditions for depoliticising watershed development through its vision of decentralized, participatory community-based projects at odds with the realities of social differentiation and power relationships. The chapter details the three principal elements of such a discourse: community, equity and local institutions, each of which is treated in apolitical terms.

Chapters 4–6 present my empirical research in the states of Andhra Pradesh and Madhya Pradesh. In Chapter 4, I examine the impact of the wider context of decentralization and the nature of politics and political competition more generally on the watershed machinery in each state.

I demonstrate that watershed reform cannot be isolated from the larger dynamics of decentralization; instead these dynamics vitally influence the prospects for a discourse of depoliticization to be actively pursued by watershed authorities. The chapter illustrates that political and institutional policy initiatives for decentralization are deeply intertwined with prevailing regional patterns of dominance, both in the ways in which they are motivated and interpreted. The chapter also illustrates the types of 'political' pressures that technocrats experience and the very different responses they produce. In Chapters 5 and 6 respectively, I pursue more specifically the very different dynamics surrounding two particular characterizations of politics that seem to abound in the depoliticized discourse of participatory watershed development: the first with respect to panchayats as the embodiment of politics and watershed committees as their conceptual opposite, and the second with respect to the use of individual and collective consent as indicators of apolitical participation. Chapter 5 interrogates the notion that it is possible to create new apolitical watershed committees that are dramatically different from the older political panchayats. It discusses the micro-politics of the four case study villages to demonstrate the impossibility of this project. It shows why the attempt to negate politics by giving it a particular association fails for different reasons. It does so by unpacking the underlying factors that influence both the motivations of village elites to 'capture' new project bodies as well as of project implementing agencies to either passively respond to or actively steer local politics. Chapter 6 examines the use of consent as an indicator of participation by the different project agencies. It traces the remarkable and worrying transformation of a concept with definitively political underpinnings into the symbol of an apolitically harmonious existence in the context of contemporary community-based participation. It delves into the details of project life in these four villages to show that not all project agencies pursue consent apolitically, but more significantly, that the dialectics of consent are never apolitical. The final Chapter concludes.

In the chapters that follow, I hope to have shown that, upon a closer look, the juggernaut of development as the anti-politics machine appears less menacing. There is little doubt that the tendency to depoliticize development is pervasive, its fulsomeness at least derived in part from the ease with which it is possible to detest politics. In unhinging the expectation that the constituents of the so-called machine necessarily pursue projects of depoliticization, my book will have achieved its modest purpose. It is here that it seeks to offer its readers hope, perhaps ephemeral, and the opportunity to relate their experiences of the daily compromise and subversion of depoliticization in its various treatments.

Chapter One

THE IDEA OF 'ANTI-POLITICS'

The Machine that Depoliticizes

In 1990, James Ferguson wrote a book called *The Anti-Politics Machine: "Development", Depoliticisation and Bureaucratic Power in Lesotho*. This book contained an anthropological analysis of the disproportionately large donor-driven development machinery in this small landlocked country in southern Africa. Its implications had profound resonances for the critical treatment of development far beyond Lesotho, in all of Africa and certainly most of the developing world. The reason for this *prima facie* appears to be a simple one, and indeed Ferguson offers it to us. No one before Ferguson or at the very least few as clearly and cogently,[1] had turned their critical attentions to analysing the actual apparatus that drove development. While scholarly analyses and critiques galore had thrashed out the political, social and economic potential of development, there was a surprising gap in understanding about the development industry itself. The existing literature in the field was dominated by the ideas of 'insiders' or 'sympathetic outsiders' who believed in development planning and therefore scrutinized it with a fix-it attitude, or at the other extreme, by radical Marxist and dependency theorists for whom the entire development effort was a great capitalist sham. There was little insight into how the bureaucrats, experts, consultants and planners that populated development organizations and establishments actually operated and the effects their operations created beyond their own proclamations.

Interrogating the limits of such analyses, Ferguson posed a somewhat different question. What if the real issues lay not in deciding whether or not a development project was a 'success' or 'failure' in relation to its stated objectives, but instead in the unintended effects that result from the actions of development bureaucrats? Were we not in danger of missing out on understanding key aspects of social reality that resulted not from intentional actions alone, but from unintentional ones as well, and were intentional actions important in a way other than that imagined by their architects? Inspired by Michel Foucault, Ferguson thus problematized the complex relationship between the 'intentionality of planning' and the 'intelligibility of outcomes'

(1990, 20). In doing so, he developed his central thesis – the anti-politics machine – which he characterized as the two-fold 'instrument effect' of a large rural development project funded by the World Bank and the Canadian International Development Agency (CIDA). While the first effect was an 'institutional' one as it strengthened the hold of bureaucratic state power, the second effect was 'ideological' as it 'depoliticized' both poverty and the state. In other words, Ferguson explains, much like an anti-gravity machine popularized by science fiction stories, the anti-politics machine seemed to be able to suspend politics from even the most 'sensitive political operations' at the symbolic flick of a button, all the while reinforcing its own power. So even though the project was a 'failure' – which Ferguson unambiguously concluded it was – such failure was accompanied by the very significant effects of depoliticization and the entrenchment of state power.

Ferguson's study went on to spark much interest both in the form and content of the metaphor of the anti-politics machine. The idea of the development apparatus, and development discourse more generally, eschewing politics seemed to strike at the heart of the problem of development itself. The 'depoliticisation' of development acquired tremendous currency. A number of scholars have commented on how fundamentally political issues are articulated or framed in an apolitical idiom. They noted that such an idiom had little bearing with the reality of development thinking and practice and was misleading with seriously detrimental effects. In his well-known study *Depoliticising Development: The World Bank and Social Capital,* John Harriss attacked Robert Putnam's well-known conceptualization of social capital (1993, 2000) in a 'realm apart from politics and government' (2001, 60), which had resulted in the denial of issues of context and power, the attribution of a dubious causality to social capital, and the depoliticisation of poverty and social justice. Sangeeta Kamat's *Development Hegemony: NGOs and the State in India* also explicitly evoked the anti-politics machine idea, to show how the law is used by the Indian state to decree all development activities and agencies as non-political (Kamat 2002).[2] In her interpretation, such deployment of the law was specifically aimed at excluding any 'radical' or 'militant' action, both ambiguously defined, from the fold of development with fascinating effects. A rich literature has since emerged on the myriad ways in the rational models and technical discourses of development 'naturalise poverty and objectify the poor and depoliticise development' (Mosse 2004, 643 citing Long 2001, Ludden 1992, Scott 1998, Skaria 1998 and Tsing 1993). Admittedly, many of these authors may not engage directly with Ferguson's anti-politics machine metaphor but the broad thrusts of their arguments endorse his depoliticization thesis. Ferguson's work symbolizes the central concerns of the many scholars who have commented on the depoliticising thrust of development.

There were many others that recognized Ferguson's ideas on depoliticization as influential, but were less convinced of particular aspects of his analysis. Mosse (2004) in particular is doubtful of the extent to which Ferguson pushes his case for the (unintended) effects of development which apparently occur 'behind the backs or against the wills of even the most powerful actors' (1990, 18). Tordella (2003) is milder in his appraisal, but equally uncertain about the merits of assuming the 'inevitability' of depoliticization. In his view, it would be more helpful if the analysis could be directed at understanding 'where development planning tends to "go wrong" and what specific assumptions must be discarded for more effective interventions' (2003, 5). Also, critics are less than convinced by Ferguson's verdict that the infuriating tedium of development, with its cycle of 'failed' projects, is no mystery but in fact is a clear outcome of the very concrete expansion in bureaucratic state power accompanying development. Even if Ferguson is not suggesting a conspiracy theory he does argue that development project work is simply too convenient for development planners for them to abandon their endeavours at lack of success. Kumar and Corbridge (2002) have argued that the Indian state simply does not need to sponsor failed development projects in order to strengthen its power.

The larger persuasiveness of Ferguson's argument about depoliticization stems from its resonance with several important critiques of neoliberal and neo-institutional economic theory that have dominated development discourse since the 1980s. Neoliberal thinking in particular has had an overarching influence on the stripping away of politics from development discourse, for it constructs all individuals as 'rational egoistic utility maximizer(s)' (Mueller 1979). Not only does this formulation glide over cultural differences, it also accentuates the economic traits of individuals in governing their behaviour. A very narrow construction of individual behaviour in the market place becomes a template for regarding individual behaviour more generally, in a social as well as a political context. Neoliberalism staunchly advocates market-led development on the grounds that markets allow for the best expression of individual preferences (Self 1993, Colclough and Manor 1991). In contrast, states are held to act in the private interests of a few, and neoliberals seek to reduce the role of the state in economic-decision making. The relationship between individuals and states is understood principally in terms of how the aggregation of individual preferences can check the corrupt and rent-seeking tendencies of the state. Over attention to these aspects of the individual-state relationship has resulted in the disregarding of very profound political questions, as those concerning the responsibility of the states towards its citizens, its accountability as well as its legitimacy (see Pateman 1985, Habermas 1975). Moreover, the practical experiences of neoliberal economic reform following the Washington Consensus revealed serious contradictions with neoliberal theory. Several writers have commented on the sheer fallacy of the neoliberal anti-state rhetoric, arguing that neo-liberalism actually relies on more not less of state intervention to further its cause, which in fact is in the limited interest of a powerful few (see the many contributions to Saad-Filho and Johnston 2005).

The dismal experiences of neoliberal economic reform and the rise of the East Asian developmental states generated an intellectual response to the Washington Consensus within the World Bank and its associates. The PWC recognized that it was not enough to propagate free markets, and that it was necessary to work with social and political institutions more generally. This stance was theoretically underpinned by the 'new institutional economics' (NIE) which turned attention away from competition and markets alone to the problem of human cooperation (which had no place in neoliberal theory) and the role of institutions in this respect.[3] This was an important development, and it is easy to see how much of the good governance agenda is derived from the new institutionalist emphasis on institutional reform. However, radical critics like Ben Fine (2001) argue that the PWC did not mark a paradigm shift in economic thinking from the Washington Consensus. Although PWC allowed policy makers to get out of the 'trap' of minimal state intervention, according them greater freedom to discuss measures relating to the state, it continued to base its analysis on taking individuals rather than social structures as its starting point. The new consensus continues to rely on methodological individualism, where the economy is still conceptualized as comprising an aggregate of individual agents, all of whom maximize utility. Fine explains how the capitalist economy is seen as a construct of imperfectly informed individuals, imperfectly coordinated through the market place, an approach that utterly disregards concepts of power as reflected in unequal social structures.

More generally, new institutionalism has been attacked for being 'profoundly apolitical' (Bates 1995, 46). The core emphasis in new institutional economics is on choice, not on constraints, and thus what is omitted from the accounts of NIE is that institutions are often imposed, not chosen, and that being backed by the power of the state, institutions provide the means whereby some individuals can and do benefit more than others. Although prominent theorists like Douglass North (1990) recognize that institutions are not created to be socially efficient and that at least the formal rules are created to serve the interests of those with the bargaining power, yet politics and the state find no explicit treatment within new institutionalist economics. This orientation has had far-reaching influences on development thinking. It has been abundantly argued that the explosion of interest in 'community-level institutions' reflects the enthusiasm about communities possessing 'self-governing capacities' but without due consideration of the historical linkages between local communities and the state at different levels (Sundar 2000, Agrawal 2005 to name a few). New institutionalism has been sharply criticized for providing a 'predictive and generalising theory' of the economic and social conditions for collective action while also creating homogenising myths about all communities being self-sufficient and harmonious (Mosse 2003, 274).

While the rise of new institutionalism has made it possible to talk about wider social and political institutions, as opposed to the excessively market-oriented approach of the 1980s, prescriptions following from a new institutional philosophy often do little to strengthen states in developing countries (Doornbos 2000). The pervasive influence of neoliberalism has meant that there is a limited ability to respond to common problems of 'deinstitutionalization'. In other words, it is quite possible to talk about state reform without actually engaging seriously with it, in any ways other than presiding over its fragmentation. There is a genuine disquiet about how the rise of social capital has blocked any serious treatment of the developmental state. While it has made it possible for those who opposed the free-market consensus of the 1980s to engage with development discourse, it has simultaneously circumscribed the terms of such engagement. There is not much space for power in such analysis; capital is simply a 'non-physical atomized resource' as opposed to a social relation, and society itself is interpreted on the basis of the micro-foundations of macroeconomics rather than with the concepts of radical political economy such as class (Fine 1999, 13). Most conveniently for the World Bank and its associates, their awkward stance of state minimalism is a thing of the past, but without conceding the basic neoliberal orientation towards the role of the state and of politics in development (Moore 1999).

The rise of good governance in development studies came about following the realization that politics could not be disregarded, but much of the treatment of governance since has been criticized for being technocratic and universalistic in emphasis (Chhotray and Stoker 2009, Chhotray and Hulme 2009). The agenda of poverty reduction pursued through poverty technologies like the Poverty Reduction Strategy Papers (PRSPs) and the top-down Millennium Development Goals has also been attacked for reinforcing the 'rule of experts' (Easterly 2006) and not treating politics explicitly and seriously enough (Hickey 2008). The debate on whether politics has truly made a return to development and to development studies is raging on.

Where Anti-Politics Began

It would seem politics is the unsung hero of development. Politics as power, politics as expression and resolution of social conflict, politics as the relationships between unequal structures of social organization, politics as state: time and again, it is these facets of politics that critics complain are missing from development thinking and policy-making. In a general sense, such depoliticization of development discourse reveals the disturbing dominance of neoliberalism and new institutionalism, and a rich and varied literature has established this. Indeed, the history of development is testimony to the ascendancy of neoliberal economics and the marginalization of radical political approaches within the orthodoxy (see Kothari 2005). This chapter will not probe this point any further.

It will explore whether there are any other explanations for why it becomes possible for the experts, planners, bureaucrats and consultants that constitute Ferguson's metaphorical machine to shun or appear to shun politics. How did development come to be associated with such a strong antipathy to politics, and why does politics become such an easy theme to manipulate into a negative image, especially for the purposes of development? Where did the idea of anti-politics originate? In particular, are there other theoretical as well as philosophical explanations that might help us account further for the sheer potency of the idea? Let me offer two propositions to respond to this question, and to organize the following discussion. The first is that development has been closely associated with the economy. A number of historical factors have contributed to the conceptualization of the economy as a domain that is principally autonomous of society, culture and politics. This process has been the subject of very lively intellectual debates which will be briefly summarized. The second is the lingering influence of a tradition of thought about politics which depicts political behaviour in very dark and unflattering terms, and appears to dominate over other traditions of thinking about politics. A very negative view of politics has further abetted the zealous restriction of development to this 'autonomous' economy. At the core of these two conceptualizations also lie judgements about individual economic behaviour as rational and necessary for development, and in contrast, about individual political behaviour as irrational and unnecessary for development. While such views are widely reflected in popular or lay perceptions of the economy and of politics, these are not without deeper theoretical underpinnings.

Construction of Economy as an Autonomous Domain

Two factors seem to play a part in the forging of an intimate relationship between development and the economy: one, capitalism; and two, colonialism leading to the emergence of the modern nation-state. The rise and consolidation of capitalism is seen as the first step in the creation of economy as a domain autonomous of society, in the sense of broader social relationships. The growth of colonialism is viewed as critical with respect to the imagination of a nation-state. And here, it is thought that the realization of the economy as a separate field of operation served as the basis of new powers of 'planning, regulation, statistical enumeration and representation' (Mitchell 1998, 91). These powers have variously been claimed by nascent nation-states in pursuit of development which is constituted as progress (Escobar 1999).

The 'Disembedded' Economy

Karl Polyani takes pride of place amongst thinkers who have commented on the making of the modern economy. In his masterpiece *The Great Transformation* (1944), Polyani documented what he regarded was the disastrous emergence of a new type of economy in England in the early 19th century, followed by the rest of the industrialising world. This economy was essentially of a market-capitalist variety. Polyani argued that it was unique in its 'disembeddedness' from wider social relationships following the processes of commodification of the factors of production, mainly land and labour. Pre-capitalist economies on the other hand were 'submerged' in their social relationships. Land and labour were accessed through social ties of kinship such as birth, adoption and marriage as well as other relationships within the community. Polyani assigned an important role to the classical economic thinking of Adam Smith (1904) in shaping the discourse on the 19th century capitalist economy. Indeed, for Polyani, such classical economics or the 'liberal creed' as he called it, 'was as much a discourse on, or about, 19th century British "market society", as the ideological force shaping it' (Fourcade-Gourinchas and Babb 2006, 534). Moreover, such 'disembedding' of the economy continued with the rise of the self-regulating market but was counteracted by measures of state socialism (or the welfare state) in order to 'check the action of the market relative to land, labour and money' (Polyani 1944 as cited in Isaac 2005, 15). This 'double movement' characterized the 19th and 20th centuries.

Polyani proposed a distinction between two meanings of the 'economic' to emphasize the contrast between capitalist and pre-capitalist economies. In the 'formal' sense, 'economic' referred essentially to choice-making within conditions of insufficient means (as apparent in such words as 'economical' or 'economising'), whereas its substantive meaning derived from 'man's dependence upon nature and his fellows' (Polyani 1957). Therefore, Polyani argued that formal economics was relevant *only* for understanding market economies where the insufficiency of means regularly requires individuals to make choices. It was not suitable for understanding pre-capitalist economies, where economic relations were still embedded in social relationships through redistribution and reciprocity and an individual's livelihood referred not to a 'definite situation of choice' but 'interchange with his natural and social environment' (Polyani 1957, 243). So even though pre-capitalist economies may have had markets, these were not integrated with the rest of the economy through exchange – as was the case in capitalist economies – but through reciprocity and redistribution. Polyani's 'substantivist' school came under meticulous and prolonged attack from the 'formalist' school[4] for drawing historical and institutional linkages between the 19th century European market economy with a very particular kind of economic analysis, i.e. that of classical economic liberalism (Cook 1966). Proponents of the formalist school argued that the limitations of classical liberal economic analysis may have reflected the state of thinking in the late 19th and early 20th century, but such thinking was soon refined by subsequent theoretical developments and that it was erroneous to equate the capitalist economy with one particular form of economic analysis. They also believed that formal microeconomic theory was applicable across cultures since all individuals everywhere made economic choices that were intended to maximize utility. For these reasons, the difference between pre-capitalist and capitalist economies was not one of kind, as Polyani and the substantivists regarded, but of degree.

Polyani was not alone in the endeavour to understand capitalism by contrasting it with its past. Modernization theorists drew a stark opposition between traditional and modern societies by attributing a few essential features to the latter and then defining the former in terms of their perceived absence. These constructs reflect the dominance of evolutionary thought in the 19th century (presenting a schema of stages from 'primitive origins to a civilized present') (Roseberry 1989). In this viewpoint, tribal and feudal societies become the key counterpoint to the capitalist present. Marx (1964, 1977) too was fundamentally concerned with contrasting capitalism with pre-capitalism (as cited in Roseberry 1997). So while the hallmark of capitalism was the separation of producers from control over the production process, producers in pre-capitalist societies were united not only with the means of production but also with a community of producers. In drawing this contrast, Marx presented an unproblematic view of the pre-capitalist 'community' disregarding its various prevalent forms of exploitation. Other theorists of peasant populations, both Marxists and non-Marxists (like James Scott who is a key proponent of the moral economy school) are also guilty of romanticising class relations in precapitalist settings and of ignoring the complex histories of proletarianization and the development of capitalism.[5]

Weber's (1981 as cited in Roseberry 1997) ideas on the development of a rational spirit with the emergence of capitalism have been particularly significant in relation to the making of the modern economy and the modern economic individual. He defined capitalism as a system of 'rational capital accounting' and suggested that the development of such a system required not just a 'new spirit' but a whole new institutional complex including the 'appropriation of all physical means of production....freedom of the market... rational technology... and the commercialization of economic life' (Weber 1981 as cited in Roseberry 1997, 255). All this has enabled freedom, disposability and calculability in a way that was not possible in pre-capitalist economies. The search for profit moreover was unbounded within capitalist societies, with no reference to the circle of the kin and community as in precapitalist settings. For Weber, the capitalist spirit was a rationalist one that reduced all considerations to a cold calculability (Roseberry 1997, 256). In a similar vein, Werner Sombart (1967 as discussed in Roseberry 1989) contrasted the 'capitalist' and 'bourgeois' spirits with the 'pre-capitalist' spirit equating the former with the 'greed of gold, desire for adventure and love of exploration' and 'calculation, careful policy, reasonableness and economy' and the latter with 'sufficiency and existence'. Such emphasis on rationality and rational calculability as an attribute of individual character within capitalist conditions was also conveyed through accompanying ideas about money. Money became a favoured tool with which to draw neat oppositions between the traditional and the modern or the natural and commodity or market-capitalist economy. Such oppositions resulted from the belief that 'whether for good or ill', 'money is often credited with an *intrinsic* power to revolutionize society and culture (Bloch and Parry 1989, 3). While one strand within the western intellectual tradition generally condemns the use of money as going against the grain of man's 'naturally self-sufficient' character (Aristotle 1962, and ultimately, Marx (1961) through his labour theory of value, cited in Bloch and Parry 1989, 2–3), the other regards money in benign terms following a general view of the individual pursuit of monetary gain as a natural outcome of 'man's propensity to truck, barter and exchange' (Adam Smith 1904 cited in Bloch and Parry 1989). Within this spectrum of varying ideas are to be found, what Bloch and Parry (1989) describe, a general 'fetishism' of money.

For Simmel (1978) for example, money unambiguously promoted the rational calculation of social life and the rationalization of modern society in general. Marx too associated money with the growth of the individual spirit and the annihilation of community solidarities, emphasising that the capitalist phenomenon of production for exchange necessitated an 'abstract money medium'. According to these views, money and market exchange had ruined the shared interdependence of the old world where production was meant for use, and replaced it with the 'explicit, relentless and egoistic calculations of capitalism' (Bloch and Parry 1989, 4). In all of this, money acquires an impersonal, anonymous and highly calculative character that depersonalizes social relations and dissolves solidarities. These viewpoints, however, have come under heavy criticism from anthropologists like Bloch and

Parry on the grounds that it is not the adoption of money that has given rise to a particular world view, but instead that the rise of particular world views gives rise to particular representations of money. There are a wealth of works in this tradition that show how the meanings invested in money are as much a result of the 'cultural matrix' in which it is incorporated as of the 'economic functions' it performs (means of exchange, store of value and so on). Indeed, Bloch and Parry argue that all cultures, and not just capitalist ones, make some space for 'exchanges' which exhibit some of the 'impersonal, calculating and opportunistic' behaviour that Simmel, Marx and others attribute to the use of money. The creation thus of 'false histories' to characterize the capitalist economy and of 'rational' behaviour within it has been challenged.

The Economy as a Field of Intervention

Polyani and other thinkers interested in defining the nature of capitalism were influential in developing the construct of the economy as a domain detached from wider social relationships. The use of the economy, however, as a distinct 'field of intervention' amenable to regulation by the state and therefore integral to its power has been described by a range of scholars inspired by the works of Michel Foucault. Foucault was fundamentally concerned with differentiating government from sovereignty, proclaiming famously that governance required that 'we cut off the King's head' and pay attention to the ways in which we direct conduct through the systems of the body of society (1980, 121). He explained that the ultimate end of sovereignty is nothing but the exercise of sovereignty which is in turn equated with the common good; this however is not true for government, which concerned itself with governing things and, therefore, its ultimate end is not common good, but an end that is convenient for each of the things that is to be governed. As such, the population acquires a special significance for government and the identification of problems pertinent to the population is what marks the constitution of the economy as a distinct field of intervention. The making of the economy underpins government rationality or 'governmentality' that allows 'the exercise of this very complex form of power, which has its target the population' (Foucault 1991 as cited in Rose 1990, 5).

Foucault's ideas have deeply influenced scholars interested in understanding state practices relating to the economy. The colonial period was of special interest in this regard, as management of the economy, often in ways described by Foucault, became seminal to the basis of colonial state power. 'Colonial governmentality' in India, writes Kalpagam, sought to 'effect a new relationship between resources, population and discipline' (2000, 418). It was moreover a 'knowledge producing activity' whereby the modalities of 'measurement, accounting and classification' enabled the constitution of the economy. With the streamlining of the colonial administrative system, there was a massive attempt to standardize diverse accountability procedures and accounts. In the invention thus of the first 'proto macro-economic accounting framework', lay the genealogy of the 'Indian economy'. An array of regulatory practices ushered in standardized units of measurement of money and goods as well as calculations that were regarded as more 'rational' and generated a massive record of commercial transactions on an unprecedented scale. Enabled by a Weberian calculating rationality, colonial governmentality allowed the Indian economy to be conceived in 'the modern economic categories of income, wealth, production, exchange, distribution and consumption' (Kalpagam 2000, 421).

Interestingly as well, the use of numbers in colonial information gathering in India had two purposes, justificatory as well as disciplinary (Appadurai 1996). In the first sense, since numbers were used by colonial administrators to comprehend the colonial experience, they also became prone to use – regardless of their 'accuracy and relevance' for 'major social resource or policy initiatives' (1996, 119). They were used to fuel struggles and conflicts throughout the bureaucratic chain, from Indian officials at low positions to the Governor-General of India. In the second sense, the use of numbers in revenue assessment and accounting comprised an element of a complex system of discipline and surveillance through which 'numerical habits' were instilled in 'native functionaries', setting the stage for the many practices of enumeration concerning human communities that would dominate colonial rule, and constituted a pedagogical training of sorts for human census takers and tabulators at many levels. Appadurai presents the fascinating case that several other non-European states, such as the Ottomans, the Mughals and various Chinese dynasties also generated 'enumerated communities', but the colonial endeavour was different in one central respect. Quantification and classification were not separate concerns but went hand in hand instead, generating 'a colonial political arithmetic' in which 'essentializing and enumerating human communities became not only concurrent activities but unimaginable without one another' (1996, 133). The colonial population was comprehended thus through the language of numbers, and then subjected to familiar state practices such as taxation, education and sanitation. The relevance of numbers to colonial state imagination thus reinforces the centrality of the economy as a field of political regulation.

The colonization of Egypt has also been explained within a Focauldian framework of governmentality (Mitchell 2002). After crushing a popular revolt against government misrule and European financial control, the British government urgently embarked upon a 'vast project of calculation'.

Central to this project was the production of a 'great land map of Egypt' which specifically aimed to collect, collate, store and manipulate very detailed information about the land and its people. This project essentially signified the massive production of knowledge of population and territory, i.e., governmentality, to bolster the power of the state. Within a decade of its introduction in 1898 the Egyptian countryside had been transformed into one of the most mapped terrains in the world. However, what distinguished this regime of calculation was not necessarily its accuracy, nor its quantity, but in fact its effects of redistributing knowledge to new sites (2002, 92). As a consequence the whole question of accuracy was rephrased into one of correspondence of the object world (such as land) on the one end and its representation on the other (map). It was this curious effect that gave rise to new objects and forms of calculation, the economy.

Unlike other scholars who have used Foucauldian analytical tools to make sense of the modern economy, Timothy Mitchell notes that Foucault, like Polyani, overlooked an important aspect of its history. 'No political economist of the 18th or 19th century', remarked Mitchell, 'wrote about an object called the economy' (2002, 4). During this time, the term carried its older meaning of thrift and largely referred to the intelligent management of resources. This is what Polyani refers to as the 'formal meaning' of the economic, evident in words like 'economical' or 'economising'. As for Foucault, his ideas about economy were expressly derived from the art of governing a family or household, where thrifty husbanding of resources was important. Akin to Foucault's notions of government, classical political economists 'expanded' the meaning of economy to refer to proper or intelligent management of resources at the political level. This approach meant that '"political economy" was concerned not with the politics of an economy, but with the proper economy, or governing, of a polity' (Mitchell 2002, 4).

In turn, Mitchell offers us a cogent explanation. The economy in its modern sense did not emerge until the mid-20th century. At this time, it came into being as a 'self-contained, internally dynamic and statistically measurable sphere of social action, scientific analysis and political regulation' (2002, 4). Mitchell takes pains to emphasize that this was not merely a figment of social imagination or a social construction, but occurred as the reorganization and transformation of processes into a fundamentally new object. A very significant aspect of this change related to key conceptual innovations within the discipline of economics and general social theory. This included the pioneering work of John Maynard Keynes (1913 cited in Mitchell 2002) that led to a whole new branch of economics called macroeconomics, the growth of econometrics as well as national income accounting. The ensuing imagination of a 'national economy', as a natural and bounded entity that could be subject to political management provided a much needed intellectual vocabulary to new nation-states, created between the 1930s and 1950s. This was a significant development given the new international context of the time, when the collapse of the British Empire and decolonization meant that the world was increasingly understood in terms of independent nation-states with their separate national economies. There were new claims to expertise, new forms of values, new kinds of equivalences, all practices – ranging from planning to regulation, enumeration to representation, management to government – that arose following the 'realization of the economy' as a distinct field of operation for the first time.

Once the economy emerged as a distinct entity, it became necessary to define, equally and with as much vigour, that which it was distinct from. In a very visual sense, the economy was a confined enclosure whose boundaries were fixed by economists and econometricians and, thus, there arose the question of what specifically lay outside this boundary. Mitchell considers that both the state and the household were excluded from the economy: the first as it was the site that regulates and plans the latter, and the second as it was based on productive transactions and activities that did not involve money (1998, 92–93). Such fixing of boundaries created a novel situation, where the non-economic (spheres of the state and household) depended on the existence of an economic sphere. Consequently, the economy became a construct, a 'hermetic field', in relation to which existed a whole variety of other spaces, including politics (broadly synonymous with the state), law, science and technology and culture (2002, 82). Within these dichotomies, the economy was thought to be distinctive for it stood for the material aspect of life, the real and the concrete, amenable therefore to rational and numerical calculations. Mitchell carefully asserts, however, that this real does not stand in rigid opposition to the imagined. The economy is not simply a 'cultural construction of the 20th century', he notes, but in fact it is an artefact, made out of processes that are as real as abstract, as material as cultural. Indeed, such bifurcations do not precede the making of the economy. The economy itself is a 'set of practices for producing this bifurcation' (2002, 82). The ostensibly non-discursive 'real' is intimately intertwined with the discursive non-real. That, for Mitchell, is the power of the construct of the economy.

Rationality, Planning and Development

Polyani (1957) and Foucault (1980) adopt different approaches to describe the making of the modern economy. Yet, it would not be inaccurate to say that an element common to the two is the association that is drawn between rationality and the economy. Of course, the particular nature of the association remains somewhat distinctive. Broadly speaking, in the approach heralded by Polyani (including thinkers like Simmel 1978, Marx 1964 and Weber 1981), where the emphasis was to contrast the modern capitalist economy with pre-capitalist economies – albeit with different explanations – rationality and rational calculability become the dominant nature of individual behaviour accompanying the rise of capitalism. In the approach led by Foucault, and refined by Mitchell, where the purpose was to highlight the emergence of the economy as a distinct field of regulation by the state – both colonial and postcolonial – rationality is the defining quality of its regulators. Both of these associations are deeply significant for the enduring antipathy that is drawn between the economy and politics, i.e., the antipathy that is the intellectual motor of the anti-politics machine.

Nothing captures the significance of rationality better than the rise of modern planning. The core idea of planning is the formulation of a deliberate and authoritative vision of the future, and the role of planners is to guide the allocation of resources towards this vision. In this basic sense, it is not hard to see why planning – particularly at the national level – became a key ingredient of the development endeavour. The modernist influence has resulted in the deeply ingrained view that development occurs in a linear path, from one stage to another (consider for instance, the famous stages of economic growth by Walt Rostow 1990). This view was particularly popular in the 1950s and 60s, a time of decolonization and nation-building around the world. Writing in the case of India (though his argument is more generally applicable in newly independent states), Chatterjee makes a powerful case that an ideology of development was a 'constituent part of the self-definition of the post-colonial state' (1998, 86). He emphasized that development implied a linear path towards 'a goal, or a series of goals separated by stages' and definite priority setting between short-term and long-term objectives. Echoing this sentiment, Gellner describes development as a post- (rather than pre-) revolutionary experience, as 'collective, deliberative and imitative and not individualist, unconscious and endogenous' (1964 as cited in Robertson 1984, 24).

In this context, planning acquires a very particular role. Chatterjee (1998) roots his explanation in the two contradictory relationships that the newly independent Indian state possessed with its people. On the one hand the state represented its people, but on the other it also directed economic development on their behalf; and here arose the dilemma. What the people expressed through their representatives via the political process was not necessarily the best option for economic development, and what the state deemed as the best option was not necessarily easy to ratify through the mechanisms of representation (see also Robertson 1984, 3 for a similar view).[6] Insofar as development itself was premised on the whole or collective interest, it was predicated upon a single 'consciousness and will', one that could 'subsume' particular interests. This created the need for 'the rational determination and pursuit of these universal goals', i.e., planning. Chatterjee specifically describes planning as a 'bureaucratic function', 'above the particular interests of civil society and institutionalized as such as a domain of policy-making outside the normal processes of representative politics and of execution through a developmental administration' (1998, 88). In its aggregative role, therefore, rational planning was crucial for generating the single or unified consciousness or will that was needed for development. In this way, rational planning, conducted coolly outside the realm of hot-headed politics, became integral for the state to be seen to be pursuing the well being of its people as a whole.

Planning thus became integral to the exercise of state power; but who precisely were these planners[7]? We know that they were ostensibly rational in temper and disposition, but what exactly was their claim to such rationality? Chatterjee's (1998) account of the composition of India's first National Planning Committee formed in 1938 is very interesting in this respect. The Committee of 15 included 4 industrialists, 5 scientists, 3 economists and the remaining 3 who had been invited on the basis of their 'political credentials' (a Gandhian, a labour leader and Nehru himself). It is quite clear from this that the majority of the committee's members were deemed to be rational for two reasons: one, the scientists and economists for their ostensible 'expertise' in fields that were presumed to be rational as opposed to being relativistic[8]; and two, the industrialists for their stewardship of the economy, an arena which was widely seen as embodying the rational spirit (apropos the Polyani approach). As for the remaining 'political' invitees, Nehru's presence accentuated the 'scientific' overtones to the Committee's proceedings given his beliefs about economic development through modernization and industrialization. The Gandhian, J. C. Kumarappa, proved an inconvenient presence for his attempts (eventually unsuccessful) to stray the Committee off the path to industrialization. His was precisely the sort of influence that was not welcome in the way of this rational committee's 'scientific' approach to planning. Luckily for Nehru, the institution of planning allowed him to glide over the impasse, enabling key decisions pertaining to the economy to be taken 'outside the squabbles and conflicts of politics' (Chatterjee 1998, 85).

With this formulation, the contours of Ferguson's anti-politics machine become more visible. Ferguson was centrally concerned with the ways in which the development apparatus neutered complex issues of politics – like poverty – precisely through the strengthening of the state bureaucracy. Planning undoubtedly anticipated the ways in which the newly independent state in India would exercise its power. It did so by the constitution of a body of 'experts' whose role would be to decide upon the priorities of a young nation, its organization and allocation of resources and the reconciliation of particular interests, all as a matter of technical evaluation to determine choices on scientific grounds. Here Chatterjee is right to observe 'self-deception' on the part of the state; however intimately the state allies itself with its role as a planner, it continues to be the site where the particular interests of the nation 'interact, ally and contend' with one another. Thus, even as the state transforms the discrete 'subjects' of power in society into 'objects' of knowledge that can be tied into one interconnected whole through planning, the planners themselves are objects within a larger configuration of power. This is a 'paradox from which a "science" of planning can never unravel within its own disciplinary boundaries' (1998, 91). When viewed from the domain of planning, the political process appears to pose an external and needless constraint. But the fact remains that planning and politics are inextricably intertwined, for the simple reason that the domain of 'rational planning' and the domain of 'social power' are both equally constitutive of the state. To separate one from the other may be the fond hope of planners, but it is fundamentally impossible.

The Dark Side of Politics

Most readers interested in development are by now familiar with these links between a constructed economy, rationality, regulation, expertise, technocracy, planning and state power. However, these provide only a part of the intellectual explanation for the idea of anti-politics. The issues described earlier concern the factors underpinning the construction of the economy and of individual behaviour pertaining to the economy (both as constituents and regulators). In the course of these conceptualizations implicit references were made to politics as the realm that was distinct from the economy, or to individual behaviour in the realm of politics, but these are not very clear. We may conclude that – by virtue of being so starkly opposed to the economy – politics is the realm of 'irrational' behaviour and that politicians are hot-headed and capable only of pursuing their vested interests, unlike planners who can adopt a holistic perspective pragmatic for all. Is this simply some quirky attribution of character to politics and political behaviour stemming from popular discontent with the behaviour of some politicians? Or are there deeper philosophical underpinnings to why politics, as a sphere in which a particular kind of individual behaviour is countenanced, is deemed to be so distinctive from the economy and, by extension, so unsuitable for development. Is there is a tradition of thought about politics that can help us understand how and why politics becomes such an easy prey to negative characterizations, in contrast to the economy?

Much of the disdain for politics stems from the classical political economists, notably Smith, Fergusen and Steurt (Chandhoke 1995). Following their view that the development of society stemmed from changes in its material organization, social norms and life itself reflected the logic of the economy. The implications of such a view are well known. Civil society emerged as the natural setting of an individual's daily life as this is where private wants were fulfilled. It was the sphere of 'universal egoism' where individuals interacted with one another not out of any mutual interdependence, but to satisfy their own ends (Avineri 1972). However, even though individuals were self-interested, classical political economists saw no contradiction between such egoistic behaviour and social harmony at large. Indeed, these individuals had gained full control over their passions through reason and were 'endowed with the faculty of knowing what they want and how to go about it within conditions of sociability' (Chandhoke 1995, 94). Such reasoned and controlled behaviour ensured collective harmony and well-being, and therefore there was no need for any external regulation by the state.[9] State intervention in the economy was not only regarded as unnecessary, it was also considered to be destructive as the state comprised vested private interests that squandered money and did not treat it as capital.

It would seem that Smith's description of politicians as insidious and crafty animals (1976a cited in Chandhoke 1995, 97) is not only succinct, it is also persuasive. Indeed the downgrading of politics by the classical political economists contradicts a much older view of politics, put forward by Aristotle in his masterpiece, *Politics*. This work 'echoes the judgement that there is a special sort of human association, one concerned with rule among free and equal human beings (Aristotle 1932, 1255b) and at its best aiming at the supreme human good, that this association is deeply in harmony with what human beings and the world really are like, and how they ought to be (Aristotle 1932, 1252a), and that humans who do not belong to such an association are sharply diminished by failing to do so (Aristotle 1932, 1252b)' (Dunn 2000, 13). Clearly, this is not how politics is widely perceived. If it were Smith's word versus Aristotle's that captured popular sentiment about politics today, Smith would win hands down! Some of the most popular contemporary perceptions about politics have been captured by Leftwich (2006) and endorsed by Stoker (2006). Politics, Leftwich writes, is regarded by many as 'extraneous nuisance', citing Alexander Pope's memorable remark that 'For Forms of Government, let fools contest: Whate'er is administered, is best' (Pope 1734 as cited in Leftwich 2006, 23). This reflects the view that politics is messy and distracts from the 'straightforward and commonsense administration of things'. Related to this view and following closely in Smith's footsteps is another widely prevalent notion of politics as dishonest manoeuvring and of politicians as untrustworthy in word and deed. To Isaac D'Israeli, politics was the 'art of governing mankind by deceiving them' (quoted in Crick 1964, cited in Dunn 2000, 10). It follows, and as Leftwich rightly remarks, that these views accompany a sense that politics is a 'discrete and isolable field of human activity' (2006, 24). So unlike the economy which is linked glowingly with a positive sort of human conduct that is rational, self-interested but reasoned, politics becomes associated with essentially vile behaviour. It is another matter that there are elements within Aristotle's philosophy that lend themselves to interpretation even within negative views of politics, which will be revisited later. The point remains that these popular perceptions of politics have deeper theoretical underpinnings, and the purpose of exposing these is to understand better the antipathy to politics that Ferguson immortalized in the metaphor of the machine.

John Dunn (2000) writes that in order to understand what politics is, we need to ask why politics at all exists. This question relates our frameworks for understanding politics to conceptualizations of human nature. Is it the case that the idea of anti-politics derives much more from one sort of explanation for why politics exists than it does from others? Dunn proposes four answers to this seminal question, and it would be instructive to discuss these briefly.

In the first view, politics exists because human beings are apt to behaving badly. Their ill behaviour stems from base feelings and they are prone to failing miserably from keeping to well-intentioned conduct. Politics thus is the direct output of human misbehaviour, which of course exists in abundance. This view sits rather uncomfortably with modern democratic ideas of individual entitlement to act as they desire, provided they do not infringe on the rights of others to act similarly and act within the scope of the law. Dunn labels this the 'theory of original sin' where human nature is viewed 'with alarm, perhaps even panic' (Dunn 2000, 37). Human beings are credited with very negative impulses, such as 'anger, pride, cruelty, greed, hardness of heart and the will to dominate one another' (ibid.). This theory has a bold explanation for the existence of rule, the Aristotelian sine qua non of politics, in human society. Human beings needed rule as they were 'not fit to be free' (Maistre 1994 as cited in Dunn 2000, 37). Or more famously, without rule, human life would resemble the Hobbesian state of nature (Hobbes 1991 as cited in Dunn 2000). Of course, this did not quite explain why some humans were more fit to rule than others, and a large chunk of modern political thinking has been devoted to answering this question. A little less drastic in its assessment of human character is the theory of 'moral error' which regards that humans could always choose to act better, and when they did not it was no one's fault but their own. It accepted that even though humans have base passions, these may result in less malicious outcomes, and the judgements they employed could be used to subordinate baser instincts. Human beings thus are not destined to act badly but are faced with continuing and real choices. Nevertheless, in both these versions politics occurs because of the sort of creature human beings are. There is an unambiguous correlation between the nature of the human psyche, which is regarded in obsessively negative terms, and politics.

Dunn remarks that there is no doubt that politics is shaped by human motives as well as judgements. Not taking this into account is the great weakness of rational choice theory informing neoclassical economics that assumes (incorrectly) that all human beings are 'well-formed and inherently sensible agents' (2000, 40). Classical economists are more sagacious in this respect in that they recognize that human beings are not without their 'dark side' but place faith in the overriding role played by reason in controlling such passions (Chandhoke 1995). Even so, the theories of original sin and moral error face grave limitations. First of all, the assumption that human beings are very dangerous or nasty animals cannot really indicate exactly how dangerous or nasty they are capable of being. An initial premise of character cannot act as a reliable predictor of conduct, for the plain 'range of possible human action is so vast and so limitlessly intricate in variation' (2000, 40). At a more profound level, Dunn raises the question of whether indeed there was a 'single, coherent way' in which all individuals should conduct themselves. And if all human beings were liable to err, whose judgement were we to trust about this single coherent way? As Locke said the 'great question in politics is who is to be Judge' (1988 as cited in Dunn 2000, 22).[10] Dunn argues that even if, for the sake of argument, there was such a way and humans were agreed on ideal values and goals, they would still need to cope with decision-making in the face of disagreements about how these values and goals ought to be pursued. He regards that even if 'some of politics comes from human depravity', some too, 'comes from discrepancies in practical judgement' (2000, 20).

The second view of why politics exists stems from 'partiality, force and idiosyncrasy' in human judgement. Human beings are prone to judging their values as well as interests and, equally, to taking their own judgements very seriously. Dunn (2000) writes that it is quintessentially human to intuitively regard one's own judgement as superior to that of others, and where we detect lapses in judgement, we are quick to attribute these to failures of character. This trait lends itself easily to endless hostility and ill-feeling amongst individuals. However, even amongst those of us who are 'nicer', clashes in judgement are inevitable. Dunn writes authoritatively, 'partiality, therefore, is no prerogative of the ludicrously self-satisfied' (2000, 27). Moreover, the undeniable and enveloping intricacy of the total context in which human beings act and the complex judgements that they need to adopt in order to respond to this intricacy together create conditions in which individuals take their own judgements so very seriously. If politics, as Hobbes regarded, was 'the civic experience unsentimentally considered' (1983 as cited in Dunn 2000, 28), then politics was teeming with such conflicts in judgement. Clashes in judgement then, in this view, are both the 'source' as well as 'site' of politics (Dunn 2000, 30).

Dunn lends his support to this view of why politics exists, taking pains to distance himself from interpreters who might attribute the perception of partiality in human judgement to the influence of particular and bounded conditions in history. So while some (since Macpherson 1962) might argue that the dismal view of man and the human condition adopted by Hobbes was the product of a distinctive and corrupted Western individualism distorted by capitalism that might not exist in other societies and times, Dunn does not regard that Hobbes' emphasis on 'self-righteous individuality' is an 'idiosyncratic and misguided western apprehension' (2000, 43). On the other hand, it is a comment on a more enduring, basic even, 'biologically grounded feature' of the human condition (ibid.). While certain cultures may amplify or enhance the exercise of individuality of this sort, but as long as humans socially co-exist, it cannot be done away with (Dunn 2000).

The third view of why politics exists is a more familiar one, as it is do with the presence of historically created and sustained conflicts of interests amongst human beings. Karl Marx is its best known proponent (though he too, as we discussed earlier, is guilty of romanticising certain periods in history as conflict-free). For Marx, human life started without conflicts and therefore without politics (primitive communism) and may progress through history to a final and ultimate stage without politics (full communism). Importantly, unlike the previous two views, politics does not inevitably arise from human nature. It appears only when society is dissected by fundamentally opposing interests of groups of human beings or classes. These interests are related to the respective stakes these groups hold in the productive activities of society. Though he regards Marxism to be a bold and exciting theory, to Dunn the clarity of its intellectual assumptions regarding historically created conflicts of interest also constitutes its weaknesses. His objection to the 'conflict of interest' theory is this: understanding stark oppositions in interest depends on certain causal judgements about how reality might be if these schisms did not exist, i.e., a certain view of how conflicts could be transposed into commonalities. Since judgements of interests depend on incredibly 'complicated and hazardous causal judgements', it is extremely unclear and also uncertain that they can be decisively resolved (2000, 25). Taking a step back, Dunn muses whether individuals can ever know 'what exactly' is in their interest (though he scarcely doubts that they take judgements of their own interests most seriously). As an explanation of why politics exists, he considers this view to be inconclusive as 'what the interests of any human being really are, is a first-order political judgement in itself' (2000, 26).

A very different approach to understanding politics in terms of conflict is adopted by German theorist, Carl Schmitt, who wrote during the times of the Weimar Republic. Schmitt (1976) argued provocatively that the way to understand politics was by focusing on the concept of the 'political'. Though politics was commonly understood through its equation with the state, Schmitt argued that this framework was thoroughly inadequate to explain politics in contexts where the state and society penetrated each other. In such a state, everything was potentially political and so the state could not be used to refer to any specifically 'political' characteristic. Consequently, it was crucial to understand the concept of the political in terms of its own distinctions, to which 'all political meaning' could ultimately be traced. The specific political distinction, he considered, 'to which political actions and motives can be reduced is that between friend and enemy' (1976, 26). Schmitt thus set about theorising the political as 'the most intense and extreme antagonism', explaining that 'every concrete antagonism becomes that much more political the closer it approaches the most extreme point, that of the friend-enemy grouping (1976, 29). In this view, politics is tantamount 'to fighting for and against someone, not for and against something' (Heller 1991, 333). The dichotomy in values between friend and foe in politics is thus no less than that between beautiful and ugly in aesthetics or good and evil in morality. In this radical perspective, anything short of direct mass action, in which friends are mobilized against foes, falls short of politics. Schmitt was severely sceptical of liberalism which he regarded as fundamentally 'depoliticising' for substituting adversaries with competitors! He has been criticized for his radical, even 'tyrannical', views on the political, for the fact that he bases his approach on exclusionist criteria even as so many political institutions exist that have nothing to do with the friend-foe dichotomy (Heller 1991).

The fourth view described by Dunn relates the existence of politics to the fact that human beings coexist and therefore need to act collectively. A conundrum arises as individuals increasingly need to act collectively and on ever greater scales, but they continue to remain irreducibly human. The conditions in which individuals would find it rational to cooperate has served as a compelling question, as we know, giving rise to very sophisticated formal analysis, such as game theory. It is in the well known formulation of the 'Prisoner's Dilemma' – whereby collective outcomes to the larger benefit of all are routinely subverted by individuals who choose to act in self-regarding ways – lies the root explanation for politics. As Dunn rightly observes, situations where collectively beneficial outcomes are subverted by individual self-interest are commoner than those where they are not. Despite this, the theoretical responses to the collective action problem have attempted to find solutions to the limits in behaviour posed by the Prisoner's Dilemma. Hardin's (1968) famous 'tragedy of the commons' metaphor to describe the pessimistic future available to man following his short-sighted and self-interested behaviour aroused a wealth of theorising, notably led by Elinor Ostrom (1986, 1990). Ostrom's work has inspired a generation of theorists who have gone on to document the conditions in which individuals find it rational to cooperate in order to manage and govern their common resources, without resorting to state control.

These four views of why politics exists may not be comprehensive, but they do cover a very large spectrum of explanations. They encompass varying degrees of optimisms about human nature, from one who is willing to subvert the interests of everyone around him or her in a mindless pursuit of their own unreasoned self-interest, to one who is able to see that individual self-interest lies precisely in cooperation with others. The explanations that lie in between these two extremes characterize the ongoing state of human affairs, one where individuals are prone to taking their own judgements seriously, from which arises an indisputable perception of conflict.[11] It should be noted as well that depending on which view of politics one adopts, the explanation for conflict varies accordingly as well. While conflict itself is regarded as mindless and constitutive of the base human condition in the first view, the second view perceives conflict as endemic to the partial judgement of human beings, and the third regards conflict as the organising principle of social interaction between antagonistic social classes. The fourth view theorizes rational cooperation as an antidote to selfish disinterest and conflict. Although each of these viewpoints offer a different characterization of politics, it is easier to reduce politics to a negative phenomenon in one view than another.

The point has thus been clearly made that the anti-politics idea rests on the first view of politics more than it does on others. It finds its closest affinity with the first view of why politics exists in human behaviour as despicable, base, conflictual and totally out of order (as described by Dunn). Politics, as the sphere in which such undesirable human behaviour is observed, thus encounters a fundamentally negative explanation (though ironically fulfilling a necessarily positive function, one of instilling order through rule!). It also draws from some aspects of the second and third views, emphasising that human nature thrives on partiality in human judgement, and thus politics is rife with conflicting judgements of values and, by extension, perceptions of conflicting interests. However, there is little or no embracing of the idea that politics as conflict may also constitute a progressive force. Further, in the rush to portray politics as negative, the anti-politics idea does not treat cooperation as politics. Dunn's fourth view of politics is in fact least relevant to development's ant-politics machine which, though obsessed with predicting cooperating behaviour through institutional formation – following the triumphant entry of new institutionalist thinking and social capital – does not view cooperation as constitutive of politics. Here, precisely, the anti-politics machine assiduously sticks to a view of individuals as inherently and detrimentally conflict-ridden that it assigns both to political behaviour and to politics more generally. It denies a rich tradition of political thinking, including communitarians like Rousseau who presented a less bleak picture of what human collective existence could potentially be, and Marx and subsequent Marxist scholars whose works emphasised how the making of collective decisions is the lifeblood of politics. Cooperation is not viewed as an essential counterpoint to conflict in the making of politics. This is explanatorily unacceptable. As Dunn puts it succinctly,

'Do they (humans) cooperate only to compete more effectively...? Or is competition forced willy-nilly upon them, because only by competing can they get what they urgently need, or what, whether they do really need it or not, they cannot help desiring with even greater urgency? In a sense, of course, each. Both the conflict and cooperation are implacably there. Neither explains the other away. Neither can be explained without taking the other into account.' (2000, 133–134)

Conclusion

This brings me to the cornerstone of my larger argument. The idea of the anti-politics machine draws as much from a particular view of the economy as from that of politics. These are regarded as discrete spheres of existence and this is achieved by resorting to characterizations of the type of human behaviour that each sphere is expected to witness. The extensive literature review earlier describes how rationality and rational calculability in human behaviour came to be associated with the making of the modern capitalist economy. In contrast, politics is associated with the baser instincts of human nature. Interestingly enough, similar qualities attributed to human nature acquire inverse implications depending on how they are being constructed. So economic self-interestedness is construed as pragmatic, rational and, as the classical political economists would have us believe, even compatible with sociability given that passions are controlled by reason; political self-interestedness, however, is regarded as the fount of vile behaviour, alluding to the free run of human passions uncontrolled by reason.

We have already seen the historical and theoretical hollowness of these constructions. In the case of the economy, we have seen how resorting to oppositional frameworks to describe the economy and economic behaviour are dubious. The views of economic anthropologists who decry the fetishising of money, markets and above all rational behaviour by resorting to some primordial instincts of communal solidarity destroyed by capitalism are particularly significant here. No doubt the role of rational expertise in regulating and planning the economy has a very special place in the history of modern state building. The chroniclers of colonial state building, as Chatterjee (1998) for India and Mitchell (1998, 2002) for Egypt, however, have in their unique ways deconstructed the precise ways in which the production and privileging of expertise itself is an exercise of a very specific sort of political judgement. Further, the a priori association of a particular and very limited kind of rationality with expertise has been subject to its own set of attacks (Flyvbjerg 2001). As for politics, Dunn wisely reminds us that human beings are certainly capable of depravity, but are also capable of overcoming these follies. This view has two different connotations, both of which are equally important for us. One, that human propensity to value differently – with all its implications for conflict and contest – has a timeless quality to it and therefore it is futile to confine it to any one aspect of human existence or behaviour (as the idea of anti-politics might purport to do). Two, there is boundless resilience in human nature to come together and overcome conflict and any understanding of politics that attempts to undermine this only serves to deform it.

In the end, it seems clear that the idea of the anti-politics machine is a very powerful metaphor to convey in one stroke, in one single phrase, different, even disparate theoretical ideas about the economy and about politics. It is effective in academic parlance as a description of what development's architects allegedly create in their discourses, by allying themselves closer to specific ideas of the economy and of their rational expertise, and by distancing themselves from the 'unreason' and indiscipline of politics. This chapter has tried to expose the intellectual motors of the anti-politics machine. It has shown that there are deep theoretical underpinnings to each of these ideas pertaining to the economy and to politics, and also that these ideas are questionable. The analysis here should not be read as a criticism of Ferguson's metaphor, which is extraordinarily successful, but rather as a guide attempting to explain further its intellectual origins. Understanding how its core ideas are constructed will help in interrogating whether, why, how and with what effects the constituents of the 'Indian anti-politics machine' create and sustain antipathies to politics.

Chapter Two

THE INDIAN 'ANTI-POLITICS MACHINE'

Is there an 'Anti-Politics Machine' in India?

This question may be justifiably asked. Is there, after all, an anti-politics machine in India? The Indian development machinery has for long served as a symbol of decisive state intervention to shape and regulate the economy. In the formative years after independence in 1947 it was the newly formed Planning Commission that provided a vehicle for the political leadership to take contentious decisions without these being subject to the wider political arena for debate. It was the planners' 'rationality' and 'expertise' that made them suitable for taking decisions in the interest of the nation at large, as contrasted with political representatives who were expected to be partisan in their views. In subsequent years, the planning commission itself may have somewhat declined in significance, but development decision-making has been prominently carried out by the bureaucracy, which is itself a mammoth, multilayered, hierarchical and overstretched organization. Even though recent years have witnessed key trends relating to state reform, notably decentralization and participatory development, the terms of engagement between the bureaucracy and relatively new actors like NGOs or international donors continue to be heavily prescribed by the former. The presence of a highly bureaucratized state apparatus and a culture of development planning that has traditionally distanced itself from 'politics' together signify that the Indian state could serve as an archetypal example of the Fergusonian anti-politics machine.

However, India also has an exceedingly complex democracy which makes the business of ostracising politics from development very difficult, if not impossible. The conditions that prevailed in 1947 that allowed the political leadership to take a particular stance with respect to planning and development have drastically changed. The intensification of electoral politics along existing social cleavages has had a profound impact on the execution of development in India. Despite the expansion and intensification of politics through increased political participation both in formal elections and in political debates in public spaces, popular disdain for politics has only grown since the Nehru years. We find resonances of the antipathies to politics as captured by Dunn's first set of explanations of why politics exists within this intriguing political culture, but the linkages are not straightforward. This chapter seeks to understand how precisely the politicization of Indian democracy has unfolded since independence. In what ways have the trajectories of democracy brought politics into the centre stage of public imagination, and what do these processes signify for the discourses of politics that are influential in India today?

There are three parts to this chapter. The story begins in the British colonial period when the seeds of a rationalist discourse of rule were sown. This discourse would deeply impact on the state's approach to planning and development after independence. The second part describes in some detail the emergence of the newly independent Indian state for its decisive influence on the making of the Indian anti-politics machine. It also discusses the disastrous consequences of 'depoliticized' planning for development in India, given the attempt to use project planning as a rationalist and technocratic process that would operate 'above' or 'outside' politics. The third part swiftly outlines the unfolding of Indian democracy particularly from the 1960s coinciding with the end of the Nehru era. There is no attempt to be comprehensive here as the purpose is merely to provide a flavour of the plural pressures that appear to have been irrevocably unleashed. Lastly, the chapter considers how these processes have generally created the conditions for particular meanings of politics to predominate which, together with the legacy of rationalist-technocratic administration, create the conditions for state actors to distance development from 'politics'. These conditions also reveal the fragility of such 'depoliticization' discourses given the sheer inextricability of development, democracy and politics in India.

Colonial Rule and the Nature of Rationality

Before the British consolidated power in India, they were confronted with the task of making sense of a very unfamiliar social terrain. There was no clearly articulated concept of a state that presided over society. Sudipta Kaviraj (1994) has described traditional Indian society as having been 'decentred in a peculiar way' where the dispersal of power amongst dominant groups according to economic assets, political power and ritual status made it harder to identify the structure of dominance. The state, often personified by rulers, enjoyed great ceremonial eminence but had rather limited powers to interfere in this social organization. Importantly as well, while the state extracted its rents from particular sectors, it did not attempt to restructure or shape them.

Further, sectors associated with commerce and the economy were treated as politically insignificant in traditional Indian social thinking. The attempt by a commercial company to claim political power and create a unified state would therefore fundamentally alter social relations.

The making sense of India by the British was in reality the making of India, as there was no pre-existing India that was readily conquered by the British (Kaviraj 1994, Khilnani 1998). The British relied on a grand rationalist discourse that was intricately tied-in with the Enlightenment in Europe and the spread of extractive capitalism. The hallmark of this discourse was an unfaltering optimism that pledged the possibility of translating all knowledge into technical control over the world, thus controlling a large and diverse society. While Enlightenment theory acknowledged the rational equality of all men, it also held that not all men were able to attain it in equal measure (Kaviraj 1994, 37). For the colonial rulers, the difficulty arose from the fact that the British colonial state had to justify itself not only to its colonial subjects, which it did mainly by force, but also to the metropolitan public, which made it necessary to forge its own discourse within the broader post-Enlightenment European discourse (Chatterjee 1994, 82). Precisely because of its dual context, a straightforward transfer of rational norms and principles from Britain to India was hardly possible. The British resorted to a principle of 'colonial difference' to explain away the continuation of certain practices that rationalist discourse would otherwise deem inappropriate (such as when Indian judicial officers were disallowed the same rights as their British counterparts to try cases where Europeans were involved) (Chatterjee 1994). Moreover, even as the colonial state tried to comprehend Indian people through acts of enumeration and classification (as briefly discussed in Chapter 1), it portrayed colonial conditions and practices that appeared to be different from European ones as deviations from a universal norm. By creating a scale of differences, the colonial power was able to justify 'rational' practices that were close to the norm in order to advance along the scale (Chatterjee, nationalism chapter 1994). This would be called 'improvement' or 'progress' in the 19th century, and 'development' in the 20th.

In order to commence the process of state-building, the British undertook systematic initiatives to introduce the logic of modernity into Indian society. These included economic reforms of various kinds, a brand new legal system and the introduction of an unprecedented vocabulary of liberal rights in the economic and social fields (Kaviraj 1991, 79). It soon became clear to the British that the initiatives that entrenched colonial authority could not be justified within the traditional 'common sense' that was prevalent in Indian society, with its segmentary arrangement of social power and a distant state. So began a conscious and deliberate project of reconstituting this common sense, a project for cultivating a 'local elite' that would be 'Indian in colour and blood, but English in tastes, in opinions, in morals and in intellect' (Khilnani 1998, 23). This led to the imposition of English as the 'language of politics', a step which had profound consequences for it created a divide between those who knew English and those who did not, and even within the former category it separated the immaculately educated anglicized elites from the rest. This amounted to the 'slow extraction of power from society' (Khilnani 1998, 23) and its concentration in a type of state that had not existed before in India. Chatterjee regards this process as an integral part of the 'hegemonic project' of the colonial state that required 'the transformation of indigenous tradition into the universal forms of a rational and scientifically ordered social life' (1994, 83) and depended on its newly created protégé for the purpose.

Kaviraj is more cautious in treating this project as a plan for the 'rationalization of the social order' and believes this conclusion severely 'misjudges' the 'crucial' and rather 'limited instrumental intention' of the British (1984, 227). He argues that the British made exemptions in this rationalising mission for the lower orders of the bureaucracy and in fact followed a policy of 'studied non-interference' in the social institutions of the colony. For Kaviraj, 'bureaucratic functioning' in India has continued to be afflicted by two cultures, that of the modernist maker at the upper end of the hierarchy and of the 'village clerk' (typifying lower and more vernacular orders of the bureaucracy), which shared no common language with one another. Making a similar point, Hansen (1999) argues that colonial rulers were not entirely successful in their attempts to 'fixate' the social world of India through their 'technical governance' and far from creating finalities, new policies only engendered further languages of contention and opposition. This was particularly the case also because newly created Indian intellectuals felt distinctly uncomfortable with the selective reading of history, as was implicit within the rationalist-colonial narrative. They resented the glorification of ancient European civilization leading up to post-renaissance Western Europe on the one hand and the bleak view of the decline of the Indian civilization on the other (Kaviraj 1994).

There remained little doubt in the minds of Indian nationalists that if the rationalist discourse propounded by the British was to be believed, then the British themselves were the biggest impediment to the 'full flowering of a rational and modern society' (Chatterjee 1994, 83). For Nehru, the very construction of rationalism as European appeared to be wrong and unjustified, and he regarded it important for Indians to claim a narrative of progress and modernity. We know that Gandhi did not share Nehru's views, but the discourse of nationalism soon moved away from his rigid opposition to Western modernity to Nehru's vision of a modern India. However, the same social structure that had necessitated the creation of an elite that would share the language and thinking of the colonisers now militated against the more general popularization of a rational vision. Kaviraj argues that the nationalist elite, led by Nehru, rather failed to make themselves understood by the vast subaltern groups in the country. This divide created debilitating problems of the lack of intelligibility between what the large majority of ordinary Indians regarded as democratic and what modernist elites aspired to in their attempt to import essentially Western principles of secularism and democracy (Kaviraj 1991).

Nevertheless, the coming of the British had effected a fundamental transformation. They had brought to India the concept of a state. While it may be true, as Kaviraj observes, that the new state dug deep into rural India to create an Indian economy but did not find its cultural counterpart, it still remained that the state had been underpinned by a distinctive disciplinary power. A key occurrence in the 19th century had been the standardization of measures, as this had the effect of integrating localities into a transactional system. This led to the constitution of India as a 'cognitive terrain for development' (Ludden 1992), creating a strong and irreversible foundation for imagining and shaping the Indian economy as one systemic entity. The disciplining of knowledge by the colonial state had led to a regimen of the 'cognition, collection and transmission of facts that universalized as it concealed state power' (Ludden 1992, 257). While those controlling the state would change, this regimentation of knowledge would remain. Besides, though Indian economic nationalists (Dutt, Ranade, Naoroji) backed a radically different concept of development from that pursued by the colonial regime, they were more or less unanimous in advocating an active and central role for the state in the process of economic development (Chandra 1989). To Ludden, Indian nationalism had much in common with other bourgeois nationalisms of the West, but lacked the means for 'real' political expression. Its struggle was grounded in a bourgeois experience of discrimination and racism under a foreign power. When its economic programme began to emerge, it pledged that its state would do everything that the British state had done, but 'do it better, and do more' (1992, 264). The language of rights appeared, 'not as negative rights but as entitlements to be secured and granted by the state' (Hansen 1999, 48). Chatterjee (1998) argues that the basis to the illegitimacy of the colonial regime was its exploitative nature, and not that it was an alien rule on grounds of race or religion. This led to the demand for self-government on positive grounds, that it represented a historically necessary form of national development. Development constituted the 'rationality of the new state' (Chatterjee 1998, 86). The basis to India's development regime had already been laid.

The Newly Independent State

The newly independent state appeared to hold a clear victory for the modernist forces championed by Nehru. Nehru ambitiously imagined an India where not only would the state take charge of economic development, but its activities would also be 'legitimized by appeal to four mythologies of rule: those of socialism, secularism, federalism and democracy' (Corbridge and Harriss 2000, 22). Patel's death and a series of internal political alignments left Nehru isolated in his own party, where he received very little support for his views (see Kaviraj 1991, Khilnani 1998). His own support base lay within members of the modern elite, who were thinly dispersed throughout the governmental and 'modern' sectors. Bolstered by their tacit cultural approval for his modernising views, he turned to the bureaucracy to carry out his vision for a social transformation. This was a crucial moment, and from our point of view, left an indelible mark on the making of the Indian anti-politics machine, for it embodied the belief that transformation of society was not to be (or indeed, need not be) achieved through a mass movement that reflected a wider political debate or consideration of issues, but through competently orchestrated bureaucratic supervision. The marriage of sorts between the 'scientific experts' of the Planning Commission and a particular kind of politician, projected as 'enlightened' and of 'superior moral fibre' became the hallmark of the Nehruvian era (Hansen 1999). Nehru's personal influence lent greatly to the authority wielded by the Planning Commission and contributed to the construction of a distinctly elitist political culture that became integral to the emergent anti-politics strategies of the Indian state.

The basic problem with this approach, according to Kaviraj, was that the bureaucracy was singularly unsuited for the tasks being charted out for it, as it was being expected to do what classical bourgeois revolutions in Europe achieved through a transformation in the 'institutional map through a politics of discourse' (1984, 231). No equivalent bourgeois leadership capable of undertaking a political negotiation of problems facing the task of transformation was existent in India. The Congress had demobilized from its 'militant political form' to 'ordinary Ministerialism', and while its mixed character made it an excellent vote winner, it was not as appropriate an agency for social change. So unlike Europe, where basic structures had been formed by civil society, in India the state intervened to create these structures. The excessive bureaucratization of social life in the absence of the structures of civil society only created the conditions in which problems like poverty were sought to be solved by elite bureaucrats and experts. Kaviraj describes this as the creation of 'a sort of elite confidentiality around the vital decisions about politics and society' (1991, 90), from which the large majority of Indians were excluded.[1] The vernacular divide that separates the elites from the masses only heightened the extent of this exclusion.

The strains of following this sort of approach have been abundantly felt in two ways. The politico-bureaucratic leadership of the Indian-state found it extremely difficult to steward the economy in the desired direction and soon the resources of the state began to dwindle under the pressure. The failure of the Indian state to achieve its stated objectives both of economic development and of social transformation is undoubtedly the most written about theme in Indian politics. Scholars of Marxist, liberal-democratic and new political economy persuasions have each offered explanations. These seem to be particularly important for they reveal the precarious embarrassments faced by the Indian anti-politics machine. The attempt to keep 'mass' politics out of development was itself predicated upon a very particular set of political circumstances, it did not seem to be working and it was also producing unprecedented difficulties.

Using a Marxist framework of analysis, Chatterjee (1998) argues that the Indian state resorted to planning because of the peculiarities of a late capitalist transition. In classical forms of capitalist industrialization, the original processes of accumulation had occurred through a variety of coercive means long before the arrival of political doctrines of legitimation through a general concept of the social good and the production of consent through representative political processes. In India, where the 'expropriation of subsistence producers' associated with accumulation was necessary for industrialization to occur, it could not possibly be legitimated within representative political processes. Thus, it was left to the institution of planning – deemed to embody the 'universal rationality of the social whole' by virtue of its location outside the political process – to tower over particular interests and resolve conflicts within a predetermined universal framework of the social good, laying down costs and benefits accruing to respective social groups.

Moreover, the Indian state had to play a key role in the transition to capitalism as capitalist classes had not been well formed, they lacked indigenous capital and, besides, forms of capital co-existed with pre-capitalist forms (Kaviraj 1988, 2429). Chatterjee describes this as a Gramscian 'passive revolution' where 'new claimants to power, lacking the full strength to launch a full scale assault on the old dominant classes, opt for a path in which the demands of a new society are satisfied by small doses, legally, in a reformist manner' (Chatterjee 1998, 94). In effect, the political logic of the passive revolution amounted to a strategy that promoted industrialization without taking the risk of agrarian political mobilization that would disturb the structures of power in the countryside. While industrialization was presented as being in the general interest of the whole nation through modern planning (especially the 2nd and 3rd plans), the absence of land reform in the 1950s was seen as a necessary pre-requisite for the incorporation of entire structures of pre-capital to be incorporated within capital's passive revolution. The second objective of the passive revolution was to contain class conflicts and 'manipulate the many dispersed power relations in society' to further accumulation. However, conflicts could scarcely be avoided in a democracy and the Indian state took to dealing with conflicts by handing out 'economic' solutions that would be compatible within the overall 'rational' strategy of capitalist development.

Pranab Bardhan (1984) takes a firm view that the Indian state was 'weak' at shaping the economy from the very beginning. In his view, India's political sociology is composed of three proprietary classes (industry, rich peasantry and professionals) which comprise a conflict ridden, heterogeneous, dominant coalition as their economic interests do not coincide, and each of these classes competes for the control of state power within its democratic framework. The personnel of the 'relatively autonomous state' are a proprietary class in themselves, 'based on their possession of human capital in the form of education and by way of de facto possession of public capital assets' (Sridharan 1993, 8–9). Yet, the autonomy of the Indian state, Bardhan observes, is reflected more often 'in its regulatory and patronage dispensing role than in a developmental role' (1992, 323). Kaviraj explains that while political demands on the state have grown exponentially since independence on account of increased mobilization, the state's resources to cope with these has remained static. This has resulted in a structural crisis which has greatly trivialized the question of economic development alongside the enormous growth of state resources and patronage. The inability of the planning project to operate 'above' politics has only produced 'violent strains' in the arrangement, producing what Kaviraj calls a 'crisis of structure' where even a Gramscian 'passive revolution' did not succeed precisely because of this 'late, backward, increasingly unreformist capitalist order' (1988, 2431).

Liberal-democratic explanations for the abysmal performance of the Indian state at social transformation by limiting political engagement with the development process have focused on the contradictions underpinning the formal state apparatus constituted at independence. These contradictions related to the basic debate between democracy and development, in the concern that democracy brings 'political and economic life' too close together for 'sober, long term' calculations in development decisions (Kaviraj 1996, 122). The 'compromise' that was struck was through India's liberal-democratic form where civil and political liberties of its citizens would be sanctified by the Constitution, but the goals of development, both of redistribution as well as growth, would be achieved through economic planning (Indian National Congress 1954 as cited in Frankel 1978, 18). However, governing elites were 'surprisingly insouciant' – as Khilnani wrote (1998, 34) – about the types of concerns that had haunted the advocates as well as critics of democracy in 19th century Europe. There was an unwitting disregard for the implications of according one man one vote in the political arena when it was clear that fundamentally unequal social and economic structures would militate against the realization of this principle. The Constitution of India seemed to inscribe this basic contradiction within itself.

Indeed, an important part of the political consensus that prompted centralization of state power was the understanding that the 'goals of social transformation would be pursued outside the arena of party politics' (Frankel 1978, 23). While state-initiated capitalist development was carried out through the 'rationalist instrument of planning', it duly refrained from undertaking any direct attacks on the propertied classes. Besides, the concessions being made to the propertied classes 'slowed down the tempo of institutional change' as also the 'government's capacity to raise additional rural resources for development programmes' (Frankel 1978, 202). This also reflected a fundamental line of tension within Indian politics i.e. between the centralized state and local provinces. Since the Congress at the centre depended vitally on the landed upper castes of rural India, its ability to undertake structural reforms had been severely compromised. The matter of social and economic reform was left to the regional legislatures 'where the landed elites could bring local pressure against redistributive moves' (Khilnani 1998, 36). As a result, little or no attempt was made at agrarian reorganization even as the ruling elite launched a full-scale plan for heavy industrialization and there was a massive growth in the bureaucracy. This was the emergence of the 'weak-strong' state that grew in size but not in capacity (Rudolph and Rudolph 1987). Liberal-democrats have also commented on the breakdown of the consensus for centralization that had been articulated through the parliamentary democratic system and a monolithic Congress party. This breakdown has resulted in the transformation of the Indian political economy into an 'elaborate network of patronage and subsidies', 'deteriorating' mechanisms of conflict management and, ultimately, the growing inability of the state to meet its stated goals of economic development (Bardhan 1992, Toye 1993).

The New Political Economy (NPE) explanation for this turn of events concerning the Indian state is true to its basic view of the state as predatory or rent seeking. In contrast to Marxist and liberal-democratic viewpoints, however, there is relatively little attempt to problematize the attempt of the Indian state to operate outside or above politics. This is logical in a sense, as for NPE theorists it is precisely the very negative influences of politics that produce the rent-seeking behaviour of the state, leading to the prescription that only the downsizing of the state can cut down or eliminate unproductive expenditures by it. Politics here is loosely equated with 'interest group activity' and fiscal intervention by the state only expands the arena that is subject to these rather unnecessary influences. Thus, within the NPE perspective, state-power is fundamentally about state-led accumulation and an interventionist fiscal policy, the former resulting in the creating of inefficient public enterprises and the latter in rent seeking.[2]

In this line of argument, the entire span of India's political economy is viewed purely in terms of how 'India's trade and industrialization policies had produced the general set of economic distortions' (Toye 1993, 120–121). Toye comments on the naiveté of this approach since three different policies, i.e., first, state promoted industrialization, second, over valued exchange rate as the instrument of state protection of industry and third, a bureaucratically discretionary method of restricting imports and sanctioning investment in industry, were being simply 'lumped together as a single syndrome of "dirigisme" or "interventionism"' (1993, 121). These critiques gained ground in the 1980s and India was labelled a 'rent seeking society'. Krueger's (1974) concepts and terminology were extended to India, 'without her own self-restraint with regard to political conclusions'. Toye comments that 'it would have been more precise to label India as a society with a rent-seeking government; since on neo-classical assumptions about economic motivation, all individuals will be rent seekers' (1993, 122). In any case, the NPE prescription is unambiguous in its call for the reduction in the domain of state activity. Interestingly enough, even as India went on to adopt market-friendly liberalization policies reversing the policy emphasis of the 1950s and 1960s, the size of the Indian state involved in economic decision-making has not commensurately declined. No clear explanations for this phenomenon have been forthcoming from the NPE school of thought, confirming its general impoverishment of thinking around the state.

The Unfolding of Indian Democracy

Most narratives in Indian historiography mark a break at the end of the Nehruvian era. Indian politics took on a different course after Nehru died. There was a general perception of the 'weakening' of the centre in terms of its growing inability to negotiate the demands of various newly mobilized social groups and the ensuing decline in political standards and institutional legitimacy. Astute observers agree that these trends originated precisely from the limitedness of the reforms undertaken in the Nehruvian era (Kaviraj 1984, Corbridge and Harriss 2000). Congress under Nehru comprised a detailed institutional mechanism for negotiating 'power, resources and mandates' both among districts and also between the centre and the states (Hansen 1999, 135).

While this approach may have worked with reasonable success at a time when a dominant political party enveloped not just the state's administrative machinery but also its (elite) political processes, it quite simply faltered when more and diverse actors appeared on the political arena. This produced a general impression of things 'getting out of hand', a description that can generally accommodate most popular views of the state of Indian democracy and politics today.

The attempt to restrict the role of politics more generally in early development strategising did not just emerge from the concerted efforts of colonial and later Nehruvian administrators to administer and develop India in a rational and orderly fashion, away from the unreason and chaos of politics. It was also grounded in a beguiling construction of the 'high politics' or of politics as a 'virtuous vocation' that emerged during the nationalist movement and acquired currency in the first few decades after independence (Hansen 1999). The projection of national political leaders selflessly and prudently guiding the masses in the new context of a 'secular' and 'democratic' India lay at the heart of this imagery. Clearly then, the anti-politics strategies of the Indian state were not about excising this sort of politics. Hansen persuasively argues that these normative ideals had a firm basis in the beliefs of 'cultural nationalists' like Gandhian communitarians who valorized the 'inner life' and 'spirit' of local communities as embodying the 'pre-political site' of the nation (1999, 58). These views lent credence to a narcissistic faith in the ability of virtuous (invariably upper caste) men and the concomitant imagining of a society that was far removed from the 'almost unbearable profanity of ordinary politics performed by lesser men' (1999, 58). Hansen suggests that this expedient construction of politics became an essential part of the prose of the Indian state, as evident through initiatives like the Community Development Programme (CDP) of 1952, which allowed high-caste, middle class politicians to patronize the poor through their involvement in 'voluntary schemes'. Conveniently then, politics of this sort was 'normatively reversed' even though its advocates preached the utopia of pre-political communities, but the same did not apply to the visible proliferation of the low politics, typified for instance by 'vulgar' clientelism, bargaining, bribery, corruption and so on.

Hansen's ethnographic research amongst middle-class professional families in Pune in western India leads him to link contemporary disdain with politics with notion of caste purities and impurities. These are evoked as a result of the increasing and more visible engagement of marginalized social (religious and caste) groups in politics. The compelling logic of democratic political mobilizations is responsible for 'plebianizing' politics, a trend that social elites cannot pardon, despite the extent to which they may be implicated in the very practices they disdain.[3] The argument about low politics appears to 'underestimate' the extent to which 'clientelist populisms' have become naturalized elements of Indian political culture, acquiring widespread legitimacy in 'quotidian forms of political common sense' (Hansen 1999, 136–137). From this point of view, a pejorative view of politics may have had elite origins but certainly appears to have been mainstreamed into popular discourses as well.

Hansen argues that these discourses of politics are intimately tied into the logic of democratization, which is fundamentally about the 'spreading' of the political field to other realms of society and as evidenced in the Indian case the 'circumscribed' but inexorable questioning of hierarchies and authorities. Indeed, it is testimony to the richness of India's democratic experience that attempts to control and limit the logic of democratic politics through strategies of anti-politics have consistency failed. The technical language of development devised by Nehruvian planners and bureaucrats may have succeeded in imposing a 'new categorical order' on the social world but failed in terms of checking the 'political uses of the new authorized identities, legal entitlements and institutions' (Hansen 1999, 58). Equally important is the burgeoning diversity of social groups that have laid claim to these political uses, an undeniable reality that has increasingly blurred the boundaries between 'high' and 'low' politics regardless of how staunchly these distinctions are made.

The story of the unfolding of Indian democracy has been told innumerable times by a range of scholars (see Kohli 1990, Kaviraj 1991, Khilnani 1998, Hansen 1999, Corbridge and Harriss 2000, Jaffrelot 2003, Luce 2006, Guha 2007 among many others). It is not the purpose of this chapter to present a detailed account of India's democratization, but it will focus on two themes to illustrate the ways in which politics has come to occupy a central place in public imagination, not just of a small elite population but also of a very large section of ordinary Indians. The first is the gradual though increasingly confident entry of India's lower castes into the democratic game and the second is the remarkable strengthening of the forces of Hindu communalism that have contributed significantly to the reshaping of the democratic arena, coinciding with the decline of the Congress system. These processes have decisively shaped the engagements of ordinary people across the social hierarchy with the expanding domain of electoral politics, contributing immeasurably to widely held discourses of politics. Simply put, caste and religion are the main alphabets of the language of politics and politicization in India. I want to comment briefly on the key processes that have expanded the arena for radical and confrontational politics, contributing to a less mainstream though no less significant discourse around politics.

Pluralization of Politics in India and the Rise of the Lower Castes

Several important changes in the political arena unfolded during Indira Gandhi's term in power. There was a gradual bifurcation between national and state-level politics which was soon institutionalized by Indira's tactical decision to delink national and state-level assembly elections in 1971 (see Corbridge and Harriss 2000, 71 for details). There was also a building-up of significant regional opposition against the Congress following a split in the party in 1969. Besides, radical and frequently violent revolutionary action (Naxalites in West Bengal) heralded a new phase of 'extra-parliamentary' political mobilization producing a dramatic expansion in the breadth as well as depth of politics (more on this later in the chapter).[4] Accompanying this context of general political disorder and social conflict was the relative stagnation of the industrial economy and of agriculture, demonstrating a serious crisis of planning. Despite her ideological posturing as one committed to radical socialist transformation, Indira Gandhi failed to match her rhetoric with suitable policies and went down the road of outright populism instead. Her populism raised expectations to unattainable levels escalating disappointment and subsequently dissent, even violently so, producing a highly authoritarian and unprecedented response in the form of a national emergency in 1975. She was disinterested in party reorganization or in the legitimacy of political institutions, contributing to the 'deinstitutionalization' of Indian politics (Kohli 1989, 1990, Rudolph and Rudolph 1987 and others). Her direct appeals for popular support marked a clear breach of established practices of Congress working through a vertical hierarchy of state and local party bosses, factional leaders and intermediate elites (Corbridge and Harriss 2000, 74).

Peasant mobilization linked to a larger social transformation was underway since the green revolution of the 1960s. New agricultural technologies made available to the rich peasantry, especially in Punjab, Haryana and western Uttar Pradesh, boosted their capacities to mobilize support through caste, kinship and patronage relationships across the spectrum of rural society (Corbridge and Harriss 2000, 82).[5] These processes contributed to the weakening of traditionally dominant high caste elites, especially since they coincided with the rise of horizontal mobilizations amongst the backward classes. Indeed, the coming together of Charan Singh – a leading peasant leader in North India – who campaigned for peasants from his own caste group ('jats') but also from other lower castes, and the Socialists who had taken to mobilising lower castes on the issue of reservations was a key moment in the political future of India as whole (Jaffrelot 2003). For in this marriage lay the basis of the Janata regime, India's first organized political opposition to the Congress at the national level. The experiment was short-lived however, and also regrettably indistinguishable in its general approach to ruling from the Congress that it had sought to replace (see Kaviraj 1988 for a lively account).

By 1981, the Congress under Indira Gandhi was back in power. Nevertheless, the political trend towards increasing regionalism in politics appeared to be irreversible, with the growth of regional bourgeois interests as well as strong regional parties all over India (Rudolph and Rudolph 1987). The Congress adjusted itself accordingly to accommodate these regionalisms and played one regionalism against the other and absorbed regional leaders, sometimes unleashing regional demands for greater political and economic autonomy from the Centre (Kaviraj 1988, 2440). Moreover, the end of the emergency had created the space for a new phase of rural agitations, as it became increasingly evident that rich peasant power could not be easily accommodated within the 'rural power bloc' (Chatterjee 1997 as cited in Corbridge and Harriss 2000, 90–91). So while the 1970s were quite clearly the decade of the political mobilization of the peasant or cultivating castes in northern and western India, they were also the decade of the growing political assertiveness of the cultivating and landowning non-brahmin groups in southern India (Hansen 1999, 141). Jaffrelot (2003) would argue that this process started even earlier in the south where the intermediate cultivating castes acquired a steady ascendancy within the Congress system, either by collaborating with the Brahmins (as did the Vokkalingas and Lingayats in Karnataka) or by gaining momentum at their expense (as the Kapus and Kammas in Andhra Pradesh). This was conspicuously not the case in northern India where the Congress' exclusion of the aspiring peasant castes was responsible for the conservative character of Indian democracy as a whole.

By the 1980s, the lower castes – between the dominant landowning groups and the scheduled castes – also entered the political arena through distinctive processes of political mobilization.[6] This was to assume profound significance in altering the course of Indian democracy given their numerical strength, their historical marginalization in politics and most importantly their seeming inability to organize collectively (given that individual castes were typically small, dispersed and also poor) (Church 1984 as cited in Hansen 1999, 254). The ensuing proliferation of regional parties – such as the Akali Dal in Punjab, the Dravida Munnetra Kazhagam (DMK) in Tamil Nadu, the Telugu Desam in Andhra Pradesh or CPI-M in West Bengal – generated the need for cultivation of new electoral constituencies which were in turn provided by this motley but potent group, though not without struggle (see Corbridge and Harriss 2000, 98). However, there was an important difference in the trajectories of lower caste mobilization in north and south India. In the southern states, low caste mobilization commenced early on (in cases even before independence) based on 'an ethnic identity and the use of reservation policies introduced by the

British' (Jaffrelot 2003, see chapter 5 in particular). In the northern states in contrast, the politicization of the lower castes only commenced in the 1970s with the recognition that they needed to organize to demand reservations for affirmative action. Charan Singh's efforts to strategically combine peasant politics with the Socialist Party's quota politics to demand reservations for the lower castes were important although without much success.

In 1980, the Mandal Commission recommended the reservation of 27 per cent of all educational seats and governmental jobs for the 'Other Backward Classes' (OBC), a residual administrative category that had been created way back in 1950. This important event led to the use of the OBC denomination as a 'rallying point' for a range of upwardly mobile groups that fell within these categories (Hansen 1999, 142). Given that numerous farmers' movements were continuously drawing support from this ambitious social group keen to acquire political as well as economic power, it was not long before 'mandalization' became the dominant theme in Indian politics. Political parties – faced with a compelling need to secure stable electoral majorities – indiscriminately transformed the lure of government jobs and educational opportunities into clientelist strategies to garner electoral support from the underprivileged groups. Interestingly, the general strength of the non-brahmin sentiment in the southern states guarded against open political conflict; northern elite response however to the prospect of sharing social privilege was violently hostile. These conflicts reached breaking point in 1990 when the National Front government led by VP Singh acted upon the recommendations of the Mandal Commission. While it is clear that this regime too was cynically courting its electorate, there remained little doubt that the forces this single act had unleashed were beyond its limited control. The OBCs earned a new voice to stage an 'intensified democratic revolution' (Hansen 1999, 144), and for the first time in history governments led by the lower castes came to power (as Mulayam Singh Yadav's regime in Uttar Pradesh and Laloo Prasad Yadav's government in Bihar).

This new age of democracy included the political mobilization and rising of the Scheduled Castes (SC) or 'dalits' as well, despite a painfully slow start. Through the 1950s and 1960s, dalit mobilization was hampered by three interrelated aspects that revealed the ideological legacy of Mahatma Gandhi: the valorization of organic social unity, elite domination and clientelism and, finally, consistent efforts to weaken any attempts on part of the lower castes, especially dalits, to organize by resisting separatist claims (recall Gandhi's conflict with Ambedkar) and co-opting their leaders (Jaffrelot 2003). Ambedkar's inspiring legacy was carried forward by the formation of the Republican Party of India (RPI), but the latter found it extremely difficult to mobilize support amongst the scheduled caste population given the Congress's hold on these communities. High caste politicians then (and now) continued to exploit the divisions amongst the dalits and indeed, before the formation of Bahujan Samaj Party (BSP), no single party claimed to represent their collective interests. Kanshi Ram, an SC leader who had formed various social organizations to promote dalit interests in the late 1970s and early 1980s, was its principal architect.

The expression 'Bahujan Samaj' literally refers to the community of the greatest numbers, and Kanshi Ram sought to unite the 85 per cent bahujans from the 15 per cent manuwadis to unite the former through a 'common history of exploitation (Kumar 2007, 2239). His sole aim was to win political power for the dalits and he aimed at building an independent dalit political leadership in a party that was led and dominated by the dalits. However, he also believed that the BSP was not a solely dalit party but was representative of the bahujans, a group that was to be created through a larger alliance of dalits with other backward castes and also Muslims (Nigam 2004). Kanshi Ram and Mayawati have together led BSP to remarkable electoral successes in Uttar Pradesh, transforming a state that has historically been dominated by elite-led politics into the liveliest theatre of lower-caste political mobilization (see Kumar 2007 for more details). Most recently, Mayawati led the BSP to a resounding electoral victory, garnering nearly 77 per cent of the total dalit vote (Kumar 2007).

Three serious issues complicate any easy conclusions of lower caste empowerment at such electoral successes, even though these are undoubtedly important signs of the manifestation of a collective dalit identity in the political arena. These will be briefly discussed here. First of all, it is hard not to notice that the BSP (as also the Samajwadi Party) has been led by 'a small elite of scheduled and middle castes that has developed since independence' (Dube 1998 as cited in Corbridge and Harriss 2000, 216). Second, dalit political leaders have entered very questionable alliances with the Bharatiya Janata Party (BJP) – the principal party of the Hindu Right – despite the proclaimed ideological opposition to the latter. The formation of BSP-BJP governments in 1993, 1997 and 2002 can only display cold electoral calculations that give the lie to the party's supposed beliefs. Conversely however, the BSP has found it difficult to build and sustain partnerships with the Samajwadi Party, which stands for the interests of the backward castes in Uttar Pradesh. More generally too, the unity of scheduled castes and backward castes has been hard to maintain, as for instance in Bihar (see Corbridge and Harriss 2000, 221). Third, the Mandal issue and the hostile reaction it has engendered has created a distinct focus to the mounting resentment amongst upper caste groups and facilitated a growing responsiveness within these groups to Hindu nationalist discourses. I will explore this last issue in somewhat greater detail for it resonates deeply with the second major theme of politicization in India, i.e., religion.

The Rise of Hindu Nationalism

The spectacular rise to power of the BJP and the forces of Hindu nationalism in the 1980s and 1990s has raised a number of very interesting questions regarding the nature of politics and politicization in India. This ascent coincided with the decline of the Congress party's apparently monolithic hold over Indian democracy, but the question of whether this was entirely coincidental remains. The transformation in BJP's national status could not have been predicted in the 1980s (Corbridge and Harriss 2000, 113). The Rashtriya Swayamsevak Sangh (RSS), a quasi-military organization of men, had lost a lot of dynamism despite the presence of a strong cadre base across north India. It was the Vishwa Hindu Parishad (VHP or the World Hindu Council), however, that was instrumental in initiating an unprecedented campaign of Hindu mass mobilization at this time. In 1984, it started a campaign for the 'liberation' of Hindu sites that it projected as having been taken over by Muslims, the most famous of these being Ayodhya (the mythical birth place of the Hindu God Ram). Buoyed by popular television (the Ramayana television series), a key judicial verdict that reopened the disputed site to the public, unleashing of a new phase of disputes between Hindu and Muslim bodies and later in 1989 a remarkable acknowledgement by Congress leader Rajiv Gandhi in an election rally that he supported the VHP case, the 'ramjanmabhoomi' or 'mandir' issue became absolutely central to the political debate of the time.

Ironically too, the Congress did its bit through this decade to contribute to the 'communalization' of Indian politics (Corbridge and Harriss 2000, 114). It opportunistically deployed 'secular' and 'communal' tactics as it needed, appeasing its traditional electoral constituency of rural and urban elites, Muslims and the scheduled communities and also courting the Hindu vote shamelessly. However, this was a fragile strategy. For one, with the rising forces of Hindu nationalism, Congress overtures towards appeasing the Muslim vote (as in Rajiv Gandhi's endorsement of the Muslim Women's Bill in 1986 in the Shah Bano Case) were quickly spotted and described as 'pseudo-secularism' that had continuously 'disadvantaged' the majority Hindu community. Equally, Congress vacillation over the recommendations of Mandal commission had antagonized many upper-caste Indians, even though many of them may have enthusiastically backed Rajiv Gandhi's modernist strategies through his term in power. Naturally, this large and heterogeneous group found little solace in the National Front/Janata Dal either for its backing of the reservations policy. It was in this context that many upper caste Indians turned to the BJP.

The accompanying changes in the social context both in urban and rural India played an important role in this transition. The emergence of a 'new Indian middle class' meant that political parties had to keep up with new aspirations, and the BJP with its conscious image of a disciplined and authoritarian party seemed to be more appealing to this constituency than the Congress which seemed to be beset by corruption and divisive factionalism. The composition of this so-called middle class is diverse and dynamic. While it had long comprised the 'petty bourgeoisie' (small industrialists, businessmen and traders), corporate sector employees and middle ranking professionals and civil servants, it grew to encompass large numbers of rich farmers in the 1980s (Corbridge and Harriss 2000, 125). The argument that disgruntlement at the reservations issue drove the middle classes towards the BJP is certainly persuasive and it is difficult to say just how significant 'religious' considerations were in playing a part in the emergence of BJP's new support base. Jaffrelot (1996) considers that these considerations played a relatively minor role. Equally, there is other evidence to show that the significance of religious identities for the shaping of the new middle class cannot be as easily dismissed. For example, Dubey (1992 as cited in Corbridge and Harriss 2000) has observed that a large number of middle class people in Delhi and western Uttar Pradesh have tried to find the social equivalent of their newfound economic status through 'religious observance and congregational activities'. Fuller (1998 also cited in Corbridge and Harriss 2000) has described the rapid rise of 'temple renovation rituals' to respond to the strengthening of temple-focused Hindu revivalism in Tamil Nadu.

The remarkable penetration of Hindu nationalism into the social and political imagination of the nation as evident in the rise of the BJP has raised a further set of profound questions. The most important of these is whether this rise can be attributed to a 'negative triumph', where the particular conjuncture of factors – notably the decline of the Congress party and also the continued failure of the Indian left – have created a space that this party and its associates have been able to exploit, or whether its rise can be attributed to the presence of an intrinsically persuasive and appealing ideology that it has come to represent. This question is deeply related to the debates around the wisdom of adopting a Western-style secularism as the official code of conduct for the Indian state.[7] Scholarship on Hindu nationalism can be broadly divided into two strands: the first that explains its rise in terms of decades of meticulous organizational work and the use of imaginative political strategies (Jaffrelot 1996, Hansen 1999); and the second that interprets the success of Hindu nationalists in historical and cultural terms (notably the work of Peter Van der Veer 1994 who argued that the most important imaginings of the nation in India continue to be religious, not secular).

The first set of explanations is particularly relevant here as it focuses on the use of religion and religious identities by politico-social organizations to negotiate the trajectories of Indian democracy. Hansen (1999) is an important advocate of this view. He considers that the Hindu nationalist movement emerged as a result of 'a massive and protracted labour of organization and ideological promulgation' and not because it expresses 'essential cultural differences or new social and religious practices in India' (1999, 13). In his view, the notion of a single Hindu culture that is 'incommensurable' with Islamic or western epistemes and organizational forms is a 'real fiction' and the outcome of sustained projections by the constituents of the 'Sangh Parivar'. He has tried to understand the rise of Hindu nationalism precisely in terms of the various 'precarious' processes through which the scattered, everyday grievances and sentiments of ordinary people in Indian society have been reframed by the discourse of Hindu nationalism. Hindu nationalists have consistently tried to negotiate the instabilities of democracy by imposing a 'matrix of a naturalised, eternal and essentialised Hindu culture' upon society (1999, 19). However the approach adopted has been to project religion and culture as 'apolitical' and above the impurities of politics. The ensuing dichotomy between a 'sublime culture' and a 'profane politics' has served as the basis from which the Hindu nationalist movement has built its organizational campaigns and networks (1999, 10). In a strange way, therefore, Hansen concludes, the Hindu nationalist movement in India is both an 'expression of politicization of Indian public culture' (through democracy that is), 'and a reaction against it' (1999, 9).

The appeal of Hindu nationalism to the upper castes, especially in the context of lower caste entry into politics, follows also from the reluctance of Hindu nationalist organizations to transcend the divide between middle class society and the residual masses that form the object of state 'governmentalities'. Conspicuously therefore, the Hindu nationalist movement is very keen to develop a new creed of leaders that can imbibe 'the paternalistic spirit of reform', echoing the sentiment to create politics as a virtuous vocation as opposed to the 'rot' that it had come to be. The BJP's attempts to pursue 'principled' and 'clean' politics needs to be seen in this light. However, clearly the demands of electoral pragmatism have meant that the BJP has had to embrace coalition politics and all manner of ideologically incompatible coalition partners in tow. These compulsions have also created tensions between the RSS, which remains deeply committed to an overall vision of control and organizational unity for the whole 'Hindu' society, and the BJP, which has had to reinvent itself to cope with the demands of the pluralization of politics. This tension has often been portrayed as a conflict between 'ideological purity' on the one hand and 'pragmatic politics' on the other (Hansen 1999, 225). It has been played out in the communal agitations (like Kashmir) pursued by the Sangh

Parivar on the one hand and the BJP's attempt to go beyond the 'middle-class, higher-caste cocoon' by promoting a lower-caste public face on the other. Hansen is cautious to point out that the BJP's lower-castes approach combines a mixture of 'paternalistic condescension' and 'the promotion of the Hindu community as *the* encompassing national community' (1999, 227). Besides, entering power-sharing arrangements with lower caste parties has had limited success. The BJP-BSP combination in Uttar Pradesh between 1991 and 1993 only antagonized the upper-caste stronghold of the BJP, intensified intra-party factionalism and reinforced its image as an 'upper-caste, middle-class party' (Hasan 1996 as cited in Hansen 1999, 226).

Although it is clear that BJP has been keen not to be seen as a single-issue party, its status as a national political party that commands national loyalties remains unconvincing. It has failed to take a clear stand on the construction of the mandir in Ayodhya – much to the annoyance of the RSS and VHP – sending out a diluted message to an emerging Hindu constituency. Besides, the combined will of other parties to keep the BJP out of power saw the return of the Congress from 1991–1996. After the frenzied years of Mandal and mandir, Indian politics was dominated by a somewhat different set of political debates revolving around the adoption of economic liberalization. The Sangh Parivar's response to these debates revealed its internal contradictions once more. The RSS was vehemently opposed to foreign investments particularly in the consumer goods sector but favoured these in high-technology sectors. "Potato chips, no; Computer chips, yes!" was the slogan in 1996 (Hansen 1999, 220). However, other allies like the Shiv Sena in Maharashtra were much more eager to partake of the 'products of modernity'. Pressed on by these forces, the BJP-Shiva Sena government in Maharashtra resumed negotiations with the disputed electricity giant, Enron. The redrafting of the project without any major amendments served to disappoint observers that the practices of BJP leaders were no different from their Congress predecessors.

Other electoral developments at the time seemed to confirm the uncertain rise of the BJP. The 1996 general elections saw the BJP emerge for the first time as India's largest single party but it did so without expanding its support base 'numerically, socially or geographically' (Corbridge and Harriss 2000, 133). It only stayed in power for 13 days and succumbed to a shortfall in the required numbers to make up a parliamentary majority. Support for it seemed to be confined to the Hindi belt. In 1998 when it consolidated its position over 1996, gains seemed to come in from the east and south India – traditionally weak bastions for the BJP – but this was attributed to the regional alliances that the party had forged 'without any considerations of principle' (Hansen and Jaffrelot 1998 as cited in Corbridge and Harriss 2000, 139). The highpoint of its term in power was undoubtedly the testing of nuclear devices, a move that earned the BJP a huge surge in support. The move revealed how important the pursuit of 'Hindutva' remained for the BJP and how cardinal an influence the teachings of Veer Savarkar who, as the ideological father of Hindu nationalism demanded that it should 'Hinduise all politics and militarize all Hinduism' (Corbridge 1999, 240), continued to exercise over the party's actions. Importantly though, the nuclear explosions showed that the BJP could not remain true to its efforts to present itself as a moderate party.

Was the bomb a sign that that a particularly militant Hindutva had a broader appeal, or did it show that the BJP needed to court its conservative constituency given that it had been more moderate in its rhetoric lately? The 1998 manifesto was remarkably moderate as compared with the ones in 1991 and 1996, and the BJP campaign emphasized issues such as law and order, a stable and honest government and a cautious economic nationalism that appeased the 'swadeshi' lobby without alienating foreign investors. The answer is not entirely clear. On the one hand, the BJP poses a threat to non-Hindu south Asia and its activities are underpinned by a very well-organized network of party members and followers who support the hard core Hindutva ideology. On the other hand, the BJP constantly needs to balance this loyal constituency with an equally compelling imperative to win power in a democratic polity by appealing to a wider social base. The 'shock' results of the 2004 election, which saw the Congress-led United Progressive Alliance win over the BJP-led National Democratic Alliance, further revealed these tensions. BJP suffered maximum losses amongst its core supporters from the upper castes and classes, an outcome that led commentators to argue that the BJP paid the price for not paying attention to its core cadres (Yadav 2004). Others viewed that the situation was more complex, and a party seeking to be predominant nationally cannot really homogenize all Hindus into a single category through its focus on Hindutva (Pati 2004). Yet, although the BJP has tried to pursue economic reform as a conscious poll strategy, this cannot be viewed as evidence of the party abandoning its communal strategies (its support of Gujarat's Narendra Modi being a case in point) (see Palshikar 2004).

Radical and Confrontationist Politics

An account of the intensification of India's democracy would be incomplete without a discussion of the radical confrontations that have constituted key moments in the process of democratization itself. These have brought into the fold of Indian politics elements of violence, illegality and state oppression, to add to the colourful yet humdrum routine of ever more contested elections. Movements of popular mobilization and struggle now encompass a range of crosscutting issues to do with peasants, tribals, lower castes and women as well as environmental movements among others (see Raj and Choudhury 1998, Rao 1978 and 1979 and Ray and Katzenstein 2005 for good overviews). Peasant mobilizations linked with the left political parties in the country illustrate well the linkages as also tensions between electoral and extra-electoral politics. The Communist Party of India led the peasant insurrection in Telangana (then a part of the princely state of Hyderabad) during 1946–51. Subsequently, differences regarding ideological sympathies with China as a major communist power led to the birth of the CPI (M) in 1964. But the newly formed party was torn apart by disagreement regarding the readiness for 'revolution', and while the leadership of the CPI (M) opted for participating in legislative politics (leading to the formation of a United Front government with CPI-M support in West Bengal in 1967), a whole host of 'extremist' groups within the party remained extremely critical of this move. The Naxalbari peasant uprising of 1967 further exacerbated schisms within the party and several extremist radical groups were 'either expelled or they dissociated themselves with the Party' (Mukherji 1978, 24). The subsequent grouping of a number of different extremist groups spearheaded by the Naxalbari and Peasant Struggle Assistance Committee (NKSSS) led to the formation of the All India Coordination Committee of Communist Revolutionaries and the CPI (Marxist-Leninist) in 1969.

Having crystallized their ideological and political bases in different states through this new party, the Naxalites stepped up their political momentum but through the adoption of a rather different strategy from that in the 1967 peasant uprising. While then the focus had been on massive peasant participation in the forcible occupation of 'benami' land (which typically refers to land registered by large landlords in the name of a fictional individual to escape land ceilings), the new strategy was broader and much more radical with its objective of complete class annihilation through guerrilla tactics. By going 'underground', the political movement escalated and spread quickly and by the 2nd of April there were 46 places in India where the movement had struck, with West Bengal and Andhra Pradesh being its hotspots (Mukherji 1978). State response to these developments was brutal, and with the unfortunate passing of the charismatic Naxal leader Charu Mazumdar, the movement received a further blow. Indira Gandhi left no stone unturned in pursuing acts of repression and torture and by 1973, nearly 40000 activists were in jails. However, as Mukherji (1978) writes, these did not at all signal the dissolution of the CPI (ML). On the contrary, a very large number of groups emerged claiming to be the real CPI (ML) and there was the re-emergence of Naxalism both in West Bengal (Nadia) and Bihar (Sahar) in the late 1970s. In contemporary times, the intensification of Maoist struggles in a number of states (West Bengal,

Bihar, Orissa and Andhra Pradesh) has opened a new chapter of violent and extremely dangerous politics.

Back in the 1970s, there were a very large range of protests against the Indian state, then personified by Mrs Gandhi. In 1975, Gandhi had taken recourse to a quasi-fascist, totalitarian mode of governance by declaring a national emergency to bypass the judgement of the Allahabad High Court setting aside her election to the Parliament. There were radical student movements like the Chhatra Yuwa Sangharsha Vahinee and a range of women's movements such as from Maoist movements in Hyderabad (the Progressive Organization of Women) and Maharashtra (Purogami Stree Sangathana and Stree Mukti Sanghatana) (Ray 1999). Women's issues received national legitimacy through a report on the status of women published in 1974 and also by the UN Declaration of 1975 as International Women's Year. However, women's movements like other resistance movements had been driven underground in 1975, but these burst into the political scene after the fall of Indira Gandhi's government in 1977. There is a rich literature documenting the trajectories of women's activism in India (see Basu 1992 and Ray 1999 in particular).

It is important not to forget that there is a clear legacy of non-violent political activism originating in Gandhian thinking, as manifest most clearly in the 'Sarvodaya' movement. This reached its peak in the 1970s through the 'Bhoodan' or voluntary land redistribution movement initiated by Vinoba Bhave in 1951 and later taken forward by JP Narayan and others. The movement embodied key tenets of Gandhian socialism including the dignity of labour, equitable distribution of wealth and communal self-sufficiency. An interesting parallel has been drawn between the 'gramdan' movement (which attempted to replace individual land ownership with communal ownership) and the early Naxalbari movement in that both eventually broadened out from their initial objectives (Mukherji 1978). While the Naxalbari movement aimed at total class annihilation in order to go beyond the 'narrow economic demands' of previous peasant struggles, the 'sarvodaya' movement 'relapsed into a mystic trust in a change-of-heart that would usher in a new society' (Mukherji 1978, 83). Many groups that have descended from the bhoodan and gramdan networks continue to function locally although there is no significant presence of any one group on a national scale.

Finally, a general theme of contention in research around social movements in India appears to be the extent to which these have played out within a "'master frame of state-led development' (LaRocque 2006, 522). Various different studies have commented on the strong-hold of the monolithic Congress party and Nehruvian developmentalism on the scope and expression of particular movements.[8] However, in the decades since there has been a burgeoning of new social movements that have grown both in 'autonomy' from the state as well as 'hostility' to it (LaRocque 2006, 523) making the subject of state-social movements' relations an extremely fertile area for research. The growing assertiveness of social movements has to do with factors that have been described in this chapter, such as the pluralization of political claimants, and also with the seemingly inexorable entry of neoliberal influences on development which have eroded state responsibilities, deepened existing differences and created new disgruntlements amongst vulnerable sections. Popular mobilization and social movements as forms of resistance have generally served to widen the political arena, taking it beyond the realm of electoral politics alone, although these have in no way been divorced from one another.

Conclusion

It is possible to come to four main conclusions on the basis of the discussion contained in this chapter all of which have implications for the story that unfolds in the rest of the book. First, the Indian state inherited a rationalist discourse of rule from the British but this was fraught with contradictions, especially in the attempt to transpose social transformation from above, given the chasm between the elite English-speaking protégé of the colonial rulers and the vast majority of Indians. The emphasis on development as a fundamentally scientific-bureaucratic endeavour followed with the victory of Nehruvian modernism and as Kaviraj rightly observed, this was a triumph over the question of social design, i.e., should the political order try to reshape traditional society or should it adhere to its logic (1984, 230). Although the development project started off flamboyantly, with a highly regarded Planning Commission assisting Nehru, the approach had shaky underpinnings. The bureaucracy was being expected to undertake social transformation but it was clearly unsuitable for the tasks ahead. This was especially because the 'ruling bourgeois leadership' both refrained from and was unable to undertake the necessary political negotiations and power struggles for social transformation to be seriously pursued. The bureaucratic core of the Indian state developed steeped in a tradition of rationalist-administration, but with little or no engagement with the difficulties of social transformation.

Second, this meant that the development project from the Indian state echoed a Fergusonian depoliticization from the very outset. It was conceptualized as a technocratic and apolitical endeavour, relating to an autonomous economic domain that could be kept aside from the distractions of politics. This was most visibly conveyed through the adoption of a planning approach to development that would keep development 'outside' or 'above' politics. At the same time, leading commentators on Indian political economy, whether of Marxist or liberal persuasions, have no doubt that in this approach lay the basis of the fundamental failures of the Indian state to achieve its development objectives. In a manner of speaking, the more the state tried to keep development away from politics, the less it was able to achieve developmentally and the more it had to squander by way of satisfying the growing demands of innumerable political claimants on its resources. Moreover, the reliance of the ruling Congress party on the landed upper castes of rural India and its anathema to undertaking serious redistribution therefore rendered doubtful any argument that claimed development to be seriously apolitical. And yet, the rationalist-bureaucratic instruments for pursuing development have endured.

Third, the growing pluralization of democratic processes has had two very interesting implications for the depoliticization discourse pursued by the Indian anti-politics machine. On the one hand, the decades since the 1960s have seen a very large and ever growing popular political mobilization. Caste- and religion-based political discourses have produced an unprecedented broadening of the political arena, bringing a very large range of issues into its fold. Lower caste groups now have their own political parties that claim to pursue their interests and are also actively courted by other parties for the sake of electoral majorities. At a purely instrumental level, such mobilization has had the effect of multiplying the numbers of political claimants on the state's resources. Many lower caste leaders (like Mayawati) have ridden a wave of popularity through promises of empowerment and used their tenure to repeat the excesses of upper caste leaders elsewhere. All of this has meant that politics now appears to be all-encompassing. The singular achievement of democracy has been the politicization of different arenas of life. It could be argued that this has made it much harder for the Indian state to deploy credible discourses of depoliticization. If politics is everywhere, how can it possibly be done away with?

On the other hand, it is precisely the volume and nature of political engagement that has produced a striking discourse around politics as the realm of the profane. The growing involvement of the lower castes and Muslims in political contest has contributed to elite discourses that construct 'ordinary' politics in pejorative terms and their own ensuing involvement with Hindu nationalist politics in virtuous ways. One significant effect of this has been the rise in support for the BJP's heroic (though understandably unsuccessful) claims to pursue a 'clean' and 'principled' politics through self-styled disciplined (authoritarian) governance. These negative notions of politics are not restricted to elite discourses. The sheer symbolism of democratic politics with the heat and dust of electoral rallies, rhetorical speeches, leaders and cronies, wheeling and dealing have associated politics with the seedy manipulations of electoral arithmetic and vested interest-seeking more broadly as well. Depending on the position of particular groups of individuals in the socio-political spectrum, political engagement may be circumscribed or extensive, but most would regard politics as the necessary evil, whether overtly or covertly. The unfolding of democracy has only produced ever more fodder to substantiate negative views of politics. So while in 1947 Nehru may have perceived politics as a source of unruly distractions, unsuitable for discussions around development, the evidence now is even more compelling if this line of argument were to be pursued!

Finally, even though the predominance of negative discourses of politics create conducive conditions for the metaphorical Indian anti-politics machine, it needs to be clarified that such discourses are ultimately tied to the logic of democratization and can therefore change. For the many resistance movements that have brought in an unmistakable radical tension to political engagement across the country, politics is more than electoral competition. It is about broadening the arena and content of political debate, sometimes through peaceful albeit noisy protest, at other times through violent means. Politics within discourses of resistance subscribes to other meanings, whereby profanity, if any, is derived not from an 'excess' of politics as it were but a dearth of it! The point simply is that with a multiplicity of actors and processes engaged in the Indian democratic process, it will be extremely difficult to predict which meanings of politics predominate in which contexts and why. Much more attention therefore needs to be paid to unearthing the particular conjunctures, conditions and constrains within which different actors comprising the so-called anti-politics machine find themselves. This is imperative if we are to obtain a fine-grained and contextualized understanding of the meanings of politics that predominate. Depoliticization it would seem is hardly about the doing away of politics, but about the selective uses of particular meanings of politics with significant implications and consequences for development. John Dunn would agree!

Chapter Three

THE ANTI-POLITICS WATERSHED MACHINE: THE MAKING OF WATERSHED DEVELOPMENT IN INDIA

Part I: State Power, Depoliticization and Watershed Development

Watershed development (WSD) in India has come to embody the dilemmas around state power, decentralization and depoliticization that this book is about. A watershed or catchment is quite simply 'all the land area from which all water drains to a common point' (Kerr 2002, 1387). The term 'watershed' above any point on a defined drainage channel is used to denote all the land and water areas that drain through that point. In effect, anywhere that one lives is part of a watershed, usually classified as micro, milli or macro in size. The transformation of what was narrowly defined in the past as soil and water conservation all around the world into a comprehensive intervention for rural development (Farrington et al 1999, Hinchcliffe et al 1999) can be clearly observed in India over the recent decades. WSD programmes now encompass core development objectives of the Indian state, most notably agricultural productivity, environmental conservation and poverty reduction. These objectives have been variously important to the state at different points of time, but their convergence as core pursuits has lent WSD an unparalleled significance for the Indian state. The central ministries of rural development and agriculture devote considerable administrative and financial resources to WSD. As a result, WSD programmes are perfectly poised to be intricately bound with the exercise of state power. In other words, WSD constitutes a 'rational' development project for the state to follow (Chatterjee 1998).

The exercise of state power is not particularly straightforward however. Since the mid-1980s a number of different influences, both from within and outside the country, have pushed state policies to take on a more decentralized and participatory flavour. This is in keeping with the decentring and regionalization of politics discussed in Chapter 2. Specifically, this trend has accompanied the embracing of an 'integrated' approach to managing land, water and forest resources and the emergence of the micro-watershed (a land and water area of 500–1000 hectares contributing runoff to a common point) as an ideal unit of planning and local involvement. Although the interplay between non-governmental, donor and governmental initiatives and policies around WSD is complex, the clearest evidence of a shift in state policy came in 1994 when the central Ministry of Rural Development (MORD) issued new policy guidelines. These guidelines reinvented various existing schemes in favour of a new decentralized administrative structure and participatory methods of working through specially-constituted village-level watershed committees. Since 1994, there have been at least three subsequent iterations of MORD's guidelines (2001, 2003 and most recently in 2008)[1], in addition to their adaptation by the central Ministry of Agriculture (MOA) in 2000, and these revisions have revoked and intensified existing debates around community-based participation and decentralization in India. Practices of decentralization and participation in the WSD programme have also complicated the exercise of state power and greatly multiplied the arenas of interaction between governmental and non-governmental actors at a range of levels.

This chapter will trace the institutional and ideological shifts embodied within watershed development, with a view to establishing how the anti-politics orientation of the Indian state finds its particular expression in this field. It argues that there are three ways in which the Indian state's tendency towards a Fergusonian depoliticization manifests itself: a naively idealistic conceptualization of local communities; an insufficient treatment of the problem of ensuring equity without any reference to power relations; and finally, a formulation of the decentralization debate in India in excessively institutional terms (casting one local body against another). Firstly, however, the chapter offers a historical account of the key influences that have contributed to the making of watershed development in India.

Early Influences: Soil and Water Conservation

Colonial regimes in Africa and India seriously pursued soil and water conservation (SWC) works, widely regarded as the forerunners to contemporary WSD. Erosion was regarded as both costly and damaging, and states held that the 'poor' management of soil and water by farmers was the principal factor (Hinchcliffe et al 1999, 2). This view echoed dominant narratives of global environmental change rooted in neo-Malthusian perspectives that attributed environmental degradation to demographic pressure, and later poverty, and disregarded indigenous understandings of local environments. Powerful parallel technological developments, as among agricultural authorities in the USA starting in the late 19th century, influenced the formulation of a definite 'top-down' SWC strategy with complex multiple objectives of checking degradation and also increasing productivity. The latter was particularly significant during the colonial period, following bulk exports of agricultural and mineral raw materials from the colonies on which the colonial economy flourished.[2]

Conservation gradually became an important area for state intervention in the 1930s with respect to soil and water as well as forestry (Sivaramakrishnan 2000). In India, the Royal Commission on Agriculture established in 1928 had recognized soil conservation as a problem of special importance, and had noted work already in progress.[3] The Bombay Land Improvement Scheme Act of 1942 was a prominent instance of a regional initiative at this time. The Famine Enquiry Commission of 1945 later indicated that the large-scale experiments conducted in Bombay had produced results sufficient to warrant replication on a wider scale (Hinchcliffe et al 1999, 5–6).

The essential principle of this strategy was a 'transfer of technology paradigm', in which technologies were developed by scientists and 'extended' to an 'eager' population (Mazzucato and Niemeijer 2000, 834). This technological response was articulated through a process of planning, which was not local, and involved central official planning authorities devising blueprints on which large-scale projects were to be based. There was no question of planners discussing the suitability of the method being adopted with the farmers themselves (Hinchcliffe et al 1999, Farrington et al 1999, Pretty 1995, Pretty and Shah 1994, Kerr and Sanghi 1992). SWC at this time, therefore, was a matter of scientific and policy response of the state, in line with prevailing principles of applied environmental science.

These histories have been frequently evoked in later arguments for reverting centralized state governance of soil and water. The influential report *Dying Wisdom: Rise, fall and potential of India's traditional water harvesting* published by the Centre for Science and Environment reinforced 'new traditionalist' arguments about the deleterious role played by British colonial rule in the erosion of centuries old indigenous water management systems (Sinha et al 1998), and the destruction of 'risk-reducing' and 'surplus-generating' village economies in which they were rooted (Mosse 2003, 10). The 'new traditionalists' of Indian environmentalism may constitute one strand of thinking amongst others, but have undeniably contributed to powerful narratives around the revival of community-based management. And yet, not only have the simple dichotomies between the colonial state and local communities been abundantly questioned (Chakravaraty-Kaul 1996, Skaria 1999, Sundar 2000) but assumptions regarding the sheer transformative capacity of the colonial state to shape various environmental resources have also been challenged (Sivaramakrishnan 1999 cited in Mosse 2003, 10).

SWC works after independence continued to be large-scale, taking the form of treatment works in the catchments of river valley projects to reduce the siltation of reservoirs. The agriculture strategy concentrated on higher food production, which led to a thrust towards developing irrigated lower river basins. As a result, catchments were seriously neglected leading to premature siltation of riverbeds, tanks and reservoirs. The first major government response, Soil Conservation Works in the Catchments of River Valley Projects Scheme (RVP), was launched in 1962–63, and still continues in the catchments of many reservoirs. However, continuing high proportions of siltation led to the need for prioritization of deep ravine watersheds in order to address the problem of land degradation. A national policy on ravenous watersheds was declared in 1967 and ravine reclamation projects in Uttar Pradesh, Madhya Pradesh, Rajasthan and Gujarat were started. Later during the 6th five-year plan (1980–1985) the government also started another scheme called Integrated Watershed Management in the Catchments of Flood Prone Rivers (FPR). More recently, the 9th plan (1997–2002) merged FPR and RVP together. These schemes are implemented by the central Ministry of Agriculture (MOA).

India's first soil and water conservation efforts were confined to over-silted and degraded lands. These areas however were not perceived by the state as lucrative from the point of view of agricultural production, a primary national imperative of the newly independent Indian state. In this period of 'post-independence developmentalism' moreover (Gupta 1998), agricultural productivity was accorded a higher priority than checking environmental degradation. In the 1960s and 70s, several newly independent African countries also experienced reductions in attempts at environmental conservation, as these were 'subordinated to imperatives of agricultural production' (Woodhouse et al 2000, 9). No significant correlation was made between SWC and agricultural productivity, contributing to its relative insignificance in the agricultural strategy of the following decades.

The Green Revolution, Drylands and Rainfed Agriculture

The food crisis of the mid-1960s marked a turning point in Indian agricultural policy (Rao 1995, 1997 and Vaidyanathan 1994). The central government responded with the introduction of a New Agricultural Strategy (NAS). This essentially growth-oriented programme was to be concentrated on better endowed, higher productivity areas thus continuing an experiment that had been initiated in the early 1960s. The NAS heralded India's famous 'Green Revolution' which revolutionized irrigated agriculture in the country, brought about self-sufficiency in food grains and also changed the face of inter-regional disparities.

There seem to be three principal reasons for this strategy. First, by the late 1960s, India was confronted with the pressures of having accepted food aid (under the Public Law 480 or Food for Peace, commonly abbreviated as PL 480) from a US dominated food regime. The regime that came into existence following the internationalization of US technology/policy model after the Second World War had disastrous consequences for agrarian structures and food supply in Third World nations (Goodman and Redclift 1991, 133–166). Not only were countries like India filled with a false sense of food security, they were also pressured by America to acquiesce to its agricultural policies, curb population and depreciate currency (Frankel 1978, 246–292). Food sufficiency thus became articulated as a matter of national sovereignty. Second, in this international context, central planning agents were influenced by neo-Malthusian fears about growing population pressures and inadequate food production (Gupta 1998, 60–62). Finally, launching a 'technical' strategy to spur intensive cultivation suited the ruling Congress party domestically as well. It was able to make concessions to agitating farmers' groups in the 1970s (Frankel 1978, 237).

The Green Revolution marked the 'productivist shift' in Indian agriculture in no uncertain terms. The productivist approach had a single dominant objective, to increase agricultural yields in order to raise the country's food production. It called for a shift from major and medium irrigation works, which had been the focus of the first and second plans, to minor irrigation. The emphasis on irrigated areas in pursuit of productivity led to a visible neglect of the country's dryland areas. Drylands are 'areas where agriculture is rainfed, depending mainly on the rains for soil moisture supply', and occupy nearly 52 per cent of the total geographical area (Shah et al 1998, 121).[4] The planning process mirrored the higher priority accorded to irrigation and flood control, compared with SWC that is typically concentrated in the drylands. By the late 1980s, 'the amount allocated for irrigation and flood control projects in the 7th plan was nearly 22 times the amount envisaged for soil and water conservation; in the 3rd plan, the amount was only 9 times the amount spent on the latter' (Vaidyanath 1994, 49). These trends confirmed that the state was disregarding rainfed agriculture in dryland areas, but it soon became clear that this strategy was undermining the productivist strategy on the whole. Independent analyses that followed confirmed that dryland areas were extremely important from the point of view of increasing food security, and that it had been unrealistic to rely on irrigated areas alone, for meeting the country's food needs (Shah et al 1998).

Yet, while unrecognized in mainstream planning until 1985, rainfed agriculture and drylands research acquired a higher profile through the efforts of a number of state scientific institutions to respond to the inadequacies of the Green Revolution. The Central Soil and Water Conservation Research and Training Institute (CSWRTI) and Central Research Institute for Dryland Agriculture (CRIDA), affiliated to the Indian Council of Agricultural Research (an autonomous body affiliated to MOA), were established with the specific mandate to promote research in dryland farming in India. In 1970, CRIDA together with ICAR launched the All-India Coordinated Research Project for Dryland Agriculture (AICRPDA) in 22 centres in different agro-climactic regions throughout the country. In 1972, the International Crop Research Centre for the Semi-Arid Tropics (ICRISAT) was established in Hyderabad. Many other scientific institutions, especially state level agricultural universities, have also undertaken significant initiatives in dryland agricultural research.

By 1985, the 7th Plan document of the Government of India (GOI) officially recorded the government's admission of neglect of the country's drylands. It stated that decades of neglect had led to dryland areas being caught in a vicious circle of high risk, low investment, poor technology and low production. This situation was the result of an agricultural strategy that had concentrated on irrigated lands and confined soil and conservation works to over-silted and degraded lands. Further, it had not taken adequate measures to address the state of remaining lands, which although cultivable were erosion prone as well. It became amply clear that issues of agricultural productivity and degradation of biophysical resources could no longer be compartmentalized. In the mid-1980s, the Indian Council for Agricultural Research (ICAR) decided to implement the findings of its dryland agricultural research in 47 model watersheds around the country. In 1984, the World Bank initiated its pilot project for 'Watershed Development in Rainfed Areas' in Karnataka, Madhya Pradesh, Maharashtra and Andhra Pradesh. In 1990, MOA launched the National Watershed Development Programme for Rainfed Areas (NWDPRA) as a counterpart project to the World Bank's pilot initiative, making NWDPRA the country's premier dryland farming scheme on a watershed basis. By 1991, the World Bank launched the second phase of its project called the Integrated Watershed Development Project (IWDP) with separate components for hills and plains. These initiatives reflected the changing view of the Indian state towards its drylands. Watershed development was no longer just about soil and water conservation, but encompassed broader objectives relating to the sustainable development of rainfed areas for production and livelihoods.

Water Harvesting and Participatory Watershed Development

The roots of contemporary WSD lie not only in the recognition of rainfed agriculture but also in decades of local level innovations in soil and water conservation through water harvesting. Regions like western Maharashtra, where a number of successful water harvesting initiatives are located, experience severe scarcity of water but have favourable topography that offers opportunities for water to be harvested and then used for irrigation. In these parts, for example, water can be harvested in small dams where plateaus slope down to the plains and porous soils favour percolation of harvested water into groundwater aquifers following which water is pumped up for irrigation use (Kerr, Pangare and Pangare 2002). The best known local water harvesting initiative which has become iconic in its inspiration for other individual innovations as well as subsequent state policy is that led by Anna Hazare in a village called Ralegan Siddhi in western Maharashtra. Hazare galvanized local involvement through his personal commitment to Gandhian ideals of self-sacrifice and social reform, spearheading a dedicated movement to harvest water and intensively manage the four village watersheds. A drainage system, trenches, check dams, drainage plugs and percolation tanks were developed with the efforts and participation of the villagers themselves to trap every single raindrop.[5] The results have been spectacular and irrigated area in Ralegan Siddhi has shot up from 'virtually zero to about 70 percent of the cultivated land over the last 25 years' (Kerr, Pangare and Pangare 2002, 8). The effective use of water harvesting through watershed development in an area where rainfall was too meagre (barely 500 mm a year) for rainfed farming established the link between soil conservation and water harvesting (Kerr 2002), and encouraged later project designers to see the value of irrigation development through water harvesting and watershed development.

At least two other village-level projects also led by visionary individuals – Sukhomajri in Haryana under Parasu Ram and the Pani Panchayat initiative in Naigaon in Maharashtra under Vilasrao Salunkhe – also initiated in the 1970s reinforced this link between water harvesting and soil conversation turning villages 'from barren wastelands into green, productive oases' (Kerr 2002, 1390). Both leaders pursued environmental regeneration with extensive involvement of their village communities. Both initiatives were remarkable in the innovative institutional arrangements that were devised to share the costs and benefits associated with gains in productivity and conservation (Kerr 2002). For instance, under the pani panchayat's principles which have now been adopted by a number of villages across Maharashtra, water is regarded as a common property resource with equal rights and access to all villagers. Irrigation schemes are undertaken for groups of farmers rather than individuals, water is allocated in proportion to the numbers of persons in each family rather than the size of the landholding, cropping is restricted to seasonal crops with low water requirements and all members including the landless have the right to water.[6]

These initiatives were widely hailed and stimulated further state attention to the watershed approach. The attractiveness of a watershed approach lay in facilitating an interrelated treatment of land, water as well as forest resources, where scarce water resources could be harnessed, soil erosion could be checked and natural resources more generally could be conserved. Treatment follows a ridge-to-valley approach, from the upper to the lower reaches of watersheds. The Government of Maharashtra launched the Comprehensive Watershed Development Programme (COWDEP) by combining the Employment Guarantee Scheme's budgetary resources and the technical provisions of the 1942 Bombay Land Improvement Schemes (Kerr, Pangare and Pangare 2002). Large-scale bureaucratic coordination continued to be a major problem leading to the initiation of the Jal Sandharan programme in 1992 which brought four concerned administrative departments under one umbrella. Unlike NWDPRA and the World Bank rainfed farming projects, Jal Sandharan treated the village as its unit of planning, implementing projects in micro-watersheds that lay within village boundaries. The Government of Maharashtra's adoption of the watershed approach soon resonated in the central government's schemes as well. The reformulation of the Drought Prone Areas Programme (DPAP), originally a rural works programme established in 1971, to focus on area development for drought proofing through land and water resource development was a significant step in this direction. By the late 1980s, DPAP almost exclusively became a WSD programme.

While both the central as well as a number of state governments like Maharashtra embraced the watershed approach during the 1980s, their initiatives (as also of the World Bank's large-scale interventions) continued to be associated with 'top-down, inflexible technology' with little attention being paid to local institutional arrangements (Kerr 2002, 1390). They were influenced by the technological approaches used in Ralegan Siddhi, Sukhomajri and the Pani Panchayat villages but the lessons of evoking local participation through careful social organization were much harder to learn. Kerr (2002) also notes that these projects scarcely recognized that the costs and benefits from watershed projects were typically unevenly distributed and devoted no extra effort to address these issues through collective local involvement (more on this issue later in the chapter). A number of studies concluded that while many of these projects showed 'good technological and economic performance' especially in the early project years when the project staff was still on site, sustaining benefits beyond the project duration proved to be much harder (Farrington et al 1999, Government of India 1994a, World Bank 1990 all cited in Kerr 2002, 1390).

It was the parallel engagement of a large number of NGOs and donor agencies in small-scale watershed interventions in the late 1980s that contributed to the momentum towards participation being taken seriously by the state. MYRADA[7] in Karnataka, the Aga Khan Rural Support Programme in Gujarat, the Social Centre in Maharashtra and Sewa Mandir are fine examples of NGOs that introduced WSD as a part of broader activities and complemented these with non-land based activities in order to target the needs of the poorest (Kerr 2002). Attempts to organize the politically and economically marginal sections of the village communities for the initiation of 'self-help' activities were integral to these WSD interventions. A key challenge of WSD is that different groups of people use the upper and lower reaches of the watershed for different purposes which may be incompatible with one another. It is not atypical for large tracts of uncultivated common land to be located on the upper reaches. WSD projects aim to restrict access to these common lands to prevent erosion, and while the benefits of such measures are felt by wealthier farmers downstream, it is the poorest who suffer given their disproportionate dependence on the commons. Many NGOs recognized the special needs of the landless, often in unconventional ways. MYRADA for example favoured villages where the total percentage of the landless was less than 10 per cent to implement WSD on the grounds that fewer people were cut off from the common lands.

Before long, the rush to incorporate participatory practices and institutional arrangements for social organization at the village level for watershed development had begun. NGOs, bilateral donors and government agencies were all drawn in, inaugurating an era of inter-institutional collaborations. In Maharashtra, the 'Adarsh Gaon Yojana' was launched to replicate the Ralegaon Sidhi 'model' in nearly 300 villages by combining the technical staff of the Jal Sandharan programme with NGOs sensitive to 'social orientation'. PIDOW or Project for Participatory and Integrated Development of Watershed was launched in 1985 jointly by SC, MYRADA and the Government of Karnataka in Gulbaraga district. The Indo-German Watershed Programme (IGWDP) initiated in 1993 was another example of governmental and non-governmental collaboration seeking to scale-up the practices of smaller NGO WSD interventions (Farrington and Lobo 1997 as cited in Kerr, Pangare and Pangare 2002, 16). By June 2002, IGWDP had undertaken WSD programmes in 146 villages, covering about 137,000 hectares and involving 78 NGOs. The Danish International Development Agency (DANIDA) embraced a participatory approach in its WSD projects in Karnataka and Tamil Nadu in the early 1990s. In most of these projects, participation was principally pursued through the organization of people in self-help groups, the formation of local institutions and 'shramdaan' or voluntary community work.

These developments confirmed the firm arrival of discourses of participatory, community-based development and decentralization which had taken hold of practitioners around the world by the 1990s. By this time decentralization of powers to local government bodies, and increasingly to locally based NGOs as 'facilitators' of community-based development, became an important component of community-based natural resource management (CBNRM) with a more general emphasis on a 'plural, institutional landscape' (Evans 1996, Ostrom 1996, Woodhouse et al 2000). Decentralization in land and water management acquired a key place in the linked agendas of poverty alleviation and environmental conservation, central to Agenda 21 and the Convention to Combat Desertification (CCD) of the United Nations Commission for Environment and Development, first formulated at Rio in 1992 and subsequently ratified in 1997. Both in terms of internal momentum and the conduciveness of international conditions, the stage seemed to be set for major reorganization of state policy in watershed development. Participatory watershed projects had become the norm, and top-down as well as centralized state interventions were beginning to look seriously out of place. Decentralization would offer the way out.

Bureaucratic Responses

Growing evidence was signalling the need for urgent rethinking by the state with respect to its soil and water conservation strategy. By the late 1980s, the significance of drylands agriculture and rainfed farming had been acknowledged for overall agricultural productivity, but the staggering extent of the problem of degradation, both present and in the imminent future, was yet to receive its proper response. In 1994, the Government of India instituted a High Level Committee on Wastelands Development called the Dharia Committee to analyse the results from the latest Land Use Survey. Its empirical findings presented the following year compelled a rethinking of the existing soil and water conservation strategy. The summary of the latest land use statistics available to the committee is presented below. Out of 329 million hectares (mha) of land, information is available for 304.9 mha which are being used as follows:

Area under non-agricultural uses	21.2 mha
Barren & uncultivable lands	19.7 mha
Net area sown	142.2 mha
Forest lands under good tree cover (40% and above)	38.6 mha

Miscellaneous tree crops and groves	3.7 mha
Forest lands under poor tree cover	29.3 mha
Cultivable wastelands	15.0 mha
Current fallows	13.8 mha
Old fallows	9.6 mha
Permanent pastures and grazing grounds	11.8 mha
Total	304.9 mha

The Committee assessed that if the first two items are excluded from consideration, the total land resources of the country that possess any material for 'biotic production' are no more than 264 mha. Assuming that forest lands under poor tree cover and the permanent pastures and grazing grounds are almost bereft of poor tree cover, these along with the cultivable wastelands, current fallows and old fallows amount to 79.5 mha, and can be regarded as wastelands. So the amount of wastelands is almost one third of the total amount of land that is available for biotic production (i.e. 264 mha). This however does not mean that the remaining area of 184.5 mha (264 minus 79.5 mha) is in good health. The land use survey also revealed that the extent of the land area that suffers from degradation, to a greater or lesser degree, is nearly 175 mha (independent figure not in the table above). Since this figure includes wastelands, it follows that the area of lands that are still productive, but are suffering from degradation is 95.5 mha (175–79.5). The committee also concluded that this area of 95.5 mha must necessarily be a part of the 142.2 mha of lands that are under agriculture. This means that nearly two thirds of our agricultural lands are sick to some extent or the other, and that only 46.7 mha (142.2–79.5) are in good health.

These figures led the committee to arrive at the following inferences. It noted that efforts at preventing soil erosion in India had been unsatisfactory and wasteful of money. It strongly disapproved of the restriction of soil conservation efforts to the reclamation of over-silted lands. It advised that as wastelands had gone out of production, the protection of erosion-prone lands was of utmost importance. This meant that 95.5 mha of 'degraded lands' required urgent attention without which they too were in danger of being converted into wastelands. The committee also estimated that nearly 50 per cent of the wastelands were non-forest wastelands which if treated properly could be made fertile again. Further, the committee cautioned against complacency about good agricultural lands as these, presently under a dosage of multiple cropping, irrigation, heavy pesticides and fertilizers, could be depleted under the long run. Besides, these lands were also in danger of being converted into non-agricultural uses that are socially unproductive, such as farmhouses for the new rich.[8] In response, the Dharia Committee unambiguously recommended that SWC efforts should not be confined to the reclamation of over-silted reservoirs, but to all lands, whether degraded or currently in good shape, in order to prevent further deterioration and depletion.

The other major problem with the existing soil and water conservation strategy was the absence of a comprehensive approach that treated the three biophysical resources – land, water and forests – in an interrelated manner. This was largely due to the rigid compartmentalization between departments that were responsible for managing these different resources. For example, of the 'good lands' estimated to be about 89mha, nearly 39 mha were forests that warranted particular yet integrated treatment (Dharia Committee 1995). And yet, all forestlands are the responsibility of the Ministry of Forests which does not deal with general issues of land and water. Moreover, as the existing SWC approach mainly concentrated on the conception and planning of reservoirs alone, it did not look at the multiple uses of water in totality. In the attempt to ensure that maximum water and minimum silt find their way to the reservoir, most efforts were concentrated on building 'heading type engineering structures that break the velocity of water, and then guide the silt flowing downstream to ultimately reach the reservoir' (DFID et al 2000, 4). As a result, benefits were marginal to poor people, who typically owned land along the ridgeline. In contrast, rich people who owned land in the lower reaches of the drainage divide or watershed received greater benefits.

Also, very worryingly for the large majority of poor people, the degradation of village wastelands was seen as the direct outcome of their demand for fuel wood and food which was producing the loss of tree cover. The National Wastelands Board established in 1985 to promote popular participation in afforestation programmes and to regenerate India's wastelands therefore concentrated on the production of fuel wood when soil erosion was much more linked to run-off from rainwater (Saxena 2001). This typically reflected the difficulties arising from the lack of integrated treatment of natural resources, as it is not possible to 'stabilize water regimes even for crop lands' without controlling runoff (Saxena 2001).[9] Whereas the main thrust of programmes implemented by the National Wasteland Board ought to have been activities relating to soil conservation, pasture development and water resources conservation for the entire watershed, they concentrated merely on afforestation on wastelands (Saxena 2001). Equally, it was not quite justifiable to address the degradation of common lands – a problem of growing seriousness throughout the country (Jodha 1986, Blair 1996) – in isolation of other issues including the low productivity of crop lands in rainfed areas (Farrington et al 1999). Indeed these holistic perspectives were conspicuously absent in various government programmes.

The Dharia Committee concluded the need for an urgent reorientation in focus towards an integrated approach to biophysical resource conservation on the basis of a micro-watershed. This no doubt reflected the various innovations and initiatives related to the watershed approach that had been unfolding around the country. The normalization of a micro-watershed as a 'rational' unit of planning for integrated conservation, management and development of land, water and forest resources has followed abundantly: 'It [choice of watershed as a unit of planning] is *natural* because it allows planners to focus on all the effects of downhill runoff in a given area and to plan accordingly for it' (Tideman 1998, 7, emphasis added). The committee's recommendations marked the potential transformation of the watershed from a geo-hydrological divide to integrated watershed development comprising complex development objectives. These include checking degradation and promoting conservation, integrating land use, improving on-site (and thereby national) productivity and also alleviating poverty among a host of other associated aims. The convergence of objectives imparted to WSD a flavour of 'catch-all development' responding to key imperatives of the Indian state. This has obscured a thorough discussion of the difficulties involved in poverty reduction through WSD (more on this later in the chapter). In subsequent years, strategies concerning the promotion of livelihood security in general, like the formation of women's micro-credit groups, grain banks, the cultivation of valuable tree and fodder crops and soon, have been added on to the array of watershed objectives under the banner of 'watershed plus'.

The Dharia Committee's recommendations proved to be immensely consequential for they resulted in concrete bureaucratic reorganization to facilitate the transition of soil and water conservation into WSD as a rural livelihoods programme. They complemented the 1993 review of the DPAP and the Desert Development Programme (DDP) by the CH Hanumantha Rao Committee commissioned by the central government. DPAP had started as a Rural Works Programme in 1971 but had become almost exclusively a WSD programme by the late 1980s. DDP had been launched in 1978 and aimed to mitigate the adverse effects of desertification and restore the ecological balance of the area. Both schemes were being implemented by the central MORD, previously called the Ministry of Rural Areas and Employment. The Hanumantha Rao Committee review advocated that a number of other ongoing schemes with related objectives such as SWC, wastelands development and drought proofing be coalesced together with DPAP and DDP and be implemented under a 'common' approach which would be the 'watershed approach'. Following its suggestions, DPAP, DDP and the IWDP were to be implemented on a mutually exclusive basis. Also, recommendations were made for earmarking 50 per cent of funds for treatment on a watershed basis from two major employment generation schemes – the Employment Assurance Scheme (EAS) and the Jawahar Gram Samriddhi Yojana (JGSY). This would ensure that the same areas would not be treated twice to avoid previous excesses following the uncoordinated pursuit of similar development schemes.

As a result, all of these schemes went on to constitute the largest coordinated watershed based intervention by the Indian state in history. The central MORD became the 'nodal' government authority. By 1999, following a Department of Land Resources (DoLR) that was vested with the powers to address conservation issues in *all* types of land had been established within MORD. DoLR was responsible for WSD in all types of land: waste, degraded, drought-prone or vulnerable. Although this has been an important step towards promoting bureaucratic coordination, there remains a distinction between forested and non-forested lands, and watershed based development in forested lands is still the responsibility of the Ministry of Environment and Forests (MoEF). Difficulties also remain in local-level coordination of schemes implemented by MORD and MOA (like NWDPRA). Nevertheless, the tremendous expansion of scope of WSD-based intervention to all land area across the country, degraded or not, has meant that MORD and MOA were together responsible for implementing WSD schemes in over 25 different states. Over the years, financial investments for these schemes have continued to increase. Watershed Development has today virtually become the flagship programme of rural development in India, with an estimated annual expenditure of Rs 2300 crores during the Tenth Plan (Report of the Technical Committee on Watershed Programmes in India 2006 cited in Samuel et al 2006) and a target of treating 63 million hectares over the next 20–25 years with an estimated total outlay of Rs 76,000 crores (GOI 2000 cited in Samuel et al 2006, 13). The 2006 Technical Committee Report argued for a concerted increase in funding, making the case that at the current level of outlay it would take about 75 years for WSD to be 'completed', and if the government was serious about completing the work by 2020, it needed to allocate money to the tune of 10,000 crores per year for the next 15 years.

The transfer of principal governmental mandate from MOA – which had previously been responsible for WSD-related programmes – to MORD sealed the transformation of WSD into a rural development programme with the entire gamut of objectives. This transfer was both symbolic as well as substantive. It was symbolic of the state's recognition of the breadth of objectives that WSD has now come to occupy, and substantive because it paved the way for wide ranging policy changes, especially with respect to incorporating a participatory focus for the programme. MOA has followed the lead provided by MORD in making the transition towards participatory watershed projects.

The Common Guidelines of 1994: Creating Programme Structure for Decentralization and Participation

In 1994, MORD issued the recommendations of the Hanumantha Rao Committee as the 'common guidelines' applicable to all WSD schemes being implemented by the ministry. These came into effect on the 1st of April, 1995. The guidelines were unprecedented in nature as they introduced a decentralized administrative structure for the programme and incorporated an explicitly participatory focus into local programme operations. The guidelines introduced many institutional provisions that reflected wider discourses around decentralization and participatory development. The envisaged structure was uniformly applicable throughout the country, though individual states were free to improvise as long as they did not alter the essential aspects of reorganization. While marking a step forward in state-initiated decentralization, the guidelines reignited older debates around the empowerment of local bodies (panchayats) in India (more on this later in the chapter).

The administrative structure proposed by the 1994 guidelines is modelled on a typical government line department, but there were two key innovations: the first is the involvement of NGOs at different levels of implementation and the second is the constitution of a non-elected village watershed committee (WC) that would be exclusively responsible for the implementation of the watershed project in a participatory manner. Decentralization in programme administration and participation in decision-making were thus viewed as mutually constitutive, quite in line with prevailing discourses around these ideas. These discourses regarded NGOs favourably for their positive roles in promoting 'social mobilization' and participation, and programme architects clearly did not seek to confine decentralization to the intra-governmental redistribution of powers alone. As for WCs, at the time, their formation consolidated a significant new trend in the conduct of decentralized development in India, as the implementation of various natural resource management programmes like Joint Forestry Management (JFM) was also taking place through dedicated local bodies. Local management of watershed resources presents a complex challenge, and programme planners perceived the need for the development of institutions like the WC to govern the use of private and common resources (Turton 2000).

The Department for Rural Development in each state is the parent department for MORD-funded WSD programmes. There is an advisory committee called the State Watershed Programme Implementation and

Review Committee (SWPIRC) comprising departmental heads and directors of relevant technical institutions and NGOs involved in WSD related work around the state. Decentralization of powers to the district tier of the programme is the most important aspect of administrative reorganization and a direct link has been established between the central government and the district programme body for the flow of funds. The district programme body responsible is either the District Rural Development Agency (DRDA – the administrative body that typically implements rural development programmes in every district) or the Zilla Panchayat (ZP – the district level body of the three tier panchayat or local government system) if it has been merged with the DRDA following a 1995 directive by MORD to this effect.[10] This was an important move by the central government in favour of decentralization to the beleaguered panchayats, but very few states around the country implemented this merger readily.[11]

Depending on its status, the DRDA/ZP is the principal administrative tier of the programme. Thus a district level body – not the state government – is principally in charge of implementation (MORD 1994, 12). It is responsible both for the selection of watershed areas and of Project Implementing Agencies (PIAs) that are responsible for 'planning, coordinating and supervising the formulation and implementation' of the projects in selected villages (MORD 1994, 17). The guidelines require the selection of villages to which WSD projects are awarded to be strictly determined by criteria of biophysical and socio-economic indicators that must be devised at the state level.[12] Commonly included indicators are evapo-transpiration rate, rainfall, drinking water scarcity, status of groundwater as also percentage of the Scheduled Castes/Scheduled Tribes (SC/ST) population, illiterates and agricultural labour and so on. Considerations of contiguity of watershed areas and the preponderance of common lands may also prevail. The guidelines require PIAs to be selected from among a wide pool of institutions including government line departments, agricultural universities, cooperatives and banks, apart from NGOs (MORD 1994, 12). The district has considerable discretion in this matter. PIAs work through a four member Watershed Development Team, which is multidisciplinary, though individual arrangements may vary between states.[13]

As a measure of financial decentralization, funds for the programme flow directly from MORD to the DRDA or ZP, and the state government only releases a matching grant to the latter.[14] Once received by the district level authority, money for works is transferred directly to the account held by the WC.[15] As a result of this provision, a strong basis for the claim that the WC is not a nominal body has been laid. Yet it is the district that retains controls over money and has discretionary powers to innovate provisions for financial stringency. The district Collector usually has final powers of administrative sanction.[16] District level government officers from relevant departments like minor irrigation and agriculture have powers of technical sanction for different sectors within a watershed project.

Panchayat institutions have been accorded an advisory role at the district, where the nucleus of programme decision-making is located. The District Watershed Advisory Committee (DWAC) mainly comprises elected representatives to the Zilla Panchayat. In theory, the district programme body is meant to consult DWAC on policy matters. In practice, district authorities have the discretion to determine the extent of DWAC's involvement in the watershed programme. This is usually dependent on the broader political stance towards panchayat bodies adopted by the concerned state government. The 'gram' or village panchayat has a more substantial role than ZP representatives. In fact, the guidelines require that resolutions must be obtained from the gram panchayat before the commencement of the watershed project as well as regarding public contributions and the maintenance of common assets created during the programme. In institutional terms, the assumption is that gram panchayats, while not implementing the project directly would assume a cooperative role.[17] However, this advisory role notwithstanding, the denial of principal responsibility for WSD to panchayats has been abundantly criticized as the latest ploy by the central government to deflect powers away from panchayats.

Perhaps the most remarkable aspect of the 1994 guidelines is their detailed account of the procedures that ought to be followed at the village level to form watershed committees and subsequently in relation to their functioning for the duration of the project. These procedures codify bureaucratic imagination of local participation. They are also at the heart of the argument to distinguish WCs from panchayats and presented as *more* suitable than the latter for the imperatives of participatory watershed development. Unlike panchayats, which are elected local bodies, the process of committee formation is meant to be consensual and not through competitive elections. The guidelines prescribe that the committee should be appointed by the larger collective of all residents in the watershed area, termed the 'watershed association'. Prior to the formation of the committee, the PIA is responsible for initiating the formation of user and self-help groups in the village, which it envisages will be formed with the help of 'village volunteers' identified in the course of participatory rural appraisal (PRA) exercises in the 'community organization programme' that precedes each project.[18] The watershed association is required to nominate four representatives from the self-help groups and five from the user groups as members of the watershed committee, and the remaining two members are nominated by the village panchayat and the Watershed

Development Team (WDT). The committee elects a Chairman from among its members, and appoints a Watershed Secretary, who is a full-time paid employee of the association. The guidelines thus emphasize collective action by the community in facilitating these local institutions. Seats are reserved for the SC/ST community and for women, in tune with the state's affirmative reservations policies for disadvantaged sections.

The guidelines also offer a ready blueprint for how a model watershed committee ought to function. Each WSD project is implemented on the basis of a four-year action plan,[19] which proposes measures upon careful consideration of the topography of the micro-watershed. Their objective is land and water resource management within the watershed. There are usually three points of emphasis – on-farm soil and water conservation and surface water harvesting that primarily involve the construction of structures on land, and afforestation through planting of trees. The guidelines envision that the action plan would be prepared not in government offices, but in the village by the watershed committee, through a 'participatory and gradual' process involving deliberations with user and self-help groups, which may extend until the end of the first project year. This provision allows policy makers to claim successfully that the programme subscribes to a philosophy of decentralized planning. It is primarily through the action plan that the government expects persons living in watershed areas to have a say in the implementation of the project. The guidelines also lay down a number of methods for 'collective decision-making and participation', such as regular public meetings, that it expects the watershed committee to adopt. There is a provision for creating a Watershed Development Fund (WDF) through voluntary contributions of cash or labour, to be used by the community for post-project maintenance. The PIA and its WDT are the critical links between the village watershed committee and the rest of the project structure. Yet, while charting a course for participatory decision-making, the guidelines are cautious in maintaining that the PIA is not a substitute for the watershed committee, which is portrayed as the real node of decision-making. District authorities in charge of the programme can monitor the activities of PIAs within their general powers of implementation.

Part II: The Anti-Politics Watershed Machine

It is precisely through their imagination of community-based participation and decentralization to locally created institutions that the policy guidelines of 1994 create the conditions for depoliticising watershed development. The ways in which this depoliticization is sought have to do very largely with disengagement with the particular issues of power rooted in political, economic and social differences but also disavowal of the very discourses that structure these unequal relationships. Not only are differences not seriously recognized beyond the nominal mention of 'weaker' sections like the SC/STs or women, it is also presumed that individuals acting from the vantage point of their particular positions (dominant or subordinate) will temporarily suspend these asymmetries while interacting during 'participatory' processes as the 'local' is unquestioningly valorized. This perspective reflects a common failing of participatory approaches to regard the fluidities of power and its presence and movement beyond the 'macro' and 'central' levels alone (Kothari 2001). In doing so, they seem to disregard that the interactions that structure participatory processes, outcomes and indeed the articulation of local knowledge are not isolated from power relationships but are 'embedded' within them (Kothari 2001, 141). These interactions include the entire range of village-level social relations as well as between residents of project villages and project staff, as also amongst different tiers of the project administration.

The implications of this stance for the large numbers of practitioners who are involved in the interpretation and implementation of the guidelines are immense. For reasons set out below, the chapter will argue that the guidelines project a social vision of community-based WSD that has little bearing to reality. In doing so they create conditions of incredulity (in other words, we do not really expect the practitioners who implement them nor village residents who are subject to them to believe in them), but at the same time, they allow for an available discourse of depoliticization that can be suffused with pertinent meanings to suit a variety of ends, depending on the positions and political contexts of key actors.

Community

The cornerstone of decentralized and participatory decision making as espoused by the 1994 guidelines is their view of local communities. This view is heavily influenced by contemporary ideas that exaggerate the ability of 'communities' to engage uniformly in cooperative behaviour and develop their 'own' institutions. The formation of such institutions, watershed committees, is depicted through lengthy descriptions of procedures (MORD 1994, 27–30). These procedures make four important assumptions, and though these remain unstated they appear to guide the spirit of the descriptions. In this respect they are no different from an entire generation of participatory policies that have been deployed in various countries, and have also been abundantly criticized (see Mosse 2001, Kothari 2001). The first assumption is that the individual, and indeed *all* individuals, would find it equally reasonable to participate in the development project and would indeed do so harmoniously. Second, they assume that participatory projects contain *equal potential* for the development of the local community in its entirety and make no distinction on grounds of caste, class or gender. Third, they regard that institutional mechanisms are sufficient to *peacefully* reconcile differences among members of the local community, should these even arise, and that differences must be expressed through public mechanisms of deliberation. Finally, the guidelines believe that the participatory project is equipped to secure *perfect consensus* or unanimity in the local community.

These assumptions individually and collectively reveal the influence of particular theoretical traditions that have come to dominate development discourse in recent decades. The influences are by no means straightforward however. The first two assumptions for instance are at least partly derived from liberal theory (see Williams and Young 1994), though as the chapter will argue, subsequent assumptions distort basic liberal principles.[20] The guidelines presume that all individuals would find it in their best interest to participate in the project. This relates to a notion of the individual as 'autonomous', rational and free choosing that is central to liberal thinking (Kymlicka 1990, 198), and was later extended into the economic realm by the New Political Economy (NPE) school. Drawing from the liberal tradition, the NPE adopted a view of the human as a 'rational, egoistic utility maximizer' (Mueller 1979, 1–2). The economic traits of the individual were 'assumed to be universal, underneath the superficial variety of culturally conditioned behaviour' (Williams and Young 1994, 97). The participatory project is deemed to be attractive to all individuals who would therefore find it rational to participate. Moreover, the effacing away of all differences amongst individuals in liberal theory lends itself to the assumption that the participatory project makes no distinction amongst persons on the basis of their socio-economic backgrounds or their gender.

The dissonance between liberal theory and contemporary participatory discourse surfaces most clearly with respect to the treatment of divergences and differences. Liberals are passionate about the idea of a liberal public sphere in which ideas are publicly exchanged, associations formed and differences articulated. In effect, liberals not only recognize the diversity of interests specifically they also provide that free deliberation involves explicit disagreement. In so far as liberal democratic institutions claim to provide successive opportunities for resolving differences, disagreement is expected to be a constant feature in human interaction mediated by an ostensibly neutral state. Moreover, individuals continue to participate in liberal democratic institutions as the hope of resetting political institutions on the next rung of deliberations is a powerful one (Kaviraj 1996). Although participatory projects imbibe a similar spirit of a neutral public within which individuals may express their views freely, they contain a far less tolerant view of disagreement. The guidelines expect the necessary reconciliation of differences in a public setting where the outcome is nothing short of consensus. There is a huge difference between the liberal-democratic backings of majority rule (where the minority can be expected to provide continuous challenge as well as an electoral reversal) and the embracing of total agreement or consensus during a finite participatory project where grievance and exclusion are not adequately addressed.

This schism can at one level be explained through the simultaneous influence of communitarian and new-institutional ideas on participatory discourse that do not quite sit comfortably with the liberal notions described earlier. Communitarians have attacked the liberal view of the self as 'false', proposing instead the significance of community as a 'unity', in which every member regards the 'common good' as their own (Avineri and De-Shalit 2001, Sandel 2001). Communitarians argue that reconciliation of competing views of the 'good life' involves choosing a common conception of life, which in turn requires a 'shared inquiry' and not an autonomous one as liberal individualists suggest. Liberals and communitarians also disagree about the proper role of the state. The latter see the state as the arena in which common 'visions of the good' can be formulated and the former view this stance as tantamount to the collapsing of boundaries between the public or political (closely identified with the state which must mediate differences) and the private or social and economic (where such differences must necessarily be expressed). Participatory discourses heartily endorse the identification of a common vision with the 'community' though they do not similarly associate the community's agenda setting with the state. With respect to the state, they bear the overwhelming imprint of new institutionalism (NI), which has led to influential theorising casting community as an alternative to the state for the resolution of collective choice problems.

NI theory responds to the quintessential collective choice problem of why rational individuals would find it in their interest to co-operate with one another and act collectively (Olson 1971). Both Olson and Hardin (1968) justified state formation as the only means of providing order and security to rational individuals. These ideas gave rise to further interpretations of the 'contractualist' view of state formation as the product of conscious decisions amongst individuals and the search for explanations beyond the state to explain collective action. Communitarian theorists as Michael Taylor (1987) used the principles of NI to discuss the strengths of the community in providing solutions to collective choice problems. New institutionalists led by Elinor Ostrom (1990) argued that communities that shared particular characteristics could develop their own institutions that would facilitate cooperative behaviour, or indeed, collective action amongst rational individuals.

NI theorists are principally concerned with the problem of collective action and therefore a large part of the literature has developed in relation to common property regimes, i.e., 'the problem of understanding and *developing principles which would encourage* collective action to conserve common pool resources' (Johnson 2004, 412). NI theories have consequently become predominant in agency discourse about the social science of community. They have contributed to the development of a 'hypothetico-deductive' model (Mosse 2003) based upon assumptions of individual decision-making and rational choice. Subsequently, NI has been fiercely criticized as a 'predictive and generalising' theory of the economic and social conditions for collective action (Mosse 2003, 274). Its implicit 'universalism' creates expectations of 'community-like' behaviour that may be unsubstantiated within particular contexts (Sinha 1999). These critiques have in turn produced a rival scholarly tradition that emphasizes 'the historical struggles that determine resource access and entitlement, and the ways in which formal and informal rules create and reinforce unequal access to the commons' (Johnson 2004, 409).

This combination of partial influences of liberalism, communitarianism and new institutionalism is potent in its implications for creating the conditions for depoliticization within participatory discourse as set out by the 1994 guidelines (as other similar policies elsewhere). The uniform treatment of all individuals – as in liberal and later NPE theory – is potentially catastrophic in its denial of power and difference (how can a male landholder possibly occupy the same position in project proceedings as a landless woman?). The exaggerated emphasis on the community's articulation of its perceived common interest is clearly communitarian in spirit, and threatens to gloss over the structural differences that stratify any community. With respect to watershed development, a land-based development intervention, these differences are significant. Micro-watersheds essentially include multiple property boundaries (both private and common), and encompass diverse as well competing uses of natural resources. The size, location and quality of land owned greatly impacts the extent to which landowners may benefit from programme interventions and the landless are more precariously poised to gain, if at all. The enthusiasm with which the guidelines expect communities to consensually form a local institution, one that will address common issues and facilitate collective action, derives from new institutionalism and retains its familiar silence on local politics that militates against such idyllic processes.

The guidelines' projection of community-based participation can also be critiqued from a broad Foucauldian perspective for greatly simplifying the nature of power. Foucault's analysis is useful in 'understanding the everyday nature of social control' (Kothari 2001, 143), which constitutes the daily politics of dominance and subordination, performance and silence, consent and dissent. All of these have a part to play in the enactment of the processes that are imagined by the guidelines but are unsurprisingly disregarded. Critics have observed several serious problems with the 'publicly articulated consensus' approach on this basis. Mosse has rightly pointed out that the public conduct of participatory methods of information gathering masks the 'real structure of power' in the community, and creates a context where the selective presentation of opinion is most likely (1994, 510). Mosse also argues that participatory techniques privilege the general over the particular given their keenness to identify a homogenous and recordable 'community view'. It follows that neither 'chance happenings' nor 'unplanned and irregular occurrences' (Kothari 2001, 147), let alone conflict, are easily accommodated. Besides, presence at these meetings is at best a partial indicator of consent for individuals who create private domains of resistance that are not sufficiently articulated in the public sphere (Scott 1990). Moreover, for those who attend these meetings but do not feel free to voice their views, 'the very act of inclusion, of being drawn in as a participant can symbolize an exercise of power and control over an individual' (Kothari 2001, 142). Their presence may suggest a form of 'adverse incorporation' (Wood 1999) or 'insidious modes of inclusionary control' (Cohen 1985) that further reduce spaces of conflict and confrontation. There is also a rich literature on participation as 'performance' where what we see as a part of the rituals of PRA-based processes are interpreted as an act, both by dominant elites and subordinates, to manipulate the process to suit particular ends (Mosse 1994, Goffman 1997, Kothari 2001).

It is perhaps unremarkable that most of these critiques that have been levelled against participatory initiatives elsewhere are also applicable to MORD's 1994 guidelines, for they reiterate the wider domestic and international leanings towards community-based development, participation and decentralization. This chapter has drawn on many of these influences that have shaped WSD programmes in India. Depoliticized treatments of community have been pervasive. At the same time, it is important to emphasize that state learning is necessarily selective; so while it may have been quick to incorporate politically naive conceptualizations of community and participation, it has been tardier in learning from the real life experiences and difficulties accompanying participatory development that have also been documented not just by academic critics but practitioners themselves.[21] Many of these issues resonate in the way in which the guidelines approach the problem of equity.

Equity

The 1994 guidelines listed three key objectives for WSD in the country: 'economic development' of the village community which is directly or indirectly dependent on the watershed, through optimum integrated use of its biophysical and human resources (through employment generation and other savings-enhancing economic activities); 'restoration of ecological balance' through 'easy and affordable technological solutions and institutional arrangements that make use of local technical knowledge and available materials' and 'sustained, community action for the operation and maintenance of assets created'; and improvement of the 'economic and social condition' of the 'resource poor' and the 'disadvantaged sections of the watershed community' such as the asset-less and women through more 'equitable distribution' of the benefits of land and water resources development and greater access to 'income generating activities' (MORD 1994, 5–6). The first two objectives confirm the eventual convergence of productivity and conservation as key aims of WSD, following a long history of neglect where the two were not correlated. The recognition that the productivity of India's drylands could be secured best through rainfed farming achieved with low cost SWC, together with the understanding that SWC must be extended to *all* lands (and not just those that are over-silted) produced a spectacular expansion in the scope of WSD based state interventions across the country. The complementarity of productivity and conservation objectives is generally acknowledged in the literature (Kerr 2002). What is rather less clear is how WSD is to serve the interests of the poorest sections of the village communities it claims to benefit. In fact, there is considerable disagreement over whether poverty reduction can be central to WSD at all. A large number of extremely thorny issues thus threaten to undermine the ostensible equity objective mentioned by the guidelines.

The following comment by N. C. Saxena, a civil servant who has held important positions in key environmental ministries in the central government, captures the dilemma well: 'It should be stressed here that WSD programmes should only indirectly address the problem of poverty or unemployment. They should be aimed at increasing or stabilising the carrying capacity of land and water resources in rainfed areas. As poverty is both a cause and effect of over-exploitation of natural resources, successful implementation of watershed development programmes would result in sustainable reduction in poverty. On the other hand, if production is not emphasized as the goal, one may end up by achieving neither reduction in poverty nor employment' (2001).[22] Another perspective on this issue is that WSD is undertaken in areas that are generally poor (following the nature of biophysical and socio-economic criteria being adopted) and therefore 'addressing this concern of generic poverty is more important that addressing the issue of inequity in resource allocation and access' (Samuel et al 2006, 88). These authors however acknowledge that such an approach can hurt the 'relative vulnerability' of certain sections, especially those without assets.

Uncertainty about how precisely to factor in poverty reduction as well as the equitable distribution of benefits through WSD has resulted in these objectives taking a backseat during implementation. The important point of course is that the very nature of WSD makes it only too easy for the interests of the landless, the asset poor and within these categories, of women who may often be doubly disadvantaged, to be disregarded. As WSD is typically implemented using a ridge-to-valley approach, common land area in the upper WSD needs to be conserved and access shut off; and while this approach may benefit richer landholders downstream, poorer persons most dependent on the commons receive little or no compensation. Kerr's (2002) authoritative analysis of 70 villages in Maharashtra that were the site of a medley of government, NGO and donor programmes came to two significant conclusions: first, projects faced a potential trade-off in the sense that the projects 'most successful in achieving conservation and productivity benefits also had the strongest evidence of skewed distribution of benefits towards larger landholders' and second, although WSD requires the poor to offer a 'valuable environmental service to the wealthiest landowners, few projects have framed the situation in this way and thus they have not addressed sufficiently the poverty alleviation trade-offs' (Kerr 2002, 1398).

The guidelines are not silent on the equity issue as they state: 'The WDT must recognize that people have different economic and social interests and they need to reconcile these differences to cooperate and work together for the holistic development of the watershed and at the same time ensure that the benefits are shared equitably with a tilt in favour of the poor and the weak, particularly when public investments are being made for the creation of common assets' (MORD 1994, xx). However, they remain resolutely silent on how exactly this is to happen. They do not once acknowledge that the primary beneficiaries of WSD are landholders and benefits therefore will echo existing inequalities in resource ownership and property rights. There is no mention of the critical role of location in landownership (upper or lower reaches of the watershed) in the distribution of benefits. Beyond the prescription that problems relating to common lands in the watershed must be 'tackled' the guidelines do not consider that access to common lands can be highly contested and inequitable. And as far as the all important issue of where water harvesting structures like check dams must be constructed, the guidelines naively presume that this will be determined on the basis of need alone, where fully functioning user groups comprising concerned individuals (whose lands are likely to be impacted by the construction of structures, either adversely or beneficially) will work cooperatively with the WDT.

Women, both from poorer and richer households, are adversely affected by processes accompanying WSD projects in many ways. The guidelines take no firm stance on dealing with such challenges beyond mentioning that some seats must be reserved for women in the watershed committee. The general approach to men and women's respective roles in the participatory watershed project confirms a 'sexual division of labour' where men are involved in coordinating, planning, implementing and monitoring, and women either work to assist men through wage labour or are involved in a range of ancillary 'income generating' (like basket weaving) and 'saving' (through the formation of thrift and credit groups) activities that have become popular in later generations of watershed projects.[23] They also treat all women as constituting a 'homogenous' group[24] and are blind to the very different implications of WSD for women from different socio-economic backgrounds. When WSD interventions curtail access to common lands, they concomitantly reduce access to fuel wood and poorer women often have to walk farther to obtain fuel (Kerr 2002). Kerr's study also concluded that loss of access to common lands also deprived women of many sources of income that they had held independently of men, such as the collection of marketable products like tendu leaves and tamarind pods. As for women from wealthier households, an increase in cropping area or crop production following expanded irrigation can result in undue increases in their services as agricultural labourers without any reduction in household work or child rearing duties.

Employment generation is a stated objective in the 1994 guidelines and generally regarded as a key instrument for compensating the landless and small holders who may not benefit from WSD interventions as much as those with larger landholdings. There are two ways in which this is expected to happen: the first through the provision of wage labour on project works and the second through expected increases in labour opportunities through increased agricultural activities following the WSD project. While the first approach is often thought to relieve the effects of closing access to common lands, most acutely felt by the landless (Kerr 2002), the second is designated as a 'trickle down effect' to equity (Samuel et al 2006, 94). But as practitioners are well aware, the allocation of wage labour is a process fraught with complexities. A common problem concerns wage rates, and if the project's wage rates are higher than local wage rates (as is often the case), then resistance by local power holders is very likely. Bigger farmers often prefer to adopt machinery instead of engaging wage labour in order to preserve status quo on local wage rates, thus benefitting contractors rather than the resource poor (Samuel et al

2006, 93–94). Ultimately as well, the question of how this wage labour ought to be selected receives no consideration in the guidelines beyond the utopian expectation that this process will be facilitated by the relevant user groups on whose lands works are being organized. However, the micro-politics of wage allocation are likely to be intertwined with different types of local groupings and caste-based 'factionalism' (Hardiman 1982) and a temporary project intervention is likely not be able to make a dent in existing practices.

The guidelines' depoliticized approach to equity issues is the result of a discussion that assumes the existence and viability of the new participatory institutions that are created at the village level. It also draws from a lack of serious engagement with the concrete structural inequalities and power relationships that impact upon the possibility of equitable outcomes from WSD. In not bringing these realities in to the fold of discussion, the guidelines are guilty of offering state sanction to a thoroughly apolitical projection not just of the village community but also of the actual dynamics of local working and interaction. Equity itself has not fallen off the radar of state attention however, and subsequent committees constituted by the central government (like the Eswaran Committee established in 1998 to review issues of training and capacity building) have continued to emphasize the need for more equitable sharing of watershed benefits. There is specific attention to the issue of sharing net benefits in the 2000 guidelines adopted by MOA. The 2006 Technical Committee (also dubbed the Parthasarathy Committee after its Chairman) has staunchly argued that principles of equity should be extended to 'conflict sharing, beneficiary selection and benefit sharing'. It has pointed out the need for special provisions to be made to ensure that dalits (or SCs) and landless persons do not lose access to common lands, and also the creation of a separate women's watershed council among other measures to protect their interests. The latest 2008 guidelines have imbibed this spirit and mention 'equity and gender sensitivity' as the first guiding principle for WSD projects all over the country.

Local Institutions

The 1994 guidelines created an exclusive local body – the watershed committee – for implementing WSD projects at the village. This reflected the international move towards CBNRM driven by the idea that to decentralize means to establish 'self-governing non-state' regulatory institutions that build on coherence within local communities (Hulme and Woodhouse 2000, 227). In India however, this sparked a special controversy because by creating dedicated local institutions for WSD, the guidelines did not confer direct responsibility for programme implementation to gram panchayats, the lowest of the three tier panchayat or elected body system in India. Panchayats in India have long suffered neglect and disempowerment at the hands of the bureaucracy and political leaders at various levels,[25] and this was interpreted by many as an unacceptable blow. This was especially since the 73rd and 74th constitutional amendments, enacted in 1993, had accorded constitutional status to these bodies, laying down powers, resources and responsibilities that would be mandatory for state governments to devolve.

In the 16 years since 1994, a very large number of actors have become involved with implementing WSD projects across the country and the 'panchayat versus watershed committee' debate has drawn a lot of interest and opinion. The central government has clearly been sensitive to these debates because in the intervening years it has changed the common guidelines three times (2001, 2003, 2008), and a key point of the change has been to shift responsibility from one institution to the other. While these debates are extremely pertinent and have brought a lot of very important issues to the fore, there is also a danger that the guidelines have engendered a discourse of depoliticization to rationalize the appropriateness of watershed committees that is then serving to obscure other conflicts and interests. Here depoliticization is the express outcome of particular meanings being attributed to politics, which are then transposed on to panchayats.

Following the guidelines' rather idyllic description of local communities, watershed committees were imagined to be the outcome of pristinely cooperative processes, a peaceful aggregation of the smaller user and self-help groups that are ostensibly formed prior to the first general meeting of the watershed association. Majority voting is generally regarded as unsuitable for the formation of these bodies for it would 'give an official status to the existence of disagreements' which is incompatible with the image of community being pursued (Sangameswaran 2008, 394 citing Platteau and Abraham 2002). The obvious contrast here is with panchayats for they are typically integrated with mainstream party politics and may be characterized by contest, violence and factionalism. A senior civil servant, among the principal architects of the 1994 guidelines, stated: 'Panchayats are not participatory, but representative institutions. It is precisely due to this that they end up representing sectional and vested interests. Political factionalism finds easier conduits of reflection in these bodies' (Interview, 2000, New Delhi). In contrast, it has been widely expressed that WCs can be insulated from 'politics'. Baviskar describes how this view was expressed by administrators and officials of WSD projects in Jhabua district in Madhya Pradesh, 'The panchayat is not participatory; the sarpanch (elected head) becomes a contractor. The panchayat is a delivery system. The watershed committee involves everybody. The panchayat is too political' (2007, 300). Manor (2005) comments how user bodies like watershed committees in Zambia, South Africa and Bangladesh as well as several Indian states are routinely described as 'apolitical'. Interestingly here, the politics that these bodies are supposedly distant from is not really specified; all that is implied is that politics is pejorative because the argument is made to promote watershed committees (and other user bodies) for positive reasons. It is this space that allows for the notion of politics to be filled with particular meanings, depending on the context.

With respect to panchayats then, watershed committees are being portrayed as bodies that can be insulated from the contestation for political power. There is the expectation that despite sharing a common social context with panchayats, they would not be affected by the cleavages of caste, class and ethnicity that are the basis of the irreversible politicization of social life in India. Manor rightly dismisses this notion as a 'dangerous myth' (2005, 205) and concludes that any attempt to 'exclude' politics from the watershed arena can only ensure that a certain type of politics dominates. The actual differences and similarities between panchayats and watershed committees in various locations should be empirically ascertained before universal claims are made regarding the particular attributes of these institutions. Even so, the debate on the appropriateness of panchayats versus WCs for participatory watershed development has continued to hinge on this very issue of politics. Manor remarks that 'many people continue to cling to the myth, some out of naivety, while others do so out of cynicism' (2005, 205). His discerning comments capture the essence of the dynamics that will be described below.

The 1994 guidelines led to acrimonious debates between two rather fluid camps over the WC issue. The first accused these guidelines of being another attempt by politicians and bureaucrats of depriving panchayats of legitimate power, particular as WSD is one of 29 subjects identified by the constitution for transfer to panchayats. The second dismissed such views as 'panchayat-purism' and further justified why panchayats were not appropriate as direct implementers of WSD. Typical arguments that were explicitly made included the assertion that panchayats (and their officials like the panchayats secretary) are rather over-burdened or too 'big' to focus on a single development activity (Baumann 1999). Fears that panchayats would divert watershed money (to the tune of 2 million rupees or more for a single project over five years) into other activities were less openly articulated. The former camp argued that panchayats are enduring local bodies with constitutional recognition and ought not to be marginalized for this reason alone (Baumann 1999).

In the meantime, between 1994 and 2003 there has been the general endorsement of the role of non-elected local bodies (WCs, user and self-help groups) in facilitating participatory WSD. This was true not only of the large numbers of proactive NGOs around the country and prominent donor agencies like UK's DFID, but within the state itself. When MORD revised its 1994 guidelines in 2001 it made certain alterations to other aspects (like increasing cost norms from 4000 rupees per hectare to 6000 rupees per hectare) but left the original format of user groups, watershed committees and watershed associations untouched. When the MOA adopted a new set of common guidelines imbibing the participatory approach in 2000, it followed in the same mould, and the same was true of the CAPART (Council for Advancement of Rural Action and Peoples' Technology) guidelines. In this context, the MORD's 2003 *Hariyali* guidelines introduced a sharp chord of dissonance. These guidelines reversed two key aspects of the existing policy. First, they did away with WCs altogether and laid down that the gram panchayat shall implement the watershed project under the 'overall supervision and guidance of Project Implementation Agencies', which as a matter of priority were to be the intermediate (or block) panchayats. If the block panchayats did not have the requisite capability, the Zilla or district panchayats could either act as a PIA itself or appoint a 'suitable line department'. So the second major change came with respect to the status of NGOs as potential PIAs. Whereas the previous guidelines had adopted a very favourable attitude towards NGO involvement, the Hariyali guidelines displayed lukewarm enthusiasm, hedging the very limited provisions about NGO engagement with all manner of restrictions to do with demonstrated experience. At points, there was discernible hostility, as for example in the mention that 'the NGOs blacklisted by CAPART or other Departments of State Government or the Government of India should not be appointed as PIA'.[26]

NGOs unsurprisingly were very piqued. At a formal level, perhaps the most concrete outpouring of disagreement came through the 2006 Parthasarathy Committee which drew upon consultations with the most active and influential NGOs working in watershed development throughout the country (including MYRADA, Samaj Pragati Sahyog and the Development Support Centre amongst several others). The Report agreed that the Hariyali guidelines were an important step in empowering panchayats, but argued that making gram panchayats directly responsible for implementing WSD was not the way forward (2006, part 2, 8). All the reasons cited echoed with the initial factors that had led to the constitution of watershed committees in 1994, the diverse responsibilities of panchayats being the foremost one. The Report also made a renewed plea for the continued involvement of NGOs in WSD projects on the grounds that the success of WSD depends on developing different types of collaborations (between scientists and farmers for example), and an active engagement of the civil society with the state, including panchayat institutions (Shah 2006).[27]

While these reasonable tones were being articulated in the public domain, informal conversations with a number of NGO practitioners (in Hyderabad) and mid-level MORD bureaucrats in New Delhi in early 2005 revealed anger and accusations of vested interests. These suggested that the debate between watershed committees and panchayats was being transposed into a covert tussle between NGOs and the bureaucracy. NGOs' ire over the abandonment of WCs in 2003was interpreted by MORD officials at New Delhi as nothing but disappointment about losing their own privileged PIA position under the 1994 guidelines (Interviews with MORD officials, 2005, New Delhi). NGOs and other policy analysts interviewed retorted that the 2003 guidelines were not really about empowering panchayats, for the executive functions at each tier of panchayat institutions are vested in a non-elected government official.[28] They argued that the bureaucracy's championing of the panchayat cause was in itself suspect given its historical resistance to panchayat institutions. The official discourse within MORD was simply that 'The (1994) guidelines did not provide a pivotal role to the PRIs and it is time to do so by bringing in suitable revisions' (MORD 2003, Foreword). On further probing, some mid-level officials stated that the change was a hurried pre-election move by the ministry's top political leadership to curry favour with panchayats and their local constituencies. Given the timing and the rather isolated and secretive formulation of the Hariyali guidelines,[29] this is the explanation for policy change that finds the widest currency, certainly outside the government, and perhaps even within it.

The debate is clearly far from over as the more recently adopted 2008 guidelines have reverted to the institutional arrangements provided for in pre-Hariyali guidelines. Watershed committees have been officially reinstated, as one of the many committees of gram panchayats that have once again been accorded overall responsibilities of coordination. The valuable services offered by NGOs (or Voluntary Organizations) as PIA have also been recognized though a long list of essential criteria to guide the selection of NGOs has also been laid down.

These dynamic developments over a 14 year period show that the debate about which type of local institution is appropriate for participatory WSD cannot be held without also taking on board the entangled interests of the very many actors that are engaged in programme implementation. If watershed committees share the same social contexts as panchayats, it will need more than mere attributions of characteristics to ascertain precisely why and how the two institutions are different, in what ways and for what reasons. A proper treatment of decentralization therefore cannot just be about the projected institutional attributes of two types of local bodies but about the comprehensive politics of their relationships. The assumption that WCs can be apolitical in a way that panchayats cannot obscures the pervasive politicization of social life, and reiterates the same naive projection of communities that underpins the bureaucratic projection of participation. It also offers a way out for selective meanings of politics to be adopted and the conditions established for implementers to turn a blind eye to all that is equally the lifeblood of politics.

Conclusion

This chapter has discussed the transformation of soil and water conservation into a comprehensive watershed development programme for rural development. Two aspects to this transformation, namely a broadening out of objectives to include conservation, productivity and poverty reduction and the adoption of an integrated approach to managing land, water and forests have contributed to the enormous expansion of the scope and scale of intervention by the state in the attempt to treat all lands on a watershed basis. The third element of change has been the incorporation of a decentralized administrative structure and participatory decision-making at the village level by the principal state-led programmes implemented by MORD, and other central government ministries have followed suit. The 'normalization' of a micro-watershed as a rational unit of planning and participatory involvement in state policy has been driven by the many remarkable initiatives spearheaded by individuals, NGOs and donor agencies across India through the 1980s. The influences exercised by the more general discrediting of neo-Malthusian approaches, the affirmation of faith in indigenous knowledge and community capabilities for collective action in international development discourse, and the importance of decentralization in land and water management have also been significant in effecting such transformation.

The history of evolution of WSD reveals the many different reasons why the programme is of considerable importance to the Indian state. It seeks to satisfy key development objectives and since the 1994 guidelines were issued, the central ministries of rural development and agriculture have reiterated their commitment to WSD through revisions in policy and scaling up of financial resources. Indeed the embracing of decentralization and participation have provided ever new grounds for state stewardship of policy making, as the successive iterations of the 1994 guidelines might indicate. The 1994 policy framework is in itself a landmark document that codifies in the clearest possible way the bureaucratic imagination of village level participatory decision-making and the decentralized roles played by project agencies at different points in the programme hierarchy.

The chapter has considered in some detail the elements of an 'anti-politics watershed machine'. At the core of this is the guidelines' projection of a village community in India, upon which it builds its entire discourse of participation, the possibility of equity and the role of local institutions. The vision of community is divorced from reality in critical respects, reflecting a tangle of theoretical influences, and the result is an improper treatment of power and difference, disagreement and exclusion. This together with an exaggerated and unsubstantiated emphasis on collective action, cooperation and publicly manifest consensus amounts to a discourse around community that is severely depoliticized of politics as power. Equally, the guidelines depoliticize the equity issue by remaining silent on the inescapable implications of structural inequalities and the micro-politics of village level organization and decision-making on project outcomes likely to have a bearing on equitable sharing of watershed benefits.

And finally, the guidelines have been instrumental in unleashing an enduring debate around decentralized local bodies by presenting watershed committees as the obvious (though formally unstated) antithesis to the panchayat (as is popularly perceived). So while there is no formal or explicit mention of this contrast – for the guidelines present a picture of institutional harmony between the panchayat and the watershed committee – there have been no dearth of interpretations that describe watershed committees as apolitical compared to the undeniably political panchayats. With subsequent guidelines going back and forth between WCs and panchayats as the favoured body directly responsible for implementation, the debate on decentralization is being cast in excessive institutional terms where the interests of other programme actors and the social contexts of these bodies are obscured.

The larger aim of this chapter has been to argue that the so-called anti-politics watershed machine has through its 1994 and subsequent guidelines put in place a pliant discourse of depoliticization that is ready and available for those who want to use it. But this does not imply that the medley of actors engaged in programme implementation necessarily employ strategies of depoliticization. Besides, if so many of the ideas that constitute this discourse of depoliticization are so easily challenged, should we expect implementers who are deeply involved with their contexts of operations to believe in them? The point therefore is no longer to prove that the anti-politics machine exists, but to demonstrate which constituents try to depoliticize watershed development, in what ways, under what conditions and why. In India moreover where the meanings being attributed to politics are many and difficult to predict, the depoliticization discourse may unfold in unpredictable ways. This, as contended in the chapters to follow, has significant implications for the exercise of state power.

Chapter Four

TWO LANDSCAPES OF DECENTRALIZATION

Looking into the Watershed Machine

This chapter takes a closer look at the conditions in which the key actors implementing the 1994 watershed guidelines were situated in the two Indian states of study. Since I started this investigation in 1999, Andhra Pradesh in southern India and Madhya Pradesh in central India have been the subject of much interest and fascination for their simultaneously unfolding albeit distinctive initiatives regarding decentralization (see Manor 2000 and 2002, Jenkins et al 2003 and Johnson, Deshingkar and Start 2005). Curiosity has endured in the popular media about the two men – Chandrababu Naidu in Andhra Pradesh and Digvijay Singh in Madhya Pradesh – who as Chief Ministers spearheaded bold reform processes in their ten-year stints of power,[1] which in seeming political synchrony ended roughly around the same time. Naidu's Telugu Desam Party (TDP) lost to the Congress in Andhra Pradesh in 2004 and Singh's Congress regime succumbed to the BJP in Madhya Pradesh a year earlier, in 2003. While the reasons for their defeat were rooted in state-specific factors, what is of interest here is the contrast that has been drawn between their respective attitudes and policies towards decentralization. Both Naidu and Singh projected themselves as proactive governance reformers, of which decentralization was the ostensible cornerstone. Naidu's governance reforms emphasized technocratic efficiency of the bureaucracy, popular mobilization through strictly monitored government initiatives (Janmabhoomi for example), and the unabashed promotion of local user bodies for local participation, but did not attempt to integrate these initiatives with panchayats (Reddy 2002, Mooij 2003). Singh's governance reforms also endorsed improved performance of the bureaucracy (mainly by founding dedicated 'missions' for different development programmes) but he consciously sought to empower panchayat bodies at all levels and integrate district panchayats with the nitty-gritty of district administration (Behar 2003, Baviskar 2007). But did these differences in overall political and administrative context bear any implications for the watershed machines of the two states? More specifically, did the prevailing environments of decentralization impact upon the readiness with which key watershed authorities embraced a discourse of anti-politics or depoliticization?

My second aim in this chapter is to present the regional dimensions of dominance as manifest in Andhra Pradesh and MP and in particular in Kurnool and Dewas districts, the places described in this book. The dynamics of domination and subordination in the two states are remarkably different. Politics in Andhra Pradesh has been marked by decades of contest between dominant peasant caste groups, particularly the Reddys and Kammas, growing political mobilization of the numerous OBCs (like the Boyas, Chakalis and Waderas) and as well as the dalits, though tempered by abundant processes of accommodation and dilution of their rising aspirations (Srinivasulu 2002, Suri 2002). Brahmins may have been dominant historically, but have clearly suffered as a result of the 'anti-brahminical' tone of Reddy and Kamma ascendance. Politics in Madhya Pradesh is dominated by the forward castes, notably the Brahmins and Rajputs. The corresponding absence of a strong component of backward castes, which despite their numbers remain fragmented, together with the scattered presence of dalits, divided by language and culture across the vast geographical spread of the state, has limited the emergence of low-caste solidarities and leadership (Jaffrelot 2003, Gupta 2004). The very large component of scheduled tribes or adivasis in Madhya Pradesh is routinely subordinated and exploited by non-tribals (Shah 2005, Baviskar 2007). This chapter will explore the ways in which these dimensions of dominance interact with the watershed machinery to impact upon two critical decisions that need to be taken at the outset: the selection of PIAs and the selection of project villages. In what ways did the watershed authorities in Kurnool and Dewas respond to these broader dynamics? As I will show, while pressures to privilege dominant persons and places have been experienced in both these districts, the response to distance the programme from such pressures has not been couched in a technocratic discourse of depoliticization in quite the same way. This has had profound consequences.

Decentralization under Naidu and Singh

Chandrababu Naidu wrested control of the TDP from his father-in-law and party patriarch NT Rama Rao (NTR), despite the latter's massive election victory in December 1994. Naidu was hailed as a 'prudent and pragmatic' leader by TDP ministers and Members of Legislative Assembly (MLAs) who were growing tired of NTR's ceaselessly 'populist and autocratic' politics (Suri 2002). Once in power, Naidu embarked on an earnest drive to reform the government's economic policies and boost professionalism in politics as well as the bureaucracy (Naidu with Ninan 2000). The new government White Papers revealed a shift from NTR's 'welfarist/populist' agenda and emphasized that government subsidies were unfeasible, expenditure on welfare schemes had to be reduced, state controls had to be lifted and foreign private capital was to be encouraged. His vision of the state as a facilitator of private enterprise and promoter of business also included a philosophy of development where people had to change their 'mindsets' from being mere recipients of state benevolence to one where they took control, so that the state could be a 'facilitator' rather than 'provider' (Government of Andhra Pradesh 1999 and Srinivasulu 1999 as cited in Suri 2002).

And so was launched the 'Janmabhoomi' in 1997, conceptualized as a process of 'social mobilization', that aimed to extend democracy beyond the 'confines' of representative institutions, and make the government more accountable and transparent.[2] The programme proposed to bring government to the people (through public discussions of the performance of government schemes in the presence of mandal-level[3] officers who would visit villages periodically), promote 'community contributions' to a 'Janmabhoomi fund' for the construction of schools, roads, or any other required village infrastructure, and facilitate micro-level planning at the grassroots through village-based self-help and user bodies (Reddy 2002, Mooij 2003). Naidu took the programme seriously. A 'Janmabhoomi think-tank' established in Hyderabad devised intricate village-level institutional mechanisms with the aim of initiating community-development plans through the Janmabhoomi. Money for the Janmabhoomi fund, previously called the ;shramdaan' fund, was drawn from almost all the ongoing schemes of the state government and additionally from a Government of India (GOI) yearly allocation under the head of decentralized planning. All public contributions received that were not yet tied to any specific community work were meant to be transferred to the Janmabhoomi fund maintained at the district level with the District Collector.

Naidu's Janmabhoomi initiative, much like the vast array of other development initiatives that he endorsed, did not involve panchayats directly. Instances of these include local water users' associations for participatory irrigation management, education committees, thrift and credit associations and youth groups. It is this aspect of his decentralization policy that he has been judged most harshly for, as some critics saw through his shrewd attempts to 'pack' such committees 'with party supporters', funding them generously and empowering them 'precisely because loyalists dominate them' (Manor 2000, 824, and 2002). The realities may be somewhat more blurred. With the Janmabhoomi for example, no doubt there were allegations especially in rural areas that the programme acted as a subterfuge for TDP supporters to gain privileged access to contracts for Janmabhoomi works.[4] However, despite this disillusionment the programme was cleverly drafted, cutting across party lines, and the 'rounds' by mandal officers to select villages in rotation had to be conducted everywhere, even in areas that were dominated by opposition parties. Local journalists interviewed in Kurnool district were of the view that opposition parties' leaders rarely boycotted Janmabhoomi proceedings, and used it as a forum to challenge the TDP government, in the process lending it some legitimacy.

The allegation about disregarding panchayats however needs to be taken seriously. Although Andhra Pradesh was among the first Indian states to introduce the panchayat system in 1959, successive state governments have subordinated panchayats to party interests. Nearly three decades of Congress rule in the state after independence gave way to the TDP in the early 1980s, and NTR tried to improve his party's strength at the grassroots by 'capturing' panchayat bodies that had been dominated by local Congress supporters. Through a range of measures that included capturing the positions of Zilla Panchayat chairmen, Rao systematically created a political climate where panchayats were clearly subordinated to party interests (Raghavulu and Narayana 1999). Naidu has continued this trend throughout his stint in power (Manor 2002). In the period after the 73rd constitutional amendment, important pro-panchayat steps like the merger between DRDAs and ZPs have not yet been taken. The state government has still to empower District Planning Committees (DPCs), which were created by the Constitution (Article 243-ZD) to integrate urban and local planning, but continue to lie as defunct bodies in most states of the country. The principal development agency at the district level is the District Development and Review Committee (DDRC), chaired by a state cabinet minister. Panchayat elections have not been convened regularly.[5] The fear that strengthening panchayats would enhance local political leverage of the Congress has posed a constant dilemma for the latter. At the same time, the argument that empowering panchayats would have necessarily gone against TDP party interests needs to be made with some caution. Suri (2002) points out that between 1996 and 2001, when the Janmabhoomi was launched and various 'parallel' user bodies were initiated, the TDP controlled all 22 Zilla Parishads (district panchayats) and nearly two-thirds of the Mandal Parishads. Manor (2000) is firm in his contention that it was harder for Naidu to 'exclude' representatives of opposition parties as effectively from panchayats compared with the water and education committees which he has 'set *against* the decentralized councils in order to weaken the latter further' (2000. 824–825; italics in original). These differences apart, the main point that panchayats in general found an inhospitable patron in Naidu remains.

Naidu clearly placed a lot of emphasis on a competent bureaucracy. In fact, the cornerstone of his appeal to voters to choose TDP over the Congress was his claim that the former stood for 'development, stability and SMART government' (Suri 2002, 39, Mooij 2003). An acronym for Simple, Moral, Accountable, Responsive and Transparent government, SMART, acquired much currency after the *Vision 2020* document (Government of AP, 1999). His personal style of functioning moreover meant he frequently prioritized civil servants over party loyalists in his daily meetings and it was well known that he gathered information 'less through his party' than through 'private polls and information technology systems staffed by bureaucrats and independent consultants' (Manor 2004, 267). His reliance on the bureaucracy came with the firm belief that it should be free of 'political interference' and he thus embarked on a zealous mission to monitor it obsessively, which yielded in an overtly target-oriented approach (Mooij 2003, 11–12). This unsurprisingly produced deep resentment down the bureaucratic hierarchy at all levels, for officials across different development programmes had to bear the burden of excessive reporting.[6] Nevertheless, as long as Naidu remained in power, he favoured intimate bureaucratic involvement in development programmes and the fastidious maintenance of records and information, which he could call upon at any time. This over-controlling technocratic stance was an integral constituent of his larger discourse of the state facilitating development rather than doling out welfare.

Digvijay Singh shared more similarities with Naidu than was commonly conceded, except after both suffered resounding defeats at the end of their respective second terms in office. If Naidu lost out to the Congress in 2004 for his image of promoting hi-tech solutions to state problems and being oblivious to the concerns of the rural poor (which were thoroughly compounded by farmer suicides following crop failure and indebtedness), Singh succumbed to the BJP a year earlier for his failure to provide 'bijli, sadak and pani' (electricity, roads and water).[7] Both had shared very similar visions of reform: 'Like Naidu, he had begun as a young technocratic modernizer, an idealist innovator committed to transparency and accountability. His efforts to computerize the state administration had drawn international attention. Foreigners came in larger numbers to study his innovative "best practices"' (Pant 2004). A key innovation undertaken by Singh was the adoption of the Rajiv Gandhi Technology Missions for the tasks of universal primary education, watershed development, control for diarrhoeal diseases and elimination of iodine disorders, rural industries and fisheries development. In effect, each of these technology missions developed a distinct political association with the Congress Party. However, the stated purposes of following the mission mode were 'clarity of strategies and objectives, action within a definite timeframe, fast-track procedures, committed team, inter-sectoral effort, collective action, close monitoring and transparent evaluation' (GoMP 1998b cited in Baviskar 2007, 294). It was held that the mission approach would be most conducive for achieving targets. A key feature of this approach was the direct access it would allow mission directors (usually Indian Administrative Service or IAS officers, handpicked by the Chief Minister) to Singh himself. However, as the government left the larger institutional structures of the administration with its rigid boundaries between departments and agencies intact, the principal enthusiasts for these missions were those IAS officers selected to lead the missions (Baviskar 2007). Many within the bureaucracy resented this imposition.

Where Singh differed consciously from Naidu was in his concerted attempts to reform and empower the panchayat bodies, both at the village level as well as at the district level. After Singh assumed power in 1993, Madhya Pradesh became the first state to introduce the new panchayat raj system following the 73rd and 74th amendment. Further, the Madhya Pradesh Panchayat Raj Act of 1997 provided for 100 per cent reservation at all levels of the three tier panchayat system. These measures revealed that Singh was not being merely rhetorical in his pledge to devolve power to the people, and he was re-elected in 1998 (Gupta 2005). Manor observed that unlike Naidu, Singh did not try to 'pack' the different user and local committees in existence with his own party loyalists and was 'content to see people from the main opposition party (the BJP) involved in such committees' (2000, 826). In his second term, Singh went further and initiated a bold and extremely controversial system of 'Zilla Sarkar' or district government. Zilla Sarkar is a popular name given to the constitutionally created District Planning Committees (DPCs) that remain as defunct bodies in most states of the country including AP. In 1999, the state government of Madhya Pradesh amended the District Planning Committee Act of 1995, with the principal objective of creating a second tier of administration in the district, second to the state level, and doing away with at least 293 divisional offices of different departments. The Act placed all departments functioning at the district level under the newly empowered DPCs. These measures have been adopted with the intention to transform DPCs as 'decision-making bodies' instead of being planning units only. Government officials described this process of transformation as the 'de-escalation' of the authority of government to the district.[8]

DPCs are composed of elected representatives of ZPs and urban local bodies in 4:1 ratio, as well as of all Members of Legislative Assembly and Members of Parliament (MLAs and MPs respectively) elected from the district. Any other political appointees of the state government are also included. The Chairman is a minister of the state government, designated 'in-charge' of the district and is called 'Prabhari Mantri'. The Collector is the only bureaucratic representative in the DPC, and acts as its Secretary. Other important district level officers such as the Chief Executive Officer (CEO) of Zilla Panchayat, who is in charge of its administrative matters, have not been included. This composition suggests that a DPC is a nucleus of the political leadership within every district. Initial reports confirmed that the initialization of Zilla Sarkar had resulted in a substantial measure of administrative decentralization.[9] However, the political leadership at the state level continued to maintain the upper hand in decision-making at the district. The appointment of ministers as Chairmen of DPCs ensured that this tier of political leadership was not excluded from the new power arrangement devised by the Chief Minister and his aides. This move needs to be viewed as a shrewd measure that would avert likely resistance from powerful state level politicians. Indeed, more retrospectively, Singh's district government initiative has unambiguously been viewed as an attempt by the state government to 'placate the established elite' that had felt marginalized after Singh's initial pro-panchayat moves (Gupta 2005, 5098).

The institution of the Zilla Sarkar has been instrumental in changing the dynamics of interaction between politicians and bureaucrats in the districts of M.P. It has undeniably contributed to a swift broadening of the interface between elected representatives and the bureaucracy. It is typical for the bureaucracy to be extremely powerful in district level administrative arrangements, with the Collectorate as the pivot of such power since colonial days. Zilla Panchayats have historically played second fiddle to district level bureaucrats, especially IAS officers, and their inclusion in Zilla Sarkar or district government has gone a long way in lending to these elected bodies a measure of state authority that they had not partaken of before. The remark of an IAS office in Dewas district was telling, 'Earlier, we would not have allowed these people into our houses, and now we have to usher them into our drawing rooms and serve them tea' (Interview, Dewas, November 2000).

Singh tried to be responsive to the realities of panchayat functioning in the initial years after his government initiated an array of pro-panchayat measures. Reports that panchayat raj was really 'sarpanch raj' (a sarpanch is the head of a panchayat) where panchayat powers and money were being unduly appropriated by a handful of men, led the Madhya Pradesh government to amend the Panchayat Act in 2001. The key feature of the change was a much acclaimed transition from 'indirect' to 'direct' democracy as all powers accorded to the elected panchayats were transferred to the 'gram sabha', the collective of all adults (who are registered voters) in the panchayat, with the belief that power must be in the hands of people and not their representatives (Behar 2001). The new system was called 'gram swaraj' and raised hope particularly amongst Gandhian activist groups and civil society organizations tired of panchayat excesses (Behar 2003). Nonetheless the realities of implementation have been sobering as key aspects underpinning the operationalization of this Act, such as regularity of meetings, quorum of members present, involvement of disadvantaged groups, and essentially the transformation of the gram sabha into a functioning agency for change, have all been visibly missing. There were a lot of local clashes following rival institutional agendas: so for example, the gram sabha was required to form its own committees to carry out different tasks but these were not properly related to the existing user bodies and committees of various government line departments including forests, education and health. The new system received a lot of resistance from the sarpanch lobby for the obvious curtailment of their privileges, and the government had to backtrack by bringing 'them back into the gram swaraj system by making them co-signatories for operating the gram swaraj account' (Behar 2003, 1928). There is also ample evidence available to show that a variety of entrenched interests continue to dominate panchayats locally, and the reservation of seats for the lower castes and women largely remains cosmetic in nature.

Differences in Administrative Arrangements for Watershed Development[10]

The creation of exclusive district-level project offices for managing MORD's WSD programmes was the most important administrative innovation in AP. This was unlike other states, including MP, where (despite the existence of a state WSD mission) there was no exclusive administrative authority responsible for programme implementation at the district. In MP, the formal charge for implementing WSD at the district level lay with the ZP-DRDA (headed by the ZP following its merger with the DRDA), a body with a multitude of functions and responsibilities. The presence of a single bureaucratic authority that was able to concentrate exclusively on WSD reflected the technocratic discourse around development that was keenly promoted by the Chief Minister, Naidu. For the watershed programme, Naidu's proclaimed attempt to ensure that the bureaucracy be allowed to work without 'political interference' was conducive to justifying an institutional mechanism that could keep elected political representatives at the district (members of the Zilla Panchayat and other politicians) 'out' of the critical ambit of programme decision-making. It is not being argued here that Naidu personally ordered the creation of these district level watershed authorities. Instead, attention is being drawn to a political climate where bureaucrats in Hyderabad, who were responsible for devising institutional arrangements for implementing MORD's 1994 guidelines, were encouraged to facilitate close bureaucratic monitoring of the WSD programme. In the process, the District Watershed Advisory Committee (DWAC), a body comprising all elected representatives in the district, including MPs, MLAs and elected members from the Zilla Panchayat in addition to some representatives from voluntary and technical organizations engaged in WSD in the district, was relegated to a marginal position (this was the case as observed in Kurnool district).[11] DWAC was one of the ways in which the 1994 guidelines had sought to create a synergetic role for panchayats to be involved with WSD.

In MP, the political move to decentralize development administration and integrate it with elected representatives from the Zilla Panchayat ensured that a similar discourse of depoliticization (where politics refers to political representatives) found a relatively inhospitable environment. This was irrespective of the actual practices of administration that were followed as a result of the Rajiv Gandhi Mission (RGM). Following the merger of ZPs and DRDAs, the ZP is theoretically in charge of programme implementation (this was the case in Dewas district).[12] The political conditions have therefore also been favourable for a more active role for DWAC to 'advise' the ZP. Besides, under the new arrangements of the Zilla Sarkar, issues relating to WSD are regularly presented to elected political representatives (following their membership in the District Planning Committees) for their consideration. However, given that the WSD is one of many functions of the ZP, matters of administrative design and innovation have typically been left to the District Collector and his team of officers. But the Collector has no dearth of duties, being the head of the police, revenue and district administration, and therefore the attention that WSD receives from the Collector may vary considerably from one official to another. Baviskar observed in the case of Jhabua district, 'The projects, however, greatly depend on the "vision" and enthusiasm of an individual collector who is soon transferred and promoted to a posting elsewhere. With the departure of the Collector, his pet project also dwindles' (2007, 303). On occasion, other government officials junior to the Collector, may take greater interest in programme provisions and formulate initiatives for reform which ultimately require the Collector's approval. This was the case for example in Dewas in 1998–2000, when the CEO of the Zilla Panchayat, an IAS officer in charge of its administrative matters, took a keen interest in the district WSD programme. This officer initiated several important changes in district level programme procedures during his tenure. Subsequent officials have not been equally pro-active or interested. The prospect of association with the prestigious Rajiv Gandhi Watershed Mission made a difference for younger IAS officers keen to impress both powerful bureaucrats in Bhopal advising the Chief Minister, and Digvijay Singh himself. Baviskar's remark that 'the watershed mission is also an avenue for dynamic IAS officers to rise to prominence' (2007, 303) is in the same spirit as my observation.

A second tier of differences existed at the level of the project implementing agency, responsible for implementing micro-watershed projects. There were important differences both in terms of the level of programme support available to PIAs in Kurnool and those in Dewas, and the extent to which they were subject to intensive monitoring. District watershed offices in Andhra Pradesh lent themselves to 'tight' programme organization with a very clearly demarcated hierarchy of monitoring and reporting. The Kurnool Watershed Office (KWO) was an exemplar of such internal organization.[13] The PD of KWO was the administrative head of the programme, and was assisted by a Multi-Disciplinary Team (MDT) that advises the PD on technical matters. MDT is a state level innovation, particular to Andhra Pradesh alone, and the main functions of its members are to co-ordinate and supervise watershed activities, in accordance with their disciplinary strengths. PIAs could be either government officers or NGOs, but irrespective of this fact a PIA had to be assisted by a four member interdisciplinary Watershed Development Team (WDT). The PD assisted by the MDT was vested with critical powers of decision-making. All junior project officers (POs), including the PIA and WDT members reported to the MDT and ultimately the Project Director (PD). Each PIA, assisted by the WDT, was typically in charge of seven to eight micro-watersheds (and no more than 5000 hectares of land in all). NGOs were accorded responsibility for micro-watershed projects if they were able to satisfy criteria laid down by KWO. WDT members worked exclusively and full time on projects entrusted to them, constituting the 'face' of the project and operating in close proximity to the villagers. They were typically hired from the open market through temporary contracts.

In Madhya Pradesh too, each micro-watershed project was implemented either by a government officer or an NGO. But unlike Kurnool where every PIA had to work through a four member WDT, village level programme arrangements in Dewas varied between government and NGO PIAs. When a government official designated as PO was in charge of project implementation, he worked with the assistance of individual officers who were designated as PIAs. A PO was usually assigned charge of a milli-watershed, which comprises six to seven microwatershed projects. A PIA was in charge of one to two micro-watersheds. Thus, a PO supervised the work of three to four PIAs in the entire milli-watershed. NGOs entrusted with project implementation were free to improvise their own village level arrangements. This meant that government project staff in Dewas were extremely overburdened, as they held charge of six to seven micro-watershed projects (but without the same level of assistance from multidisciplinary WDTs as in Kurnool) in addition to discharging other government duties. Also, district level-monitoring of programme implementation in Dewas was highly diffused given the overlapping responsibilities of the ZP and the Collectorate. As a result, the pressures on government as well as non-governmental project agencies to comply with reporting requirements here were insignificant compared to Kurnool, where a very clearly defined mechanism for 'upward' reporting had been put in place for all parties involved. These differences would prove to be extremely significant for the interpretation of the 1994 guidelines and lead to very different compulsions regarding depoliticization.

Regional Dimensions of Dominance

Politics from the perspective of the Indian anti-politics machine frequently refers to demands that emanate from actors and agencies that are dominant or aspire to be dominant,[14] in their attempts to steer development's gravy train. However, as has been abundantly pointed out (especially in critiques of state planning, see Chatterjee 1998), the machine itself is not situated outside of the structures of power and therefore the attempt to transform 'subjects of power' into 'objects of knowledge' that can be planned and directed above particular interests is an exercise in self-deception by planners. Nevertheless, it is extremely interesting to unravel how exactly planners in different watershed machines responded to the 'political pressures' within which they themselves are situated. The chapter will unpack how different configurations of power and political contest arouse fairly dissimilar responses relating to how such 'pressures' must in fact be dealt with. It will discuss briefly the regional dimensions of dominance in Andhra Pradesh and Madhya Pradesh as a necessary preface to this exercise.

The large-scale political mobilization of prosperous peasant castes and the agrarian poor, many of whom are also from the scheduled castes, is a defining feature of domination in AP. The agrarian struggles in the late 19th century in coastal Andhra and Telangana[15] contributed to the emergence of a 'peasant stratagem belonging to the Kamma and Reddy castes respectively' (Srinivasulu 2002, 7). In coastal Andhra, the educated elites of three peasant castes – the Kammas, Reddys and Kapus – were instrumental in spearheading caste-based mobilization against Brahmin domination. They were also at the forefront of the anti-'zamindari' and 'kisan' struggles which ultimately led to the abolition of the zamindari system and the tenancy reforms in the early years after independence. As a result, 'ryots' (or tenants) from the peasant castes were able to obtain direct access to most of the fertile lands. The trajectory of change was somewhat different in the Telangana region, where landed gentry comprising both Muslim 'jagirdars' as well as Hindu 'deshmukhs' (from the Reddy, Velama and Brahmin castes) constituted the support base of the Nizam (Srinivasulu 2002, 6). The landed gentry exploited farmers, often evicting them whimsically in the absence of any secure rights bestowed by the Nizam and regularly extracting free goods and services (a practice known as 'vetti'). In the early 20th century, the Andhra Mahasabha – initially dominated by pro-Congress elements and later led by the Communists – led an agitation against the Nizam and other feudal forces demanding 'land to the tiller'. Interestingly however, the armed squads that led these struggles were dominated by Reddys and Kapus, and this had a significant effect on the land redistribution. While they appropriated the lands of the Hindu deshmukhs, the dalits who had also fought in these armed squads were left practically landless, with nothing but common and waste lands to their lot (Srinivasulu 1988 cited by Srinivasulu 2002).

In the initial years of its rule, the Congress party propounded a progressive image and pursued a reformist agenda that consisted of the abolition of the zamindari and jagirdari systems. However, following the sharp differentiation of the peasantry along caste lines, the core support base of the party lay predominantly within the rich peasantry of the Reddy, Kamma and Kapu castes (Srinivasulu 2002, 8). By the time the first three panchayat elections were held in the state in 1959, 1964 and 1970 the control of these richer peasant castes over the Zilla Parishads and most Panchayat Samitis was firmly entrenched. But if there was one caste that clearly dominated over the Congress, especially in the early decades of its rule, it was clearly the Reddy caste. N. Sanjeeva Reddy and K Brahmanana Reddy, both Congress Chief Ministers from 1956–71, were extremely powerful. Their term also accompanied the decline of the Brahmin influence in the State Assembly (Elliot 1970 cited in Srinivasulu 2002, 9). The image of the Congress as a party for the Reddys contributed greatly to a general feeling of marginalization amongst the rural rich belonging to the Kamma and Kapu communities particularly in the rich coastal belt of the state. So when the TDP came to power in 1982, the Kammas 'gravitated' easily to it, and following the successful mobilization of Kammas across the state, NTR became AP's first Kamma Chief Minister in 1983. The rise of this new regional party provided a legitimate organizational basis for factional politics within the dominant castes and thus continued patterns of political co-optation already established by the Congress.

While politics in Andhra has been dominated by the Reddys and Kammas on the whole, it has also been 'marked by increased space for the representatives of the backward castes and the *dalits*' though lower-caste mobilization has also been simultaneously accommodated by leaders of dominant communities (Suri 2002, 62). After the TDP came to power, tensions between upper caste communities and the dalits grew, and dalits were disenchanted as much with the TDP which they dismissed as 'kamma raj' as they were with the Congress which they described as 'reddy raj' (Suri 2002). Atrocities by Kammas against dalits in Prakasam district in Coastal AP led to the formation of the Dalit Mahasabha or the DMS in 1985, which soon became a common vehicle for dalit assertion all over the state. Dalit politics took on a new shape with the arrival of BSP leader Kanshi Ram on the political scene of AP and his efforts to ride the wave of dalit mobilization. Kanshi Ram's clarion call was for all dalits to unite against the exploitation of the Brahmins, which he argued included Kapus, Kammas and Reddys. However the BSP was a 'non-starter' in Andhra Pradesh politics and performed dismally in the 1994 assembly elections following reports of a clandestine arrangement with the Reddy-dominated Congress (Suri 2002). The poor showing of the DMS in this election also hurt the credibility of well-regarded dalit leaders. Like elsewhere in the country, the dalit movement here rapidly became a movement for dignity and self-respect, but there was no 'sustained engagement with the materiality of cultural degradation' (Srinivasulu, 2002, 50). In later years, the growing electoral importance of the dalits in Andhra Pradesh has been marred by internal caste-based divisions within the SCs (between the Malas and Madigas) and continuing attempts both by the Congress and TDP to exploit and deepen these (Srinivasulu, 2002).

AP has a large percentage of OBCs (nearly 46 per cent) that have grown considerably in influence since the 1980s. The important feature of OBC mobilization is that it has taken place within the existing framework of political co-optation, and a number of factors have led to these castes rallying around the TDP as opposed to the Congress. It was in the 1970s and early 1980s that an educated peasant middle class emerged from OBCs like the Munnuru Kapus, Padmashalis, Goudas, Kurmas and others mainly following the Green Revolution (Srinivasulu 2002, 13). They were able to enter the rural credit system, be part of co-operatives and run small businesses. They also entered educational institutions and the state bureaucracy following reservations in government education and employment. This process had started earlier in the more developed parts of coastal Andhra compared to Telangana and other parts of the state. Around this time the OBCs began to feel greatly disenchanted with the Congress party, which they regarded as being interested only in wooing the SC vote, and as a result, voted 'overwhelmingly' for the TDP in 1983 (Suri 2002). The Congress tried to respond by organising meetings with various backward castes' associations. In order to check the Congress moves and to further consolidate his growing backward caste support, NTR's TDP government accepted the Muralidhar Rao Commission Report on reservations for backward castes in education and employment from 25 per cent to 44 per cent (Suri 2002, 35). The state was soon engulfed in a tremendous backlash from those opposing the reservations policy, and the Andhra Pradesh High Court struck down this increase as unconstitutional. The Government had to withdraw this order.

The 1990s were marked by even greater political mobilization by a range of backward castes' associations who began to organize state-level meetings with the TDP as well as the Congress party to articulate their demands. There were attempts by OBC leaders to bring in Mulayam Singh to rally the OBC vote in AP, especially following the coalition victory of his Samajwadi Party together with the BSP in Uttar Pradesh in 1993. BSP leader Kanshi Ram's visit to Andhra Pradesh in 1994 attracted wide publicity among the politically marginalized elite belonging to the OBCs in addition to the dalits under his slogan of the 'bahujan' or majority. However, the BSP was unable to cut into the social support of the Congress and TDP, a failure that has been attributed to its 'internal differences' and inability to 'cut into the hegemonic politics of the state' (Suri 2002, 56). The TDP led by NTR was victorious in the 1994 election on the basis of extremely populist promises including subsidized rice, free housing and the supply of cheap cloth to rally weaker sections amongst the OBC as well as SC. Chandrababu Naidu subsequently announced a new era of fiscal austerity and reversed several of NTR's core populist schemes (such as by raising the price of rice supplied through the pubic distribution system, increasing power tariffs for the farm sector and lifting prohibition on Indian Manufactured Foreign Liquor). However, he too proved to be every bit the shrewd election strategist and months before the 1999 election Naidu outdid his predecessor in announcing a plethora of schemes for the benefit of the weaker sections, especially women (Suri 2002). Naidu's alignment with the BJP in this election helped sway some of the upper caste (from the Brahmin and Vyasa communities) votes in his favour, and he continued to earn the support of the relatively 'forward' within the backward castes (Suri 2002, 42).

The highly polarized caste environment of AP has generated intense conflicts making it much more difficult for 'politicians to sustain political parties and, at times, to govern' (Manor 2004, 258). There have been sustained conflicts in every part of the state. The economically backward Telangana region has twice been the site of secessionist movements since Andhra Pradesh was created in 1956. The first in the late 1960s and early 1970s was tackled through accommodation by the Congress (in the form of senior posts being offered to Telangana politicians), but this only evoked bitter resentment from Rayalseema and Coastal Andhra. The second in the late 1990s was brought about by Congress politicians who saw separatism as a political strategy to check the TDP from winning a second term in office, and though it gained some strength in 2000 (with three other Indian states being created), it could not be sustained for long (Manor 2004). Telangana has also witnessed an armed insurgency by leftist and Naxalite groups against prosperous sections of society as well as the government for years, concentrated in particular districts. In coastal AP, which is the most prosperous region in the state, organized violence by 'groups of thugs' has been on the rise especially since the TDP came into power in 1983 (Manor 2004, 260). This violence, Manor argues, is more reflective of social conflict on the basis of caste, class and other economic interests rather than with partisan rivalries alone.

Finally, there is the Rayalseema region to the south-west, of which Kurnool district is a part. Caste-based alliances and factional networks have penetrated deep into society, and bitter tensions between castes and factions have persisted at both local as well as higher levels. A faction denotes a 'vertical' organization that typically comprises members from different castes, who are held by 'transactional' ties to a leader (Hardiman 1982, 199). According to Hardiman, factions – in addition to cutting through castes – are supposed to link high caste patrons to low caste clients. Factional networks have allowed leaders from dominant castes (typically Reddys on account of their economic preponderance, see Wade 1990) to draw on the support of the numerous backward castes in villages. On occasion, factionalism in Rayalseema is also loosely used to describe groupism and conflict more generally, with faction-based conflicts being anchored in old family rivalries around property or the sharing of political power through panchayat control. Factional networks that cut through different castes are often embroiled in these conflicts, as observed in the villages studied. Moreover, as will be discussed in some detail in the next chapter, conflicts in Rayalseema can often be extremely violent and bloody. Rayalseema reportedly has a high crime rate and a major percentage of this is owed to petty quarrels and fights leading to murders.[16] A vivid depiction of caste and factional tension in Medak, another district within the Rayalseema region, has been provided by Marguerite Robinson (1988). Manor observes emphatically that 'specialists in the study of society and politics in the state have repeatedly stressed to this writer, over three decades, that factional infighting at these levels within this region is particularly vicious' (2004, 259–60).

The regional dimensions of dominance in MP are remarkably different in three key respects: the continued domination of the upper castes (Brahmins, Rajputs and Banias), the notable absence of mobilized intermediate or middle ranking peasant castes and large numbers of Scheduled Tribes that exist in dense pockets amidst non-tribal majorities (Gupta 2005, Shah 2005). According to Gupta, the upper castes – especially the Brahmins – are more numerous in MP than in most of the country. At the same time, the numbers of 'high ranking middle castes' are very small (unlike the Reddys and Kammas in AP), whereas the 'lower ranking middle castes', now classified as OBCs, though numerous comprise various distinct caste groups and are not particularly well organized. The entrenched domination of the upper castes has continued through decades of Congress rule in the state, and although opportunities for the representation of the OBCs and dalits have improved, this has not been systematic. The BJP (previously Jana Sangh) has historically been identified with the upper castes but it has begun responding to the political upsurge especially amongst the upper echelons of the OBCs (Jaffrelot 2003).

Political elites in Madhya Pradesh have historically lacked an identity particular to the state, with there being little in common between elites from the different regions that comprised Madhya Pradesh (Gupta 2005). Until its division in 2000 with the creation of Chattisgarh, Madhya Pradesh comprised: Madhya Bharat, a union of states in the Malwa Plateau region; Vindhya Pradesh, a union of states in the Vindhya mountain region; Bhopal, a centrally administered princely state; and the Hindi-speaking portion of the Central Provinces in addition to the previously amalgamated Hindi-speaking areas of Chattisgarh. Wayne Wilcox has commented that contemporary Madhya Pradesh was created from the 'left out portions of different states combined into one heterogeneous unit' (cited in Gupta 2005, 5094). The relatively inaccessible terrain of the state, far away from coastal areas and from European traders had two important consequences: the lack of influence of anti-Brahmin social enlightenment movements (which were holding sway in neighbouring Maharashtra for instance), and the powerful presence of local traders and moneylenders. Gupta argues that Madhya Pradesh lacked a cohesive societal group that demanded industrialization, and the industries that appeared in Indore (in the Malwa plateau) had more to do with 'contiguity with the developed economic enclave of western India' than with 'indigenous entrepreneurial effort' (2005, 5096). Trading interest groups are consequently extremely powerful in Madhya Pradesh and wield considerable influence both over the Congress and the BJP.

The Congress party in its various periods of rule has made attempts to further the interests of marginalized communities, but lower caste groups have consistently been 'unprepared in utilising these state-initiated reforms to their advantage' (Gupta 2005, 5098). The Congress in Madhya Pradesh had acquired a 'radical image' since the 1960s, because of its stand on the abolition of privy pursues for princely states (compensation packages in lieu of their merger with the Indian Union).[17] Most princes switched their political allegiance to the Jana Sangh as a result. In the 1980s, Congress Chief Minister Arjun Singh initiated the appointment of the Mahajan Commission to list the backward castes in the state and identify their needs even though there were no social pressures for such initiatives (unlike other states like Uttar Pradesh and Bihar that followed but primarily after the implementation of the Mandal Commission Report). Arjun Singh also promoted Subhash Yadav as his political protégé. Yadav belonged to a middle caste and Singh saw his rise as an essential strategy to woo the backward caste vote at a time when the social base of the Congress in the Hindi heartland needed invigoration (Gupta 2005). When Yadav lost to Digvijay Singh in a party contest in 1993, Arjun Singh walked out in protest to symbolize his commitment to the 'backwards' cause. Digvijay Singh continued the policy of positive discrimination initiated by his predecessor through the Bhopal Declaration, also known as the Dalit Agenda for it envisaged land redistribution in favour of the dalits. It is no coincidence that these Congress gestures coincided with the rising prominence of the BSP in MP. By all accounts, this was an unsuccessful initiative as it met with stiff opposition not only from the upper castes but also from emerging agro-capitalists from the 'upper backward' castes (especially in the fertile Chambal region) who deeply resented Congress overtures towards the dalits. In a large number of cases, land deeds given to dalits were in areas that were still under the effective control of the OBCs, and this antagonized the latter greatly. Moreover, the Congress could not even make as many gains into the dalit vote as it had expected, mainly because of competition from the BSP.

Gupta (2005) has argued that though the Mahajan Commission Report did not create 'social stir' in Madhya Pradesh the same way as perhaps the Mungeri Lal and later the Mandal Commissions did in Bihar, it did contribute to 'stoking the political consciousness' of the upper backwards (2005, 5097). OBC representation in the state assembly has increased since the 1980s but this was not a linear trend and greatly depended on the party that held office (Jaffrelot 2003 cited in Gupta 2005). OBCs were better represented in Congress regimes than in BJP cabinets which were dominated by the upper castes. Moreover, politicians from the OBCs that rose to prominence within the Congress, and later within the BJP for that matter, were typically accommodated because these parties wanted to be seen to be sympathetic to the backward castes and rarely because of a broader articulation of political aspirations of caste-based associations unlike in AP. The BJP – a party whose social base had largely catered to Brahmins and banias throughout the country – also tried to respond to the assertiveness being displayed by OBCs throughout the Hindi heartland. When the BJP defeated Digvijay Singh's Congress government in 2003, it was Uma Bharti whom the party appointed as Chief Minister. Bharti was from the OBCs and the BJP tried to project her as an 'organic leader' of the backward castes of the state. When she had to step down from her post for being charge-sheeted in an old case, the man appointed to replace her was Babu Lal Gaur, also from the OBCs. However, Gaur was much more in the mould of the 'sanskritists' of the party who had in the past raised doubts regarding the reservations policy favouring the backward castes for fears of 'fragmentation of Hindu society' (Gupta 2005, 5094). Traditional elites in the

BJP want to accommodate OBC leaders but not devolve any significant power to the social groups to which they belong. OBC leaders have commensurately remained isolated within a larger canopy of upper-class caste dominance and are fairly pliant as a result.

So why has MP, situated as it is within the Hindi heartland, experienced relatively little political assertion from amongst the OBCs and dalits, despite no dearth of pro-OBC and dalit overtures by successive state regimes? In addition to the factors responsible for perpetuating the dominance of the upper castes discussed so far, Gupta (2005) has also argued that the absence of social mobility amongst the backward castes in Madhya Pradesh has to do with the particular nature of agrarian relations. In particular, the conditions that have produced social conflicts between landlords and tenants leading to socialist and farmers' movements in states like Bihar and Uttar Pradesh have been absent. Roy (2002) explains that Madhya Pradesh had different kinds of tenurial relations that were imposed over existing systems following the late introduction of colonial rule in this area. As the state was thinly populated and agricultural surpluses were difficult to generate, the landowning class was not particularly interested in rent collection. In effect therefore, a system of 'ryotwari' was being practised with a direct relationship between the state and the peasantry. Drawing from Roy, Gupta argues that this lack of productivity underpinned the eventual 'alienation' of the peasantry because it 'precluded the possibility of social mobility and also subjugated the masses to a process of complete subordination, in the context of a largely static agrarian society' (2005, 5095). So if peasants did not mobilize themselves against the landowning class, it was not because the landowners were benevolent, it was because frictions were never severe enough for the peasantry to challenge the existing relationships of domination and subordination.

The third dimension of dominance and one that is resolutely central to politics at local and regional levels in Madhya Pradesh is the economic and political marginalization of the large numbers of Scheduled Tribes and their continued exploitation by non-tribal majorities. Tribal populations here have suffered through their lack of landownership, settlement on poor quality and marginal lands, land alienation and indebtedness since pre-colonial times (Prasad 2002). Tribals have historically led 'semi-sedentary' lives marked by seasonal migration and their control over land was established through 'pattas' during the cultivation season. Prasad writes that these strips were 'demarcated through mutual understanding and oral agreements' a practice that was not compatible with notions of property rights in pre-colonial and colonial India (2002, 259–260). Reports of the 'settlement' attempts of the colonial government through recognition of individual cultivators and landholders noted, for example, how Gond cultivators mostly had poor quality and unproductive lands and were typically unable to pay rents for these fallow plots. They were impoverished and frequently in debt 'even though they could hold formal rights over their lands' (Grigson 1940 cited in Prasad 2002, 260). Various other settlement reports pertaining to a number of districts in the state reveal how tribals often held very small 'jungly tracts' (like the Gonds in Chhindwara) and being subject to tremendous pressures on land that was 'inferior' in the first place, depended on the forest for their subsistence (as the Gonds in Seoni) (see Prasad 2002 for more details). The common history behind all of these situations that tribals found themselves in lay in their relationship with non-tribal (and usually absentee) landlords who typically exploited them through extraction of rents and payment of low wages, and ultimately through alienation from their lands. Given their fragile relationship with the lands they cultivated, tribals have vitally depended on forests, but a host of state policies towards forests since colonial times have jeopardized this link as well.

Baviskar (1995) has documented in some detail the extractive policies levied by the British on the Bhils, especially by tightening the system of taxation both in areas where they ruled directly as well as indirectly through the Rajput princes. She writes that taxation 'compelled adivasis to participate in the monetized economy to a greater extent' (1995, 110). Adivasis were being pushed towards disregarding their practices of shifting cultivation, but at the same time, the forests on which they depended were being appropriated by the state and sold for revenue. In Alirajpur, a region in south-west Madhya Pradesh where Baviskar carried out her research, state revenue receipts from the early 20th century reveal a ten-fold rise in forest revenue from timber sales over a thirty year period (citing Luard 1908). This alienation has severely impacted upon the ability of tribal people to provide for themselves, made survival precarious, and forced them to migrate particularly during the bad years to the plains of Gujarat and Nimar. Tribal dispossession of forests at the hands of the state has continued after independence, with the state viewing forests in terms of an 'irreconcilable opposition between national objectives and needs of the local people' (Shah 2005, 4896).[18] With state pursuit of industrialization, moreover, tribal areas with their rich natural resources have been targeted as prime areas for exploitation in the wider national interest. Various restrictive rules and regulations have only created more avenues for petty officials to intimidate adivasis or negotiate bribes and 'gifts' in exchange for breaking the law (Baviskar 1995).

Tribals throughout the state, and perhaps across the country, have coexisted with non-tribal populations on unequal terms over generations. The idea that they have been living a 'secluded' life in 'habitual isolation' has therefore been roundly dismissed by many historians. Sarkar (1989) writes, 'Apart from some isolated and really primitive food gatherers, the tribals were and very much are a part of Indian society, as the lowest stratum of the peasantry subsisting through shifting cultivation, agricultural labour, and increasingly coolies' recruited for work in distant plantations, mines and factories' (Sarkar 1989, 44). Baviskar (1995) has usefully commented on the 'preservation' versus 'assimilation' debate that has dominated anthropological writing on tribals. She argues that while the former was never a 'realistic option' for dynamic tribal communities interacting continuously with 'larger institutional structures, the latter is simply a 'euphemism for economic impoverishment, political marginalization and the complete loss of cultural autonomy' (1995, 108). Indeed, not only have tribals had to contend with commercialization and growing interaction with the state, they have also encountered 'Hinduisation' to adopt the 'ritual practices' of upper caste Hindus in order to improve their social status (Baviskar 1995).

Dewas district, located in the south-west of the state, starkly embodies the principal dimensions of dominance that I have described. It is a part of the Malwa plateau, and is divided into two by the Narmada valley: the economically prosperous area above is known as 'ghaat-upar', while the relatively less developed area below is referred to as 'ghaat-neeche'. The ghaat-upar areas constitute the fertile Malwa uplands, and benefit from a long tradition of irrigated cultivation and industrialization, which have in turn facilitated several ancillary businesses such as dairy. Indore town lies about 50 kilometres west of Dewas, and has remained the hub of industrial and trade activities since well before the colonial times. The ghaat-upar region, primarily on account of its economic advantage, is the politically important area of the district, and politics here is dominated by upper caste groups, irrespective of whether it is the Congress or BJP that is at the helm of affairs. Both the Congress and BJP have strong and weak pockets throughout Dewas district.[19] There is also a large shifting population, which constantly changes its party loyalties. It is common for caste groups in villages to support one party or another.[20]

The ghaat-neeche areas are relatively less fertile in contrast and have suffered continuous resource degradation. They also include large concentrations of Bhil and Bhilala tribals that are interspersed with non-tribal majorities, and have generally been marginal to state or district level politics and power. A brief exception to this rule was when Kailash Joshi, the MLA who had represented Bagli constituency (which falls within the ghaat-neeche area) for eight successive terms became Chief Minister of the state in 1977, with the fall of the Congress party after the emergency. Joshi belonged to the Jana Sangh, then a part of the rival Janata Party, but his leadership was challenged by younger leaders from the Sangh and in 1979, Sunderlal Patwa replaced him as the Chief Minister for another year before the Congress came back into power. Nevertheless, Joshi's short-lived stay at the helm of power could not have made any significant difference to the general patterns of exploitation experienced by the tribals of ghaat-neeche.

The Bhils and Bhilalas of Bagli 'tehsil' in the ghaat-neeche areas were originally inhabitants of neighbouring Dhar district, and had been relocated to Bagli at the instance of the colonial government in the early 20th century presumably to occupy large tracts of cleared forestland of the ghaat-neeche areas.[21] They settled down in almost wholly tribal villages, but they continued to be a minority in a predominantly non-tribal tehsil, and district. The non-tribal neighbourhood, moreover, comprises relatively prosperous cultivators, most of whom were already practising large-scale cultivation at the time migrants arrived. They had dug wells and later tube wells on their lands for irrigation. The new entrants by contrast were given small pieces of land by the government. Although this had the effect of eliminating landlessness, most farmers continued to practice only marginal cultivation and sought wage labour on the lands of their non-tribal neighbours. Tribals have since been working as agricultural labourers, often obtaining less than minimum wages. They have also succumbed to a tortuous routine of annual migration to the Malwa uplands, where unlike ghaat-neeche villages, irrigated cultivation continues for the 'rabi' crop as well as during the summer.

Depoliticization and the Politics of Selection

Even before watershed projects are implemented in villages and encounter micro-level politics, district watershed authorities typically experience 'pressures' from influential political leaders to privilege their electoral constituencies and appoint NGOs that are in their favour. It is not particularly surprising that WSD is extremely attractive to elected political representatives as a development programme laden with spoils. As a programme that aims to improve soil and water conservation, increase availability of water for irrigation and drinking, provide employment, and reduce migration, it has all the right elements of a 'catch-all' rural development programme. Politicians seeking power by winning elections can capture voters' imagination by proclaiming the entire range of likely benefits available through watershed development. Besides, the prospect that about two million rupees or more will be spent in a single micro-watershed project over four years is most attractive.[22] Transfer of 80 per cent of these funds, that comprise the works component of the budget, to the village watershed committee, greatly enhances the selling point of the programme. Announcement of new watershed projects in electoral constituencies is seen to work to the advantage of politicians, earning them assured support from their local supporters. Requests for appointment as PIAs typically come from NGOs that are keen to work in watershed development, but believe they need to approach the watershed authorities through an influential politician to be selected. More often than not, politicians clamouring for watershed projects soon lose interest in them, after decisions regarding project allocation have been taken. They rarely take stock of the progress of such projects or pursue serious issues that may arise from their implementation.[23] This could be because of the nature of watershed development projects, which do not yield an impression of instant gain, unlike roads or large dams for example. Project structures are typically small, low-cost and visibly unimpressive, and project results usually take a minimum of two years to appear.

The 1994 guidelines do include a ready instrument to depoliticize programme decision-making of such politics. This instrument comes in the form of selection criteria, which are posited to be neutral and scientific, and are an integral part of planned development interventions. From my investigations in Kurnool and Dewas it was clear that key officials engaged in implementation – the PD in Kurnool and the CEO of the Zilla Panchayat and the Collector in Dewas – were well aware of attempts to lobby but their responses to 'depoliticize' the programme through recourse to selection criteria, or otherwise, were remarkably different. These differences, will be argued, arose from the larger political and institutional landscapes of decentralization that the two watershed machineries were situated within.

Kurnool

In a lengthy personal interview to me in his office chamber in Kurnool in January 2001, KWO's PD, a young and enthusiastic civil servant from the Indian Forest Service, set out clearly the pressures experienced for selection of watershed areas and agencies and explained how the watershed office was responding to these under his stewardship. The first point he made was that there was absolutely no scope for any politicians to influence the selection of villages or watershed areas in Kurnool. His claim was that KWO had been able to expunge decision-making on 'political' grounds which implicitly referred to the narrow interests intended to serve short-term electoral gains. 'No, not even a single square inch', he said, 'All villages in the entire district have been prioritized within a district action plan.[24] Each village's area is there, and we have entered details of how much area has been treated in the past (under different departments), and how much area remains untreated. We have details of the potential for treatment in every mandal and village. Without bias to anyone, whether to ruling or non-ruling party, we have been giving watersheds. So that has gone a long way to increase the confidence of the political will.

Whatever is happening is happening neutrally. Nobody raises any bias (sic)'. Interestingly however, his discourse of depoliticization was not an insipid one for it included a clear view of the role that elected political representatives in DWAC (or DPAP governing body) could perform in relation to WSD. While he did not think they should be influencing selection, he explained that they could use their resources to improve 'political awareness' about projects in their areas. In his view, they could make a difference to the projects that were not functioning 'properly' or 'on hold' due to the 'lack of cooperation'. He said that he had passed on all relevant information to political representatives, but also that this had not elicited much of a constructive response.

The PD was explicit about the requests, pleas and pressures he received on a daily basis for appointment as PIA, especially from NGOs. At the time of the interview, nearly 500 applications from NGOs were with him, and these were routed through 'friends, colleagues, and senior officers'. 'Everybody comes after me', was his exasperated expression. Of course, politicians in the governing body also tried to influence such postings ('they request me to put a certain man somewhere') but not necessarily with success. However, the Director took care to explain that politicians were usually amenable to reasoned responses: 'If I explain to them the requirements of the programme, and we discuss whether the person can do the required work or not, they usually listen'. He was quite clear that while NGOs were very eager to be appointed as PIAs, the same was not true for government officials who did not seek this additional responsibility. He elaborated further that government PIAs were better at adhering to rules compared to NGOs that were all too often caught in misappropriation of finances and other problems stemming from 'lack of experience, lack of exposure in handling this kind of money, lack of exposure in dealing with administrative problems and zero technical experience'. He justified his position on the basis of the 69 PIAs that he was responsible for monitoring intensively, maintaining throughout that ultimately he was not bothered about whether it was a government officer or an NGO that acted as PIA, and that 'nobody in their right mind would remove a good NGO in favour of a bad GO'.[25]

While government officials were recruited as PIAs on the basis of their 'performance' in other jobs (and internal bureaucratic hearsay plays an important role here), the PD devised his own set of criteria for prospective NGO PIAs. These included aspects such as age of the organization, experience in field of work and demonstrated competence in handling finances. Later iterations of MORD's guidelines have included similar specifications for NGOs, following more general concerns that too many organizations had mushroomed in response to the opportunities created in state-sponsored watershed projects without the requisite credentials. In Kurnool, at the time this fieldwork was carried out, there did seem to be a paucity of vibrant and active NGOs. The large number of organizations registered as NGOs shared a similar character in that they had been formed by politicians or retired government functionaries, with a cobbled membership to meet the minimum requirement of five laid down by the Indian Societies Registration Act of 1862. Given this context, the PD's impressions of NGOs in Kurnool ('maybe there are one or two NGOs working well here and there, but this cannot be said for the bulk of the NGOs') were not entirely surprising. Kurnool in this respect was remarkably different from neighbouring Anantapur district, the site of operation of a very large and well-established NGO called the Rayalseema Development Trust (RDT). It was also not representative of the high level of NGO involvement in WSD programmes throughout the state, federated at the state level in the form of an extremely organized and pro-active network called WASSAN.[26]

In keeping with the general pattern of NGO engagement in WSD in Kurnool, one of the projects that was studied (in a village called Lilapuram) was being implemented by the Kurnool District Rural Service Organization (KDRSO), a small NGO that at the time comprised only of six members.[27] A retired government functionary in Kurnool formed KDRSO in 1995. It survived as an organization by receiving government money to implement development projects.[28] The main individual in charge of the NGO implemented the project through a four-member WDT, like any other project in Kurnool district. KWO did not require, or indeed trust, KDRSO to make any separate or extra efforts beyond what is prescribed for initiating the watershed project. As the NGO did not have considerable resources of its own and received a meagre two per cent of the designated funds for administration earmarked for each project, it was considerably worse off than government PIAs which were able to depend on official resources and infrastructure. The second project studied was in a village called Malligundu, had a government officer as the PIA (from the department of agriculture and veterinary sciences) who similarly acted through his WDT.

Once watershed areas and agencies had been carefully selected, KWO attempted a second level of depoliticization in the villages identified on the basis of their position in the district-level priority list. The PD in his interview was relatively more reticent to put this strategy in words beyond his mention of projects being stalled due to 'lack of cooperation', but a fuller account of KWO's approach was obtained through informal and recurring interactions with the many WDT officials from the projects in Lilpauram and Malligundu over a three month period. The villages of Kurnool, being a part of the Rayalseema region, embody to varying degrees the intense caste- and faction-based conflicts that have been described earlier. In project parlance, villages with explicit and ongoing factional conflict were referred to as 'faction-villages'. Faction-villages were unambiguously regarded as 'problem-villages' and KWO meticulously avoided working in these places. Crucially though, this definition did not include villages that are not 'united', or more importantly appeared to be so.

In this respect, the depoliticization discourse following the 1994 guidelines acquired a highly specific and regional flavour. KWO frowned upon conflictual forms of factional politics, and since this sort of politics was amply reflected within local panchayats, the guidelines' exclusion of panchayats from direct programme implementation found favour here. The equation of politics with factional conflict amounted to the adoption of a selective meaning of politics that reflected the wider nature of political contestation in the region and the state. Moreover, watershed committees (WCs) clearly fit into KWO's technocratic orientation, as institutions that could be created, and their working procedures codified and monitored, without the 'messy politics' that continued in panchayat forums. The larger political environment in the state, where panchayats have not occupied centre stage in decentralized development, greatly facilitated such a rationalization. Both Malligundu and Lilapuram passed the project's information 'co-operation and unity' criteria. On closer examination however, this was possible because local power structures (factions) were incorporated into the project morphology, rendering KWO's attempts at depoliticization unsuccessful in reality. This will be the subject of the next chapter.

Dewas

In her account of the Rajiv Gandhi Watershed Mission in Jhabua district of MP, Baviskar explains how the watershed approach essentially rests on the attempt to use 'bureaucratic convenience' in 'rendering legible and manageable unruly ecological complexities (2007, 289 citing Scott 1998). The idea that ecological and administrative categories (the micro-watershed and the village) will converge had been adopted for administrative convenience, but in fact was likely to generate contradictions. This disjuncture could arise from potentially conflicting selection criteria, especially since the programme prioritises villages with a suitable 'political orientation'. This is similar to Kurnool, where watershed projects were not extended to villages that could not reconcile their internal differences in order to participate with the state, except that at the time of my fieldwork the criterion regarding participation was not formally stated. Baviskar argues that this approach has led to the effective skewing of stated priorities, for areas with the most 'intense ecological degradation' and therefore more in need of soil and water conservation have been left out (2007, 290).

In Dewas, the absence of a singular bureaucratic authority responsible for WSD meant that a clearly articulated technocratic discourse around selection was missing. My interviews with the Collector and CEO of the Zilla Panchayat, both IAS officials partially responsible for implementation, revealed that they commonly received requests from elected representatives for awarding watershed projects and choosing PIAs. The situation in Dewas was different from Kurnool – where a combination of political and institutional conditions meant that the PD could take a firm stand against selection being subject to 'political pressures'. Here, the merging of the Zilla Panchayat with the DRDA and, eventually, the constitution of Zilla Sarkar together masked lobbying activities under the formalities of sanctioned protocol. The guidelines of the RGM clearly mention that watershed areas are to be selected by DWAC, which mainly comprises of ZP representatives. Moreover, the dispersion of the programme's administrative powers among the Collector, Zilla Panchayat and DRDA officers implied that a strict adherence to the selection criteria through tight bureaucratic control was not always possible. Local NGOs tried to avail of the opportunities for watershed project implementation by using political contacts to influence the district administration. A senior journalist and geo-hydrologist in Dewas, who requested anonymity, revealed that it was difficult to be selected as a PIA without political contacts and influence. He had applied to the CEO, Zilla Panchayat's office, for a PIA's position and had been waiting for nearly two years for a response at the time of interview in October 2000. Interest in WSD projects by political representatives remained very largely opportunistic however. A senior member of the Dewas Zilla Panchayat gave me a detailed account of how WSD related issues were keenly discussed in the meetings of the Zilla Sarkar. But interest in them did not last beyond the initial period and dwindled once decisions regarding project allocation had been taken, even though they remained as items for formal review.

The relative absence of a depoliticization discourse regarding selection in Dewas manifested itself in very interesting ways. Embodied in the selection histories of the two villages I studied were entirely different political processes. The first set of processes underscored dominant caste politics by awarding the district's first WSD project to Kishangarh, a large and prosperous village in Tonk-Khurd tehsil in the ghaat-upar area. Kishangarsh is a part of Budasa milli-watershed, which lies in close proximity to Dewas district headquarters.[29] Milli-watersheds are identified using a ridge-to-valley approach, as advised by the national guidelines and RGM, and their constituent micro-watersheds are treated separately.[30] The most important reason influencing Budasa's selection was its location in Tonk-Khurd tehsil for it included the electoral constituency of Suren Varma, a BJP leader, who was the MLA when this programme came to the district. Varma wanted the first watershed project to be given to an important panchayat in Tonk-Khurd.[31] The ghaat-upar part of Dewas district, especially Tonk Khurd and Dewas tehsils, has in recent years become a BJP stronghold.[32] Besides, ghaat-upar being generally more important than ghaat-neeche in District politics and political economy, it was not particularly difficult for elected politicians (and bureaucrats at the helm) to accede to Varma's request. And so Tonk-Khurd in ghaat-upar was selected first, even when large parts of the district were drier, more degraded and housed poorer tribal populations, as in ghaat-neeche. This contradicted the basic tenet of the watershed guidelines to prioritize resource poor areas laid down in the programme's selection criteria.

Kishangarh village embodied the real political appeal of the Tonk-Khurd tehsil for four reasons. First, it is a big and populous village, comprising nearly 4000 residents, while the average village in this region has 1000–1500 residents. The larger the size, the greater is the electoral potential. Second, it is economically prosperous, and most farmers here practice large, irrigated soybean and wheat cultivation. Third, it has an independent panchayat, which because of its size receives a greater share of panchayat funds. Funds for development schemes to be implemented through panchayats are allocated on a per capita basis. Fourth, all its neighbouring villages are considerably smaller, although some of these have their own panchayats. Kishangarh's economic and numerical strength made it the predominant panchayat in Tonk-Khurd tehsil. Leaders from both Congress and BJP have consistently tried to woo Kishangarh's residents over the years, and awarded its panchayat generous shares of Madhya Pradesh and MLA discretionary funds.[33] While there may be many other villages in Dewas district that share some of these features, the combination of Kishangarh's locational, political and economic coordinates contributed to its appeal. Its selection indicated that political leaders could effectively influence the programme's selection procedure. The interface between the bureaucratic structure and elected representatives at the district level greatly facilitated this process.

Remarkably however, in the very same year a watershed project was awarded to Neelpura, in Bagli tehsil, to a predominantly tribal village within its ghaat-neeche portion. What was even more remarkable was the appointment as PIA of an NGO that had from 1992–1995 unleashed a spate of confrontations with local power holders in Bagli (including sub-district revenue officials, landholders and sarpanches), all non-tribal, in a concerted attempt to resist their multi-faceted exploitation of poor Bhilala tribals in Neelpura as well as other villages. In the context of a state divided by high caste domination and tribal subordination, this warrants closer examination, especially as reports from other districts in Madhya Pradesh did not confirm similar stories of the state warming up to 'activist'

NGOs. In her account of WSD programmes in Jhabua, Baviskar writes the following: 'The watershed mission carefully selects villages to ensure that "troublemakers" are left out. This means that villages mobilized by groups such as KMCS that have a history of being critical of the state, protesting against state action rather than collaborating with it, are excluded' (2007, 290). There was nothing particularly surprising in a village like Kishangarh being selected, for it affirmed the cynical influence that politicians were able to exercise in a political and institutional environment that made such opportunism relatively easy (as compared to Kurnool). However, that it was possible for a marginalized and electorally unimportant area to be selected under the aegis of an ostensibly non-conformist NGO is testimony to the extremely complex decentralization processes unleashed in Madhya Pradesh at this time. The awkward embracing of 'contentious' politics by a state development programme also proved that state actors were not subscribing to a uniform discourse of depoliticization. Simply put, the relative absence of a depoliticization discourse in Dewas may have facilitated the blatant accommodation of dominant politics in one part of the district, but it simultaneously allowed the inclusion of agencies that were challenging these very same dominant politics in another. Some preliminary remarks are offered below about the particular conditions that made this possible, as this case will be drawn upon in greater detail in later chapters.

The NGO that was selected as a PIA for a watershed project in Bagli is called 'Samaj Pragati Sahyog' (SPS – in Hindi, meaning 'Support for Social Progress'). The organization originally comprised a small group of eight friends who arrived in Bagli in 1992. It has grown considerably since amassing more than a hundred members, with established links with the state and central governments and various assorted donors. In 1992 though, group members were new to Bagli town never having lived there before. When they set up a temporary office with their personal savings and registered themselves as an NGO, they were the subject of much local curiosity and interest.[34] Local curiosity about the newly formed SPS only increased when its members attempted to acquaint themselves with Bagli and the ghaat-neeche villages. Group members recounted how local officials and politicians, based in Bagli, were distinctly unfriendly. According to the group, they were most perplexed because SPS, unlike other NGOs in the district, was not there to implement any particular development project. Indeed when SPS arrived in Bagli, it had no ready development projects under its belt, and group members felt very strongly that their motivations were much broader than simply obtaining government funds for development projects. This was very different from KDRSO, the NGO in Kurnool formed by a retired government officer that might have found it difficult to credibly claim otherwise!

In lengthy conversations with me in Bagli, a number of different members reiterated that their larger strategy was to build a 'peoples' organization' that would engage in grassroots work and advocacy. They explained they had chosen Bagli because they wanted to form 'a critical mass within policy making, so that marginalized tribal areas would get the benefit of increased state intervention and public investment'. They were very clear in that their engagement with the 'state' had to be a 'positive' one, and distanced themselves from the pro-tribal, radical, violent Naxalite and Maoist modes of activism that are widespread in parts of AP, Bihar and Orissa. A prominent member of the group said, 'It is much easier being an activist. Activists have no stakes and can afford to raise slogans and use other attention seeking tactics. When you combine activism with serious developmental work, it is the hardest combine'.

Such development work commenced soon after, when SPS initiated well-digging and water conservation projects in Neelpura, a small poor village, conveniently located close to the main road and comprising almost entirely of the Bhilala and Korku tribes. It obtained funds from the Tribal Development Department of the Government of India in 1992, a project from the Department of Science and Technology, GOI, in 1993 and two more projects from CAPART in 1993 and 1994. During its implementation of the well-digging and water conservation projects in Neelpura, SPS stumbled upon two types of exploitative practices in the region. These revealed the nexus of domination by anti-tribal forces in the ghaat-neeche area. It detected that the overall wage structure, especially for public works, in this tribal belt was not in keeping with the equal minimum wage laws of the country enacted in 1948. Both large farmers and panchayat sarpanches (acting through contractors), who engaged labourers for the execution of construction works, perpetuated this injustice. SPS also discovered that land records of poor tribals throughout the ghaat-neeche had not been updated in accordance with the MP Land Revenue Code of 1950, and essential information, such as correct rates for land transactions, was being kept out of their bounds by the local revenue bureaucracy. This included both the village 'patwari' as we all the sub-district magistrate of the revenue division, who stood to gain monetarily from such malpractices.[35] The absence of any challenge to their exploitative practices had allowed these junior state officials to act like veritable local autocrats!

SPS decided not to look away from the situation, and acted to confront these power-holders in two ways. It insisted on paying equal minimum wages to all its hired labourers, antagonising large farmers, sarpanches and contractors in the ghaat-neeche, all of whom were equal perpetrators of below minimum wages on the fields and in minor construction and other works carried out with panchayat money. There were also individuals in Neelpura who felt very upset at these developments and distanced themselves from the NGO. SPS then approached the District Administration with a proposal to organize a 'land records camp' in order to rectify the appalling records situation. The District Collector lent her support to SPS and in January 1995 such a camp was organized in Neelpura village. It was tremendously successful and more than 13,000 tribals travelled from faraway villages to attend. The district collectorate even followed this initiative with two other similar camps. This turn of events constituted an important moment in the life of this NGO and its eventual trajectories of work in the ghaat-neeche area. It marked the beginning of antagonistic relationships with junior officials (like the sub-divisional magistrate), whose vested interests suffered following SPS's intervention, but more favourable relationships with senior district and state-level officials, who had no such interests at stake. Not long after these dramatic developments, SPS was contacted by the Dewas district administration to become the PIA for the first Rajiv Gandhi Mission watershed project in the entire ghaat-neeche area, and Neelpura was the selected village.

How did an NGO that had clearly defied the status quo receive an invitation of partnership from the state? SPS had been willing to challenge the exclusionary forms of rule that commonly characterize the functioning of a multi-sited and plural state apparatus, and yet senior state officials lent it their support. State policies frequently require actors engaged in development work to look away from political phenomena like the denial of rights or the abuse of authority, and promote a 'depoliticized' engagement with development. Consider the Charitable Trusts Act of 1950 which applies to voluntary organizations: 'The achievement of a political purpose, in the sense of arousing in the people the desire, and instilling into them an imperative need to demand changes in the structures of the administration and the mechanism by which they are governed....is not a charitable purpose as being one "for the advancement of any other object of general public utility within section 9(4) of the Act"' (cited in Kamat 2002, 56). So what led to SPS obtaining support from key district officials in Dewas to rectify old and contentious practices within this larger history of state antagonism towards radicalism? While a certain familiarity in background and ease of communication with senior government authorities might have helped – members of SPS are all educated and English speaking, while fluent in Hindi (the principal regional language), and from a relatively privileged social background – there were other more important factors. First, in SPS's case, the confrontation it spearheaded was underpinned by an idea of the Indian state as a guarantor of rights, and therefore of the need to uphold legislation (minimum wages, land records) that no civil servant could possibly disregard in public. But for the fact that it had discovered malpractices in relation to existing law, it too may have been in trouble with its funding agencies (notably CAPART). Second, SPS's location in ghaat-neeche, the site of subordinate politics within the district, proved to be crucial, as opposed to ghaat-upar where SPS might have found it a lot harder to campaign for change.

A senior member said to me 'It is very different here, just to think that such a different world exists between tribal and non-tribal areas. Kishangarh is a different story. It's a government-led thing. Much of this Neelpura chaos will not be there. The whole tribal thing does not exist there. The whole tribal aspiration which one sees here will not be present...There it is more of a caste thing and the dominant politician'. Of course, even in ghaat-neeche SPS experienced considerable resistance from elected political representatives. Sarpanches together with the local Congress MLA tried hard to 'oust' the NGO from the region by complaining to Chief Minister Digvijay Singh, on the grounds that it 'was corrupt...it bypassed panchayats...and misappropriated their money' but were unsuccessful in the end. This was a time when sarpanches throughout the state were feeling rather unassailable on account of Singh's very overt pro-panchayat gestures. Even so, their relative lack of clout in the larger politics of the district translated into their inability to use the district Zilla Panchayat to block SPS's selection for watershed work. SPS was publicly acquitted of charges being levelled by the angry sarpanches by an inquiry committee headed by the Zilla Panchayat and also commended for its 'good work'. Top bureaucrats in the district were inclined to involve SPS as a PIA for watershed projects in the villages in Bagli's tribal belt, not least as the NGO was already working on water conservation in the area. Besides, it was always difficult finding motivated government officials who would be ready to work in the formidably dry, remote and inhospitable parts of the district. In this way, the watershed machine in Dewas became party to a situation where an NGO that was challenging deeply entrenched politics of domination became a formal partner of the state.

Conclusion

The main purpose in this chapter has been to show that the constraints and conditions that prompted state actors implementing the watershed programme to pursue a discourse of depoliticization have been very different in Kurnool in AP and Dewas in MP. These differences have arisen not simply from the institutional arrangements for implementing the WSD but from the larger landscapes of decentralization of which this development programme is a part. In many ways, this has been a timely comparison as the two political leaders at the helm of these reforms have been the subject of much fascination and curiosity for the similarities as also dissimilarities in their approaches. The chapter has illustrated that political and institutional policy initiatives for decentralization are deeply intertwined with prevailing regional patterns of dominance, both in the ways in which they are motivated and interpreted. It has tried to trace the main elements of these relationships in order to reveal political influences, stemming from regional configurations of power, over respective watershed machineries with respect to the selection of project villages and agencies, and analyse the responses these have elicited.

In AP, sharply contested party politics between the Congress and the TDP has framed competition between the two dominant peasant castes, the Reddys and Kammas. It is also a state that has witnessed steady political mobilization of the OBCs and dalits, and while much of this mobilization has also occurred within the existing framework of political co-optation, bitter conflicts between dominant and ascendant castes have manifested themselves in trenchant factionalism. Chandrababu Naidu's leanings towards creating a 'modern professionalism' in governance driven by a competent bureaucracy 'free of political interference' stemmed in large measure from his own personality. The policies he ultimately devised, however, were clearly in line with the history of his party to capture panchayats rather than promoting them as viable institutions of local government. His Janmabhoomi initiative has been widely regarded as more of a ploy to boost the position and clout of local party supporters and less of an initiative to facilitate community development and bottom-up accountability. Besides, we know that Naidu's talk of a lean state was very largely rhetorical, manifesting in extremely tightly monitored bureaucratic systems, and when it came to populism, Naidu outdid NTR in his announcement of welfare schemes for the poor before the 1999 elections. In Kurnool, in the heart of the Rayalseema region, these two aspects – Naidu's emphasis on technocratic and 'apolitical' governance and active factional conflicts in villages – combined to produce the imperatives for the watershed machine to be subsumed within a dedicated bureaucratic authority and a definition of politics (as factional conflict) that all KWO watershed projects should avoid.

In MP, the forward castes (notably Brahmins, Rajputs and Banias) have held sway through decades of Congress rule and have not been challenged similarly by the very scattered OBC and dalit population across the state. While other parties like the BJP and BSP have grown in significance, this has mostly had the effect of splitting the Congress hold over the upper caste vote. All political parties have tried to woo the backward castes and dalits, but this has not resulted in any systematic increase in their political representation. The historic subjugation of tribals by non-tribals is experienced across the state and the major political parties, subsumed within dominant caste politics, have been instruments of tribal exploitation. Dewas district fully embodies these dimensions in the domination of upper castes in ghaat-neeche politics and the continued marginalization of the tribal areas in ghaat-neeche. Digvijay Singh's efforts to modernize the bureaucracy were different from Naidu in that he also emphasized decentralization of powers to panchayats and tried to integrate elected political representatives with bureaucrats at the district level. In these circumstances, a Kurnool-style watershed office was not established, despite the creation of a Rajiv Gandhi Mission at the state level to promote unimpeded bureaucratic access to the Chief Minister. The absence of an articulated discourse of depoliticization in WSD projects stemmed as much from the political context of decentralization in this state, as from the relatively diffused administrative arrangements for overseeing the watershed programme. If elected political representatives were being legitimately involved at all levels, how possibly could bureaucrats talk about getting rid of their influences? Stemming from this, the regional politics of domination and subordination impacted on critical decisions regarding selection, though as we have seen in different ways: elected politicians (like the BJP MLA in Tonk-Khurd) were able to influence the selection of Kishangarh, whereas key district officials (like the Dewas Collector) were instrumental in selecting Neelpura with SPS as PIA.

Ultimately, the chapter shows that decentralization of state power and depoliticization to entrench state power shared a definite though unpredictable relationship. The state at particular levels may want to depoliticize contentious issues in order to avoid difficult questions, but decentralization disaggregates the state and brings innumerable actors into the scope of decision-making and interpretation, making such depoliticization far from uniform or indeed certain. These actors do not function whimsically. Quite on the contrary, they are deeply embedded within particular configurations of power, political and also socio-economic, and cannot be divorced from their contexts. We have seen so far that watershed authorities in both the districts studied experienced 'political pressures' but their responses were very different. The next two chapters will examine the micro-level counterparts of these responses in greater detail.

Chapter Five

DEPOLITICIZING LOCAL INSTITUTIONS? PANCHAYATS AND WATERSHED COMMITTEES

Discourses, Agencies and the Micro-Politics of Local Bodies

The watershed machineries in Kurnool and Dewas embodied the constraints and opportunities presented by their wider political and administrative environments of decentralization. These were most strikingly manifested in the extent to which the two adopted discourses of depoliticization regarding the selection of watershed villages and agencies. However these machineries were not homogenous entities; they comprised a hierarchy of officials and, in cases where NGOs were engaged, then actors from 'outside' the formal state apparatus. As the implementing agencies of watershed projects, these actors came into close contact with villages. They were responsible for initiating the formation of watershed committees in a peaceful and cooperative manner, as these would be at the fulcrum of the participatory decision-making that the 1994 guidelines so eagerly espoused. But they also had to take a stand with respect to village panchayats, which are typically maligned as bodies torn apart by 'pointless politics' arising from the domination of entrenched interests as well as seemingly endless contest. As my previous chapter has illustrated, whereas the discourse to distance panchayat politics from the watershed programme was clearly articulated by officials at different levels in Kurnool, this was not the case in Dewas, where integration of decentralized development with panchayats was a state priority.[1]

This chapter will empirically ascertain the extent to which watershed committees could be distanced from the respective panchayats in the four villages where the fieldwork was carried out. It will present the details of the interactions between project implementing agencies and village residents that have prefaced and accompanied these efforts. The larger purpose here is to challenge the idea set out in the guidelines that it is indeed possible to create local bodies that embody an outpouring of inclusive and community-based goodwill as well as co-operation, when there are other bodies, i.e., panchayats, in the same village that evidently do not exhibit these traits. The evidence presented will critique the dominant tone of the communitarian and new institutionalist influences on development discourse regarding the abilities of communities to form local institutions. The chapter is mainly concerned with revealing the micro-politics of power in these villages and exploring the different ways in which they shape panchayats as well as watershed committees, as two deeply interrelated phenomena and not as unrelated and separable institutions, as is assumed by the policy guidelines and within dominant debates. While the explanation for why panchayats and watershed committees often exhibit overlapping identities boils down to the fact that they are each dominated by the same elites, the chapter analyses the specific reasons why dominant elites found the prospect of association with the watershed programme appealing. It will differentiate between the factors that led different project agencies to privilege respective dominant elites, for these were not the same. It will argue that these differences bore important consequences for the nature of dominance they exercised, which had further implications for the participatory operations that unfolded in these villages (a subject that is explored more fully in the next chapter).

The chapter will also interrogate the particular actions and strategies adopted by agencies in charge of watershed projects while manoeuvring the formation of watershed committees. Following the introductory discussion to the book, it engages with a core insight from 'actor-network theory' that 'all actors produce interpretations and powerful actors produce interpretations into which others can be recruited for a period' (Mosse and Lewis 2006, 13). In this case, such interpretations concern the dedication with which agencies pursued the project agendas of creating depoliticized watershed committees or not, but the chapter is also concerned with understanding why and how they pursued these agendas. The village ethnographies presented here reveal that key officials assumed identities in relation to their strategies of interaction, but further that these strategies were born out of their positioning within the project hierarchy as much as their evolving relationships with various village elites and power-holders.

This chapter will demonstrate how watershed officials in Lilapuram and Malligundu were indifferent to the issue of keeping panchayats out of the watershed programme and turned a blind eye to local elites who dominated panchayats also to exercise control over watershed committees, as long as this meant that committees could be formed peacefully and factional conflict could be averted. It will describe the Kishangarh case and the lesson it offers that not all elites wished to dominate watershed committees, and key watershed agents did not need to worry about distancing the committee from the panchayat in the same way. Finally, SPS's experience with watershed committees and panchayats in Neelpura was different from that of the three other villages studied because it was inextricably intertwined with its own struggle to establish itself in the ghaat-neeche at a time when panchayats were the ascendant power.

Part I: The Kurnool Villages

The dry and dusty villages of Kurnool are regularly marked by the factional politics and violence for which Rayalseema is infamous. In such a setting, the army of project officials sent out by KWO strove to form watershed committees in a consensual and 'conflict-free' manner. They encountered a range of experiences which, far from affirming that KWO's projects were only being initiated in 'problem-free' villages, contained an insight into the ways in which local politics vitally shaped the form of these projects WDT members in Veldurthi mandal described the many villages where KWO was not able to initiate projects because village factions could not come to a conclusion about the membership of the committee. In L'kotalla village, neighbouring to Lilapuram, two factions wanted to exercise control over a single watershed committee and the project was nearly cancelled as no compromise could be arrived at. In Bomireddypalli, another village close to Malligundu, a year went by before the PIA could successfully initiate the formation of a watershed committee because factional disagreement was so intense. In yet other villages there were no clear factions and the village was 'united' under the strong influence of one leader who then exercised complete control over all project activities. Chirakulapadu and Kosinapally were both controlled by a very powerful Reddy landholder, Narayan Reddy, and no action could be initiated without his consent.

Contrary to the brazen realities of the local permissions and resistance from competing power-holders that project officials regularly encounter, the articulated discourse from officials at all levels tended to convey a rosy impression of this process. During formal interviews in Kurnool town, junior officials would regurgitate the proper procedures laid down by the guidelines and adopted by KWO, and then in more casual conversations on the road the same individuals would describe the difficulties with which they would get projects going in line with these procedures. A PIA, assisted by the WDT, worked in a number of villages and was usually well aware of the state of affairs in the surrounding villages, especially if there are prominent leaders or ongoing factions. When a decision to approach a particular village for starting up a watershed project was made, project officials did not violate local protocol and usually made contact with village leaders to organize the larger public event that announced the project to the village. A team of officers, sometimes led by the PD, arrived at a public venue in the village organising a convivial event marked by song, dance and drama to announce the arrival of the watershed project. Despite the acknowledgement of local leaders that often preceded the public event, project officials interacted with villagers in a manner that tended to downplay local power relations. Such performance by project officials during these 'entry point' meetings, where they explained the meaning of watershed development, proclaimed the benefits of soil and water conservation and described its relevance to all, agriculturists as well as the landless, men and women, necessarily required a matching performance by local elites (who appeared to sanction it) and also by various subordinate groups (who had to keep their incredulity to themselves). Such a 'public transcript' (Scott 1990) was thus essential to project continuation and success, and it is when projects were unsuccessful in generating such transcripts that they were disrupted or discontinued.

Matters were clearly complicated by the fact that it was the responsibility of the PIA and especially of the WDT, all of whom were essentially outsiders to the village, to initiate the peaceable constitution of a watershed committee that was equally accessible to all if the project's promise of participation was to be a credible one. Of course, project provisions devised by KWO, in line with the national guidelines, couched these ideas in apparent reasonableness. For instance, they stated that the committee had to be formed 'over a period of time' and be preceded by the formation of user and self-help groups among the population. Once these groups had been formed a meeting of the 'entire village' (known as the watershed association in project parlance) was convened, where these groups nominated their representatives who then constituted the watershed committee. KWO was particular about following the guidelines regarding committee membership, including the reservation of seats for SC/ST groups and women. Implicit in this process is the notion that the entire body of a village community would form the committee 'consensually'. It would, moreover, overcome its internal inequities and divisions to agree on the composition of such a body and, equally, express such agreement in public. There was a clear attempt to project the committee not as a representative body, akin to the panchayat, but instead as a mediating unit between the smaller collectivities of user and self help groups and the larger village body, or watershed association.

KWO was able to initiate committee formation in Lilapuram and Malligundu villages smoothly. In both villages, project officials started their entry-point meetings with clear statements that they were not interested in dabbling with 'village politics'.[2] However, this proved to be the critical opportunity by which the obtaining power structures of the village were officially incorporated into the project morphology. In Lilapuram, where the covered area was fortuitously large enough to allow two committees (as two watershed projects were awarded to ensure that entire village lands were treated), the two rival Reddy groups led by large Reddy landholders manned one for themselves. It did not matter that one group controlled the village panchayat as well. In Malligundu, where also two committees were formed, the lone leader and sarpanch of the village, a Boya man who was not particularly landed (with only five acres of cultivable land) but possessed a loyal following in the village and a history of committing violent crimes, exercised a quiet surveillance over the two committees. He encountered no opposition, and was able to man the bodies with his active Boya supporters. So did project practitioners succeed in depoliticising their watershed committees of the vested interests that were so often articulated in factional fighting through panchayat elections and functioning throughout the mandal? On the basis simply of expressed agreement, could the watershed committees of Lilapuram and Malligundu be described as apolitical, conceptually and practically distinct from their respective panchayats? In order to consider these questions carefully, the chapter will delve into the minutiae of village-based stratification and their implications for the attractions that the material and symbolic resources of the watershed projects held out for those who dominated.

Interrelatedness of Caste, Land and Labour in Lilapuram and Malligundu

Lilapuram

Lilapuram is a moderately sized village with an approximate population of 2500.[3] Here, as in most other villages in Andhra, caste affiliations are usually described in three neat categories – OC for other castes (referring usually to the 'higher' or forward castes in the Hindu caste hierarchy), BC for BCs and SC, an older and more familiar term, short for SCs. In Lilapuram, OCs mainly comprise the Reddys, Vaishyas and a handful of Muslim families. The BCs are in majority[4] and the village has a small population of SCs, known simply as Harijans.

This book deliberately refrains from the idea of a single and unchanging 'dominant caste' in deference to the more recent debates that have challenged the notions put forward by Srinivas (1955), Dumont (1970) and Dube (1968). These scholars identified different characteristics that allowed a caste to be dominant: numerical preponderance combined with economic and political power by Srinivas, ownership or possession of superior rights in land by Dumont, and internal unity by Dube. In later debates, several scholars including Srinivas (1998) who revised some of his previous propositions and Mendelsohn (2002) have discussed the implications for the rising tide of democratic and electoral forces for caste-based domination. My earlier discussion of lower caste mobilization as well as the rise of Hindu nationalism in some detail both reiterates the complexities that underpin domination and underscores the profound variations in factors responsible. Similarly, while it has become much harder to sustain 'relational' or 'hierarchical' values in the public domain (Beteille 1996, Dirks 1996 and Fuller 1996) following the sustaining of the discourse of universal democracy, the entry of the lower castes into mainstream political parties and political competition has contributed to more privately articulated discomfiture and distancing from 'politics' as a low culture (Hansen 1999). Bearing these issues in mind however, the fieldwork for this research revealed local conditions that ensured the relative dominance of a particular caste over a period of time.

Caste relations in Lilapuram reflect the principal links between caste and politics illustrative of Rayalseema. Reddy 'domination' in the region, through important positions in government and politics, is perhaps the most typical caste feature of the region.[5] In general, Reddys in Rayalseema draw upon their relatively 'high' caste status and ownership of large land holdings as the principal bases of local power, and their numerical strength varies significantly between villages. The principal political parties in the state, i.e., Congress and TDP, both have Reddy support bases with local variations and there is no clear caste-party identification. In Lilapuram, Reddys control the reins of local village power and use their caste position in effective conjunction with large-scale ownership of land in the village. The distribution of land ownership in the village is severely stratified.[6] A handful of farmers, all Reddys, control the agricultural economy in the village through land ownership.[7] Vaishyas here are relatively prosperous having diversified their incomes from agriculture to other petty businesses within the village. However, typically, they do not represent a threat to the Reddys in Lilapuram.[8] Most BCs in the village own medium and small landholdings and in addition to working on their lands work as wage labourers on the lands of Reddys and other large landholders. The SCs, a majority of whom are landless, are treated as untouchables. They do not share drinking water facilities with other castes in the village and their houses are constructed in a cluster, separate from the rest.

In addition to being the largest landowners in the village, several Reddy farmers also have the best access to water as they have individual wells. This allows them privilege of access to 'rabi' or winter cropping, which is practically absent in the region as agriculture, being primarily rainfed, is limited to the 'kharif' or rainy agricultural season. All cultivated land in the village is privately owned and there is no significant common land area within the watershed. Poor people meet their fuel and firewood needs from the adjoining hills and reserved forests respectively.[9] There are few common sources of water in the village. These are a 'cheruvu' or tank which stores water seasonally,[10] the 'lothu-vagu', a free flowing channel of water that cuts through village lands and retains water only in the rainy months, and five 'kuntas' (small ponds), water from which barely suffices for occasional paddy cultivation by a few farmers with adjoining lands. As a result, single crop agriculture in the rainfed kharif season is the majority practice. Groundnut is the principal kharif crop and a few farmers raise it as an irrigated crop in the rabi season.

Agriculture is the predominant occupation in Lilapuram. The nine kilometre long road to the village, dusty and undulating, is still 'kutcha' (impermanent). Apart from minor opportunities for stone cutting around the village there is a dearth of alternative employment nearby. As a result of Lilapuram's interior location and the difficulties that accompany outward travel, wage labourers are discouraged to journey outside the village on a daily basis to find alternative farm or non-farm employment. The relative absence of accessible alternative employment options exposes small and medium farmers to wage related exploitations.

Large Reddy landholders are the largest employers of wage labour in Lilapuram.[11] Moreover, it is custom for landowners here to supervise wage relations directly, unlike in the 'well-watered eastern plains of the state... where abundant rainfall and irrigation made cultivation operations sufficiently routine to be left in the hands of low status labourers, while the landowners could detach themselves from the direct management of agriculture' (Wade 1990, 23). There are no uniform methods of wage payment, which ranges from fixed wage rates in cash for certain kinds of operations to payment in kind for others. Other varying, personal and less regularized methods of payment are also in use, as generations of BC families tend to be employed by the same Reddy family. Group contracting, where a landowner hires a group of labourers for a fixed sum without determining hours of work, is a common form of wage practice. Prevailing wage rates for agriculture in Lilapuram are less than the government prescribed minimum wage. Although BC households engaged in wage labour are aware that this is the case,[12] the village has no known history of labourers organising to demand an increase in wage rates. All this indicates the presence of close relations between Reddy landowners and specific BC households.

SC households, however, experience a fair degree of social ostracism as they live in a confined area within the village and use separate hand pumps for drawing drinking water. It is common for members from SC households not to find significant employment on village lands. This affects them adversely as SCs in Lilapuram are typically landless, or in possession of marginal landholdings. Further, between the months of January and May agriculture comes to a complete halt and dryland villages like Lilapuram offer no employment. In contrast, agriculture through canal irrigation continues in the eastern parts of Kurnool district (the Kurnool-Cuddapah canal) and the coastal plains of the state (Nagarjuna Sagar Project). These areas are highly fertile and irrigated agriculture in the rabi season continues at least until March, with large-scale cultivation of cotton, chillies, tobacco, paddy and jowar seeds. There is a shortfall of local wage labourers. As a result, thousands of workers from dry, western parts of the state migrate seasonally. SCs in Lilapuram, deprived of wage employment in the village, are the worst affected and are regularly driven to distress migration. Rural-rural migration from the western parts of the state to its coastal areas is the principal form of migration in the region. A few families from Lilapuram have also migrated permanently to neighbouring towns like Veldurthi and Kurnool for employment, and this phenomenon is not restricted to any one caste.

Gender based relations in Lilapuram vary between castes. Women from the 'higher' Reddy caste do not interact greatly with men or women from the other castes. This is mostly because Reddy women belong to large landowning families where they may not be required to work on fields or conduct any 'public' dealings with 'lower' caste individuals, as these are largely left to men. In addition, notions of Reddy pride also account for stereotypical roles for women 'indoors', even when the family may not be as economically prosperous. In comparison, women from the BC and SC do not lead similarly 'private' lives as they have to work outside their homes to supplement the family's income.

Malligundu

Relations of caste, land and labour assume a strikingly different pattern in Malligundu. Malligundu is a small, poor, dry village, with a mixed caste composition. In this village, with approximately 2000 residents, BCs mainly comprising the Boyas are in majority, followed by the Reddys and Vaishyas that are second largest in number. There are a handful of SC families in this village, nearly all landless, but some have more recently been able to purchase small plots of land from the SC Corporation at concessional rates since 1998–99.[13] No one caste can claim economic dominance by virtue of land ownership in Malligundu.[14] Further, even large farmers possess huge tracts of dry land, and only eight to ten large farmers in the village derive the combined advantages of large landholding and irrigation. There are no common water sources in Malligundu and agriculture is primarily rainfed. The land in Malligundu is primarily of the black cotton soil type. High clay content in the soil makes well digging, particularly of the kutcha or temporary variety difficult. Poor people cannot afford to have cement walls or stone pitching for their wells, without which a dug-well is almost sure to give way especially in the rainy season. The small area of common land (seven hectares out of a total land area of 886 hectares) is badly eroded and gullied and hence useless even for grazing or meeting the firewood needs of the population. Besides, this land area is tightly encircled by private property on all sides. This has led to encroachment by private landholders and further restriction of free access. Most villagers attend to their fuel and firewood needs from the neighbouring Dastagiri and Venkateswara hills.

The homogeneity of economic deprivation and suffering in Malligundu acts as an effective counter to the caste hierarchy. In addition to being prone to the vagaries of dry, subsistence agriculture, all villagers also suffer from an acute shortage of drinking water as underground water in Malligundu is contaminated with fluoride. Malligundu is extremely resource poor, without the few common water resources of Lilapuram even, and there are no canals, tanks or ponds that farmers can avail water from. A thin channel of water that separates Malligundu from its big neighbour, Magarpalli, serves as an occasional resort. However, this is no solution to the water problem, as access to the channel is a matter of serious contention between the residents of Malligundu and Magarpalli. Water crisis, particularly for irrigation, is exacerbated by the lack of electricity. There are massive power shortages and an entire portion of village agricultural lands, called Lachappakunta, has no electricity supply to date. Malligundu received its first power connection in 1955.

In Malligundu the absence of large farmers along with intensive cross hiring and the availability of accessible alternative employment in nearby Kurnool town insures against exploitative wage relations. Its farmers, however, suffer due to acute indebtedness and extortion at the hands of private moneylenders operating from outside the village.[15] No official figures are available that determine its extent but oral interactions with farmers confirmed this. Malligundu is also deeply locked into the migration cycle of Rayalseema and practically the entire village is deserted during lean agricultural months. Unlike Lilapuram however, migration is not restricted to any one section of the village. Economic homogeneity that has softened an otherwise rigid caste hierarchy in Malligundu impacts gender relations as well. Women from all castes, with the exception of a few Reddy households that own large landholdings, are regularly engaged as labourers on each other's fields. This creates the basis for several informal relationships among women that are not restricted to caste barriers.

The relative sameness in economic condition partly explains the absence of Reddy domination within the village, a feature commonly observed in Rayalseema. Reddy domination has also been checkmated due to potential challenge from the Boyas, an ascendant OBC group that is well known in the region for its 'proclivity' to aggression and violence. Economically powerful Reddys did not have access to political power in the village, which was vested almost entirely in the hands of one Boya man called Chandra Mohan Naidu.

Politics and the Panchayat

Lilapuram

Panchayats in both these villages fully subsume the relationships of dominance. For nearly the last fifty years or so one large Reddy family has dominated Lilapuram and its various members have held all public positions of significance in the village. The head Viraj Mohan Reddy was the largest landowner here and also the sarpanch of the village panchayat for a continuous spell of 25 years, from 1970 to 1995. For the first time in 1985, two of VMR's cousins, Harekrishna Reddy and Gangadhar Reddy contested him in panchayat elections, but lost. Their actions also caused an enduring split in the family with VMR's numerous cousins taking respective sides. At the time of fieldwork in 2001 and then again during a second visit in 2004, the panchayat was being managed by VMR's nephew Satya Reddy. Interestingly enough, at both times he was the 'proxy-sarpanch'. In 2001, when the seat was reserved for a woman, his mother was sarpanch, and then again in 2004 when an OBC member had to be sarpanch, his nominee was appointed with Satya Reddy officiating as the vice-sarpanch. These occurrences are widespread throughout villages in the region.

The divide within the dominant Reddy family has not translated into public animosity and there is no clear rift within the rest of the population, although each group has its supporters from within the BCs. BC families that work on the lands of one Reddy group do not work on the lands of the other. Besides, Gangadhar Reddy and Harekrishna Reddy are prominent landholders and well respected for their contributions to the village.[16] Publicly, the Reddys maintain a cordial relationship, addressing each other as 'Anna' (brother) and agreeing to sit together on common forums if required. Villagers do not easily admit to any rift between the two Reddy families, preferring to address them equally venerably as 'pedda-manshis' (respectable elders), and approaching them to mediate even in their personal matters.

Reddy brothers on either side of the divide profess 'distinct' political identities, projecting their mutual distancing to be an outcome of principled political differences rather than petty personal bickering. The village has been a stronghold of the Congress Party since independence. Since 1985 however, coinciding with the first contested election to the village panchayat, Gangadhar Reddy and his brother have changed their loyalties to TDP. Mirroring a state wide trend, the district as a whole has been transformed into a TDP stronghold in the 1990s. Veldurthi mandal however, is an exception, and is one of two mandals in Kurnool district that does not have a single TDP representative. Whatever the scene politically, party affiliation at this level is no more than a sort of branding and local supporters do not usually attend party meetings. Yet, despite being fairly tenuous at most times, party political links assumed a sharp identity during elections. In Lilapuram too, the 'dignified' equation among members of the two Reddy families has been known to give way during high points of electoral tension.[17] Members of both families found unflattering mention in the local police records for inciting and responding to petty fights and violence including stone pelting, and were under police observation for their well-known involvement with the unlawful sale of liquor in the village, for Lilapuram is a prohibition centre.

Contest to panchayat seats (11 excluding the sarpanch's post) has increased since 1985. Both Reddy families nominate their respective candidates to each position. Yet, increase in contest to the panchayat does not indicate any real expansion of claim to local power beyond the Reddys. Subordinate groups comprising the BC and SC households have no real representation in the panchayat. Women, from both the dominant and subordinate castes and from different categories of land ownership, are equally irrelevant to the panchayat beyond the constitutional requirements of reservations. Satya Reddy is a well known contractor in the area and manages all panchayat works by hiring wage labour from amongst his own pool of BC supporters.[18] There is no question of putting these works forward for wider discussion even to the rest of the panchayat's members,[19] let alone to the village in a gram sabha, which is rarely convened.

The two other local bodies in the village are a Water Users' Association (WUA) to manage the village cheruvu and a Forest Protection Committee or Van Suraksha Samiti (VSS) to protect the adjoining reserved forest from the felling of trees. The composition and functioning of both, which I can only briefly discuss here, also reiterate the general relationships of domination in Lilapuram. The WUA was formed in 1997 following the enactment of the Andhra Pradesh Farmers Management of Irrigation Systems Act aiming to facilitate participatory irrigation management (PIM). In Lilapuram, a perfunctory informal system of tank-management was already in use much before this body was set up, involving the appointment of one watchman who also regulated the shutter located at the mouth of the tank. Nobody in particular was responsible for repairs to the main tank and individual farmers carried out minor works on the feeder canals that watered their lands. The labelling of the existing 80 strong group of cheruvu users as a WUA did not make any real changes to these practices, except that the four member committee that was drawn from it now formally included two big Reddy landowners, one from each 'group'. However the post of Committee President went to the Reddy from the VMR group (which already managed the panchayat) in the process excluding Harekrishna Reddy who had been instrumental to the construction of the cheruvu in Lilapuram. The WUA thus poses no challenge to the panchayat as a rival source of power, for the prestige associated with heading it is shared within the family. Besides, the scale of operations of this WUA is fairly restricted, unlike those of the coastal districts of the state where all residents of one or more villages may be a part of the WUA and the President 'can be more important than even the local MLA'.[20]

The VSS was instituted at the behest of the Divisional Forest Officer (DFO) following the initiation of joint forest management (JFM) policies across the country, especially since 1988. The forest front needing protection is four kilometres long, and all members of this committee were drawn from medium BC farmers whose landholdings encircled the forest. The entry point is manned by guards drawn from amongst members in rotation. Members also have to perform other tasks like the plantation of seedlings and the construction of check dams in the forest lands. The watershed committee of the village is not allowed to take up any activities here. The VSS is of little interest to the dominant Reddys, mostly because richer landholders meet their fuel and fodder needs from their private holdings and do not rely on the forest which is principally of concern to poorer households in Lilapuram. Committee members act according to the DFO's directions and there is usually little need to engage labourers from outside the body. One WDT member shrewdly remarked about the lack of interest shown by the Reddys in the VSS, 'There is no money to be earned through VSS, only hard work'!

Malligundu

Chandra Mohan Naidu, a small landholder from the Boya caste, has been the undisputed leader of Malligundu since the late 1980s. He also held the position of sarpanch right from the time the village was granted its own panchayat in 1995 until 2004 when he was replaced by his nephew, although he continues to exercise a strong influence on village affairs. In this sense, leadership in Malligundu presents a remarkable exception to the usual pattern of Reddy domination that characterizes villages in Rayalseema. The three biggest landholders in Malligundu are all Reddys, but none have demonstrated ambitions to acquire political power in the village, either in the panchayat or outside. Until 1995, Malligundu was a hamlet to its neighbouring village panchayat in Magarpalli, dominated typically by a powerful Reddy family. This caused a widespread feeling in Malligundu that their village received little attention from the panchayat and was disadvantaged in accessing shared resources, especially the channel of water dividing the two villages. Naidu spearheaded agitation over this issue and when it could not be satisfactorily resolved he 'banned' all residents from Malligundu from crossing over the channel to visit Magarpalli and also 'ordered' them not to allow any visitors from the other village into their own.

Irrespective of their caste affiliations, villagers are 'united' in their obedience to Naidu. The reasons for this lie in the brazenly violent manner in which Naidu has asserted his position in the village. In 1985 he killed another Boya man from within Malligundu inside a state corporation bus at a bus stop just outside the village, in broad daylight. When his attempts to negotiate a power-sharing arrangement with the dominant Reddy family in Magarpalli failed, he contested the panchayat elections in 1988 but lost. He was convinced that the election was unfair and retaliated violently. This sparked off a chain of daring murders, with Naidu and Ragireddy from Magarpalli attempting to kill each other and 11 of their relatives and supporters were murdered between 1988 and 1995. As it became impossible to contain the escalating violence the village was finally granted a separate panchayat. The additional superintendent of police from Veldurthi mandal formed a peace committee comprising Naidu, Ragireddy and their followers, and the moment of resolution captured through photographs of the smiling, garlanded men.

Since then, Malligundu has *appeared* to be united, but Naidu's penchant for violence and crime are well known here. The local police records contain vivid details of daylight crime committed by him. When Ragireddy was interviewed in Magarpalli in 2001, he mentioned that hostilities between him and Naidu continued and that he was compelled to respond to Naidu's endless acts of provocation. Few in the village were willing to come out and talk openly about it. Naidu's past criminal activities within the village have had a broad undertone of Boya-Reddy hostility. A few Reddy families had to leave the village altogether as they had fallen out of favour with Naidu and were simply too afraid to continue living there. The remaining Reddys in Malligundu do not oppose him and there is no rival power centre within the village.

This situation is amply reflected in the village panchayat. Throughout the period that Naidu was sarpanch, the panchayat was manned entirely by his henchmen. In 2004's panchayat election his nephew became sarpanch but there was no contest. Like Satya Reddy, Naidu is a well-known contractor in the region and is eager to undertake works in villages other than his own. This regularly brings him into conflict with local power holders in those villages (like Ragireddy in Magarpalli). However, the absence of any factions within

Malligundu and unanimity, though clearly of a coercive nature, has still earned this village a good name in the perception of project officials.

Effects of 'Depoliticization' in the Kurnool Villages

The particular discourse of depoliticization articulated by the senior project management of the KWO rested specifically on a view of politics as factional conflict that was frequently expressed through panchayat elections and functioning (Chhotray 2007). As both Lilapuram and Malligundu had functioning watershed committees that had not been disrupted by factional conflict, and were nearing completion at the time of fieldwork, project practitioners regarded these villages as problem-free. It is yet possible to argue that KWO did not succeed in 'depoliticising' its watershed projects in these villages because the watershed committees fully embodied the politics from which the projects were trying to distance themselves. In fact, the project that was conceived as a genetically different entity than the village panchayat ended up obtaining the same coordinates. Moreover, the project in either village could proceed with its 'participatory' activities only once locally dominant interests had been accommodated.

In Lilapuram, the dominant Reddy groups manned one committee each, and given that group leaders were also the pedda-manshis (respectable elders) that junior project officials (WDT) members relied on to initiate project proceedings, this came as no surprise. It was in fact a matter of some relief for these officials that a balance of power could be achieved within project morphology in the village, as they were well aware that senior project management highly valued village-level 'co-operation'. As long as this could be achieved it hardly mattered if those who were controlling the panchayat were also at the forefront of the watershed committees.[21] For the residents of Lilapuram, the association of the main Reddy leaders with the project could not have been less surprising given the state of affairs in the village. The initial proceedings of the project (the entry-point public meetings and the proclamations of participatory decision-making) certainly marked a sharp departure from regular social intercourse in Lilapuram. With the Reddys at the helm it was not long before widespread incredulity regarding the project's promises turned into the realization that the business of watershed development would be conducted no differently from other village works, like the engagement of wage labour or the operations of the panchayat. The next chapter describes in greater detail the moulding of participatory operations in Lilapuram to preserve the outward sanctity of project protocol.

For the Reddys, the watershed project held out tremendous symbolic as well as material appeal. Social stature and a dignified public appearance was an integral part of their authority, and they took pains to preserve this facade even when relations between the two families deteriorated greatly. The project's accoutrements, especially the opportunities it ushered of visible association with government officials in public meetings where important announcements were being made, were terribly attractive to them augmenting further their more traditional sources of domination. Gangadhar Reddy, the ex-VAO who officiated as the watershed secretary of one of the committees saw the project as a way of earning a 'good name' with the government authorities. He regularly wrote letters reporting his immaculate record-keeping not just to the project office but also to the Chief Minister![22] Importantly as well, as both Reddy groups thoroughly controlled the participatory protocol required by KWO, they were in a position to ensure that the modes of participation required by the project office would neither deter nor disarm them from playing their traditional role of deciding for the whole community. I will substantiate this argument further in the next chapter.

In Malligundu, the project claimed to have steered clear of politics especially as it followed in the relatively peaceful aftermath of the bloody years that have scarred the collective memory of the village. In their initial meetings project officials repeatedly emphasized KWO's intention to conduct the project consensually, a position that was immensely appealing to residents here. Naidu did not feel threatened by this approach, mainly because of the absence of any real opposition to his interests inside the village. Much like the Reddys in Lilapuram, he calculated that KWO's participatory protocol based around the watershed committees would allow him to integrate with the project without compromising his interests. In his case, supporting the project would also soften the harsh edge of his leadership that had rested so far on a string of brutalities. For Naidu, who wished to distract attention from his suspect acts and appear as a benign village leader, as opposed to a caste leader among the Boyas alone, allowing the project to continue without disruptions (while ensuring his interests are accommodated) seemed to be a positive thing to do. So he refrained from explicit interference and did not, for example, press for his Boya supporters to man the two committees in the same way that the Reddys did in Lilapuram. However, this seemingly consensual formation of the committee needs to be assessed critically. On the face of it, the project continued uninterruptedly, not alone for the much-lauded participatory practice, but for the fact of accommodating all principal interests of Naidu, his hidden agenda however discreet.

Even after Malligundu became an independent panchayat in 1995, Naidu continued to meddle in panchayat affairs in the neighbouring Magarpalli. Local police records revealed that small scuffles have occurred between Naidu and members of the long-time rival Ragireddy family. In fact, these were factional fights aimed at getting the upper hand in controlling contract works through as many village panchayats as possible. In March 2000, Ragireddy was attacked in Magarpalli, by some of his own supporters from within the village. These dissidents turned out to be Boyas, like Naidu, although some Reddys were also in the act. As a result the watershed committee in Magarpalli broke up and watershed works in the village came to a complete halt. Ragireddy needed no convincing that Naidu had a hand in this and explained how Naidu wanted to control contract works in the panchayat and watershed project in Magarpalli as well.[23]

Naidu had a clear share in cuts derived through watershed works, even in Malligundu. These were not insignificant given that the watershed committee exercised fiscal control over the budget of the project, which ran to two million rupees over four years.[24] Local POs were aware of his position and proclivity to aggression. They would rather leave him alone, as long as he allowed the project to be conducted smoothly and on time. A slightly different configuration of circumstances, with Ragireddy's family opposing Naidu within Malligundu and not in Magarpalli, might have led to a very different experience in obtaining consensus for the watershed project in Malligundu. In such a situation, Boya-Reddy hostility, which in Malligundu is now latent, might not have been so. The fact that Ragireddy who exercises full control over the bigger and more prosperous village of Magarpalli – with an independent panchayat – has pushed Malligundu beyond the extent of his activities. This has further diminished the conflict potential in the latter. This has clearly secured a smoother process of committee formation in Malligundu.

Part II: Kishangarh

Not too far away from the Kurnool villages where the watershed machinery was producing a vortex of upward representations of realities to safeguard their respective positions, a very different manner of representation was unfolding in the village of Kishangarh in MP. There were two important differences in context. First, officials did not feel the need to masquerade innate village-level politics under a garb of participatory peace because the district watershed machinery in Dewas was not interested in ensuring this as a precondition for continuation. This was especially the case in the early years of the RGM, in 1995 when Kishangarh was awarded its watershed project and there had not been much time to innovate participatory protocol. Besides, as has been previously discussed, district officials were required to lend their official support to pro-panchayat decentralization and watershed development came under the legitimate purview of elected representatives at the district. This correspondingly ensured the absence of an articulated discourse to distance watershed committees from panchayats in villages.

Second, RGM had been inaugurated with much fanfare and in Kishangarh, being the first village to be awarded the project, there were expectations from the outset for the project to be a tremendous 'success'. What will be described in some detail in the next chapter will hopefully substantiate the contention that this success was largely equated with the construction of large, expensive and permanent structures for water storage like percolation tanks, which would stand as visible exemplars of programme impact. In other words, while it was not particularly important that project officials tried to meticulously form watershed committees that would appear to facilitate participatory decision-making and be isolated from panchayat politics, it was critical that they ensured that the physical implementation of watershed works was impressive.

Interlocking Dominance of Rajputs and Khatis

Kishangarh is a prosperous village where the large majority of the population is landed and practises irrigated agriculture. It also has a small section of extremely poor persons, both marginal farmers and landless labourers. The richer segments of the population are drawn largely from the Khatis, a BC group that is numerically preponderant in the village and comprises nearly half of its 600 households, and the Rajputs that are fewer in number than the Khatis, at about 70 households. The village also comprises a small number of Brahmin households, other BC groups like the Lohars, Sutars, Nais and Prajapats, though none is as large or prosperous as the Khatis, and a few SC households. Numbers typically range from 10–15 households each. There are about 50 Muslim households.

Both the Khatis and the Rajputs claim local dominance, but the underlying factors are not the same. The public discourse of their relationship very much centres on separateness and caste affiliations are vigorously claimed. There are distinct 'mohallas' (residential colonies or areas) where persons from the two castes respectively reside, though it is not uncommon to find the odd Rajput house amidst Khati houses and vice versa. Their lands are also located in different parts of the village watershed. Khati lands are mostly concentrated in downstream areas and are more fertile than the hilly, rocky lands situated further upstream. More than three-quarters of the Khati population owns landholdings larger than five to six acres, and many have lands larger than 30 acres. While nearly two-thirds of Rajputs also have large landholdings, many of these plots are located in hilly areas and are less productive. Khatis are clearly numerically as well as economically preponderant.

Rajputs on the other hand derive tremendous clout from their traditional 'high caste' status and ownership of very large landholdings. The family with the largest landholding of over 100 acres is Rajput. There are a few large landholders from amongst Muslims and Brahmin households, but the large majority owns small and medium plots of land below three and five acres respectively. The SCs in the village are at the bottom of the economic hierarchy, owning marginal plots of land of less than an acre or no land at all. There are no conspicuous signs of social ostracism however, and the SCs do not live separately. Women, particularly from affluent Rajput and Khati families, do not go to the rival mohalla. Unlike SC women who need to work on fields, well-off women from the Khati, Rajput and Brahmin castes mostly stay indoors looking after household chores and occasionally go to the temple for worship.

My informal exchanges with Rajputs and Khatis offered interesting insights into the ways in which they represented themselves to each other as also to outsiders to the village. Rajputs have found it increasingly difficult to deride the Khatis in public but they have not stopped resenting their improved status and phenomenal rise to economic prosperity, which they partially attribute to state affirmative action through reservations. Khatis claimed that they are hardworking and live austere lives, and that is the only reason for their growing prosperity. This is implicitly a contrast to the lavish and extravagant lifestyles that Rajputs are commonly perceived to have.[25] Rajputs frequently resorted to imaginaries of their glorious 'warrior' heritage and culture.[26] Their ideas were fuelled by events such as the Rajput 'Mahasabha' (gathering), annually convened in Bhopal and attended by Rajputs from all over MP, as well as neighbouring states like Rajasthan. Many Rajputs in Kishangarh also saw themselves as the 'genuine' residents of the village and regarded the Khatis as outsiders.[27] Undeterred by fear of retribution in private conversations with me, some Rajputs also poured scorn at the 'low' caste status of Khatis, claiming that Khatis earned their name as they dug manure or 'khad' in Lord Krishna's time.

The village has a recorded history of caste-based polarization as well as crime since the 1950s. Local police records contain detailed accounts of clashes between Rajputs and Khatis as well as other BC groups over issues like non-payment of loans. A typical conflict would involve a poor person from a BC having borrowed money from a richer Rajput, followed by allegations of non-repayment which then produced a grouping together of different BC members, including Khatis, in solidarity leading to a fight. There have also been cases of conflict between Rajputs or Brahmins and Muslims as a result of petty misunderstandings around their respective cultural and religious practices. In police view, Kishangarh is a 'crime village' and needs to be observed closely.[28]

The nearest police station to Kishangarh is less than a quarter of an hour away in a town called Bhonrasa. Apart from caste-based clashes, there are numerous individual cases of thieving, abduction and murder in this village.[29] Farmers in Kishangarh and its neighbouring villages frequently suffer thefts of property such as cattle, motors, construction materials like stones and tractors. They are able to recover it only upon payment of a sum of money to a local leader or his henchmen operating in the 'tehsil' area, and no police case is filed. Villagers explain that this organized crime is linked to the activities of the 'kanjars', a migrant caste that floats in and out of this area, allying with local troublemakers who abet them in stealing from the village. There is also the view that organized crime is a large-scale operation in the region, and is executed with the connivance of political heavyweights like MLAs and ministers.[30]

Kishangarh has no common water resources, and the entire supply of water for irrigation comes from private wells or tube wells. The village alone has 18 electrical transformers for running motors that pump water from wells and tube wells. While most large farmers especially those owning lands in downstream areas own wells, smaller farmers depend entirely on the rains for cultivation. They are therefore exposed to the vagaries of rainfed agriculture and only cultivate small amounts of soybean or food crops like jowar, maize and 'toor dal' (lentils) for household needs in the rainy season. Large farmers with irrigated lands cultivate soybean and wheat commercially in the kharif and rabi seasons respectively. They benefit from Kishangarh's proximity to marketing facilities in the economically vibrant Malwa uplands. They are also able to cater to numerous soybean-based industries that have mushroomed in the industrial area near Indore. As a result, the village is marked by extreme economic differences between a rich majority that practices commercial cultivation and a poor minority that sticks to varying degrees of subsistence agriculture.

There is a huge demand for agricultural and non-agricultural labour in Kishangarh. It is common for large Khati and Rajput farmers to own over 30 acres of land, and they are the biggest employers of agricultural wage labour here. The number of landless persons together with small farmers who can spare time to work on other fields, is commonly not enough to meet the need of the village for agricultural labour, especially during peak times, such as sowing and harvesting. The shortfall of local labour is met by employing persons from neighbouring villages. Some farmers also use tractors, a practice which reduces their need for manual labour. Wage labourers here also find employment on construction works in the village during the lean agricultural season from late February to early June. In this respect, Kishangarh presents an unusual dryland situation. Most dryland areas suffer due to inadequate availability of local employment and this acts as the prime cause for chronic migration cycles. In Kishangarh, by contrast, there is an excess of employment opportunity and a dearth of labour. As a result, labourers are 'booked' by different landholders well in advance. Rich landowners themselves are detached from the direct management of agriculture. They use the services of a 'meth' or construction supervisor, whose responsibility it is to organize labourers for rich farmers. The institution of 'gaon meths' or village construction supervisors greatly reduces direct interface between the rich and the poor of Kishangarh. This symbolises an impersonal element in their relationship.

The village is often beset with common problems of the rich and the poor alike. The most acute problem is the contamination of drinking water by fluoride. There is also a shortage of fodder for livestock. The rich however manage to meet most of their fodder needs from private lands or through purchase. The poor have little option, as they are entirely dependent on the village commons which have suffered degradation over the years by excessive use and inadequate care.

Panchayat Politics

Although the panchayat is the symbol of local political power and influence in the region, it has not always been patronized by traditionally dominant persons in this village. Akshay Patel, a Rajput and the largest landowner with more than 100 acres of land, has been regarded as the village 'Patel' or headman by all castes, even the Khatis, since the 1960s. Patel however was the sarpanch of the village panchayat only for one term in 1985. His leadership drew on landed power, but equally on a claim to Rajput cultural hegemony propagated through constant reaffirmation of stereotypes such as Rajput splendour and chieftaincy. Even though such hegemony has considerably declined over the years in Kishangarh, particularly because of the steady rise in the strength of the Khatis, Rajputs continue to distinguish themselves from the rest of the village through their assertion of cultural pride. After Akshay Patel's death some years ago, his son Parmal Singh Patel is still accorded the respect of a village Patel, though admittedly his father enjoyed greater recognition. This family continues to perform functions that are strictly the responsibility of the panchayat, like the collection of crop and electricity taxes and mediation between personal disputes. Over the years however, the Patel family's intervention in Rajput-Khati disputes has ceased to make a tangible difference. Sharper polarizations between the two caste groups and a tighter watch by the police are the main reasons for change.

The principal groups in the village are clearly divided on the basis of their political loyalties. The Rajputs support the BJP, and the Khatis are generally aligned with the Congress Party, although there are exceptions. Other BCs, SCs, and Muslims in Kishangarh are broadly Congress supporters. The Brahmin population is divided in its support for these two parties. These affiliations have remained broadly stable over the last few decades. Kishangarh can be justly described as a two-party village. Until the 1990s however, there was no panchayat contest on political grounds in Kishangarh. The panchayat, for nearly three decades since the 1960s, was dominated by a long personal rivalry between two individuals, Raja Ram and Jawahar Lal Vakil. Ram and Vakil held positions of sarpanch and up-sarpanch respectively on an almost continuous basis, until the reservations policy for BCs came into effect in the early 1990s. Both these individuals are Khatis, owning 4 and 30 acres of land respectively. Both swore allegiance to the Congress Party, though in later years Vakil switched over to the BJP. The nature of their competition shows that the Rajputs clearly disregarded the panchayat, at least until the mid-1980s. They looked up to Akshay Patel for reaffirmation of their domination in Kishangarh. Subordinate castes in the village, especially the SCs, stayed out of panchayat politics.

In the 1990s however, an important departure from this trend was witnessed in Kishangarh. Akshay Patel's declining influence and death coincided with a noticeable surge in Khati economic dominance. The Khatis also received a major boost from the pro-BC reservation policies. The government insisted on permanent reservations of seats in the panchayat for BCs, in addition to seats for SCs and women. The sarpanch's post was reserved for these castes on a rotational basis. These reservations made a big difference in the village level politics of MP, as they occurred simultaneously with the empowerment of panchayats by the state government. Consequently, the panchayat in Kishangarh has grown in stature as the nucleus of village political power. The most conspicuous effect of this change has been a greater interest in contest for panchayat positions in Kishangarh. After the adoption of the new panchayat laws, post the 73rd constitutional amendment of 1993, and at the time of fieldwork, the state government had held three panchayat elections. Contrary to earlier indifference, candidates from both Khati and Rajput groups in Kishangarh contested the majority of the panchayat's 13 seats. Even the posts reserved for candidates from SCs, BCs and women, were contested through proxy candidature supported by the rival Khati and Rajput groups.

However, this enhanced local interest in the panchayat has still not broadened the process of its decision-making. In this respect, the nature of the panchayat's functioning virtually reflects that of the Kurnool villages. Despite all talk of panchayat empowerment, in practice Kishangarh's panchayat continues to be dominated by a few individuals who monopolise its decisions. In a manner similar to Lilapuram's panchayat, the sarpanch (or the up-sarpanch when the sarpanch is a dummy) of Kishangarh is in full control of panchayat money and its works. Most villagers here share the impression that it is easy for the sarpanch to make money while in office.[31]

Formation of Watershed Committees: Politics of Disinterest

The project commenced with the arrival of a project team comprising the PO and his assistant to the village. A public meeting had been convened to explain the project proceedings but remarkably unlike the Kurnool villages, there was no prolonged enactment of the prospect of participation. Accounts by the PO as well as a range of villagers of this episode did not include any memories of dance or drama to mark the arrival of a potentially transformative initiative. However, many anecdotal accounts confirmed that a long speech had been made by the PO pledging that every effort would be made to ensure representation of the different caste groups in the village. True to the spirit of the watershed guidelines there were no elections and, as two microwatershed projects had been sanctioned to cover the large village area to be treated, two committees were formed. They were deliberately formed along caste lines, one dominated by Rajputs and the second by Khatis, with a spattering of other castes. This would have been suitable also because the two main caste groups concentrated their landholdings in two different parts of the watershed.

A year into the project however, these committees were coalesced into a single body by district authorities on the recommendations of the PO. In the new committee, seven out of 11 members were Rajputs, and the remaining four were Khatis. Surprisingly, there was no protest from the Khatis. Judging by the previous experience of caste-based clashes, this was the first sign that the watershed project in Kishangarh would not suffer the same fate. The Rajput majority was not justified by the numerical strength of this caste in the village. It indicated, moreover, that the PO, a Rajput himself, had influenced the committee's caste composition. The new committee also did not have any members from the SCs and women. This violated the national guidelines to reserve seats for these disadvantaged sections.

The PO defended his decision on the grounds that there was simply no need for two committees, since most members were too busy with their private matters. However, the new committee was not any different. Its members had other subsidiary business concerns besides owning large chunks of land. Committee members, including the rich Khati Chairman, Suresh Arya, did not make any attempt to conceal their disinterest in the watershed project. He said candidly, 'I was extremely disinclined. But the PO persuaded me by saying that if he brought officers from RGM to inspect the project, where would they be made to sit? There was no respectable place in the village to seat government officers, other than my house'. The Chairman's post was nominal and the secretary had real powers. The secretary was responsible for project paperwork, and was also the joint signatory along with the PO for drawing cheques. The secretary, a Rajput called Amarendra Singh, managed the bulk of project work under the overall supervision of the PO. It is significant that no user, self-help, or women's thrift groups were formed in Kishangarh.

Neither the Khatis nor the Rajputs perceived the watershed project as a way of furthering their group or individual interests. Even those who had been politically active in the panchayat, like Raja Ram and Mayadhar Chowdury, did not claim any role in the watershed committee. The social composition of the village, with two main caste groups that were interlocked in their claim to dominance also comprising the bulk of the population, left a very small minority whose 'support' they did not need to compete for. These dynamics can usefully be contrasted with those in Lilapuram where the two Reddy families found the symbolic resources of a participatory project attractive in order to demonstrate the endurance of their 'benevolent' leadership over a majority OBC and SC population. Also, while decentralized fiscal control over project resources may have been an incentive for leaders like Naidu in Malligundu, these monies were simply not significant enough for the big farmers of Kishangarh to pose any meaningful lure. The other important difference was that key elites in the Kurnool villages who wanted to exercise control over watershed committees were also regular contractors in the area, making a profitable living from all types of contract works, but the landed farmers of Kishangarh carried out large-scale commercial farming or their own construction businesses, and did not bother about state-sponsored contract works. This was amply reflected in the relatively isolated nature of political competition for the panchayat in this village which, despite attracting greater interest from amongst the Rajputs, has not really enticed the attention of the largest landowners like Parmal Patel.

Moreover, Kishangarh presented the rather unusual situation where the large majority of the population had huge landholdings of its own as also access to private irrigation, and perceived the watershed project as an unnecessary distraction. The better-off sections actually resented the construction of field bunds encircling their landholdings (which are essential to checking the run-off of water), and simply refused permission for any activities to be carried out on their lands. Poorer groups that were either landless or marginally landed could have benefitted from more comprehensive consultation regarding their needs (especially of fuel and fodder which had grown since the village common lands had progressively suffered), but this was never done. The PO concentrated on executing the action plan through the assistance of the gaon meth or construction supervisor who hired labourers, paid them and maintained all project records like a cash book, receipts and expenditure register, voucher folder, works register and cheque register. For the ordinary residents of Kishangarh, construction works for the watershed project were simply no different from the vast maze of construction activities going on otherwise. The action plan moreover was formulated entirely by engineers in the Dewas DRDA office and laid special emphasis on meeting targets relating to the construction of larger, expensive and permanent structures. The PO pursued these targets meticulously and was fully supported by officials both in Dewas and Bhopal. Interestingly enough, the technocratic responses he encountered from key decision-makers higher up in the programme hierarchy to help cope with the numerous counts of private resistance to the project became integral to the production of Kishangarh's project success, an issue that will be revisited in the next chapter.

Part III: Neelpura

The watershed project in Neelpura started amidst unconventional circumstances. Most government PIAs only arrive in a village after it has been selected by the district watershed machinery, and a process of mutual familiarising between village residents and officials precedes local institutional formation. Later iterations of the national watershed guidelines have specified that NGOs selected as PIAs should generally be able to demonstrate competence in the field. As the discussion in Chapter 4 illustrates, the nature of organizations appealing for involvement as PIA is extremely variable as are the reasons governing their selection. Also, NGOs that have been intimately involved with particular villages have not necessarily found it easy to be selected as PIA, as Baviskar (2007)'s account of KMCS in Jhabua district indicates. In this context, for Samaj Pragati Sahyog to be awarded a watershed project in a village where it had based itself and its contentious activities for nearly three years were far from typical. These circumstances impacted upon its approach to local institutions, watershed committees as well as panchayats in Neelpura and more generally as well.

At the outset, SPS did not sign up to the 'state script' regarding local bodies. Its first interface with panchayats in ghaat-neeche was a fundamentally negative one, a potentially dangerous strategy in the mid-1990s when panchayats (and especially sarpanches) in Madhya Pradesh had received tremendous encouragement from the Chief Minister. As for instituting the watershed committee, it departed from the formal methods laid down by the guidelines preferring to choose individuals who it described as capable of 'leadership' and 'contentious decisions'. In its initial phase therefore, there did seem to be a clear distinction between the Neelpura watershed committee and the local panchayat. However, this was for reasons entirely different from those pursued by KWO, as SPS was not trying to distance itself from local politics and its arguments about leadership were decidedly political in nature. Following a series of unforeseen events in the course of project functioning, SPS was led to emphasize the lateral linkages between watershed committees and panchayats, and it turned its energies towards creating a 'cadre of local leaders'. It took many steps to galvanize panchayat functioning in the entire region, and its initiatives earned it kudos with state officials who had been instructed to empower panchayats. It was no coincidence that the more SPS established itself as a power-holder in its own right, the more comfortably it was able to articulate a quotidian discourse of cooperation with the same panchayats that it had antagonized earlier.

Leadership and Domination in a Tribal Village

Neelpura is a small village populated largely by Bhilala and Korku tribes in the Narmada valley. There are nearly 100 villages in this belt, and while they house significant numbers of tribals there is also a non-tribal minority in most of these villages, and at least 14 villages in the area are entirely non-tribal (Census Records, Bagli, 1991). The larger non-tribal villages here, like Bhimpura, are mainly populated by 'high' castes with a very small population of SCs. For SPS the decision to work in Neelpura may have been motivated by convenience at the time, for Neelpura is easily accessible from the main road, but this village quickly became vital to the identity of SPS in the region. Neelpura is almost uniformly poor, with most tribals owning lands between one and three acres in size and dry. A handful of farmers own more than six acres and only three out of the 100 odd households in the village are presently landless. This relatively egalitarian pattern of land ownership follows from government distribution of similar land plots to the new migrants, nearly a century ago. Neelpura is relatively homogenous socially since caste based polarization is conspicuously missing in this predominantly tribal village. Most tribal migrants work as wage labourers on the lands of their non-tribal neighbours to supplement their marginal, subsistence agriculture. Like other tribals in this belt, the residents of Neelpura have also had to migrate every summer to the prosperous Malwa uplands.

SPS's quest for local contacts within Neelpura to facilitate initial dialogues soon revealed the nature of power relationships in this seemingly unstratified village. Mahbub Khan, a Muslim landowner with more than 30 acres of land (of which at least ten were irrigated), was economically dominant, his social clout evident in his near exclusive engagement of hired labour and cultivation of a second irrigated crop. Politically however, Mahbub remained reclusive, and a Bhilala family that had long performed functions of tax collection and dispute resolution assumed the title of Patel or village headman. The Patels were respected within the village, and the family's patriarch traditionally acted as the sarpanch of the village panchayat, which in turn was practically defunct. Before the 73rd constitutional amendment of 1993, there were no regular elections in the state and like elsewhere in the country, 'panches' were hardly even aware of their own position. Shortly after the amendment, the state government undertook major reorganization of all panchayats, and Neelpura was unfortunately paired with its large non-tribal neighbour, Bhimpura. Lakhan Singh, a landless though politically connected individual from Neelpura, became sarpanch. Singh was friendly with other sarpanches in ghaat-neeche and with politicians at the Bagli tehsil office.

Of all three 'power-holders', Singh was most hospitable to SPS group members, perceiving them to be potential allies in the village's development prospects. SPS's relationship with Singh was an informal one and did not amount to a careful partnership with the local panchayat. As a group member candidly expressed, 'The politics of this place has changed. Earlier, when we came here there was nothing like a panchayat. We did not take it seriously as an institution. Now we are trying to get things passed in the gram sabha'. However, the lesson that panchayats and more specifically those who dominated the panchayats could not be taken lightly came at a price. As discussed in the previous chapter, not long after SPS commenced various well-digging and water conservation projects in the village it was drawn into antagonistic relationships with sarpanches in the entire region. They took serious umbrage to SPS's campaign to pay minimum wages for all labour. In one stroke it alienated big landlords as well as sarpanches in ghaat-neeche, and these included Singh and Khan in Neelpura. When SPS won a symbolic victory with its hugely successful land records camp organized with the support of the district administration in the summer of 1995, it only acquired new enemies, notably the lower revenue bureaucrats who had profited from the illegal sale of land revenue books at sky high prices.

However, greatly encouraged by its successes, SPS expanded its activities from Neelpura to other villages in the area. In the summer of 1995, it undertook the deepening of the village water tank in another village nearby called Meghapalli. The sarpanch of the village was a powerful man who resented SPS's activities there, which had ostensibly taken place on a show of written support by other members of the panchayat as also ordinary residents, but without his 'permission'. He galvanized 30 other discontented sarpanches and with the help of the local Congress MLA took a delegation to Chief Minister Digvijay Singh to complain that the NGO was 'corrupt...it bypassed panchayats and misappropriated their money' and should be 'removed'. This reaction was interesting and a testimony to the pro-panchayat (and pro-sarpanch) overtures of the state government. These allegations lacked credibility however and SPS reacted by pursuing a vigorous policy of image building as a transparent organization that worked in the popular interest. The local press further dramatized these unprecedented developments. The situation was ultimately resolved through the appointment of an 'inquiry committee' headed by the district panchayat (a clever ploy by the state bureaucracy to assuage angry sarpanches). After talking to an assembly of villagers in the presence of the aggrieved sarpanches, and physically inspecting some of the NGO's works in the village, the committee came to its conclusions. It acquitted SPS of the charges and publicly commended it for its 'good work' but also 'directed' the NGO not to bypass gram panchayats, simultaneously mentioning that SPS could play an active role in increasing awareness in these local bodies.[32]

SPS gained tremendously from public approval by the highest elected authority in the district. Its local opponents realized that the 'luxury of direct confrontation' against SPS was one that they could no longer afford (Scott 1990), although private confrontations between individual sarpanches and members of SPS ensued on a number of occasions. From being an 'outsider' to the region, SPS became an ascendant power due to its successful strategy of development, legality and positive engagement with the state, and had even been encouraged to enter into an active dialogue with panchayat raj institutions. Upon later reflection, senior members of SPS surmised that this 'negative process' or confrontation with local panchayats may have helped them 'to communicate more effectively because we [they] had to'. While these events acted as the prelude for SPS to engage more directly with panchayat bodies, a more positive impetus came from the proceedings of the watershed project.

The Neelpura Watershed Committee

SPS had already been working in Neelpura for three years when it was asked to initiate a watershed project in Neelpura. Not only did it know its people well, it had also created a measure of local allegiances for and against it, as by 1995 Khan and Singh did not want to associate with SPS at all. Buoyed by the firm support it had elicited in this village through the dramatic confrontations of the previous years, SPS was not bogged down by a literal interpretation of the guidelines. It did not attempt to follow the detailed instructions prescribed for the constitution of a local watershed committee in the guidelines, such as through 'consensual' methods in the presence of a public village gathering. In any case, the absence of a stringent upward reporting mechanism that required the representation of village-level consensus to the district office, as in Kurnool, meant that SPS suffered no additional pressure on this count.

It decided to facilitate the formation of a committee led by individuals who it perceived would be 'articulate, command social respect and possess potential leadership qualities' in order to 'be effective' and take 'contentious decisions' which commonly accompanied issues of land and water.[33] Both the persons selected (as committee secretary and chairperson) belonged to the Patel family, which had become closer to the NGO even as Khan and Singh had distanced themselves, but SPS justified their selection on the grounds that they were 'widely respected' and 'competent'. It also trained committee members to conduct works, pay wages and keep accounts and did away with the (tiresome) requirements of keeping minutes for committee meetings. It believed that 'demystification' of the project's objectives would be the best way of ensuring 'genuine devolution'.

For many in Neelpura, especially those who had reason to feel left out or disgruntled, the close and cosy relationship that some individuals (like the Patels) were developing was a very sore matter indeed. Even apart from Khan and Singh, other discontented individuals were encountered who were united in the fact that they were with the 'sanstha' (hindi for 'organization', and the term by which SPS is popularly referred to by villagers) earlier but now felt terribly bitter and alienated from it. At least ten different individuals in this category provided various different reasons for discontent. Some of them were angry about wells not being dug on their lands, others had been 'thrown out' by the sanstha for an array of reasons, and still some others found the sanstha's running objectionable as they found some people in the village were much more favoured than most others. Some ventured their own explanations to me about the basis of the NGO's strategy, including that it was able to secure village support by recruiting persons from large families. While individual allegations were difficult to substantiate, it was clear that the sanstha did not please everybody in Neelpura. A senior member of SPS said, 'We are not trying to create a beautiful Neelpura watershed committee that meets and gives beautiful representation to everyone'.[34] He went on to say that had Khan or Singh contested the committee (an unlikely prospect as the guidelines rule there are to be no elections), then SPS would have mobilized the village to exert collective pressure against such 'negative' interests. SPS refrained from following detailed prescriptions about consensual formation of the committee laid down by the guidelines; yet, the idea of consensus as the collective weight of opinion, if not total agreement, was certainly instrumental in justifying the composition of this body in the wider general interest.

There are important differences, in SPS's ability and intention to exclude what it described as 'negative' interests from the committee by resorting to the idea of consensus and KWO's attempts to deduce consensus from the brokering of a power-sharing arrangement between dominant interests in a village. The latter was justified as an apolitical process to keep out the politics of factional fighting from watershed projects, especially in higher-level official discourse, while obscuring the compromises and indifference that lower level project staff relied on in order to keep the project going. The former on the other hand was not masked under a discourse of depoliticization, and in fact the arguments underpinning its actions were unambiguously political in nature. The core issue here was the relationship between the sanstha and the residents of Neelpura, and the position that the NGO was beginning to occupy in local consciousness. Some members of SPS were more forthright than others in the way they articulated this relationship. The PO, also a senior member, said frankly that it was 'nearly impossible' for SPS to 'create a watershed committee that has an identity separate from the sanstha'. Besides, this is also not something the NGO in its position as PIA was necessarily trying to avoid, following its more generally expressed belief that it was important to create a 'cadre of local leaders' who would be 'from poorer sections', 'committed to village development' and ultimately work through panchayats. The work on watershed projects that these selected persons did, including different aspects of management and financial accounting, was seen to contribute to their training for panchayat roles later on.

In other matters, particularly concerning the nitty-gritty of daily decision-making for the project, SPS laid a heavy premium on allowing decisions to be taken 'naturally' without the unnecessary orchestration of 'democratic' or 'participatory' decision-making through formal committee meetings and meticulous minute-keepings. A senior member explained that it was not their belief to try and impose '(our) structures onto social situations' and they were in favour of letting the decision-making of the watershed coalesce into the 'natural flow of village decision-making'.[35] 'Just imagine a village where people live and work together', he said, 'it's not that they need to have a committee.... There are no watershed committee meetings [anymore]. It is a far more broad based structure which is what it should be'. A remark by a senior leader stayed with me, 'These are projects, and a project is not a village'. He believed that in Neelpura, the village gram sabha and the watershed committee had merged into one another, and even if there were opponents to the project, they could speak and the 'dialogue' was 'always on'.

At the same time, group members emphasized that rigorous mechanisms had been put into place to ensure accountability of funds.[36] As for transparency, SPS insisted that if all payments were 'made in the open in front of everyone, nothing can go wrong'. All group members shared the feeling that it was important and necessary for the NGO not to intervene in the village beyond the initial phase of setting up the project and training, and often repeated to me that villagers in Neelpura no longer wanted senior members of SPS to come to their village for the purpose of committee meetings. It remains however that the entire watershed project was closely identified with its PIA, SPS, particularly following its growing scale of operations in the Bagli area.

Horizontal Relationships

When SPS arrived in Bagli in 1992, it was keen to mobilize popular action at the grassroots to campaign for better resources from the state but it may not have been anticipated stiff resistance from local bodies of the state, or panchayats. It learnt from its early confrontations with panchayats that these bodies were dominated by entrenched interests and could be an extremely negative force to reckon with, but also that given their constitutional status (and the encouragement they received from Digvijay Singh's government) they were there to stay. In the years that it spent implementing the watershed project, it received further evidence that its methods of working were creating effects beyond the project itself. Its insistence on the open conduct of project transactions like wage payments and record keeping, was entirely new to local imagination in Neelpura and its neighbouring villages. Over time however, these practices have set a concrete example in transparency and accountability, and one that many local people are keen to replicate in reforming the panchayat's ways of working.

In 2000, a movement brewed amongst a few tribal panches of Neelpura to challenge the corrupt practices of the non-tribal sarpanch from Bhimpura in a gram sabha. They were mimicking in particular a collective agreement to regulate the management of the only common water body in the village, a stream or naala, the usage of which had historically been inequitable. SPS had facilitated this agreement right at the start of the watershed project, in 1995, and had also put it the written resolution forward for approval to the Bhimpura-Neelpura panchayat. This initiative will be discussed in greater detail in the next chapter, but it suffices here to say that the resolution created a precedent in the region, as never before in Bagli had such a written agreement been attempted in public nor had the institution of the gram sabha been taken seriously enough for a resolution of this nature to be passed at its venue.

In the summer of 2000, the Bhimpura-Neelpura panchayat had constructed a chaupal or common sitting area, in Bedipura near Bhimpura. The sarpanch Kartar Singh Nag had neither consulted other panches before the construction, nor had he disclosed the amount of money being spent for the purpose. In theory, each gram panchayat is collectively required to prepare an annual action plan, which is then approved by the 'Janpad' (block) panchayat. In practice, this plan is usually the output of a single individual, the sarpanch, who works in tandem with the panchayat auditor, a government functionary well versed with government procedures such as planning. The panchayat auditor frequently acts as the sarpanch's accomplice in manipulating records in order to retain a cut or a profit. Shortly after the chaupal's construction, a handful of panches, mostly from Neelpura and a few from Bhimpura, decided to question Nag regarding the details of expenditure on the construction, and were provided with an aggregate figure of 17,500 rupees. However, these panches were convinced that the figure was exaggerated and that Nag had made a profit in the bargain. When they demanded the details of cost and expenditure listed in the panchayat's cash records, Nag plainly refused, claiming that the panches were not authorized by law to see these records. This practice represents the most widespread abuse of sarpanch power throughout MP and typically goes unchallenged.

But the panches decided to confront the sarpanch, and just as SPS had done several times in the course of its involvement in Neelpura, they went about collecting signatures from at least two-thirds of the panchayat's members in support of their campaign to recall the sarpanch in the middle of his term (radical new legislation in the state had recently sanctioned this). The chaupal issue had raised expectations of a lively gram sabha, and a large number of people thronged to Bhimpura on that day. Several agitating panches asked Nag to show them the panchayat's cash records in that public gathering. Eventually the expected confrontation in the gram sabha whittled down to a heated argument with the sarpanch who abandoned the sabha and left and nothing more came of it. Though this pro-accountability initiative suffered a temporary setback, it had already marked a landmark in Neelpura's history of popular mobilization. For the first time, tribal panches had confronted a non-tribal sarpanch in the gram sabha, an institution that is recognized by the state as the principle locus of collective local decision-making. The public enactment of this confrontation moreover registered an extremely positive impact on tribal confidence in influencing the panchayat, despite the presence of a dominant non-tribal minority. SPS takes tremendous pride in these developments, attributing it to its insistence on transparent functioning, and the debates on accountability that these had generated. Besides, local interest in the panchayat has increased visibly, and its irrefutable evidence lay in the fact that by 2000, contest to panchayat seats in the Bhimpura-Neelpura panchayat had risen fifteen-fold in the previous ten years.[37]

Taking a cue from these developments, SPS has increasingly articulated a pro-panchayat discourse and devoted itself to strengthening processes contributing to panchayat empowerment more directly. In 1998, SPS received a large grant from CAPART which it used to establish a 'field station' about a kilometre away from Neelpura. The Baba Amte Centre was named after a respected social worker who works amongst tribal peoples in

MP, and went on to become a site for training activities for panchayats in the region. This important act marked a new phase in the NGO's life-history as it became clear to the people of Bagli and to the ghaat-neeche villages that SPS was here to stay. SPS has used the Baba Amte Centre (locally referred to as the 'Kendra') as a base to network with grassroots resources on a national scale. Its practical operations have primarily involved training large numbers of development workers in the watershed sector.[38] The agenda for networking grassroots resources included training elected representatives to panchayat bodies. SPS saw itself as an agent for decentralized development for the governance of water and also more generally in the region. It viewed that such agents are necessary if the state government's decentralization legislation in favour of local elected bodies is to be effective at all. The district government expressly extended its support to the Baba Amte Centre and local panchayats overwhelmingly expressed their wish to be involved. A new position of strength for SPS with respect to local panchayats resulted in a new toughening of stance against panchayats that did not extend their cooperation ('we send out a clear message that we want your contribution, only then can we work as partners', said a senior member, 'if you are negative, we are not going to touch you').

Conclusion

The case study villages offered evidence to challenge the assumptions regarding the creation of depoliticized local bodies that were more suitable for participatory watershed development than other existing bodies, notably the much reviled 'political' panchayats. This evidence lay in the perhaps un-startling finding that it was extremely difficult, if not impossible, to create watershed committees that did not take on the features of panchayats. If panchayats are political, it is because they reflect prevailing patterns of domination and contest and it is very likely that these will shape any other local bodies that are created. The argument therefore that a participatory development programme must be carried out by a body that is apolitical rests on a narrow definition of politics that is unsubstantiated in reality. Quite contrary to the idea that communities would be able to escape their hierarchical, divided and contested realities through the gentle prodding of project implementing agencies to form cooperative committees peacefully, the processes that accompanied the formation of such bodies were deeply mired within relationships of power and domination. As the chapter has shown, these relationships encapsulated dominant and subordinate segments of the villages as also the 'outside' agencies that had been entrusted this incredulous task. Beyond this general conclusion, the chapter offers two further insights from the differences observed in the four case studies. These concern the incentives for local elites to dominate local bodies and the factors motivating agencies to sustain upward representations of depoliticization.

The resources of a participatory watershed project were immensely attractive to elites in the Kurnool villages, but not for identical reasons. The Reddys of Lilapuram welcomed the visible association with officials and official authority to augment their traditional status in the village. The project enhanced their sense of importance as 'officials at work' through the abundant paperwork that it engendered, and it did so while proffering adequate opportunities to control decision-making. Naidu from Malligundu however refrained from visible domination, choosing to cast a watchful eye on the project's activities instead, for he did not really have much to gain from controlling project paperwork. His reputation as a noted criminal and troublemaker in the area ensured that he obtained his share of cuts from this village's watershed project. Unlike the Reddys who were too deeply ensconced within the hierarchical social fabric of Lilapuram to allow the substantiation of participatory procedures, Naidu did not find the project's attempts to involve the large majority of poor residents of Malligundu objectionable. This influenced the extent to which they wanted to be visibly in control. But watershed committees in both these villages could only be formed once local elites who also dominated their respective panchayats had been appeased, albeit in different ways.

Neither the symbolic nor the material resources of the participatory project appealed to the landed majority of Kishangarh. Despite their village being awarded a prestigious development project before any others in the district, big farmers here perceived it to be an unnecessary distraction. The project did not appeal to their polarized caste identities as Rajputs and Khatis, and nobody objected when two committees were coalesced into one. The pecuniary lure of cuts through project works simply could not compete with the large-scale commercial farming that is the staple of those who mattered. And while the PO was keen to involve prominent persons in the village, like the Khati Chairman whose house was suitably impressive for outsiders to be received, the latter did not compete for such a privilege. The relatively small numbers of poor, small farmers from other BCs and SCs were hardly consulted at all. But here too, the watershed committee was not the only local body to be affected by the general politics of disinterest. The panchayat has historically been disregarded by the most influential landowners, like Rajput leader Akshay Patel, and for many years panchayat competition was a matter of individual pursuit between two politically ambitious Khatis of moderate economic means. The more recent intensification of contest for panchayat seats reflects growing mobility amongst the Khatis who have responded to state reservation, and the proportionate response of Rajputs who resent their gradual ascendancy, but the panchayat continued to disinterest the largest landholders of this village.

More than the other three villages, the formation of the Neelpura watershed committee was entangled with the position and identity of the project agency, SPS, following its uncommonly long involvement with the village prior to the start of the project. The issue of project appeal therefore cannot be judged separately from that of local allegiances and alienations fostered by the NGO. Although Neelpura's internal stratification along the usual grounds of caste and landownership was negligible compared with the other case villages, its tribal population was regularly exploited by a coalition of non-tribal landlords, sarpanches and revenue officials. When SPS took on these power-holders in separate confrontations, it also alienated the two individuals who had enjoyed economic and political clout here. When the watershed committee was constituted, SPS justified its choice of individuals from the Patel family on the grounds that they were widely 'respected' and could lead and take contentious decisions. SPS's continued presence in the Bagli area meant that committee members were widely regarded as workers of the sanstha, their local agents, and this contributed to their prominence. While the committee possessed a different composition and character to the local panchayat, this was not the outcome of keeping 'politics' at bay as KWO was trying to achieve, but a decidedly political argument deployed by SPS as an agency stewarding local leadership. Besides, as later events beyond the watershed project illustrated, SPS related its watershed work explicitly to panchayats, articulating the significance of horizontal relationships between local bodies.

The case studies reveal important differences in the extent to which different project agencies were even trying to pursue the agenda to form 'depoliticized' watershed committees in the first place. The preference in favour of local unanimity or consensus exhibited by the senior management of KWO in a region marked by virulent caste-based factionalism unleashed a spate of difficulties for local officials. The peaceful formation of committees in the Kurnool villages depended greatly on the ways in which project resources could be distributed amongst or claimed by local power holders, who also typically controlled their respective panchayats. WDT officials had the unenviable task of ensuring that such a balance could be ensured. They were generally outsiders to the village, engaged on temporary contracts and low wages, and desperately needed continuous appointments on KWO's projects. They wanted to be associated with successful projects that were completed on time. They were eager to report that committees had been formed consensually away from village-level factionalism, while being perfectly aware of the intimate influences that were being exercised by various factions. Perhaps it could also be argued that for their purposes, consensus was not about the absence of factions (or politics, as in KWO's reading), but the successful production of compromise.

The agencies implementing projects in the Dewas villages did not need to strive hard to produce representations of apolitical watershed committees following the pronounced absence of a stringent district level monitoring mechanism comparable to KWO. Given all that has been described in the previous chapter, there were no pressures to distance watershed projects from panchayats unlike in Kurnool. But representations of a different sort prevailed upon the practices that were observed. The PO of Kishangarh was more concerned with ensuring that large and permanent structures that would impress senior watershed officials were raised, than with attempting the tiresome task of creating a charade of involvement from the prosperous Khatis and Rajputs of the village.

The project agency of Neelpura watershed project could hardly have represented consensus as power sharing amongst dominant persons in the village to any higher project body, not after the massive confrontations preceding the project. This was not its intent and it firmly approached the constitution of the committee as a political exercise in grooming local leadership. The matter of distinctness of the watershed committee from the panchayats of the region was closely related to SPS's own stance towards these bodies. As its own standing in the Bagli area grew, it increasingly articulated a discourse of working with the panchayats through training and specifically related its watershed activities to the latter. Its representation of itself as an agent of decentralized development to higher level state officials and political representatives in Dewas but also in the state was a necessary part of the story. Interestingly though, even as SPS extended its hand of friendship to local panchayats, subtle judgements about the sorts of 'negative' interests or politics with which it would not deal were observed.

The chapter takes forward and substantiates a central proposition of this book that depoliticization is not inevitable despite the availability of 'discursive resources' in the national watershed guidelines, like the creation of apolitical local bodies. These resources are variously adopted by the range of constituents of the so-called anti-politics machine, as shaped by their socio-political and economic contexts and the imperatives of other decentralization policies that are simultaneously underway. These combine to impact upon the meanings that different actors attribute to the politics that inevitably shape local institutional formation. While mostly such representations serve to entrench dominant politics in newer bodies, on occasion, changes inspired within newer constitutions may also trigger off positive processes that challenge domination within older local bodies as well as new and emerging spaces for mobilization. The final chapter will explore such variations in greater detail.

Chapter Six

THE DIALECTICS OF CONSENT
IN PARTICIPATORY PRACTICE

Consent and Community

A particular conceptualization of the local community has acted as a core
constituent of the anti-politics watershed machine. Ideas of community as
homogenous and un-stratified have vitally underpinned notions of local
bodies that are suitable exemplars of this community spirit, while drawing
a sharp and, as we have seen, often unsubstantiated contrast with the much
reviled panchayats. In watershed development policies, and more generally
in contemporary natural resources governance discourse (see Leach et al
1997), 'consensual communities' hold the key to the apolitical character of
participatory decision-making that is prized above all else. This chapter will
take a closer look at how the idea of consent becomes transformed as an active
ally in the depoliticization project.[1] The word 'project' is not used lightly, not
just because it does not necessarily succeed, but also because not all actors
are equally pledged to it in the first place. This follows Tanya Murray-Li
on the point of her divergence from scholars who emphasize the 'effective
achievement of depoliticization' (2007, 10).

While we know that the theoretical sway of new institutionalist and
communitarian ideas have yielded the apolitical formulation of communities
that we are regularly confronted with, it is not as easy to identify the precise
origins of the apolitical use of the idea of consent. In fact, here there is a
perplexing conundrum at play. In political theory, especially the history of liberal
democracy, it is the notion of consent that marks the making of citizenship
and limits the power of the state. The idea that autonomous individuals assent
to be part of political formations and acknowledge only those obligations that
are self-imposed has definite liberal roots (Pateman 1985). Equally, the idea
of consent has posed a wider problem for social theory in its use to project
particular interests as universal. 'Universalization' as mediated through the
authority of the state has been regarded as absolutely 'central' to theories of
the state (Wood 1985). In the liberal tradition, the issue of universalization

arises in order to address the problem posed by pluralism, as the society is deeply divided over numerous conceptions of the 'good'.[2] This is resolved by recourse to a measure of 'objectivity and universal generalizations' (Avineri and De-Shalit 2001, 5), as classical liberal thinkers John Locke and Immanuel Kant spoke of a 'rational consensus' on the values that constitute a 'good life' (Gray 2000, 14). They also placed their faith in a 'neutral' state which 'does not justify its actions on the basis of this intrinsic superiority or inferiority of conceptions of the good life' (Kymlicka 1990, 205). For Marxists however, universalization is viewed in terms of the functioning of the bourgeois state. Marxism, argue scholars like Hoffman, is based on the idea of consent, and contend that Marx realized that the 'reality of politics is such that a state cannot represent a dominant class unless this class domination is represented in an illusory form' (Hoffman 1984, 29). This simply means that a particular (class) interest is expressed as a general or universal interest by the state. The rational state, the state 'as the great organism', which superintends the whole now stands as a 'theological notion' or an ideal masked in illusion (Hoffman 1984, 29). In Rousseau's thinking, this has been referred to as the 'fundamental paradox of modern living' (Colletti 1972, 36–37). The general interest of the community sacrifices and legitimizes the 'disunity among men' and 'the general will is invoked in order to create absolute value on individual caprice' (Colletti 1972, 36–37).

This chapter will argue that these theoretical underpinnings of consent continue to be relevant in informing the dialectics of consent in contemporary participatory practice. For instance, on the one hand, the articulation of individual consent was used as evidence of participation and codified as such within the participatory protocol devised by the KWO. On the other, the expression of collective consent was vigorously and repeatedly claimed to legitimize struggle by SPS, and also to signify the 'rightness' of its own agency in the ghaat-neeche area. In both these respects, consent was in fact being used politically, but there were critical differences in the extent to which it was admitted as such. KWO's project strategy privileged a framework of technocratic planning within which demonstrated and recordable consent was sought. SPS was not similarly bound by a depoliticized discourse, and was more given to using a language of politics while negotiating local support or initiating confrontation. Yet, its use of consent to portray stewardship of the general interest without any explicit reference to politics or power grew strikingly in proportion to its own position.

The practices that will be described draw upon the insights inspired by Antonio Gramsci in his treatment of consent as a key constituent of 'hegemony' sought by the dominant class or groups. Gramsci well understood the fragility of such attempts (Murray-Li 2007, 22) and later Gramscian scholars like William

Roseberry argued that the concept of hegemony be used not to understand 'consent' but 'struggle' (1994, 361). The lack of finality of consent, either sought or obtained, is reiterated through the case studies presented here. The case studies also reveal the great interplay of crosscutting representations, of dominant and subordinate groups, village elites and project officials, in the course of enacting consent in public and private domains. These fully endorse James Scott's conclusions regarding the respective theatres of the 'public' and 'hidden' 'transcripts'. Scott (1990) convincingly showed that what might appear as active, willing or even enthusiastic consent on the part of subordinates is frequently only the 'public transcript', i.e., the '*self*-portrait of dominant elites, as they would have themselves seen' (1990, 18, italics in original). The 'hidden' transcript was inaccessible to dominant elites, being 'the privileged site for non-hegemonic, contrapuntal, dissident and subversive discourse' (1990, 25). My case studies showed also that public and hidden transcripts were dynamic and varied according to intended audiences, reiterating my previous argument that the need to represent as well as document consent was never uniform. Moreover, as the local bases of domination varied greatly in the four villages that were researched, these dialectics produced remarkable differences.

This chapter is organized in two parts. The first will detail the use of consent as evidence of participation in the Kurnool villages and Kishangarh, for these present different scenarios in the fulfilment of participatory protocol. The briefer second part will focus on the use of consent as a strategy to signify the general interest by SPS. It will begin however with a short prelude on how consent became such an essential aspect of participation in the particular context of watershed development.

Consent and Community in Watershed Development

Chapter 3 discussed how state policies for watershed development in India have been inspired by the experiences of collective mobilization initiated by dedicated individuals like Anna Hazare, Vilasrao Salunkhe and Parasu Ram. An excellent example of the state modelling an entire programme to 'replicate' such isolated cases was the Adarsh Gaon Yojana (AGY) launched by the government of Maharashtra with a view to mimic the Ralegan Siddhi 'model' in at least 300 villages. Even though other state and national initiatives can hardly match such a dedicated endeavour to follow on the footsteps of Hazare and others, it is possible to discern the influences that have permeated watershed thinking more generally.

Ralegan Siddhi and the Pani Panchayat villages built their reputation on the innovative institutional arrangements they devised for sharing costs and benefits equitably, thus recognizing that watershed development is very likely to engender different outcomes for different persons depending on the size, quality and location of lands owned. They brought to the fore the importance of persuading persons of different standing in the village to consent to a collective arrangement, often through concerted brokering by one or two individuals who assumed a leadership role. A number of other NGO and donor-led initiatives were soon reported to be following similar methods, albeit with varying degrees of success. The Indo-German Watershed Programme in Maharashtra succeeded in convincing the wealthier people in at least one village to grant exclusive fishing rights to landless persons in the run-off pond established within the project. MYRADA, operating in villages in AP and Karnataka, focuses on 'building consensus among different interest groups' and developing mechanisms to compensate those who lose in the process of cooperating 'for the greater good' (Kerr, Pangare and Pangare 2002, 14). This process of compensating the poor for 'externalities' is a difficult one, and several structural factors militate against the possibility of devising arrangements that are just as also equitable (the unsuitability of externally imposed 'standards', preferential treatment of landowners in groundwater legislation in India and difficulties in attributing the availability of water to watershed activities or land use patterns upstream to name a few, see Kerr 2002 and Kerr et al 2006). Nevertheless, many NGOs have tried to foster written agreements to share common land and water with landless people (Kerr 2002).

At a deeper level though, it is this 'willingness' to put the common good ahead of narrow-mindedness that constitutes a large measure of that to which persons are often asked to consent. Villages participating in the AGY initiative were encouraged to follow the five social principles of Ralegan Siddhi (family planning in addition to bans on alcohol, open grazing, cutting trees and voluntary community work or 'shramdaan'). The underlying philosophy encouraged 'self-discipline and a willingness to overcome social barriers and political factionalism to work for the common good' (Kerr, Pangare and Pangare 2002, 15). This focus on unity and harmony has served to mobilize a vision of an 'ideal community' to which participating villages (like Hivre Bazar) could aspire (see Sangameswaran 2008 for an excellent discussion). This 'reified' vision while providing a 'vocabulary of legitimation for requests to be made and pressure to be exerted' was also extremely malleable to incorporating other local or village-specific elements within this ideal goal (like indigeneity, fairness, self-sufficiency and development) (Sangameswaran 2008, 389).

Apart from the greater good idea, a second notion that has also substantiated the idea of consent in watershed development is that of demonstrated involvement in physical works and activities. In other words, a verbal agreement is not good enough, and a more concrete involvement is needed for people to have a 'sense of satisfaction and achievement' in the works they have helped to create through an 'investment of their labour' (Kerr, Pangare and Pangare 2002, 15). This is at the core of the idea of shramdaan, literally a sacrifice of labour, and now widely regarded as an integral part of participatory watershed development. It also echoes the notion that communities can be self-sufficient in providing for themselves, and cease to depend on the 'external' state. Such an expectation is not new in the history of Indian community development, as it played a central role in the Community Development Programme of 1952 and has been amply reiterated in international discourses of decentralization and CBNRM. The practices generated by shramdaan however have varied greatly, and not just in the villages that were visited, confirming the influences exercised by motives less lofty than sacrifice. In Hivre Bazar in Maharashtra where a very large number of villagers performed shramdaan, a wide range of factors were at play. Many villagers regarded shramdaan as a 'favour that could be called upon at some future time to be redeemed – such as for a recommendation for a bank loan by the headman or a job transfer (Sangameswaran 2008, 399). Some also reported social pressure as a particular percentage of shramdaan was required for the village to qualify for government funds, and abstaining villagers were faced with the 'ire' of others. Bigger farmers contributed tractors instead of their labour, and women did not offer their labour beyond the initial period for it clashed with their household duties. Both these illustrate that the practice of shramdaan reproduced power hierarchies and gender differences that permeated social life. Far from being the elixir of an apolitical and harmonious existence in this village, the expression of consent was deeply embedded in everyday life and its inevitable politics.

Part I: Consent and the Kurnool Watershed Office

The use of consent by the KWO in its participatory protocol needs to be viewed in the context of its larger history. KWO's insistence on consent cannot be viewed independently of the excessively procedural conception of participation specified in the national guidelines though, clearly, circumstances particular to the climate of governance and decentralization in Andhra Pradesh in the late 1990s and early 2000s led to these ideas being developed so fully. KWO's project strategy rested on an array of methods designed to record consent for its projects within a larger framework of technocratic planning. It used consent as evidence of participation within a strategy that was presumed to operate within the 'apolitical spaces' ostensibly created within project villages. Such a strategy left its own expertise and modes of intervention unquestioned as these could easily be justified as politically neutral, unbiased and necessary for project efficiency. The procedures described below epitomize the codification of the depoliticization discourse to which KWO subscribed, within an extremely tight-knit and upward oriented protocol that all implementing staff were expected to follow.

Technocratic Intervention: The Project Action Plan

KWO's strategy for project implementation on a participatory basis rested on project planning that listed physical and financial targets in an action plan to be executed over the stipulated four year time frame. It also rested on the innovation of implementation procedures to ensure that physical and financial operations could not be conducted without the explicit consent of concerned individuals. The action plan symbolizes decentralized planning and policy makers regard it to be amongst the most progressive aspect of reform in the watershed sector. According to the national guidelines, the village watershed committee prepares the action plan by assimilating individual work plans drawn up by various user groups comprising private landholders within the watershed area. The idea is that user groups should plan for the lands they use. Planners hope this provision would ensure that individual landholders participate eagerly in the watershed project, by contributing in cash or labour, and maintaining the structures even when the project is over. In addition, the aggregate plan is to be 'presented' to the watershed association for its final consent. Village level project staff, i.e. the WDT, has been given an 'advisory' role in the planning process. In contrast, the major responsibility for planning rests with the local people's agency in different sizes – group, committee and association.

These roles however were reversed in reality. Preparation of the action plan was a complex task that not only required an intimate knowledge of local topography but also a fair degree of technical capability. The action plan is a modern document, complete with sector wise targets and financial estimates, and its formulation required skills that immediately put project officials at an advantage over the 'locals' they sought to empower. This was especially as the action plan had to be formulated at the outset, as even the first year of the project had targets that were to be met.[3] Therefore, for members of the watershed committee to assume any meaningful role in the process a 'significant degree of technical capability development' would have to be devolved, and by the time it occurred in any meaningful way the action plan might already have been drafted (Shah 1997, 12). In both Lilapuram and Malligundu, the action plan was formulated by WDT officers (and approved by the district level multi-disciplinary team) and 'handed over' to the Secretary and Chairman of respective watershed committees. KWO's intervention in the project was framed entirely within this technical, time bound and rather inflexible action plan. Its approach confirmed a trend that has increasingly become an axiom in development practice that 'if technology and people's participation are wedded together, then prosperity will follow' (Kamat 2002, 93).

Calculations of Cost and Consent

The action plan was the yardstick by which KWO's participatory projects were to be implemented, and it could not be revised once senior officers in KWO had granted technical and administrative sanction to it. This meant that project staff officials, both at senior and junior levels, were under considerable pressure to meet the physical and financial targets listed in the plan (see Chhotray 2005). While senior officials like the PD were accountable to their superiors in the state department and had to regularly demonstrate that targets were being met, junior officials like the WDT team members had to ensure that the projects they were responsible for were up to the mark. The pressures to meet targets is no new phenomenon in development projects, but what made it doubly difficult in Kurnool was KWO's insistence that no money could be spent or watershed structure constructed without the demonstrated consent of those affected. In its attempts to combine the project's target-driven thrust with its recently acquired participatory orientation, KWO's senior management insisted that no watershed structure could be constructed without the individual consent of the private landholder or the collective consent of the village community, depending on whether the structure was to be located on private or common lands respectively.[4] However, project funds for watershed development are typically allocated on a yearly basis to four principal sectors – agriculture, minor irrigation (MI), afforestation and animal husbandry (or activities like horticulture) – and KWO's officials found it easier to meet targets in some sectors compared with others. Indeed in approaching the whole issue of target completion, WDT officials were guided by astute calculations of cost and consent, i.e. structures that cost more money and were easy to obtain consent for were the favoured ones. This would have otherwise created a tendency for meeting targets through over-spending on certain structures at the cost of others, but precisely in anticipation of this KWO banned inter-sectoral transfers of funds once the action plan had been approved. This only constrained the village-level officials further. It is worth stressing that popularising the participatory discourse, for which consent was a stated proxy, was the last thing on the minds of these officers.

A number of generic reasons underpin these calculations of cost and consent, and a finer understanding of these can help with appreciating the differences in support received by the project in respective villages (not just in

Kurnool, but also elsewhere in the country, as Kishangarh in Madhya Pradesh). To begin with, MI sector targets are, as a norm, easier to meet than those in the agriculture sector. MI includes structures for storage like percolation tanks, and erosion control like rock filled dams, check dams and check walls. It is easier to spend project money on MI structures as construction involves both material as well as labour costs. The agriculture sector, in contrast, includes earthen field bunds that circle individual landholdings. These entail only labour costs as no materials are required to be purchased. MI sector targets are easier to meet than those in the agriculture sector on account of their location as well, as this has implications for individual contributions in cash or labour (shramdaan) to the Watershed Development Fund (WDF) for post-project maintenance of works. Storage and erosion control structures are located either on commonly owned lands or across gullies and water channels. The latter, though situated on private lands, are not perceived as such because these water bodies traverse many individual landholdings. Field bunds, in contrast, are almost always built on private property. Private individuals tend to resent the erection of such structures on their lands as they are reluctant to contribute. Contributions on structures raised on common lands, in principle, should be obtained on a shared basis from landholders who are most likely to benefit. This is rarely the practice, however, because of the difficulties involved in assessing beneficiaries and bringing about an agreement among them to share the cost. As a result, poor labourers who are engaged in construction works on common lands end up paying for the mandatory contribution from their wages (Shah 1997), and such structures meet little resistance from landholders.

In addition, locals perceive some structures as more beneficial than others. This also influences how easy or difficult it is for POs to receive consent from farmers for watershed works, both on private and common lands. For example, farmers tend to be suspicious of project arguments in favour of field bunds. Bunds are typically constructed on the lower end of the slope, encircling the field. They aim to reduce the velocity of rainwater as it flows downward, eroding topsoil with it. For a total land area of one acre (4000 square metres), a field bund would take up nearly 400 square metres. Farmers are reluctant to part with this land area. They think of field bunds as unnecessary structures that result in water stagnation at the corners of their fields, causing crops to rot. In comparison, big structures like farm ponds are normally not refused by farmers because they are perceived as highly beneficial. This suits project implementers, encouraging them to pursue construction of larger, costlier and visible structures even more doggedly. Watershed activities in the afforestation sector tend to suffer for the same reason, as they involve little labour and relatively modest cost of plantations. More importantly, they are carried out on common lands which are frequently the subject of apathy. All other activities covered under the watershed project such as horticulture, animal husbandry and pisciculture are based on disbursement of project money or seeds, as the case may be. As these activities are associated with receipt of project resources they are generally popular and the issue of beneficiary selection becomes a critical matter over which project officials and committee secretaries can exercise discretion.

Itemising Participation

According to the national guidelines, the village watershed committee effectively decided on four aspects of implementation: location and timing of structures, preparation of estimates per individual structure (then approved by WDT members), physical execution of works through engagement of labourers and selection of beneficiaries for direct disbursements, like seeds and gas stoves, under the project. Within this framework, KWO introduced various measures to integrate routine implementation of the action plan with participatory decision-making. The PD explained to me that these measures had specifically been devised to help local project staff ensure that targets were met, but with the consent of those participating in the project. The result was an itemized protocol of participation in three main parts:

- Collective decision-making: KWO wanted to leave nothing to chance to ensure the collective nature of the committees' working. It initiated the practice of an 'inland letter scheme', whereby committee secretaries had to send copies of resolutions signed by all members to the project office in Kurnool each month. KWO had ruled that vouchers for works not listed in committee resolutions would not be accepted and payments would be refused. The PD hoped that these measures would provide fewer chances to the influential elements within the watershed to appropriate works by unjustifiably concentrating structures on their lands.
- Individual consent: POs (WDT typically, and MDT for structures with higher) estimates) had been instructed not to approve any structure raised on private lands without the committee first having secured a written letter of consent or 'sammati patram' from the individual landholder.
- Individual contribution: The national guidelines require individual landholders to contribute towards the construction of watershed works (the shramdaan principle) as a token of participation and endorsement. Once the decision to start an item of work was taken, it was left to the landholder to decide whether to execute the works on his own, or leave it to the watershed committee. If materials needed to be bought for the structure, the necessary purchases had to be made by the individual farmer. Once the

work was complete, the concerned WDT member (the specialist responsible for agriculture or minor irrigation for example) physically inspected the work (termed 'check measurement' in project-speak) and prepared the final bill. The consolidated amount was then paid to the farmer in the form of a cheque to return for his investment in cash and kind. Prior to payment, the bank deducted ten per cent (five per cent of the landholder belonged to the SC or ST communities) of the total amount paid to be deposited into the project's WDF. On works carried out on common lands, KWO followed the patently unfair practice of obtaining contributions for WDF from the wages of the labourers engaged for works, as opposed to a wider contribution from the village, as this would be difficult to execute.

Through its initial deductions KWO ensured the contribution even before it was made. While this may have regularized contributions to WDF it neglected the voluntarism that is integral to participation, at least in theory. KWO's approach to contributions is not unique and similar practices are carried out elsewhere through government rules and directives requiring a percentage of the minimum wage to be deducted at source (see Baviskar 2007, 298 for an account of 'voluntary' labour in Jhabua district). Baviskar rightly argues that this approach implies that all too often villagers did not even knew that their labour was 'volunteered', perceiving no difference at all between watershed works and other 'forms of labouring for the state'. This subject remains a contentious one within the wider watershed community in the country with still others arguing that without such procedural intervention landlords would be able to control 'free labour' in the name of shramdaan.[5]

Paperwork for the Project

Not content with generating abundant paperwork in its enthusiasm to pursue participatory procedures, KWO also initiated mechanisms to monitor project documentation to ensure that local project staff and watershed committee secretaries maintained records properly. Committee secretaries were required to maintain a large number of records, all of which were used as tools of surveillance by KWO. The first of these was a cashbook listing all receipts and expenditures. The committee held the watershed account for project work and the WDF for post-project maintenance. A bank maintained passbooks for these accounts, details of which had to match with those in cashbooks maintained by the watershed secretaries. Moreover, when committees sent vouchers to KWO for audit purposes, these had to be tallied with the passbooks, copies of which were also maintained at the project office. Committee secretaries were also required to record minutes of watershed meetings and committee resolutions.

KWO was categorical about correct and updated record keeping. In the year that fieldwork was carried out, it initiated the 'Community Mobilization Programme' (CMP) to increase 'public awareness' regarding the procedures of the watershed project. A CMP was held once every month in a chosen project village and attended by project staff and committee members from that village plus neighbouring project villages under the same PIA. KWO tried to cover all project villages in the district in rotation. It sent senior officers from Kurnool to attend such meetings for the express purpose of inspecting and correcting project records. The PD and his senior advisors claimed that these events aimed to increase project transparency.

At one such CMP, the session quickly transformed into a forum for senior officials from Kurnool to publicly criticize WDT members as also committee secretaries for inefficient record keeping. It was a suitable venue for KWO to show to those present that it was in charge. A circular issued by the PD, KWO, to his MDT members introducing the CMP was worded in the following manner, 'I expect that you shall become the agent of change by making people aware, by *telling them what is good for them* and thus playing the role of an enabler and facilitator' (italics added). I heard from WDT officials of Lilapuram and Malligundu of how CMP meetings became an occasion for great excitement in the village, sometimes even attended by the PD himself, who also brought with him visitors and guests to 'show off' the project. Such public demonstration of project emphasis on paperwork and record keeping may have served to humiliate those at the receiving end of criticism and amuse bystanders. Above all, it was likely to send out the message to local project managers that formal fulfilment of project criteria would be enough to satisfy senior project officials in KWO.

Public Proceedings

Most importantly, project transactions had to be conducted in 'public' in order to be participatory. Consent, whether accorded orally or through written documents, had to be expressed in public which varied depending on the nature of the transaction involved. Typically, the public venue in relation to participatory development projects is understood to be a space that is open to the 'entire' village community. This in itself is a difficult proposition as large spaces that can accommodate 'everybody' may not be accessible to all. Temple courtyards, for instance, might be out of bounds for the lower castes in a village. Smaller 'publics' were implicated as well, such as in the course of the working of the committee which is expected to meet in a convenient location, which typically was the house of the committee secretary or chairperson. If the office bearer was a landed Reddy, as was the case in Lilapuram, then SC members that were treated as untouchables would not have been able to enter their homes, or be seated in the presence of 'higher' castes. The dynamics of exclusion in public settings, so vividly described by Mosse (1994) in his well-cited paper, would have operated in at least some of the proceedings that transpired in KWO's project villages, as will now be described.

Formal Compliance and Reinforcement of Domination in Lilapuram

In Lilapuram's rigidly hierarchical social fabric, KWO's project initiation rituals lauding the virtues of inclusive and equally accessible decision-making were not particularly discordant for the dominant Reddy landholders, for the project fell in tune with the village power structure right from the outset. Indeed, its maze of procedures and paperwork created fecund opportunities for the two Reddy watershed secretaries who were fairly comfortable with document-keeping as a result of their other official roles (panchayat sarpanch for one, village agricultural officer for the other). They also easily discovered that they would be able to record consent for KWO's documentation, without in fact making much of an effort to seek it (both from committee members and other villagers), and in the secure knowledge that it would not be denied. What I will first describe demonstrates the intricate ways in which these procedures were formally complied with, often to the private anger (but not incredulity) of ordinary residents. The nature of the progress made in fulfilling targets in particular sectors (like minor irrigation and agriculture) was another indication that the watershed project in Lilapuram performed poorly in areas where concerted engagement with farmers, especially the poorest in the village, was necessary. This had implications for the general reinforcement of socio-economic domination of bigger farmers in the village, mainly comprising the Reddys. Even when projects are not 'fully participatory', wrote Mosse, 'they can have genuinely livelihoods effects' (2004, 662). Here, the absence of genuinely palpable improvements for the large majority of Lilapuram's residents further undermined general enthusiasm for the project, which played an important role in the experience of watershed development quite irrespective of the formal documentation of consent.

Rituals of Paper

The practice of securing sammati-patrams from landholders and signatures from committee members as measures of their consent was flagrantly abused.

A WDT member from the project team, who requested anonymity, told me that both committee secretaries considered it normal to start work on the lands of individuals much before any written consent was obtained. This was also confirmed by a Muslim farmer owning more than 20 acres of land in the village, among others, who quipped that it 'was hardly surprising given Satya Reddy's ways of working'. Besides, there were no cases of consent ever denied by any landholder, which only makes the matter further suspect. Most landholders who tendered sammati-patrams were not clear about to what they had agreed. Committee secretaries could exercise the option of manipulating the text since the majority could not read or write. Even if a fair transaction took place and a committee secretary presented the landholder with a request for consent, the margin for dissent was negligible. This was inevitable as the watershed secretaries were also the principal providers of wage labour in the village. Which farmer would deny permission to Satya Reddy or Gangadhar Reddy? Likewise, committee resolutions signed by all members did not count for much. Many did not even know that they were members of the committee, and as the Reddy secretaries did not conduct works in joint consultation with them, signatures or thumbprints presented only a semblance of collective decision-making that did not exist.

All works were executed in typical contract fashion and without the involvement of the large majority of user and self-help groups formed in Lilapuram at the start of the project. This violated an important procedure laid down by KWO which took 'group engagement' of labourers very seriously, even devising group payments through cheques in an attempt to institutionalize this practice. In Lilapuram, 16 user and self-help groups were formed in all, their composition was caste-based and they were all men. While a few user groups comprising the BC farmers that were regularly engaged on the lands of the large Reddy farmers also obtained employment on watershed works, most others remained uninvolved. In a number of focus group discussions with individuals listed as group members, it was discovered that there were about eight to ten BC farmers with close links to each of the Reddy groups who were engaged on works and paid through cheques but the remaining persons maintained they were not 'given' any work on the project. It became clear that a very small number of BC supporters (mostly male) were exclusively engaged on project works.

The entire SC population of the village, which was landless and had been formed into SHG groups, was denied employment opportunities. Angry SC women also told me that they had never been called or engaged by either of the Reddy farmers when I met them separately. A BC farmer named Madayya, who was close to Satya Reddy, was present at the meeting and mildly contradicted the incensed women saying that all watershed work was carried out in the summer and these women were not around in the village at the time. One woman retorted even more angrily, 'We leave the village to migrate because there is no work here. If you gave us work here, why would we want to leave our homes and undertake such a long and uncomfortable journey?' It was not uncommon for Satya Reddy to post informers at my private meetings, gaining access to what might have been a 'hidden transcript' of these poor low-caste women, but what surprised me was that his presence did not deter these women from speaking their minds. Satya Reddy for his part refused to address these issues when I spoke to him afterwards, brazenly maintaining that Lilapuram's farmers did not 'trust' works to be carried out by user groups. This of course did not make much sense as user groups are meant to comprise owners of contiguous landholdings, who are expected to work on structures raised on each other's lands.

With this attitude, it was scarcely surprising that the committee secretaries made no effort to create links with the eight 'podupulakhmi' or women's thrift and credit groups that had been active in Lilapuram since 1999. The government of AP under Chandrababu Naidu was a keen promoter of such groups and lent substantial support to the central government funded Department of Women and Child Welfare (DWCRA) groups for women.[6] In 1996, it also extended the initiative to men under a youth ('Yuva Shakti') initiative labelled as the Chief Minister's Empowerment of Youth Programme. These groups came into existence following an introduction by the Mandal Development Officer, and most designated group leaders decided to choose members from their respective castes. Three groups were formed from amongst BC women, two from SC women, one from the OCs, while the remaining two had mixed membership from the OCs and BCs. My conversations with these groups revealed that all eight were functional in a broad sense, with accounts in the Rayalseema Grameen Bank in Veldurthi. Of the 90 families included in the eight podupulaksmi groups, only five had members that had worked on the watershed projects in the village at any time, all of whom were from the BCs. They were especially outraged at this situation as they claimed that many persons employed on watershed works in Lilapuram were not residents of this village at all and had been brought in from neighbouring hamlets like L'kotalla.

While engaging labour from a small pool of supporters and usual farm hands was reasonably straightforward for the committee secretaries, manipulating the contributions that went into the WDF was harder. It required more than the seeming unconcern of WDT and MDT officials, and possibly a degree of active connivance. KWO required that all works could be executed only after a watershed committee collectively prepared estimates for these, which would then be approved by a PO (either WDT or MDT depending on the amount in question, as higher amounts were referred to the MDT based in Kurnool). In Lilapuram, the Reddys appropriated the power of estimate preparation and regularly provided for costs higher than those actually incurred in the village (since, typically, the government rates for materials and labour were much higher than those prevalent locally). They then used this gap not only to show the WDF contribution on paper, but also to pocket part of the difference. Interestingly, it was the PD who described the general occurrence of this malpractice, confirming that, as long as the gap between estimated and actual rates continued, it would be difficult to verify individual contributions.[7] The KWO's system of anticipatory contributions deducted at source while reimbursing farmers was far from effective. It was especially unjust when the project constructed works on common lands, as poor labourers had to pay the mandatory contribution from their wages. Irrespective of malpractices however, all project paperwork remained immaculate.

The interplay between junior project officials and local elites in charge of project protocol was critical to sustaining the practices of formal compliance. The nature of domination exercised by the Reddys was also significant, for they knew that keeping up with these rituals on paper was entirely consistent with their interests and position in the village. They carried on as they had always done, making not the slightest effort to reach out to the subordinate majority, but taking care not to rupture their interactions with project officials. Low salaried WDT officers on the other hand did not wish to challenge the high-caste Reddy landholders, who clearly commanded authority in the village whilst they were merely temporary visitors. Besides, they were well aware that the project could not go ahead without the cooperation of the Reddys, and accepted the terms on which it was offered. Consent of the wider population was neither sought, nor received, and judging from the successful conclusion of the project and its paperwork in the higher precincts of KWO, this did not matter.

Targets and Benefits: Difficulties in Popular Engagement

Watershed projects are supposed to commence through the undertaking of relevant 'entry-point' activities (EPAs). The idea is that some project money be spent in the first year, preceding any other project activities, with the participation and involvement of local people to fulfil a widely felt local need. Suggestions regarding appropriate EPAs should ideally be collected in the course of public meetings convened in the early days of any project. In Lilapuram, the allocated funds for EPAs for both the watershed projects were devoted to the construction of a 'community hall', work on which did not start until the second project year. Apart from the minor quibble that it did not really serve as an EPA, the choice of a community hall reflected the wishes of a few influential persons in the village and not a widely felt village need. There were other more pressing requirements, like the urgent repairs needed on the well accessed by the village's SC community for instance. In not seeking a wider consultation, the project missed an important opportunity to appear credible in its promise that the watershed project was a project for all.

The progress of the project produced more proof that both watershed committees had been able to spend money more effectively on activities relating to minor irrigation, but recorded major under-spending on afforestation. These underscored the points made earlier regarding calculations of cost and consent. From a PO's viewpoint, if money had been successfully spent on 'difficult' sectors like afforestation, it could be interpreted as a sign of a high level of community involvement. This was not the case in Lilapuram.

The figures in Table 1 are an aggregation of expenditure over the four year project period. They reveal very similar trajectories of spending by both watershed committees, confirming that the two Reddy groups operated very similarly (note that these targets were not set by the Reddy secretaries, but handed down to them in the action plans). While expenditure targets were most effectively met in the minor irrigation section (with only 0.15 and 0.16 lakh rupees in balance respectively), projects experienced major under-spending in the afforestation sector (2.14 and 3.46 lakh rupees were left over). Afforestation activities, which should have been carried out on village common lands, were of little interest to the richer farmers of Lilapuram who met their fuel and fodder needs from private lands or purchase. As village commons have deteriorated significantly over the years, poorer people have taken to grazing livestock and gathering firewood from the adjoining hills and reserved forests. Project proposals for afforestation therefore did not evoke much enthusiasm amongst committee secretaries, and as the project office had banned inter-sectoral transfers, this money simply lapsed. Dryland horticulture on the other

Table 1. Financial performance 1997–2001, Lilapuram watershed project. (All figures in lakhs of rupees*)

Sector	Watershed Committee 1			Watershed Committee 2		
	Target	Expenditure	Balance	Target	Expenditure	Balance
Agriculture	3.78	3.627	0.153	7.72	6.73	0.99
Minor Irrigation	4.84	4.69	0.15	5.25	5.09	0.16
Afforestation	3.03	0.889	2.141	4.2	0.74	3.46
Horticulture	1.352	0.934	0.418	0.57	0.63	−0.06

Source: Kurnool Watershed Office.
* 1 lakh = 100,000 rupees.

hand proved to be extremely popular. This involved disbursement of seeds or money for seeds to individual beneficiaries, and both committee secretaries were flooded with requests.

However, not all farmers in the village were able to avail of disbursements for horticulture, which was an option realistically available only to larger farmers with access to a steady supply of water. Shifting to horticulture is not a risk that small farmers could easily afford, as fruit trees do not bear fruit for at least four to five years subjecting the farmer to negative returns. Indeed, WDT members reported how large farmers who had 'exceeded' their quota for reimbursements for planting fruit trees persuaded smaller farmers to do so on their behalf. Other project 'benefits' similarly eluded smaller farmers in this village. As I have discussed in previous chapters, the benefits from watershed development mirror patterns of land ownership, and Lilapuram was no different. Typical changes associated with soil and water conservation measures in watershed projects are increased yields in existing crops and the intensification of cropping through multi-cropping and two-season agriculture. In dryland villages like Lilapuram and Malligundu, agriculture is mostly restricted to one principal crop in the kharif or rainfed season. Groundnut is the dominant crop grown in these villages. Besides, depletion of soil moisture and nutrients on account of monoculture, factors like bad rains, crash in groundnut prices and pest attacks regularly put farmers at risk, depriving them of major sources of income. Farmers also grow small amounts of red gram and 'korra' (an inferior rice-like cereal) for domestic consumption. Therefore, only large farmers owning wells have the option of growing a major second crop in the kharif season, like castor or sunflower, and cultivating their lands to grow winter groundnut, cotton and jowar through irrigation during the rabi season.

The 30 odd farmers with large landholdings above 30 acres each and private wells were in the best position to maximize opportunities available through improved water retention. The most visible project benefits were limited to this group, and many of them introduced new water intensive crops like drumstick, in addition to cultivating sunflower, cotton, castor and winter groundnut in large land areas. Each of these crops required high input costs for seeds and pesticides that only large farmers could afford. POs actively encouraged these trends, and were extremely enthusiastic in describing isolated cases of success. One large farmer, Venkataramanna Reddy, who procured a staggering 2.5 lakh rupees of profit from his drumstick crop in its first year, was regularly hailed as the 'drumstick hero'!

Project practices coupled with the nature of resource stratification in the village combined to produce an extremely unequal perception of benefits. Medium and smaller farmers reported few changes, apart from the occasional marginal increase in groundnut yields, which could hardly compare with the more concrete improvements being experienced by a minority of large farmers. The most disgruntled group was undoubtedly the landless community, almost exclusively from the SCs, who did not obtain any employment on the project and continued to conduct their annual ritual of summer migration to the canal-irrigated east. As the project had failed to improve the condition of the commons, there was no change to their fuel and fodder supply either.

Popular Mobilization in Malligundu

Unlike Lilapuram, the interplay of local domination and village socio-economic conditions yielded very different dialectics of consent for the watershed project. With a large majority of the village's population sharing the vagaries of dry subsistence agriculture, a tortuous annual rhythm of migration and poverty, village residents welcomed KWO's promise of a development project with wide ranging benefits. Equally significant was the unambiguous emphasis by POs in public meetings on KWO's intention to conduct the project consensually. Villagers, weary of Malligundu's violent and bloody history in recent years, found this position extremely appealing. Project officials were largely content to leave Naidu (and *his* panchayat) alone and this had the effect of assuring the headman that he could continue his activities with little need for a new subterfuge. But importantly as well, unlike the Reddys, Naidu did not seek a prominent role in the everyday management of the project. He did not feel threatened by the project's approach mainly because of the absence of any real opposition to his material interests inside the village, and therefore refrained from interfering with the unfolding of participatory procedures. In Lilapuram, the symbolism of controlling these procedures had been too attractive for the Reddys to resist, but this was not the case with Naidu. His domination derived principally from violence and the confidence of belonging to an ascendant caste group, the Boyas. Unlike landownership or traditional caste status, violence for Naidu was an unconventional resource, and participatory gestures like collective decision-making by the watershed committees or securing of sammati-patrams from farmers did not contradict the non-hierarchical nature of his power. Besides, he like others in Malligundu believed that the watershed project could bring in benefits, and perceived it as an opportunity to sanctify his leadership, otherwise based in brute, albeit well-masked, force.

Substantiating Consent

From the outset, the watershed project created hope and expectations amongst the people of Malligundu. The POs on their part took tremendous care that these hopes were not dashed, especially at first when popular perceptions typically swerve to cynicism. They made a judicious assessment of the village needs and acted accordingly. The inaugural EPAs included the construction of a bus shelter and a cement concrete road connecting the main village to a new hamlet where government houses for SC families were located. These fulfilled two long persisting village needs. In addition, the PIA, a government officer, obtained special permission from the PD to exceed action plan targets set up for the first year. This aimed to generate intensive employment opportunities through watershed works over summer that would put a total halt to migration, the bane of the entire village. This course of action was exceptional, given KWO's usual rigidity. It was made possible primarily because of effective communication between the government PIA and the main project office.

Popular mood in Malligundu favoured the watershed project. At this time, project WDT officials meticulously initiated the formation of user and self-help groups along the lines prescribed by KWO. Unlike Lilapuram, none of these ten groups were formed on the basis of caste affiliations. Also, two among these comprised exclusively of women. The distinguishing aspect of group formation in Malligundu was that all groups worked intimately with both watershed committees in carrying out project works. I was able to verify this through a succession of separate interviews with WDT members, watershed committee secretaries and group members. These revealed detailed attention to specific procedures and indicated the presence of a culture of work that was drastically different from that in Lilapuram.

Watershed committees engaged user and self-help groups in watershed works by rotation and no one group was privileged, ensuring that many persons in the village including the landless benefitted from project employment. At the same time, the extent of their involvement varied according to the task at hand and the consent of the landholder. Once the individual landholder (or landholders) had agreed to a watershed structure being raised on his land, he was given the option of carrying out the works on his own (by hiring labourers privately) or through a group. Committee secretaries and farmers explained that while most landholders preferred to carry out activities like field bunding on their own, for more complex constructions like check dams and walls, user groups were preferred. One farmer who has a check dam on his landholding joked, 'Most people in the village are in some or the other group anyway. How can I avoid them even if I wanted?' The choice of the group selected to carry out a particular task depending entirely on its composition, and the group that owned lands closest to the planned structure was hired. Care was taken to award work to Self Help Groups (SHGs) comprising the landless, to avoid disadvantage. There was no rigid distinction between groups attached to the respective committees, and groups sought work wherever it was available depending on their appropriateness.[8] In a variety of ways therefore, KWO's principal requirement of individual consent prior to any watershed activity was fulfilled, and not just on paper.

Since user groups were actively engaged on project works, WDT members were also able to follow KWO's directive that all labour payments be made through group leaders by joint cheque. According to procedure, the group leader distributed wages to members depending on the quantity of individual work done. During encashment, the bank deducted the amount of 'voluntary' contribution on behalf of landholders for construction of the watershed structure. However, the total amount cleared for payment by KWO included the costs of material as well as of labour, and was thus linked to the estimate for construction prepared by the watershed committee and approved by the WDT. The entire procedure, even in Malligundu, was opaque to scrutiny. It was difficult to ascertain (albeit very likely) whether committee secretaries prepared high estimates at Naidu's bidding, which would have ensured his cuts, but there was a determined reluctance on the part of secretaries and group members to say anything about this.[9]

The principle of voluntary contributions to the project was strictly adhered to in Malligundu. It is notoriously difficult to extract contributions from structures raised on common lands from landholders who benefit the most, and very often landless labourers who work on their construction end up paying from their wages. In Malligundu, however, when it was made evident that Sriram Reddy, a landholder, benefitted alone from a check dam constructed on the village common land, he was made to bear the requisite contribution for that structure. Watershed secretaries and WDT officials also initiated with some success a day of shramdaan on the ninth of every month when between 50–100 persons volunteered to clean the village. The enthusiastic WDT officer gushed that this would 'remind people to imbibe a community spirit for the watershed programme'. Newly created men's youth groups initiated in the village mimicked these initiatives through their own day of shramdaan held on the third Saturday of each month under a 'clean and green' slogan. While it is difficult to vouch for the continuation of these practices beyond the watershed project, there was a discourse of shramdaan where the idea was not scoffed at as ridiculous, at least not by a large number of actively engaged group members and watershed secretaries. This too contrasted with Satya Reddy's wry remark in Lilapuram that when people could work for wages, 'they were not stupid to work for free'.

The watershed project also took particular interest in the burgeoning activities of the nearly fifteen podupulakshmi groups in the village. These groups were initiated by the WDT social organizer in 1999, a year after the project started, who introduced the idea of saving a rupee a day to women in Malligundu. The idea proved to be immensely popular, and groups are able to practise internal lending and save money in a bank in the neighbouring Veldurthi town. Many women recounted to me how they had stopped using local moneylenders who charged extortionist rates since they became a part of these groups. The attitude of project staff and of watershed secretaries to these groups in Malligundu could not have been more different from that in Lilapuram, for they regarded them as an integral part of the project, much like the user and self-help groups. Senior officials in KWO regarded the 'performance' of podupulakshmi groups here as exemplary and requested three group leaders from Malligundu to act as 'ambassadors' for the initiative by speaking to women in other neighbouring villages. Taking the cue from these women's groups, four user groups formed for the watershed project voluntarily reorganized themselves into Yuva Shakti (youth) groups to avail of enterprise loans offered by the state government. Group members narrated to me that Naidu spotted the advertisement for this scheme in a local newspaper and conveyed the message to the user groups in the village.

The activities of nearly fifteen beneficiary groups of different types brought about a symbolic change in the character of public space in Malligundu. Before the project started, public meetings in the village, if at all, were an oddity. After the project unfolded, group meetings on the corridors of the primary school building, or under trees in the central village courtyard, became an unmistakable feature of village life. No longer would the sight of people meeting for a discussion arouse suspicion of possible opposition by Naidu or his henchmen. Rangamma, a podupulakshmi group leader, said 'Before the project started, if two or more persons were seen talking to one another outside their homes, people would suspect that something was wrong. Now everyone would think that they are only discussing some group matter'. Moreover, these were held irrespective of larger village meetings and regardless of whether convened by the watershed committee or the panchayat.

POs recognized that these meetings were important because they were an exercise in collective deliberation and confidence building. The articulation of demands in public spaces has been accorded a central place in participatory development, like the watershed programme or the state's Janmabhoomi initiatives. It is frequently reduced to tokenism because subordinate groups like poor low-caste women find it difficult to speak freely in the presence of village elites and government officials. Podupulaksmi members in Malligundu planned to demand proper lavatories in the village during the Janmabhoomi gram sabha. If they were carried out, they would constitute the 'empowering moments' that have been emphasized as the most promising aspect of participatory development (Kamat 2002, 60). The reality is also that dynamic members of these groups may put forward innocuous demands in public meetings, but hesitate from speaking against Naidu. While there were limits to what group mobilization could achieve in Malligundu, both in relation to the watershed project and beyond it, it remains that the nature of domination exercised by Naidu did not impede various types of group solidarities from emerging. These infused a positive spirit into social intercourse and offered opportunities for material advancement. Consent for the project, it would seem, was being generated in a multiplicity of fora and endorsed through a variety of popular responses. Perhaps the most interesting manifestation of this was the little time and talk devoted to fulfilling project recordings of consent in this village, for these were integrated into the actual business of working.

Targets and Benefits: Wide-scale Individual Appreciation

The trajectories of project spending in Malligundu may not appear to be remarkably different from that in Lilapuram, but there were important contrasts which speak of dissimilar project priorities as well as popular responses. The figures in Table 2 below show actual expenditures in the third project year (2001, my fieldwork year), followed by a column on the planned expenditure for the fourth and final year. The balance is estimated on the basis of what would be spent in this last year.

At first, it would seem that much like with the projects in Lilapuram, here too financial targets were most easily met in MI but not in afforestation. This was because MI structures usually cost more (both labour and material) and money is generally easier to spend. The same is not true for afforestation

Table 2. Financial performance 1998–2001, Malligundu watershed project. (All figures in lakhs of rupees)

Sector	Watershed Committee 1			
	Target	Exp in 3 yrs	4th year plan	Balance
Agriculture	3.671	3.88	0.695	−0.119
Minor Irrigation	2.455	2.46	0	−0.005
Afforestation	2.885	1.21	0.075	1.675
Horticulture	0.54	0.63	0	−0.09

Sector	Watershed Committee 2			
	Target	Exp in 3 yrs	4th year plan	Balance
Agriculture	4.69	3.67	0.99	1.09
Minor Irrigation	3.535	3.05	0.39	0.485
Afforestation	3.65	0.73	0.015	2.92
Horticulture	0.93	0.76	0.15	0.17

however where spending money is the hardest because these are low cost activities that involve little labour as well. Even here, the projects in Malligundu had lower unspent figures for afforestation than Lilapuram (1.675 and 2.92 lakhs as compared with 2.141 and 3.46 lakhs respectively). It also emerged that the projects had totally met the physical targets in at least one of the two projects, even though it had failed to spend the allocated money. This was not the case in Lilapuram where the project lagged in physical targets too as no effort for afforestation activities had been made. Fuel and fodder plantations had been undertaken in some of the village commons, and farmers owning encircling lands even contributed the fringes of their own lands to build a fence encircling the common area to prevent encroachments. WDT officers proudly described this as 'social fencing'. Avenue plantations were undertaken along the main road leading to the village and a landless man was named the 'beneficiary' and appointed to water these regularly for a small wage.

Both projects also fared reasonably well in meeting agriculture targets compared with Lilapuram, even exceeding the allocation by a small amount in one (-0.119 and 1.09 lakhs compared with 0.153 and 0.99). But the remarkable picture emerged upon disaggregating the nature of activities carried out under this sector. While in Malligundu a very large number of farmers had consented to field bunds being constructed on their lands, field bunding had been regarded as generally unworthy by the Reddys who did not pursue it seriously (in fact, agriculture works in Lilapuram included other activities like the construction of rock filled dams and stone checks as opposed to field bunds). Project works in Malligundu started with an intensive concentration on field bunding and by the third year of the project, nearly 310 hectares of land in the two watersheds had been 'bunded'. Committee secretaries pledged that another 100 hectares would be bunded in the final year. This approach signified that the project was not limited to the construction of large water harvesting structures on the lands of a few individuals alone, and ensured a wider, more broad-based interaction between farmers and project officials. More evidence that local farmers appreciated the value of their bunds came with their own efforts to preserve these new structures, and many planted 'koban' grass along these mud bunds for strength.

There was a far more uniform appreciation of the project's potential to bring about material changes for residents in this village as compared with Lilapuram. Unlike the latter, where a small section of the population received a generous proportion of project benefits, the base conditions in Malligundu made a similar bias more implausible. The village has a large majority of small farmers owning dry plots, and to its credit, the project fulfilled its promises to the poor. The most visible was the break in chronic migration cycles, which alleviated conditions for all sections of the village, even those who were most deeply entrenched. No longer was Malligundu reduced to a ghost village in the summer, with only the old, infirm and some women staying behind. Poor SC women gratefully recounted that working on the project in the summer and saving money in the podupulakshmi groups had extracted them from the clutches of moneylenders. Unlike Lilapuram, most families in Malligundu received employment on project works.

Watershed benefits relating to agriculture tend to be biased in favour of farmers with larger landholdings and access to irrigation, for they can experiment with new options of multi-cropping, two-season as well as commercial agriculture. In Malligundu however, POs had carefully assessed the needs of small farmers and encouraged project practices that would yield concrete improvements. They persuaded small farmers to plant paddy – a water intensive crop and therefore only planted by large farmers with tube wells – along their field bunds. Although the cropped area often did not exceed even a part of an acre, it was enough to meet the cereal needs of the whole family for many months. In some cases, farmers released land previously devoted to cultivating korra (another cereal), for other crops. Besides, the horticulture plantations introduced by the project became extremely popular in Malligundu. Project extension staff explained the special needs of fruit trees to all interested farmers and not merely large landholders. Although very few individuals in the village owned wells, beneficiaries were not restricted only to well owners and project staff judiciously selected landholders whose plots were close to wells. Madamma and Lakshmidevi for instance, the poor women leaders of two podupulaksmi groups in the village, planted fruit trees on their small plots scarcely measuring more than one to two acres. They borrowed water in exchange for some wage labour from a nearby well-owner. Many beneficiaries were also advised to plant jowar and groundnut as intercrops between their fruit trees for their subsistence needs to be met until these trees bore fruit. Meticulous attention of this sort enabled smaller farmers in Malligundu not to be excluded from concrete improvements. In this manner, landholders and landless, both men and women, irrespective of their caste affiliations felt enthused about the project, both jointly as well as severally. Stray cases of discontent with the project or its office bearers could not of course be ruled out.

Denial of Consent and Project Expedience in Kishangarh

Unlike project officials who worked for the KWO, implementing officers in Dewas had no participatory protocol to fulfil. But even though there was no pressing need to document – or much less create – consent for the project through participatory procedures, the dialectics of consent manifested themselves regardless. The PO in Kishangarh was confronted with a clear, if not hostile, lack of co-operation from the landed majority of this village. This translated into the systematic denial of consent for the project, which interestingly translated into project expedience for it enabled the construction of particular sorts of watershed structures that were regarded as integral to project success by bureaucrats and technocrats higher up in the ranks. Although dissimilar to the Kurnool villages in its experience of participation, Kishangarh reaffirmed that the manifestation of consent was closely linked to the structure of domination and socio-economic stratification. It also brought home the message that consent was not only sought by project officials to record participation; it was embedded within the very nature of the relationship between a 'development project agency' and the 'subject people'. In this light, the issue of consent needs to be considered holistically, in relation to power, and not in isolated terms to signify an apolitical participation.

The previous chapter described how the project was plagued by the politics of disinterest from the beginning. Rich Khatis and Rajputs alike showed no interest in managing the project, and the watershed committee was reduced from two to one, with a single Rajput man assisting the PO. In any case, the robust dynamics of group working observed in Malligundu, and even the more restricted methods of labour engagement in Lilapuram were missing in Kishangarh, because all works were carried out through the services of a 'gaon meth' or construction supervisor. The initial conditions were inimical for the sort of participation that was being emphasized in Kurnool. With a shortfall in agricultural and non-agricultural labour, it would have been difficult to argue for shramdaan. Besides, big farmers here did not welcome watershed works on their lands, and were particularly against the construction of earthen field bunds. Other low-cost structures for water conservation that are typically promoted within watershed projects, such as dykes and check dams, were also remote from their practices of irrigated agriculture for which they had private wells, tube wells and electrical motors. Once they heard that they would have to pay ten per cent of project costs by way of contribution to a WDF, they plainly disallowed any works on their lands.

The watershed programme in the district was still at an early stage, and when the PO contacted his superiors in Dewas and the RGM office in Bhopal they responded with a number of 'innovative steps'. These enabled the PO to complete the project in Kishangarh despite local resistance on private lands. The first step was taken by the CEO of Dewas Zilla Panchayat, who raised the upper limit of money to be spent on any individual structure from 100,000 to 200,000 rupees. Besides, as there was no ceiling on the amount to be spent on any one work sector, whether agriculture, minor irrigation or afforestation, POs were unrestrained from spending money by constructing large, expensive structures, regardless of their utility. Inter-sectoral transfers of funds were extremely useful in meeting overall financial targets. Second, RGM officers strengthened this trend further by issuing directions to district authorities in favour of permanent structures. The justification offered was that farmers are sceptical of field bunds, whereas permanent structures built with cement and concrete were preferred to low-cost constructions made of mud and stones, as the former were supposedly more durable.[10]

As permission to construct any structures on private lands had been refused, the PO authorized the concentration of works on village common lands, which was located on the top of a hill nearby, constituting the head of the ridgeline in the watershed. This was fortuitous for watershed development which follows a ridge-to-valley approach to treatment, bringing benefits to lands downstream. The table below shows the aggregate physical and financial achievements of the two projects in Kishangarh. These are itemized according to structures clubbed broadly within different sectors: MI, agriculture and afforestation.

As Table 3 above illustrates, the project, even to begin with, set high targets for works such as tank and underground dyke construction, as well as the raising of contour and cattle contour trenches, all implemented on the common land area. In some of these sectors, particularly cattle contour trenches, the project exceeded physical and financial targets by significant measure. In contrast, structures such as check dams, gabion structures and field bunding that typically fall within the category of individual lands, as they are built along the drainage line, were underemphasized. The skewed approach to constructing structures violated a core principle of the national guidelines which allocate money for treatment per hectare of land. The construction of large percolation tanks and other permanent structures in Kishangarh enhanced a 'prestigious' image for the watershed mission, as the flattering posters on the walls of the DRDA office in Dewas suggested, but this scale of emphasis contradicted the philosophy of low-cost water conservation and storage that is central to participatory watershed development.

Even when these were built on private lands, their owners did not pay any contributions which were simply deducted from the wages of labourers hired to do the work. This was doubly unjust as they benefited from reported increases in the availability of water for irrigation. The RGM office claims that the project in Kishangarh was a 'huge' success, with increases in irrigated area, numbers of wells and tube wells in the village. In addition, my conversations with farmers (individually and in groups) owning lands in different parts of the watershed suggested that many farmers were able to grow a second crop through irrigation, especially in downstream areas, and reported increased cropped areas in both kharif and rabi seasons. It was clear that they credited

Table 3. Physical and financial achievements under Kishangarh watershed project.

Name of work	Physical targets	Financial targets (in lakhs)	Physical achievements	Money spent (in lakhs)
Minor Irrigation				
Percolation tank	7	7.208	8	5.74
Cattle contour trench	4901 metres	1.076	22949 metres	5.494
Contour Trench	146262 metres	11.349	146262 metres	9.343
Rubble check dam (on the drain)	185.45 metres	1.465	46 metres	0.355
Rubble check dam (on the hill)	518.75 metres	0.441	358 metres	0.505
Agriculture				
Gabion Structures	4	0.90	2	0.570
Earthen bunding	8975 metres	0.648	6932 metres	0.648
Underground dykes	122 metres	4.274	138.60 metres	4.851
Afforestation and other				
Cleaning the area	67 hectares	1.09	24 hectares	1.410
Development of pastures	Area not specified	1.09	24 hectares	0.216
Afforestation	20,000 trees	0.538	20,000 trees	0.848
Any other works		0.86		0.895
TOTAL		**32.61**		**30.875**

Source: Project records, Kishangarh Micro Watershed Project, Dewas.

the project for positive improvements, but this did not make a difference to their general disinclination to support it in any way.

The project failed the poorer minority of the village in more than one way: not only did they have to bear the brunt of the contributions from their wages, the project did not address their urgent fuel and fodder needs in the slightest. There was a shortage of fuel and fodder in Kishangarh and the commons had suffered severe degradation following apathy and neglect over the years. The poor minority were not in a position to regenerate these areas as they were constrained for time, resources and organization. The remote location of village commons atop a hill only made matters more difficult. As a result, the meagre attempts made at afforestation on these commons suffered because even the poor were not motivated to go there regularly. Besides, initial attempts to protect the afforested patches failed because of frequent trespassing by residents from Nandpur village that lay on the opposite side of the hill. Nandpur, despite being contiguous to Kishangarh was not given a watershed project. Its residents therefore resented project activities on the hill, which they perceived as their territory as well.[11] This further discouraged feeble attempts at maintenance and protection of watershed structures. Local thieves also destroyed watershed structures to steal their materials. The tale of Kishangarh brings a poignant irony to Mosse's observation regarding projects that while not being participatory can bring 'positive livelihoods effects', for these effects were restricted to those who were suspicious of the project and denied to those who worked for it.

Part II: An NGO and Consent

The use of consent in participatory practice extends beyond the documentation of participation. The case of SPS and its remarkable trajectory in Dewas' ghaat-neeche revealed that the use of consent in the classical political sense as mandate, or indeed, legitimation to act (if not rule)[12] was the essential ingredient in its strategy for survival in a hostile environment and then consolidation of its own position. The difference was that state bodies like the KWO did not need popular legitimation to ensure their own continuation, as projects would have continued regardless of what people actually thought. The upward representations sustained by village elites and project officials in the Kurnool villages support this conclusion. The situation was different for Samaj Pragati Sahyog, an NGO, and its 'entrance' into an unequal world dominated by a nexus of non-tribal interests (some like junior revenue bureaucrats who were officially a part of the state) sparked off an extremely confrontationist beginning that threatened its continued existence and functioning here. SPS responded through a lived discourse of struggle and resistance, but at its heart was the idea that it had popular support for its actions. Undeniably, some even in Neelpura village felt alienated from the organization, but SPS was clear from the outset that it could not 'please everyone'. To instigate change however, SPS needed and relied upon a physical, observable and rather dramatic outpouring of consent, which it also used as its armour to ward off a variety of accusations. Its use of consent both by way of public demonstrations and through written resolutions was therefore decidedly political. As touched upon in Chapter 4, at critical stages of these very political confrontations, SPS earned support from senior state officials which challenged the idea that depoliticization was a definitive state project with predictable consequences. In line with the broader thesis of this book, these episodes revealed that senior state actors did not, and in this case could not, resort to pejorative meanings of politics from which development could be distanced.

The above however was the first phase in this NGO's use of consent. The evolving nature of its position in ghaat-neeche, which this research offered the occasion to observe, revealed a growing position of strength. From being the challenger, SPS was the defendant of a new status quo where it seemed to benefit from a more secure financial position, favour with the state and partnership on a variety of development projects and a wide grassroots network of support. It increasingly resorted to a discourse of rightness and representation of the general interest. Its projection of itself as the embodiment of popular interest constituted a new hegemonic posture that can perhaps be compared with that of the state. Unlike the first phase where consent was being used by SPS as a strategy for contest and overturning power relationships, as a counter-hegemonic power, was SPS on a path to fostering its own fragile hegemony as a force for the good?

Consenting to Struggle

When I visited Bagli, it had been five years since the dramatic events of 1995 but memories of what had passed were still fresh. Oral histories of the dramatic land records camp that I obtained from members of SPS were tinged with pride at the historic nature of what they had achieved. For the first time in the district, and perhaps in tribal areas more generally, an NGO had compelled the district administration to organize a 'land records camp'. The administration had been faced with a request that had been impossible to turn down, given that not responding would have drawn even more attention to the flagrant violation of state responsibility towards marginalized tribals. The holding of the camps however was as important for the substantive changes it inspired as for the symbolic messages of change that it contained. For the tribal majority of Neelpura, here was concrete proof that SPS was unafraid to champion the tribal cause. The public enactment of change was vital in the creation of local support for SPS in Neelpura and also adjacent villages.

Soon after this episode, SPS tried to extend its range of activities beyond Neelpura by deepening the village water tank in Meghapalli. Its sarpanch protested bitterly, for he was at one with other sarpanches in ghaat-neeche whose pride and material advantages had been seriously hurt through SPS's pursuit of minimum wages. But SPS continued on the grounds that it had received popular mandate for this work from the remaining panches and residents. It had meticulously collected letters of support signed by its supporters, and in these written documents lay the enduring proof of consent for change, inviolable through later denial. SPS greatly emphasised these letters, for these were stored carefully and shown to me when I enquired. This was perhaps the first time that the NGO was using written letters of consent to take on vested interests, but it would not be the last. Meghapalli's sarpanch, Sawant Patel was a powerful man who reacted by organising 30 other sarpanches and took the help of the local Congress MLA to lodge a complaint against SPS. The public ratification that followed from the Zilla Panchayat that headed the enquiry committee, was the second major boost to SPS's local image and critical for containing panchayat opposition. It was no longer possible to publicly allege that SPS was 'corrupt' or interested in 'bypassing panchayats'.

It was in its stewardship of local resistance against the inequitable use of the only water common body in the village that these performative and textual aspects of its strategies became most clearly evident. The episode that will be described shortly also reaffirmed SPS's commitment to using existing legal and policy spaces for campaigning for change, thus making it extremely difficult for state officials to question its interpretations. In effect, the role that it played constituted an act of political entrepreneurship to facilitate the material and symbolic overturning of local power relations within the legitimate project framework. While conducting watershed works in Neelpura, SPS discovered that the use of the village 'naala' had been improperly appropriated by a small group of upstream farmers, Mahbub Khan in particular, who drew waters continuously through 'naardas' (underground channels) and, daringly, even from the surface through the use of electric pump sets and diesel engines. With several farmers siphoning off waters upstream, downstream farmers had little access to running water or recharge for their wells. Village livestock were terribly affected since the naala ran dry after the rainy season.

Watershed works included treatment of the naala's catchment, but SPS realized that any likely benefits would be easily appropriated by a rich, upstream minority under the existing arrangement. It resolved not to act on project works until this arrangement had been overturned. It is clear that SPS was attempting to intervene in a highly contentious area, which other project agencies may have disregarded, but one which had actually been specified within its role as PIA. The national guidelines emphasized common property resources, but as we have seen in other projects, these are typically neglected. SPS interpreted the powers accorded to it as project PIA to the fullest, and went on to mobilize popular opinion in the village to formulate a collective agreement to regulate the use of naala waters. One hundred and thirty nine farmers from Neelpura and some adjacent villages signed a written resolution, which in translation from Hindi reads as follows:

> It is decided by consent ('sarvasammati') that nobody would ever draw water from the naala using a naarda. Those farmers who have wells will also not draw water from the naala using motors. Those farmers

who do not have wells have agreed to draw water from the naala on a limited basis according to rules. After the water in the naala stops flowing, nobody would draw water from it, irrespective of whether they have wells or not. This water would be kept for cattle only. *All villagers* agree to this resolution (italics added).

Mahbub Khan protested vehemently, but under the weight of collective consent and the NGO's vigilant stand, had to block the underground channels with cement along with the other farmers. Those who had water in their wells or lands on which wells could be dug had to remove motors from the naala. SPS even constructed additional wells wherever necessary, free of any contributions from the farmer. The naala agreement was a matter of tremendous pride for SPS, and it mediated this to the last detail. In the initial days after the agreement, enthused villagers set up a system of rotation to watch the naala against possible violators at night. SPS claims that the agreement benefited everyone although those with lands upstream were at a greater advantage than the rest.

Khan protested violently, even taking SPS to court claiming that he had 'easementary right' to the village naala under the Indian Easements Act of 1882. SPS was well-placed to undertake research into the legal history of the naala, and was soon able to trounce Mahbub's claims. While the Act allows a single user or group of users exclusive or predominant use over a village resource, on the basis of 'long use or prescription' where this use has been peaceable, open and uninterrupted for at least 30 years, as an easement and over a resource that is not owned by anyone in particular, The naala was actually owned by the government, which in 1993 had issued an order prohibiting villagers to refrain from its use, and Mahbub himself had claimed right of use for the last 17 years only. SPS demonstrated this to the court and Mahbub was reprimanded for coming to court with 'unclean hands' and his appeal for 'easementary right' was struck down. This had the effect of upholding the naala agreement and effectively altering the local field of power.

This agreement had several material consequences too. As a result of better availability of water most farmers in the village were able to grow and sell many new varieties of crops. SPS's well-digging activities even before the start of the watershed project had ensured that nearly each landholder in Neelpura had a new well or a deepened old well. Most landholders were therefore able to benefit from the increased retention of groundwater as a result of watershed development. This was reflected most clearly in two respects. The first was changing land use to reflect more diverse cultivation around the year. This was evident in the extension of cultivation from the rainfed kharif season to the largely irrigated rabi season, as demonstrated through Table 4. An increase in cropping intensity through the rise of double and multi-cropping, as demonstrated through Table 5, was also an important aspect of changing land use, especially since it marked the swing away from food crops to non-food crops like cotton or soybean, which are easily marketed, and within food

Table 4. Principal changes in land use, Neelpura.

	1992–93 Hectares	%	1996–97 Hectares	%	1999–000 Hectares	%
Kharif						
Unirrigated	434.38	100	446.16	98	441.45	97
Irrigated	0	0	7.84	2	12.5	3
Total	434.38	100	454	100	453.95	100
Rabi						
Unirrigated	0	0	8.14	14	13.7	18
Irrigated	30.64	100	51.32	86	62.4	82
Total	30.64	100	59.64	100	76.1	100
Gross cropped area	465.02		513.64		530.05	

Source: Project records, *Samaj Pragati Sahyog*[14].

Table 5. Land area devoted to food and non-food crops, Neelpura.

Food crops			Non-food crops		
	1992–93 Hectares	1999–2000 Hectares		1992–93 Hectares	1999–2000 Hectares
Jowar	213.91	195.03	Soybean Unirrigated	26.56	219.91
Maize	6.15	225.32	cotton Irrigated	164.48	0
Paddy	5.98	4.05	cotton	0	52.82
Tuar	3	3.7			
Other pulses	13.30	0			
Wheat	26.05	56.1			
Gram	4.60	18.9			

Source: Project records, *Samaj Pragati Sahyog.*
(Note: Figures for jowar, maize and soybean are aggregate figures for each crop. They include common areas of intercropping. For instance, 225.32 hectares of land area devoted to maize in 1999–2000 refers to the total land devoted to the maize-soybean intercrop, part of which is 'double counted' in the total land area of 219.91 hectares on which soybean is raised. The purpose of this table however is to portray the changing significance of respective individual crops.)

crops, the move from coarser, yet hardier cereals like jowar to wheat and rice. The second was a reduction in outward migration to the fertile plateau region during the summer on account of the rapid increase in on-site employment (watershed project related constructions works in particular) during the lean summer months.[13] They had previously resorted to arduous migration to the Malwa plateau as the income available from collecting tendu leaves from the neighbouring forest and work on the lands of their non-tribal neighbours ahead of the rabi season had not been adequate. Villagers unequivocally credited SPS for this welcome outcome.

These unprecedented events created ample opportunities for the NGO to be seen to be doing the right thing underpinned by popular mandate. Those in opposition could only seethe privately for the 'luxury of direct confrontation' against SPS was one that they could no longer afford (Scott 1990), although there were some isolated incidents where particular sarpanches threatened members of SPS. After a few such incidents, SPS organized a non-violent 'dharna' or 'sit-in' at the entrance to Neelpura, protesting against the hostility shown by these sarpanches. The very public manner of its protest was no coincidence and was intended to convey to wider audiences (beyond the villagers of Neelpura) that its opponents were obstructing an agency that had nothing but popular interest at heart. Villagers from Neelpura, sufficiently buoyed by the naala episode publicly expressed their solidarity with SPS. The dharna had the desired effect for in a matter of days it had earned the attention of several Zilla and Janpad panchayat members, who came to Neelpura to appease senior members. A month later, in November 1995, the gram sabha of the Bhimpura-Neelpura passed this resolution at a meeting.

The previous chapter has described the profound effects generated by this act, for tribal panches from the village tried to follow the same methods of written resolutions and public confrontations which had become associated with SPS. These methods were essentially about mobilising popular opinion to consent to struggle and change, and for these SPS deserved the fullest appreciation. Parallels may be drawn between SPS's stewardship that led to the establishment for equitable water rights in the Neelpura watershed, and the initiatives undertaken by Anna Hazare in Ralegaon Siddhi and Vilasrao Salunke in Naigaon through the Pani Panchayat. Interestingly, SPS itself did not wish to pursue such a comparison beyond a point. A senior member unequivocally maintained that that have never been interested in creating a 'model' village and that Neelpura presented a very different situation from the much-hyped Ralegaon. In Neelpura there was no comparable discourse of socio-moral transformation along the lines of an 'ideal community' that Sangameswaram (2008) for instance has described in relation to Hivre Bazar. Quite on the contrary, SPS had eschewed community consensus for its own sake, articulating a sharply political discourse around leadership instead.

It is clear that SPS greatly relied on this outpouring of local people consenting to struggle to project itself as a progressive agency for change. Despite the increased prominence of NGOs in development, there is no legal, political or indeed popular consensus to their power. SPS knew only too well that its own power had to be exclusionary, and especially in its years, it courted public and written endorsements to fights off challenges and secure its position. Despite its antagonistic relationship with local revenue bureaucrats, it also elicited state support especially from senior officials at key junctures. It never contradicted the idea of the state, drawing upon more than just its project resources, but its laws and guarantees of rights to press forward its agenda for change.

The 'Rule' of Consent

In the years since my visit to Bagli, SPS has scaled up its work to an extent that it is hardly the same small NGO that I had observed. I have not been able to return to Bagli since, but through occasional correspondence with its members I learnt that it now implements a range of development projects in over 40 villages spread over three tehsils in Dewas and also adjoining Khargone district with further plans for expansion. Indeed, over the last two decades, it has 'grown to be one of India's largest grassroots initiatives for water and livelihood security'.[15] It no longer functions from its modest offices in Bagli and has relocated to a large and impressive office building. It also employs more than 100 staff members. The main focus of its projects continues to be related to watershed development and drought proofing and funding agencies include the state and central governments, CAPART and other donors. It has also developed an 'Agricultural Programme' spread over 45 villages and an initiative for micro-finance through women's self-help groups is rapidly growing.

SPS keenly projects itself as a people's organization and does not want to be seen as a replica of the district administration. A senior member stated unequivocally to me, 'NGOs cannot replace the state'. It has increasingly sought a discourse of complementarity with government, of partnership at a variety of levels, and not just at the district. SPS has been playing a key role in advising policy reform at the national level, and played a prominent part in the 2005 Technical Committee constituted by the MORD to review all WSD programmes in the country. The intensity of collaboration with the state at a number of different levels has accorded to it an enviable manoeuvring position. It is not surprising that it has received abundant support from the state government for its panchayat training initiatives and forging of horizontal solidarities amongst other grassroots organizations like itself at the Baba Amte Centre.

While its relationship with the state has become cosier, this has not necessarily stopped SPS from continuing to resist state oppression and expressing solidarity with the politics of resistance in the ghaat-neeche. Bagli tehsil, with its forested areas, has long been the site of exploitation of the tribal population by the Forest Department and, more recently, their collective mobilization against it through organizations called the 'Adivasi Morcha Sangathan' and 'Adivasi Shakti Sangathan'. In March 2001, the Dewas district administration authorized police firings upon unarmed tribals in several villages in Bagli to ostensibly evict them from 'illegally' occupied land. The act was widely condemned in local and regional media. A volunteer based solidarity network 'Friends of the River Narmada' expressed the view that this state 'attack' was actually aimed at countering the rising political influence of the tribal sangathans. SPS played an active part in investigating the firings, compiling a detailed report of the atrocities and supporting many tribal families that had been affected. Its actions served a pragmatic purpose as well. SPS enjoys widespread support amongst tribals in ghaat-neeche and it would have been crucial to publicly express solidarity or risk damaging the key source of its legitimacy in the region.

It would appear that from being an outsider to the balance of power in the ghaat-neeche, SPS has gradually become the defendant of a formidable new status quo. This strong claim to a legitimate mandate is not surprising. It follows closely from the NGO's iteration of positive ideas of the state, as a guarantor of rights and, subsequently, as a doer of development. While SPS may have resisted state structures, or actors or processes, it never discredited the idea of the state as such and has painstakingly moulded both its organizational practice and its discourse to complement this state idea. This has made it all the more difficult for local stakeholders to oppose SPS, which stands tall in its demonstrated conviction in all the 'good things' that development might embody.

SPS straddles both popular as well as official support, and this potent blend constitutes a unique source of strength. Its continued presence through its many activities sends out the message to the people of ghaat-neeche that it is here to stay, and this has no doubt impacted upon local consciousness and the formation of allegiances. SPS itself has been aware of these dimensions since an early stage of its formation. Speaking of the difficulties of combing activism with 'serious development work', one senior member said, 'You cannot afford to take an extreme view on anything, yet you want to raise issues. You cannot afford to alienate anyone, yet alliances are inevitable because issues provoke realignments and exaggerate existing differences'. The last chapter documented the presence of a group of discontented persons even within

Neelpura village who have had to learn to live with their discontent. SPS is no stranger to opposition, but just as the nature of the opposition it receives has changed, so has its approach to tackling such resistance. In its early years here, it responded by staging dramatic public struggles where it could visibly demonstrate the support it received from wider sections of the population. This sort of public staging has been much less necessary in its later years, as the organization feels confident enough of the support it enjoys in the ghaat-neeche area in order to make fairly sturdy claims on its basis. A brief example will illustrate.

In 2000, a senior member justified the SPS decision to keep out Kartar Singh Nag, the discredited sarpanch from Bhimpura, from a panchayat conference at the Baba Amte Centre on the following grounds: 'How do you invite a person who is completely negative to you, making false allegations? *Also, I am not an individual. I represent a lot of people who have a certain feeling about this man'* (italics added for emphasis). He mused that while he had 'respect' for opposition from individuals like Majid Khan, for it embodied a 'class interest', Nag's opposition was 'baseless', it 'represented a physical threat' and 'he should be tackled'. Another member said, 'We are sending out a public message that we only wanted to initiate a dialogue with those who were positive. This one is totally negative....on the one hand, we have to let him know that he cannot have it his way, and on the other, we can extend an arm of friendship. But if we let up on the pressure, then he will think we are going down on our knees, which is ruinous'. The first member added that the local BJP leaders were also fed up with Nag. Even the local Congress MLA, I was told, who had resisted the NGO ferociously in 1995 came to 'beg forgiveness' and asked to be 'included in their work'. Given SPS's record of continuing to use consent as a progressive force for struggle and resistance, it will be incorrect to conclude otherwise purely on the basis of its growing position of strength in ghaat-neeche. Nevertheless the difficulty of opposing SPS and its immense ability to marginalize what it regards as 'negative opposition' begs the question of whether this may in the future restrict space for challenge and resistance to its own agency. I have no further evidence to answer it myself as I have not been able to return to Bagli since for further fieldwork; but when consent identified with the 'general interest' is no longer used by an agency to resist status quo, but to defend it, then could there be a reason to be critical of it?

Conclusion

Much like the idea of apolitical local bodies, the notion of apolitical consent acts as a powerful discursive resource for the practitioners of participatory watershed development, but this chapter has shown that the dialectics of consent are rich and varied. The chapter has shown that the theoretical underpinnings of consent are unmistakably political, and the problems they pose for participation are political too. Whether the issue is of individuals consenting to a particular intervention or of an agency claiming general consent to intervene or act on their behalf, consent is cardinally linked both to representation and to hegemony and thus strikes at the heart of politics. Its use as a discursive resource to signify the lack of politics in participatory development reiterates the dominance of new institutionalist and communitarian theories that do not critically interrogate the underlying politics of consent creation or articulation. The history of WSD in India moreover suggests that consent (as the cornerstone of cooperation) has been abundantly internalized as a cherished ideal, one that is ennobling for its role in uniting persons for a higher purpose, overcoming their divisions and differences. Consent is regularly contrasted with contest and conflict, but only to establish what is not political.

The trouble with this approach however, as my research shows, is that the tools of depoliticization create easy dichotomies that simply fail to capture the complexities of social interaction. The case studies demonstrate that consent was not simply the absence of conflict. Four further lessons can be drawn from Part I. First, the articulation of consent was reflective of the nature of power and domination in the village, the character of its leadership and the imperatives of agency representation to superiors in the political and bureaucratic hierarchy. In Lilapuram, traditionally dominant Reddy leaders were keen to remain 'in charge' of the project. They manipulated the recording of consent on paper so as not to compromise their usual ways of working and did not promote any substantive participatory activities either. In Malligundu however, the Boya leader Naidu did not feel threatened by the project's approach as his interests were mainly material and as long as these were assured he did not interfere in the project's participatory procedures. In both these villages moreover, the extent and nature of their socio-economic stratification mattered a great deal. The presence of a poor majority in Malligundu created conditions that were more conducive to popular mobilization and involvement than the sharply stratified society of Lilapuram. While project staff were able to interact directly with a large number of persons in Malligundu through the formation of different groups, this was not possible in Lilapuram where their interaction was mediated through a few dominant persons. Constrained by their temporary jobs, project officials were either compliant with or at least indifferent to the rituals on paper so willingly enacted by the elites in Lilapuram. In this context of upward representations, the more robust experience of generating consent for the project in Malligundu is testimony to the variety of outcomes possible even within KWO's doggedly technocratic approach.

Second, the dialectics of consent were not restricted to the arena of the big public meeting alone. Much of the critical appraisal of participatory practice has taken place in relation to the dynamics of performance and exclusion that characterize public meetings. There is the typical project requirement that individuals articulate their consent or dissent in the presence of others presuming an equality that does not exist. But in fact public meetings were not held very often in any of the villages except Neelpura (where also the conditions were somewhat different from a typical project-initiated public meeting), at least not after the initial ones. Smaller 'publics' on the other hand were created in the course of everyday interactions between unequal parties, as for example, a Reddy landholder and his BC wage labourer. The latter would find it impossible to speak his mind or deny the consent being 'sought' on the veranda of Reddy farmer's house as much as in a larger gathering. The public transcript, following Scott (1990), thus depended not so much on the venue of the theatre as it did on the audience. Hidden transcripts were harder to access, but I got some glimpse into these, as for instance through the frank revelations of WDT officials in private conversations.

Besides, project officials and village elites were guided by various other considerations in documenting consent as evidence of participation. Both in Kurnool and Dewas, government project officials were guided by astute considerations of cost and consent in relation to constructing different types of watershed structures. Big structures that cost more money to build and appeared to be impressive were more popular with farmers (especially larger farmers) than simpler, low-cost constructions. Also, common resources were typically disregarded because they did not matter much to richer sections. As a result, watershed project sectors like minor irrigation were typically more 'successful' from the point of view of project expenditure than others like afforestation. Conversely however, when sectors like afforestation did better, or when the project was able to persuade many more farmers to raise earthen bunds on their lands, then it was usually a sign that project staff had worked harder to earn the trust of village residents, and not disregarded the cares of the poorest. A careful examination of the trajectories of target completion in the two Kurnool villages revealed important differences in this respect

Third, even when consent was not being explicitly sought from farmers and documented on paper, it remained an integral aspect of project-people relationships. The Kishangarh case reiterates why consent, whether given or denied, needs to be viewed holistically in relation to power and is irreducible to an apolitical act. Kishangarh's rich, landed majority could not be persuaded to support the project, despite benefiting from it, and few structures were raised on their private lands. While this may have created serious problems for project officials in Kurnool, given the need to document consent and the simultaneous restrictions on inter-sectoral transfers, it was expedient for staff in Dewas. Here the imperatives of representations were different, and geared towards documenting big, visible icons of watershed success. There was no attempt at a wider consultation with the poorer farmers in the village either.

Fourth, the material basis of consent was clearly as important in underscoring popular enthusiasm (extending beyond village elites) for the project as its procedures for participatory decision-making. The case studies also revealed that projects that paid attention to substantiating consent were more inclusive even in the sharing of project benefits than those where consent was manipulated. The skewed nature of watershed development means that much more needs to be done by project agencies if those without large plots of land and private wells are also to partake of visible improvements. This was not the case in Lilapuram where the dynamics of exclusion were blatant with respect to all major project benefits, ranging from cropping to employment and migration. In Malligundu however, project agencies tried harder to customize project intervention to the needs of small, poor farmers, who could plant new crops, stop migrating and procure more fuel and fodder from village commons. In Kishangarh, the project received the least support from the landed majority, but served their interests the most while thoroughly disregarding the needs of the poor minority. In Neelpura, the concerted actions of the project agency, SPS, to overturn inequitable power relationships in favour of the poor, tribal majority earned it (and the project) a deep loyalty on the part of the village.

Part two of the chapter focused attention on an agency that legitimated its actions and presence by claiming the general consent of the people it sought to represent. Moreover, the imperatives for an NGO like SPS to actually substantiate popular consent, unlike state agencies, stemmed from the absence of any constitutional, legal or indeed political consensus on NGO power and the roles they may assume. The Neelpura case showed how SPS relied repeatedly on the idea of popular will or general consent to legitimize struggle, confrontation and change. In doing so, its use of consent went far beyond the documentation of participation alone, and was stridently political in that SPS was mobilizing consent in order to spearhead radical contests against power holders in the ghaat-neeche region. It repeatedly sought collective consent in the form of written resolutions from the people of Neelpura or other villages where it worked, always with a clear collective objective at stake. It used the language of power-struggle explicitly and was counter-hegemonic in purpose, seeking to expose the deceitful and exploitative practices perpetuated by state officials and local actors (like sarpanches) vested with state authority. Its use of consent to galvanize contest with actual consequences, symbolic as well as material, economic as also political, could not have been more different from the manipulation of consent on paper as a subterfuge for contrary realities in Kurnool. The public enactment, both of its attempts to mobilize consent (the naala resolution) as well as to claim it (its righteous dharna when it was harassed by angry sarpanches) revealed the extent to which its own fortunes in the valley were tied up with its interventions preceding and accompanying the watershed project.

SPS's growing position of strength in the ghaat-neeche raises age old questions about hegemony through the universalization of particular interests as general. It straddles popular support with official state support. Its strategy of never distancing itself from the idea of the state, while challenging its actors and practices, has accorded to it an enviable manoeuvring capacity. Riding on this strength, SPS has stood firm in its solidarity with tribal causes, opposing the state in unambiguous terms even on extremely contentious issues like forest rights. However, it is now a power holder in its own right, and by its own admission, opponents are either coming into its fold or can be relatively easily isolated. It is secure in its claim as *the* legitimate agency of the people, representing their general interest, but with less of a need to explain or justify its own stance or the new politics of the region it has been instrumental in creating. Whether the dialectics of consent underpinning SPS are hegemonic or counter-hegemonic in the future remains to seen, but clearly, they will be no more apolitical than the shifting balance of power in ghaat-neeche.

CONCLUSION

For the radical activists and critical scholars who encounter and observe the juggernaut of the development machine, anti-politics is a quotidian reality. States, international development agencies, NGOs and donors are, to varying degrees, accomplices in the vehement and unrelenting tendency to treat politics in the widest sense with disdain or disquiet, or both, and the desire to 'depoliticize' development is as strong as ever. This book is not trying to prove otherwise. Indeed, it is in large measure an attempt to document the making and unfolding of a definite discourse of depoliticization through the premier state-led and nationally implemented participatory watershed development programme in India. This is a country with an unequivocal history of anti-politics, since colonial times, through technocratic development planning embedded within a large state bureaucracy. Being a vibrant and dynamic democracy with a highly differentiated social fabric, India puts James Ferguson's views about development as an anti-politics machine to the test in very unique ways. While there is no doubt that there is an anti-politics machine in India, its outcomes are different from those Ferguson predicted for Lesotho. Studying the particular contours of the anti-politics machine in India is the principal business of this book, and in doing so, the book develops a distinctive approach to examining the problem of depoliticization in general. The book concludes not just that India presents a different context for the anti-politics critique of development that Ferguson levelled at Lesotho, but also that there is a need to go considerably beyond what Ferguson proposed.

Critics studying Ferguson have already injected a healthy uncertainty into the prospect of depoliticization, arguing that it is a *project* that needs to be achieved, and not an inevitable outcome (Li 2007, Mosse 2004, and Tordella 2003 among others). This is driven principally by dissatisfaction with a certain crudity in analysis. How can we be sure that all actors are evenly implicated in the alleged pursuit to depoliticize? A more nuanced understanding of how and why actors sign up to particular interpretations of discourses has become more common amongst development anthropologists (through the actor-oriented and actor-network approaches) as well as political scientists (such as through critical studies of hegemony). Ferguson has been criticized for his treatment of governmentality as an isolated rock of 'bureaucratic proliferation', where development as an apolitical and technical Endeavour allows the state to plainly 'control' social processes; Agrawal writes, '......although it is fair to suggest that development discourses colonize subjects, surely they do not colonize all subjects' (2005, 225). Similarly, it is not acceptable to treat hegemony as a finished, determinate monolithic formation, but a messy and contested process made of co-option and compromise as much as resistance and struggle (Chatterjee 1998, Scott 1985, Roseberry 1994). It has also been emphasized that Gramsci, more than his interpreters, 'well understood the fragility of hegemony' (Roseberry 1994, 358).

In this same tradition, the book treats power and potency of a discourse, depoliticization in this case, with uncertainty. It considers the realization of the discourse as a project to be fulfilled. My enquiry is about empirically delineating the conditions and constraints within which particular actors and agencies pursue the depoliticization project or desist from doing so. It is also about understanding the outcomes of such engagements, both for the actors and agencies themselves, as also for the wider communities within which such projects are situated. While this echoes a well established approach in critical development studies, the book offers an innovative treatment of the anti-politics machine through two principal arguments. First, there is a need to pay attention to the particular meanings or characterizations of politics that are in use by the constituents of the so-called anti-politics machine, if we are to understand how exactly the depoliticization discourse relies on the representation of particular processes. Second, decentralization as a contemporary development policy has profound implications for the pursuit of depoliticization as a state project, as it is a political process that redistributes state power and reorganizes state-society relationships. The first argument could be seen as further critical engagement with the content of the discourse of depoliticization itself, while the second is more directly to do with its practice.

The Significance of Politics within the Anti-Politics Machine

The anti-politics thrust of development has engaged critics of influential development discourses and practices; but this has been principally through an exposition of how experts have tried to construct an intelligible field, i.e., the economy, which is appropriate for development intervention through the application of technical expertise. Li goes beyond this by sharply maintaining that issues that are rendered technical are 'simultaneously rendered non-political' (2007, 7). I have been interested in going further, in actually understanding which meanings of politics are called upon in this rendering. For Li, who studies projects of improvement, politics as critical and contentious is counter-posed to government that tries to order and contain, and that is a sufficient characterization for such purpose. In this case however, the critical eye is turned to all those who are engaged in governing the watershed development programme, and to the particular meanings of politics that predominate in their contexts and the reasons for these. By way of a metaphor, this is akin to lifting the cloak over depoliticization.

While the larger context of the distancing of development from politics is shaped by the ascendancy of neoliberal economics, a further engagement with the precise meanings of politics is instructive, especially if we are to understand why exactly it has been easy to project politics as unhelpful for development. The theoretical enquiry in Chapter 1 drew on the work of political philosopher John Dunn who finds four answers to the question of why politics exists. It showed that the anti-politics idea predominantly projects politics as the sphere in which undesirable human behaviour is observed, and equates it with conflict, while disregarding that conflict is the essential counterpoint to co-operation in the making of politics. All this is contrasted with the 'reasonable' and 'rational' economic behaviour of human beings that is viewed as necessary for development. In the specific context of India as discussed in Chapter 2, right after independence anti-politics was not about excising a peculiar 'high' politics or politics as a 'virtuous vocation' that emerged through the nationalist movement, but much more the 'unbearable profanity' of low politics 'performed by lesser men' (Hansen 1999, 58). With the expansion and deepening of democracy, these distinctions have clearly collapsed and a discourse of politics as a repugnant activity occupies a central place in public imagination both in elite as well as subaltern discourses.

The Indian state represents a peculiar anti-politics machine. On the one hand, it is blatantly clear that dominant politics of various types has continued to strongly steer the working of the Indian state both through electoral competition and extra-electoral relationships of patronage. This means that any discourse that development is apolitical is not particularly credible. On the other hand, discourses of depoliticization remain attractive as ever for development practitioners because politics, reduced to the 'dismal' business of electoral competition and vested interest-seeking, is perceived in very pejorative terms. At the same time, the presence of seemingly inexorable democratic processes means that even though negative discourses around politics predominate and create conducive conditions for the anti-politics machine, these are not universal. Within resistance movements and popular mobilizations, the concern has been to broaden and deepen political engagement beyond that provided by the current state of electoral competition. The anti-politics machine cannot 'do away' with politics because politics is all-encompassing. It is worth repeating the words of John Dunn that were cited in the introduction: 'there is never no political dimension, and the political dimension is never trivial'. Depoliticization therefore is about the selective uses of particular meanings of politics with significant implications and consequences for development.

In Chapter 3, the book considers the makings of a watershed machine that bears a unique anti-politics orientation. The shift from top-down and technocratic soil and water conservation to a bottom-up, decentralized and participatory rural livelihoods programme was symbolic of the wider transformations being attempted by the Indian state, especially with respect to the involvement of ordinary people in decision-making. Yet, the paradox of 'participation but not politics' that sums up the attempt to depoliticize watershed development is clearly conveyed through the main policy guidelines devised in 1994, with subsequent iterations in 2001, 2003 and 2008. The core elements of anti-politics here are contained in the conceptualization of a village community in India, upon which the guidelines build their entire discourse of participation, the possibility of equity and the role of local institutions. They reveal an exaggerated emphasis on co-operation and public consensus and remain resolutely silent on the implications of structural inequalities, and the micro-politics of village level organization.

While idyllic and ahistorical conceptualizations of community have been criticized abundantly in the literature on CBNRM, this book offers two further points of critique, both of which reveal particular meanings that are ascribed to politics. The first is the stark contrast drawn between non-elected and community-based watershed committees with elected panchayats. Here politics refers to the factionalism, violence and open contest that typically characterize panchayats, and watershed committees are regarded to be non-political by virtue of being distinctive from the former. The second is the use of consent as an apolitical proxy for participation, given the emphasis on both individual and collective forms of consent to denote full-bodied community involvement. Here dissent, or 'worse', conflict is viewed as the politics from which the programme is distanced. Both these modes of depoliticization also implicate the relationship between decentralized project agencies (either government or NGOs) and local communities, which are held as neutral transactions devoid of power and representation. So it is only by attributing particular meanings to politics, and through a posture of distancing from these meanings, does the anti-politics machine come into existence. These meanings, as my empirical research shows, are at best 'discursive resources' available to the implementers of a programme like watershed development, and their very presence does not predetermine any particular set of outcomes. It is here that decentralization as a political process that is embedded within distinctive contexts of social differentiation and politico-bureaucratic power makes a massive difference to the pursuit of depoliticization as a project.

Decentralization and Depoliticization

According to Ferguson, the anti-politics machine entrenches bureaucratic state power; but it is possible to obtain a more finely grained view of this relationship with the question: how are decentralized actors enrolled into larger projects of depoliticization and do they necessarily participate in such projects? My research into the practices of decentralization suggests a complex, even contradictory, use of state power in the course of implementing watershed development. This stems from relationships internal to the official state machinery, but equally from those established with other project agencies like NGOs, and with local elites in course of executing a 'participatory' programme. Mainstream theories of decentralization gloss over these dimensions by focusing on its potential to reduce the state in favour of heightened community or private sector involvement. As reviewed at some length in the introduction, these theories have been severely criticized for their disengagement with the nature of what actually goes on within a state when decentralization unfolds.

The history of decentralization in India further establishes that decentralization has been shaped by the constraints of the central state, as well as by regional configurations of state power. Besides, the Indian state is not a 'homogenous bloc', but a complex and extremely differentiated organization that is continuously 'buffeted by contending social forces' (Corbridge et al 2005, 36). In such a context, far from diminishing the state in any sense at all, decentralization has produced its spectacular disaggregation, through the proliferation of actors and agencies, as well as institutional forums and meanings. Yet, while there is disaggregation, there is unification too as a variety of processes seek to define and sustain all the state stands for. As the SPS case shows, decentralization produces an ongoing imperative for NGOs to engage not simply with state actors and practices, but also with the 'idea' of the state to press for support in overturning unjust coalitions of power as well as consolidating their own position as doers of development in partnership with the state.

The body of the book draws on nested comparisons between two contexts of decentralization, Andhra Pradesh and Madhya Pradesh, in the 1990s and early 2000s. The cases establish that the wider context of decentralization in the state made a critical difference to the depoliticization of watershed development partly because the same institutions and actors were implicated within multiple roles, but more importantly because the key discursive resources for depoliticization were not similarly utilized. In other words, the meanings attributed to politics within the national watershed guidelines were not equally congruous within these environments of decentralization, and this impacted upon the depoliticization project. Decentralization brought new imperatives to bear upon major actors and institutions: the high level political leadership, elected political representatives, regional non-elected bureaucracy and NGOs, in both these states. In Andhra Pradesh, the apathetic state of elected panchayats combined with a strong thrust on bureaucratic management of popular mobilization through various state-led initiatives. This larger environment shaped the bureaucratic arrangements for the watershed programme, and the presence of a single district level administrative authority that was able to concentrate exclusively on watershed development reflected the technocratic discourse around development that was keenly promoted by Chief Minister Naidu. In Madhya Pradesh, the political move to decentralize development administration and integrate it with elected representatives from the Zilla Panchayat ensured that similar bureaucratic antipathy to panchayats (especially at the more senior levels of government) was not really possible. District level programme arrangements were also not as tightly organized in comparison, with responsibilities diffused between an already overburdened Collectorate and the Zilla Panchayat, and this further diluted any attempt at technocratic monitoring.

The watershed programme encountered specific political pressures arising from the regional dimensions of dominance in the two states, but their responses varied according to their distinctive approaches to decentralization. Chapter 4 detailed the nature of politics and power in these two states: Andhra Pradesh with its polarized competition between the Reddy and Kamma caste groups, strident OBC ascendancy and dalit mobilization, and Madhya Pradesh with dominant Brahmin and Rajput castes, relatively dispersed BCs and SCs and severe tribal marginalization. It described the specific regional manifestations of politics in the study districts: Kurnool in Andhra Pradesh's western Rayalseema region where caste-based alliances and factional networks have penetrated deep into society, and bitter tensions, conflict and violence between factions have persisted both at local and higher levels, and Dewas with its economically and politically dominant ghaat-upar parts of the Malwa plateau and the commensurately marginalized ghaat-neeche of the Narmada valley with tribal concentrations.

Watershed machineries in both districts received pressures from influential politicians for favouring their electoral constituencies, but their responses to 'depoliticize' the programme through recourse to 'technical' selection criteria were different. The technocratic tone of the response was fairly unambiguous in Kurnool, where the PD was acutely aware of political lobbying and categorically maintained that 'not even a square inch' of land could be claimed for watershed development on grounds of 'political' pressures. As there was no overarching political move to involve panchayats in the watershed programme, it was realistic for the bureaucrat to adopt such a tough stance. In Dewas, the larger political environment was inimical to a similar discourse of depoliticized selection with very interesting outcomes, and embodied in the selection histories of the two villages I studied were entirely different political processes. Kishangarh's selection underscored dominant caste politics, but the fact that Neelpura, a poor tribal village in the economic backwaters of Dewas, was chosen in the same year, under the leadership of a non-conformist NGO, meant that the same dominant politics could also be challenged under the aegis of a state programme. Moreover, the four sets of interactions between decentralized project agencies and local communities complicated any easy conclusions regarding the guidelines' depoliticized emphasis on local institutions and local consent.

Local Institutions and Agencies

The attempt to create local institutions that will promote 'positive' and 'constructive' engagement of communities with development interventions (as of course the actors and agencies carrying out the intervention) is pervasive in development. In general, states, donors and NGOs, are all keen to realize agendas or goals within specific timeframes, and this makes peace and harmony at the community level valuable as development resources. It has been emphasized that such an orientation makes local institution-building a key strategy of the anti-politics machine, and there are no immediate signs that this will change. The predominance of new institutionalism wedded to a larger neoliberal framework means that the plethora of development programmes and policies being crafted in India or elsewhere in the developing world are overwhelmingly as such. For example, cyclone shelter maintenance and management committees formed in the state of Orissa after the 1999 supercyclone also bear the same institutional prescriptions for cooperation like the watershed committees observed here. What this book does is to show in considerable detail the precise outcomes achieved in the attempt to form depoliticized local institutions.

The principal empirical lesson that emerged from all four villages is that the local configurations of power that manifest themselves in older, existing institutions (panchayats) also influenced new institutional processes. For any social scientist, this is an unremarkable conclusion, but the book goes beyond this basic observation. Chapter 5 presents the very specific manifestations of local politics in each case. It shows that state resources in the form of a watershed development project hold different kinds of appeal for local elites, and the nature of their domination over newly created bodies varies accordingly. For the Reddys of Lilapuram, the symbolic as well as material resources of the watershed project were both important, and their own entrenchment within the village's hierarchical social fabric meant that they were opposed to any meaningful substantiation of participatory procedures. For Boya leader Naidu in Malligundu, material incentives were important, and his status as the predominant village head with a violent past, meant that these were ensured. However, he preferred to keep a low profile with respect to the actual business of participation, shied from visible proximity to government officials, and did not obstruct the functioning of participatory user and self-help groups. In Kishangarh, neither the symbolic nor the material resources of the watershed project interested the big landholding elites, of either caste, that perceived it more as an unnecessary distraction. This was an extension of the local apathy historically meted out towards the panchayats. In Neelpura, the entire process of initiating a village watershed committee was set in the context of a dramatic confrontation between the project agency and the local power holders, including non-tribal sarpanches, and but for SPS's active intervention, the watershed committee would have mirrored this status quo as well.

And as for even attempting to form depoliticized watershed committees by distancing these from the more 'political' panchayats, the four agencies in the case study villages acted very differently. These differences stemmed from the location of these project agencies within the internal state apparatus and their subjection to particular constraints or exposure to opportunities following the larger context of decentralization. In the Kurnool villages, where panchayats embodied the factional conflict that the KWO frowned upon, project agencies assiduously avoided any village where local elites did not manage to peacefully compromise. In the process, they ensured that the local morphology of power and politics was absorbed into the project structure. Depoliticization, even when tactically attempted, did not really succeed. In the Dewas villages no such attempt was forthcoming and principally because the district watershed authorities were not interested in rigidly enforcing participatory peace as a precondition for watershed development. In precisely such a context, SPS was able to implement the state-funded project despite initiating various confrontations with local power holders, including powerful non-tribal sarpanches. In later years, it initiated a more positive process of working with panchayats by seeking their endorsement of local collective action, thus legitimating panchayat authority in the area. It sought to promote a cadre of local leaders that would be able to re-energize panchayats. Quite clearly then, the meanings attributed to politics for the purpose of contrasting watershed committees with panchayats were not similarly sustained.

Consent and Anti-Politics

The final empirical chapter shows how a concept as deeply political as consent becomes enrolled as an active ally in the depoliticization project. The watershed guidelines conceptualize village communities as harmonious entities and obscure social differences in a tradition of depoliticized CBNRM that has been robustly criticized in the wider literature. The book takes this criticism a step further by focusing attention on the precise issue of how consent, when treated apolitically, serves to project the relationship struck between project communities and project agencies as totally neutral, and devoid of any transaction of power. All the cases showed that the expression of consent for a development project is embedded in the inevitable politics of everyday life. They also showed that how a development agency approaches the issue of consent – whether to procure, record, mobilize or claim – is quite a significant indicator of how it approaches the larger issue of depoliticizing development interventions and its own role within it.

The KWO's project strategy rested on methods specifically aimed at recording consent for its projects within a larger framework of technocratic planning. Chapter 6 detailed the various measures adopted using consent as an apolitical proxy for participation. But even as the execution of these measures required a hierarchy of project officials to assume fairly specific positions (such as of indifference to local manipulation) in order to see that consent was recorded on paper, the overall strategy was to leave its own modes of intervention unquestioned. Project officials, sometimes despite personal good intentions, were more concerned about demonstrating that consent had been procured from locals to their bosses, than about trying to secure consent of the local population. Of course, the nature of domination exercised by local elites ensured that there was a degree of difference in the extent to which participatory measures were genuinely substantiated, as shown in the discussions of Lilapuram and Malligundu. The upward as opposed to the downward nature of their concerns in turn meant seriously detrimental effects for the poor, especially in Lilapuram. Project agencies in Dewas were not pressured to record consent in the same way, but there were other imperatives that came into play. Powerful landed elites in Kishangarh were disinterested in watershed development, and did not consent to the project's measures, which in effect restricted the scope of what the project could do for the poorer sections of the village. Even though consent was not specifically sought, its refusal by those whose voices mattered had significant implications for the project.

In the case of SPS, consent was actively sought to achieve radical action in the face of resistance from older power holders, and this was cast in an explicitly political language of mobilization and struggle. Here consent was not treated apolitically, and quite unlike KWO, SPS was not interested in projecting its intervention or role as neutral. This was in keeping with its general approach to development, where signing up to the state script of bureaucratically prescribed participation was simply not acceptable. There were other lessons to be learnt regarding the role of consent to legitimize or mandate the role performed by a development agency like SPS. As it moved from a more confrontationist part of its life course in the region to one of partnership with the state, SPS also claimed wider consent to substantiate its claim that it embodied the general interest of the tribal population. The marginalization of opposition and the rallying of ex-opponents to win its favour were both sweet and hard earned rewards, but signified a clear change in the local balance of power in no uncertain terms.

Depoliticization and Progressive Politics

The question may be rightfully asked if depoliticization can ever be a progressive strategy with outcomes that favour the poorest groups. The approach taken in this book suggests that the discourse of depoliticization necessarily relies on characterizing particular phenomena or processes as political, but the practice of depoliticization confirms that steering clear of such politics is never truly possible. In Kurnool, the best efforts of the district watershed office to keep their projects free of factionalism and panchayat politics did not actually succeed, and only ensured that the deeper politics of caste-class domination framed project approaches and their material consequences without being questioned. Even in Malligundu, the Kurnool village where the project delivered comparatively more benefits to the poor than in Lilapuram, this was possible not because depoliticization succeeded; instead, this was because the particular expression of local power implied the least interference with the actual business of participation as well as the concrete distribution of project resources.

The cases considered in this book do not lend much support to the idea that depoliticization as a strategy can actually produce progressive outcomes, as such a strategy is inevitably motivated by unwillingness (albeit circumscribed within historical conditions) to tackle contentious issues. But it is important to remember that while actors are constrained by their environments in choosing whether or not to adopt different types of anti-politics orientations, their choices may well be fashioned by expediency or plain pragmatism. These are not necessarily always related to cynical manipulations of politics. Further, the evidence presented here does not preclude progressive outcomes from arising within similar contexts, yet not directly as *a result of* the depoliticization strategy. Research by Johnson,

Deshingkar and Start (2005) in the same two states – AP and MP – usefully illustrates this point. The authors have argued that the non-involvement of panchayats and the involvement of non-elected mandal officials in AP actually helped to improve the effectiveness of a particular development programme, on account of there being plural channels of communication between poor citizens and the state. This was noticeably absent in MP, where the emphasis on panchayat-led decentralization translated into an over-reliance on sarpanches and a relatively narrowed base of accountability. These cases show that positive outcomes may be associated with the same circumstances that actually facilitated an anti-politics orientation: specifically, the distancing of panchayats in AP; and contrarily, in MP, where an over-reliance on panchayats made it harder to sustain a discourse of depoliticization, and actually reduced the spaces for progressive politics. This is comparable to the situation described in Kishangarh, where dominant caste politics entrenched within the panchayat system made it impossible for project benefits to reach the poor in the village.

While these findings are not inimical to the conclusions reached here, this book has a wider purpose. Its aim is to show that the adoption of a strategy of depoliticization depends on particular configurations of decentralization. And as the four case studies have shown, a range of further factors influence whether the pursuit or non-pursuit of depoliticization translates into either progressive or retrogressive outcomes for poor, subordinate people: Lilapuram in AP does better than Malligundu, and Neelpura in MP does much better than Kishangarh.

The Persistence of Anti-Politics?

My concern in this book has been to look further into the anti-politics machine and to unsettle the notion that projects of depoliticization are necessarily pursued. This does not mean that there is any dearth of anti-politics within the development machine. At a practical level, there is a technocratic urge not to engage with political analysis for it complicates the picture and runs counter to the pressures faced by development practitioners. In a world where development is about time-bound targets and limited resources, the search for concrete strategies for improvement and action is an impatient one. More fundamentally, the intention to depoliticize is generated because of the predominance of neoliberal economic theory over development policy, and the lack of serious attention to social difference and power. However, as with any project of depoliticization, the particular meanings or characterizations of politics become very important to consider. Neo-liberalism itself is a political project that rests on a type of politics that has more to do with authoritarian (if small) government and less to do with participatory or pluralistic politics (Munck 2005, Toye 1991). In a similar vein, calls for re-politicization also privilege a specific kind of politics, rooted in leftist social mobilization and redistributive reform (Harriss, Stokke and Tornquist 2004, Heller 2001, Hickey and Mohan 2004).[1] There has been a renewed call for 'progressive politics', which can be realized through the language and strategies of citizenship, but underpinned by a proper emphasis on political economy (Hickey 2010).

Anti-politics rests on antipathy to a particular kind of politics, which is political in itself. Quite simply put, anti-politics is merely another type of politics. But while projects to depoliticize may attempt to create segmented life-worlds of their own, 'sanitizing' these of politics, variously interpreted, they do not exist in a sanitized world and too many factors complicate the sustenance of these narratives. In India, the most profound challenges to depoliticization stem from within the state owing to its complex and heterogeneous nature, further complicated by the changes unleashed on account of the multiple initiatives accompanying decentralization. Moreover, the burden of depoliticization narratives needs to be borne not just at the top, at the realm of policy making, but at innumerable regional and local levels. The flux of actors embedded within differentiated social, economic and political configurations of power makes for the pursuit of depoliticization projects as much as for their abandonment. Finally, even when depoliticization projects 'succeed' on paper and as ritual, they ultimately fail because politics is more encompassing than even the most ardent architect of depoliticization would have us believe.

NOTES

Introduction

1 Remarks by the noted political theorist John Dunn at the 'Workshop on Citizenship and Democracy in honour of John Dunn', University of Southampton, March 7, 2008.

2 I am grateful to David Owen for his insights on this issue. Exchange at the 'Workshop on Citizenship and Democracy in honour of John Dunn', University of Southampton, March 7, 2008.

3 There have been three main attempts to decentralize planning: (i) in 1969, the Planning Commission issued 'Guidelines for the Formulation of District Plans';(ii) in 1978, the Report of the Working Group on Block Level Planning emphasized block level planning in the interest of integrating the many poverty alleviation programmes; and (iii) in 1984, the CH Hanumantha Rao Committee shifted the focus back to district level planning.

4 Here, I borrow a phrase used by the Rudolphs (1987) to describe the separation of national and regional voting patterns in the 1980s.

5 For a fuller account of the provisions of the 73rd amendment, see Baumann (1999), Isaac and Frank (2000), Lekha (1997), Rajaraman et al (1996), Shaheena (1999). For the full amendment, see Constitution of India at http://indiacode.nic.in/coiweb/welcome. html

Chapter One. The Idea of 'Anti-Politics'

1 Ferguson cites Heyer et al (1981), Williams (1976, 1986), Beckman (1977) and Bernstein (1977, 1979) among others as key works that have attempted to view the rural development establishment as a social institution in its own right, meriting separate analysis.

2 Kamat is referring here to the Charitable Trusts Act 1950 which applies to voluntary organizations.

3 See North 1990, Toye 1993, Clague 1997, Nabli and Nugent 1989, Ostrom 1990 and Bates 1995 for further discussions.

4 See Cook 1966, 1969, LeClair and Schneider 1968 and Schneider 1974 as cited in Isaac (2005).

5 The classic work, *The Making of the English Working Class* by E P Thompson (1963) is notable here for its treatment of the precapitalist community with 'traditional rights' that inform the 'moral economy of the poor' in uncritical terms.

6 This is in fact the quintessential dilemma of democracy and development (see Kaviraj 1995, 1996 and 1997 and Leftwich 1996 for masterful treatments of this debate).

7 Robertson's (1984) account of the rise of modern planning remains one of the most comprehensive to date.

8 This view of expertise is taken apart by Flyvbjerg (2001) in his provocative defence of the social sciences. Flyvbjerg's principal argument is that expertise is not grounded in 'calculated, analytical rationality, as is commonly presumed, but on 'intuition, experience and judgement' (2001, 21). This orientation only reflects the extent to which the social sciences have allowed themselves to be colonized by the natural sciences, with their explanatory and predictive potential. He argues that the social sciences can do better what the natural sciences cannot ever hope to achieve, and that is the 'reflexive analysis and discussion of values and interests' (2001, 3).

9 Unlike the neoclassical economists who present a very linear view of the individual as a rational economic agent, the classical economists were not unaware of the 'dark side of human passions, the destructiveness of the acquisitive instinct or of the distortions of distribution' (Chandhoke 1995, 105).

10 Communitarian thinking would approach this question very differently. Communitarians argue that individual existence can only be understood in the context of the 'community', a 'unity' with its own intrinsic value, in which all members regard the 'common good' as their own (Avineri and De-Shalit 2001, 4, Sandel 2001).

11 Dunn's approach to arriving at this conclusion is vastly different from that of Marx. Perhaps this is because the analytical starting point of Dunn's theorising are individuals and not collectives, and there is little direct engagement with the political questions posed by 'non-individualist sociability' (borrowed from Kaviraj 2001).

Chapter Two. The Indian 'Anti-Politics Machine'

1 See Khilnani (1998, 81–88) for an extremely lively account of the rise of technocrats and scientists under Nehru.

2 In the Indian context, these views were articulated in the work of Roy (1989), Lal (1988), Bhagwati (1982, 1991) and Srinivasan (1991).

3 See Hansen (1999, 145–148) for a fascinating account of the duplicitous strategies pursued by the upper caste families interviewed in Pune in their everyday engagements with the 'scandalous secrets' of politics, i.e., with its corruption and naked power. They justified this intercourse through the use of a 'depoliticized vocabulary' ('everyday business' or 'a small job') while also hiding behind a moral shield of exclusive cultural sophistication that ostensibly protected them from the vulgarities, perils and temptations of politics.

4 Refer to Isaac and Frank (2000), Rudolphs (1987), Tornquist and Tharakan (1996), Webster (1992) for a more detailed consideration of these issues.

5 Corbridge and Harriss (2000) argue that the rise of the rich peasantry exercised a decisive influence on India's development since independence but differ in their analysis from the Rudolphs (1987) who emphasized the rise of 'bullock capitalists' (agriculturists owning land of sizes between 2.5 and 15 acres) replacing very large landholders. They maintain that abundant village ethnography has demonstrated the continued dominance of a small number of landholders whose mode of operation resembles that of 'rich peasants' or 'capitalist' farmers, rather than 'of "landlords" leasing out lands to surf-like tenant cultivators' (Corbridge and Harriss 2000, 83).

6 Although from diverse caste groups, these form an economic and social stratum between the middle castes above them and the scheduled castes below (Jaffrelot 2003). This stratum comprises marginal farmers, sharecroppers, landless labourers from relatively low-ranking agricultural castes together with traditional service and artisan castes, such as barbers, carpenters, blacksmiths and so on. The proportion of this stratum varies from one region to another, but is usually about a third of the population.

7 The details of this debate will not be delved into here. See Hansen 1999, Nandy et al (1995), Corbridge and Harriss (2000) for various perspectives on this issue.

8 Chibber 2005, as cited in Ray and Katzenstein 2005, has commented on the diffusion of radical working class-organizations by the Congress in association with industrialists, Guru and Chakravarty 2005 have written about the inhibition of political mobilization around class identities through the consensus of the Nehruvian period and John 2005 (as cited in Ray and Katzenstein 2005) has discussed the reasons why women's movements became prominent only in the 1970s; please see Ray and Katzenstein 2005 for more details.

Chapter Three. The Anti-Politics Watershed Machine: The Making of Watershed Development in India

1 In fact the 2008 guidelines were jointly issued by the Ministries of Rural Development and Agriculture.

2 For descriptions of how processes of agricultural commercialization for export were introduced by colonial governments in India and Africa, refer to Bharadwaj (1985) and Woodhouse et al (2000) respectively. For a succinct analysis of the role of the colonial state in irrigation development that accompanied commercialization of agriculture, see Vaidyanathan (1999).

3 The earliest accounts show that in 1888, nearly 1200 hectares of ravines in Uttar Pradesh were treated with conservation measures to protect the adjoining town of Etawah from water erosion (PRAI 1963).

4 Shah et al (1998) emphasize that this definition must capture the 'vulnerability arising from low and undependable rainfall and the absence of adequate supplements to this meagre rain'. Conditions of intensity of rainfall are important, as are the temperature and soil conditions of the area. Rainfed areas simply can include areas with very high rainfall, and in India, at least 30 per cent of rainfed areas fall within such high rainfall regimes (World Bank 1988 as cited in Shah et al 1998). Dry regions are usually found concentrated within specific climates, such as deserts, arid and semi-arid tropics, etc.

5 http://www.fao.org/docrep/x5669e/x5669e06.htm#approachesmethods%20 used%20for%20people's%20participation

6 http://www.goodnewsindia.com/Pages/content/inspirational/paniPanchayat.htm

7 This is a non-profit organization which is widely known by its acronym alone.

8 Per capita availability of agricultural lands, which stood at 0.48 ha in 1951, is expected to go down to 0.14 hectares in 2000 (Dharia Committee Report 1995). The percentage of the Indian population dependent on land has not declined commensurately, and agriculture remains the primary occupation for more than two thirds of all Indians.

9 http://upgov.up.nic.in/watershed/ncsaxena.htm

10 There are indications that despite this pro-panchayat move, GOI does not intend to do away with the basic structure of the DRDA. It specifies that 'DRDAs will maintain their separate identity, but will function under the chairmanship of the ZP'. Besides,

in states where the DRDA does not have a separate identity, a 'separate cell should be created in the ZP, which maintains a separate identity and separate accounts, so that the accounts are capable of being audited separately' (GOI 1999, 1–4).

11　Madhya Pradesh and Karnataka were notable exceptions.

12　The revised watershed guidelines of 2001, 2003 and 2008 all mention (in different ways) that the willingness and assured participation of villagers in making contributions of raw materials, cash, labour and in operating and maintaining the assets created as an important criteria in selecting watershed areas. An interesting interpretation is offered by Baviskar (2007) who remarks that the programme is keenly extended to villages where villagers 'are likely to be willing partners of the state' (2007, 290).

13　These members are usually experts in the fields of agriculture, irrigation, forestry and 'social mobilization'. The social mobilizer is responsible for facilitating the formation of user and self-help groups.

14　Centre-state ratios for principal schemes funding the WSDP are as follows- DPAP (75:25), DDP (75:25 for hot arid non-sandy areas, and 100 per cent centrally funded for hot sandy, and cold arid areas), IWDP (100 per cent centrally funded), EAS (75:25) and JGSY (80:20).

15　Money for works comprises 80 per cent of total finances, and the remaining 20 per cent have been earmarked for administration (10 per cent), 'community organization' (6 per cent) and training (4 per cent) respectively.

16　The Collector is the head of administration of a district in India. Her functions include the maintenance of law and order, revenue collection as also developmental functions for the district.

17　The guidelines even provide for the possibility of panchayats as PIAs, though this is not practice in most states implementing the 1994 guidelines. Rajasthan is a notable exception.

18　While user groups (UGs) are typically composed of landholders, self-help groups comprise the landless (SHGs).

19　This timeframe was revized in subsequent iterations of the guidelines.

20　This argument has been developed further in Chhotray (2004).

21　A good example of such critical writing is 'The Micro Politics of Development: An Anatomy of Change in Two Villages' by Ajay S. Mehta, the President of *Seva Mandir*, a grassroots NGO based in Udaipur, Rajasthan. See http://www.ashanet.org/conferences/asha-12/T223.1.PDF

22　http://www.ashanet.org/conferences/asha-12/T223.1.PDF

23　This was also the conclusion of a case study of watershed projects in Adgaon, Maharashtra, by Marathwada Sheti Sahaya Mandal, reported in Samuel et al (2006, 97).

24　A glossary of key terms listed in the 1994 guidelines refers to self-help group as a 'homogenous group with a common identity' and examples include women, shepherds, SC/STs and agricultural labourers.

25　The chapter will not go into the history of panchayats in India here. See Mathews (1995) for an excellent overview.

26　http://www.dolr.nic.in/fguidelines.htm

27　The Parthasarthy Committee made other important administrative and financial recommendations, like the establishment of an apex governing board for watershed development called the National Authority for Sustainable Development of Rainfed Areas (NASDORA) and tripling financial allocations for the watershed programme.

28 Interview with a number of NGO officials in Andhra Pradesh and a policy analyst at the Centre for Economic and Social Studies in Hyderabad, 2005.

29 'To say that there was "no consultation" is an understatement', said an official in the Department of Land Resources, MORD (Interview, 2005, New Delhi). 'The Hariyali Guidelines were not debated; they were formulated within closed-door settings', said a member of WASSAN, a leading network of NGOs in Andhra Pradesh (Interview, 2005, Hyderabad).

Chapter Four. Two Landscapes of Decentralization

1 A leading newspaper in India *Business World* ran a cover story titled 'The Wow Guys' on Naidu and Singh in March 1999.

2 Interview with M. Tirupathaiah, Assistant Director, AP Academy for Rural Development, November 2000.

3 A mandal is a sub-district unit of administration in AP.

4 Conversations with local journalists, Veldurthi mandal, Kurnool, January 2001.

5 In AP, panchayat elections to be convened in 2000 were delayed almost by a year.

6 Interviews with district officials in Kurnool, December 2004.

7 Other reasons for Singh's defeat include his unsuccessful adoption of a 'soft Hindutva' to cope with the BJP's challenge. For a man reputed to have a modernist temperament to support the inclusion of 'jyotish' traditional Indian astrology in the university syllabus was viewed with widespread incredulity and cyncisim (Pant 2004), http://www.southasianmedia.net/Magazine/Journal/after_elections.htm. Ironically, while the BJP trounced Singh over failed promises of modernization in MP, the BJP-led NDA central government heavily backed Naidu in Andhra Pradesh over his programme of reform which also backfired.

8 Interview with S. N. Sirohi, Secretary, Planning Department, Government of Madhya Pradesh, June 2000.

9 Rajendra Chaube, Public Relations Minister, remarked that 'in the last 100 days, there was a 25% decline in the number of visitors to Vallabh Bhawan (state secretariat) for getting their work done' (*National Mail*, July 20, 1999 as quoted in Behar 1999).

10 This discussion pertains to the arrangements that were in place between 1995 and 2003, the period of the investigation presented in this book and therefore relevant to the village-level practices that will be described in subsequent chapters.

11 This is often referred to as the 'DPAP governing body'. DPAP or the Drought Prone Area Programme is one of the oldest and principal constituents of MORD's watershed intervention and the name has continued to refer to the district watershed office, also as a large part of MORD's watershed funding is directed under DPAP schemes. The governing body is meant to meet once every quarter, but this is often logistically difficult to organise given the concentration of busy political leaders in a group (Interview with Project Director, Kurnool Watershed Office, January 2001).

12 Older administrative arrangements have been difficult to replace, and in Dewas in 2000, I saw how the 'old' DRDA continued to be responsible for managing watershed funds and collating district level procedures despite its 'merger' with the ZP. As a matter of fact, one clerk in the DRDA office of Dewas was the person to speak to for any information regarding the nitty-gritty details of project funds, expenditures and latest procedures.

13 Its practices were spoken of highly in the Department for Rural Development in Hyderabad and amongst DFID staff working on the Andhra Pradesh Rural Livelihoods Programme (an initiative to complement the state government's existing watershed programme by contributing to 'watershed plus' activities and capacity building of programme officials).

14 'Domination' is used here to refer to a relatively stable and hierarchical exercise of power, and as an aspect of power relations more generally.

15 AP is divided into three regions: coastal Andhra in the east, Telangana in the north and Rayalseema to the south and west. The area excluding Telangana was a part of the Madras Presidency until 1953 when, following a prolonged demand of the telugu-speaking elites of Andhra, the coastal and Rayalseema regions were carved out of the composite Madras state and into the separate state of Andhra, with Kurnool as its capital. Telangana was part of the Nizam's composite Hyderabad State, which comprised of eight telugu-speaking, three kannada-speaking and five marathi-speaking districts. Contemporary Andhra Pradesh as it presently exists was constituted in 1956 following a left-led agitation for the formation of 'Vishalandhra' and a general national policy of support for the creation of states on a linguistic basis (Srinivasulu 2002).

16 Conversations with local journalists in Kurnool, 2000.

17 Princely states have played an important part in the post-independence politics of MP. The Scindias of Gwalior and the Holkars of Indore have been credited with driving 'modernization and industrialization' in their principalities and have not been associated with the blatant exploitation perpetuated by zamindars in the permanent settlement areas of the British (Gupta 2005, 5097). As many of the economically developed regions of Madhya Pradesh were from the princely states, not from areas governed by the British, these princes have been very successful in winning elections after the introduction of parliamentary democracy.

18 See Shah (2005) for a useful discussion of the latest Scheduled Tribes Bill 2005 which responds to debates concerning the rights of forest-dwelling scheduled tribes to forest land under their occupation.

19 It is quite common for the Madhya Pradesh and MLA of a common area to belong to different parties. An instance is the Dewas constituency where in 2000 – the year of my fieldwork – the MP, Thavar Chand Singh Gehlot, was from the BJP and the MLA, Sajjan Singh Varma was from the Congress.

20 Fieldwork in Tonk-Khurd 'tehsil', October 2000.

21 Office records, Bagli tehsil.

22 The project period mentioned in the 1994 guidelines is four years. This was later extended to five years. Proposals to increase investment in watershed projects have since been made by the Parthasarthy Committee, 2006.

23 Conversations with watershed officials and local journalists in Kurnool and Dewas, 2000–2001.

24 KWO's 12 point weighted selection criteria gave maximum importance to priority areas selected by remote sensing on the basis of evapo-transpiration, rainfall, etc., followed by the size of SC/ST population and then equal emphasis to percentage of literates, agricultural labour, drinking water scarcity, fluoride affected quality of water, presence of active NGOs, active DWCRA Self Help Groups, status of ground water, contiguity and livestock. The district action plans are in fact generated by the National Remote Sensing Agency (NRSA), Department of Space, through its Integrated Mission for Sustainable Development (IMSD) launched in 1990. An interview with the Project Director IMSD, in November 2000, revealed that Kurnool is among the few districts in Andhra that sticks assiduously to the action plans submitted by NRSA.

25 48 out of 69 PIAs in Kurnool district were from the government in the year of my fieldwork (2000–2001).

26 In the same year, out of 5960 watershed projects being implemented in AP, 922 were being implemented by NGOs. Chittoor and Nalgonda districts had the highest numbers of NGO PIAs.

27 5 members have private occupations, and serve merely formal requirements of minimum membership, under the Indian Societies Registration Act of 1862.

28 KDRSO also manages a Child Labour School in Kurnool funded by the state government's Child Labour Department.

29 Budasa comprises of seven micro-watersheds that coincide with seven villages called Budasa, Kishanpura, Pandi, Jirvai, Gallakheri, Kishangarh and Pipliyakumar. The first watershed project to be started was in Budasa itself because it is the first village along the ridgeline of this milli-watershed. However, it soon had to be disbanded, apparently following the sarpanch's refusal to allow the constitution of watershed committees, as these appeared to threaten his own position (Interview with PO, Budasa Milli-Watershed, Dewas, October 2000). POs then chose Kishangarh to initiate a watershed project, on the ground that this was the next in sequence to Budasa along the ridge. For all effective purposes therefore, Kishangarh was the first microwatershed project to be completed in Dewas district.

30 At the time of fieldwork, Rajiv Gandhi Mission in Madhya Pradesh took a milli-watershed, of 5000 to 10000 hectares, as a unit of planning, instead of a micro-watershed of 500–1000 hectares, as proposed by the guidelines. The mission believed that the use of a planning unit that is too small leads to problems in downward integration of schemes, and therefore insisted on watershed planning for the entire state on a milli-watershed basis. However, it complied with the guidelines' emphasis on micro-watersheds with respect to the execution of structures, and therefore each individual watershed project that was designed was based on a micro-watershed (Government of MP, 1994).

31 Interview with a journalist, who requested anonymity, Dewas, October 2000. I also tried corroborating this by talking to Suren Varma. Interestingly enough, Varma said that he may have been the MLA, but the Congress party being in power at the state, had pressed for this selection (Dewas, October 2000).

32 BJP leader Thavar Singh Gehlot was the MP from Dewas in 2000–01 at the time of my research. Other BJP heavyweights like Phool Chand Varma and Kailash Dalmia are also from this part of Dewas.

33 Both MLAs and MPs are granted discretionary funds per annum, which they can disburse according to their wishes. They are free to rotate such grants to different panchayats.

34 Interview with a group member, SPS, Bagli, 2000.

35 They sold land revenue books worth five rupees at a thousand rupees per copy!

Chapter Five. Depoliticizing Local Institutions? Panchayats and Watershed Committees

1 It is not being suggested that the more pervasive idea of panchayats embodying divisive interests was not expressed in MP. Baviskar's (2007) account of WSD administrators in Jhabua is testimony to this. The point is to draw attention to the strong pro-panchayat discourses of the late 1990s initiated by the Digvijay Singh government in the state.

2 Conversation with WDT members, Kurnool, 2001.

3 Demographic information for all case villages was correct at the time of fieldwork, in 2000–2001.

4 There are at least six different BCs here. These are the Pinjaris, Vaddes, Boyas, Chakalis, Mangalis and Kamaris.

5 Robert Wade's study of Kotapalle village in Kurnool district highlights this phenomenon and draws from other literature on the subject that confirm this trend. See Wade (1994, 31–32).

6 For the purposes of this study, small farmers have lands between zero to three acres, medium farmers have lands between three to six acres and large farmers have lands above six acres. This will remain the typology throughout. Also, all landholdings referred to are 'consolidated landholdings' which, for the purposes of this study, have been defined as the total number of acres that are under a single ownership, and are being cultivated jointly, under the aegis of the head of a household, and the benefits of the consolidated agriculture accrue to all families that are a part of the household. This will necessarily include the sum of all land holdings that may be registered under different 'pattas', as long as the 'pattadars' are members of this household and derive the benefits of agriculture from that land. The notion of consolidated landholdings attempts to overcome errors in reporting landownership and joint cultivation. It relies extensively on village level knowledge to verify official documentation.

7 Of the 290 consolidated landholdings listed in the latest Village Agricultural Officer (VAO) records, 89 are above six acres, and at least 30 of these are big farmers with total landholdings of 30 or more acres. Ninety-six farmers are in the middle category and have lands between three and six acres. There are 70 small farmers with landholdings under three acres. Many of these are negligibly landed, with barely an acre or less of land. There are roughly 35 landless families in the village.

8 Wade writes of Reddys in Kurnool, 'A Reddy informant said of the few Vaishya merchants, some of whom are reputed to be wealthy, 'They just make money and keep quiet" (1994, 54).

9 A reserved forest of 697 hectares borders Lilapuram on its eastern side. It is directly under the control of the Forest Department. Grazing of animals in the forest area was never a common practice because villagers prefer to graze their herds of cows, sheep and goats on the nearby hillocks. Unregulated access to the forest was stopped in 1997 with the formation of a Van Suraksha Samiti (VSS) in the village, under the state Forest Department's Joint Forest Management initiative.

10 The cheruvu has 80 users who own lands in its ayacut. In 1997, with the state government's Participatory Irrigation Management initiative, these users were constituted into a Water Users' Association (WUA) to manage the cheruvu's resources collectively. The eldest son of the largest Reddy landowner in Lilapuram has been appointed the President. The association's activities include appointing a watchman to regulate the flow of water in the rainy months, and collecting the water tax that goes to the department.

11 All crops grown in Lilapuram are labour intensive. Apart from groundnut, which is the principal crop, crops like red gram, castor and cotton that farmers grow require labour for sowing, weeding and harvesting.

12 Conversations with several members of BC households, both men and women, confirmed this (Lilapuram, March 2001).

13 The policy of land distribution involves the offer of sale of land by a landholder to the SC Corporation. The Corporation buys the land after a field inspection, and then sells it to SC applicants for concessional rates.

14 Of the 340 consolidated landholdings listed in the VAO records, 237 landholdings are in the small category (of under three acres), 72 are medium farmers holding between three and six acres of land, and only 31 farmers have land more than six acres in size. There are 30 landless families in the village.

15 The Bank Manager, State Bank of India (SBI), Veldurthi Branch, reported that very few individuals from Malligundu have asked for loans at the branch. SBI has special rural operations whereby it grants crop loans and loans for allied activities, which are usually low interest, short-term loans.

16 The former was the VAO for 40 years until his retirement in 1990, and the latter played an important role in the demand for a cheruvu or tank to be constructed in the village. Harekrishna Reddy provided a lengthy account of how the demand was first made in 1960 but it was only in 1973 that the construction actually started.

17 Lilapuram Police Records, Veldurthi Police Station.

18 The board on the door of the house where he conducts his 'official' work reads 'Satya Reddy, Contractor'.

19 At a 'meeting' of the gram panchayat attended in Lilapuram, the 'sarpanch' Satya Reddy was absent, very likely because this was because he was far too confident of his control over this body to bother about its proceedings. When the members present were asked about what they knew of the panchayat's sources of income and its activities, the most vocal amongst them said, 'We don't know, we only present our problems to "him"', referring here to Satya Reddy, thus distancing themselves from the sole nucleus of information and authority within the panchayat. However, they were keen to demonstrate their loyalty to the sarpanch by stating that the panchayat has done a lot of work in the village, whereas the 'other party' did not do anything.

20 Interview with Secretary, Department of Irrigation, Hyderabad, 2001.

21 For all KWO projects, formal panchayat involvement was typically restricted to passing the resolution authorising the start of the watershed project at the beginning. This was usually not a problem, and as the PD said to me, 'Which panchayat would have an objection to this?' Getting panchayats to pass a resolution was not the problem. The problem was of ensuring that the same sort of factional fighting that was associated with panchayats is kept out of watershed projects.

22 He showed me one such letter that was addressed to Chandrababu Naidu, with copies to the Minister for Minor Irrigation and the Minister for Endowments, Government of Andhra Pradesh. The opening lines were: 'Respected Sir, I want to submit the following lines for your kind notice and information. I have been advising all my watershed presidents, chairmen and secretaries, to do their works sincerely with good quality in a justified manner to get a good name'.

23 Interview with Ragireddy, Magarpalli, January 2001.

24 The 2001 guidelines increased project duration to 5 years and also raised the cost of investment per hectare from 4000 to 6000 rupees per hectare, thus raising the total amount that passed through the hands of a village watershed committee. There have been recommendations for increasing this amount further in subsequent iterations.

25 Rajput landlords in the village are reputed to drinking heavily during late evenings.

26 These stereotypes are reflected in ethnographic accounts. Russell (1916) writing on the castes of central India describes Rajputs as 'warriors by nature' and endowed with a regal 'shaan' or splendour (Volumes II and III).

27 They mentioned that a 'gadhi' or temple of the goddess Kalika Devi has been located in Kishangarh for many years. This is apparently of much religious and cultural

significance to the Rajputs, and is comparable to the famous *gadhis* in Jodhpur and Udaipur. The only other *gadhi* anywhere in Madhya Pradesh is in Chittorgarh (Field notes, Kishangarh, October 2000).

28 Interview with Superintendent of Police, Dewas district, October 2000.

29 Mayadhar Chowdhury, a Khati and the up-sarpanch (vice president) of the panchayat apparently committed multiple murders to get rid of opposition among the Khatis.

30 A journalist in Dewas, who requested anonymity, told me that Hukum Singh Karada, an MLA from Shajapur, manages such activities professionally.

31 Many anecdotes of misappropriation of panchayat funds were obtained.

32 These documents and press reports were examined at the SPS office in Bagli in 2000.

33 Interview with a senior member of SPS, Bagli, 2000.

34 The only landless woman in the village was included in the committee, presumably following the guidelines that recommend the reservation of seats for women, but she did not appear to be aware of the committee's work when interviewed. The main initiative undertaken by SPS for women in this village was the construction of a 'silai Kendra' (stitching centre) on the outskirts of the village, where women could go to learn the art, and sell their products on a group basis, sharing the proceeds with the landless woman. However, many women spoke of the resistance they faced from their husbands on this issue, which led to a conflict and the eventual burning down of the shelter that served as the centre! It has been a contentious issue and that SPS sometimes held its meetings with watershed committee members at the refurbished centre irked those who felt excluded from its activities.

35 We need to consider the possibility that 'coalescing' the process of decision-making of the watershed committee into 'natural' village processes may have resulted in the perception (for some) that decisions were being taken by a few individuals who were active in the committee in consultation with the sanstha. Matters were also considerably complicated by the fact that SPS had been carrying out other projects (as funded by CAPART) in the village before it commenced watershed works, and villagers found it hard to distinguish between the two, producing discontent. For example in the initial years SPS had contacted individual landholders to build new wells or deepen old wells on their lands under its well-digging projects. Although initially sceptical of SPS's offers of 'free wells' (due to bitter memories of a loan scheme in the 1970s that had led to government 'harassment' for repayment), most people had agreed. Some however had resolutely declined the sanstha's offers, but had later changed their minds and tried to plead for wells either with the 'influential' committee members or with sanstha members directly. As funds for the well-digging project had long run out, there requests could not be honoured producing a lot of bitterness.

36 All records were maintained by a committee member who had been trained to do so, and then audited at the NGO's Bagli office by a senior SPS member. The two then filled out and submitted the 18 progress form required by the district administration on a monthly basis.

37 All 18 seats to the Bhimpura-Neelpura panchayat were elected unanimously in 1990, two out of 18 were contested in the elections of 1994–95, and in the last elections of 2000, 15 out of 18 seats were contested (Janpad Panchayat Office, Bagli).

38 'There are six lakh villages in the country, of which four lakh need urgent water retention. These are situated in 1,000,000 watersheds. If you have 200 NGOs covering 50 watersheds each, you can cover this scale; for that you would need ten Voluntary Support Organizations, who will train 20 NGOs each. In this way, we can actually make the effort to upscale this to the entire country in the next 20 years', Interview with Secretary, SPS, Bagli, 2000.

Chapter Six. The Dialectics of Consent in Participatory Practice

1 The chapter is interested in both the individual and collective expressions of consent. The latter is often mistakenly projected as consensus for it disregards the significance of viable spaces for the articulation of dissent and the resolution of difference. Please see earlier critique of 'consensus' in Chapter 3.

2 Liberals think in terms of the 'priority of the self over its aim', which means individuals are free to decide the ends they want to pursue and the kind of life they want to lead, referred to simply as the 'good life' (Avineri and De-Shalit 2001, 3). By extension, this means there are competing views or indeed plural conceptions of the 'good life'.

3 The guidelines laid down a ratio of expenditure for the four year project period and, ideally, finances were to be spent in the 25:40:25:10 ratio over four years.

4 Lands that are not privately owned can be described as 'common' or 'open access' depending on whether there are rules that govern its use.

5 Conversations with project practitioners in Dewas and Kurnool.

6 Thrift and credit groups are essentially savings groups whose members must save a nominal amount of a rupee a day, and deposit 30 or so rupees at the end of the month with the two group leaders. The leaders must then deposit the 450 rupees collected into the group account at the end of the month. When the savings reach an amount of 5,000 rupees, the group becomes eligible to receive a loan from the state government, which is in the nature of a revolving fund to be used as seed capital for various enterprises and not as a loan. In 2001 at the time of fieldwork, the state of AP had a total number of 3,33,774 groups, more than the groups in the rest of India put together, and this number has been steadily increasing.

7 Other senior officers in KWO explained cynically that this was the only way any WDF contributions could be obtained from farmers, as there was the danger of very low wage rates once the contribution had been deducted and farmers would typically be unwilling to work for less than the prevailing agricultural wage rate.

8 User groups formed for the watershed project were assuming other roles too. Their members acted to support one another on farming matters, and the WDT agriculture officer briefed them on latest trends in agriculture.

9 Chengappa, one of the two watershed secretaries of this village, smiled weakly when I pressed the matter. He was a typically forthright man who was eager to talk about the work he did.

10 Conversations with officials at DRDA, Dewas, October 2000.

11 Nandpur's non-selection violated the RGM guideline that areas contiguous to one another must be taken up for treatment simultaneously. It also showed that the selection process was guided by factors other than those mentioned in the selection criteria.

12 The emphasis on 'act' and not 'rule' follows the conceptual developments proposed by post-Gramscian scholars like James Scott (1990) and William Roseberry (1994) that demystified the role of consent in ensuring ideological domination or hegemony. The principal lesson here was that those claiming hegemony did not necessarily possess the active and conscious consent of the masses (or subordinates). Of course this is not to say that dominant actors cannot *claim* such hegemony, and consent plays a vital role in their ability to make such claims. My point here is in the same vein as Scott's analytic of public and hidden transcripts: public manifestation of consent allows dominant actors to claim rightful authority, even if this is regularly undercut by subversive

remarks by subordinate actors in private. Whether we look at consent from a liberal or a Gramcian tradition, the tremendous role of consent to legitimize or mandate agency and representation cannot be denied.

13 Farmers interviewed in 2000 corroborated that minimum wages of 50 rupees and 50 paise per day were offered for heavy works ('bhaari kaam') like construction on the watershed project and panchayat works too. The PO clarified however that when SPS engaged agricultural wage labour (to work on its 'agricultural experiment plot') it paid only 25 rupees a day to match what local farmers were capable of paying to their hired labourers. He claimed that the real success of SPS's minimum wages campaign in 1992–3 had been that nobody in the region would agree to work for less than the official minimum wages for heavy works of any sort.

14 Although the project officially started in 1995, this data describes changes from 1992, the year that SPS started working here till 2000, the year of fieldwork. 1996–97 has been taken as a mid-point in this eight-year period.

15 www.samprag.org

Conclusion

1 I am grateful to Richard Palmer-Jones for this insight.

REFERENCES

Abrams, P. (1988) 'Notes on the Difficulty of Studying the State', *Journal of Historical Sociology*, Volume 1, no. 1, pp 58–89

Agrawal, A. (2005) *Environmentality: Technologies of Government and the Making of Subjects*, Michigan

Appadurai, A. (1996) *Modernity at Large: Cultural Dimensions of Globalisation*, University of Minnesota Press, Minnesota

Arce, A. and Long, N. (2000) 'Reconfiguring modernity and development from an anthropological perspective' in Arce. A. and Long, N. (ed.) *Anthropology, Development and Modernities: Exploring discourses, counter-tendencies and violence*, Routledge, London

Aristotle (1932) *The Politics*, translated by Racham. H., Harvard University Press, Cambridge, Massachusetts

Avineri, S. (1972) *Hegel's theory of the modern state*, Cambridge University Press, London

Avineri, S. and De-Shalit, A. (2001) 'Introduction', in Avineri, S. and De-Shalit, A. (eds), *Communitarianism and Individualism*, Oxford University Press, Oxford

Bardhan, P. (1984) *The Political Economy of Development*, Oxford University Press, New Delhi

Bardhan, P. (1992) 'A Political Economy Perspective on Development', in Jalan, B. (ed.), *The Indian Economy*, Viking, Penguin India, New Delhi

Basu, A. (1992) *Two faces of protest: Contrasting modes of women's activism in India*, University of California Press and Oxford University Press, New Delhi

Bates, R. H. (1995) 'Social Dilemmas and Rational Individuals: An Assessment of the New Individualism', in Harriss, J. et al (eds), *The New Institutional Economics and Third World Development*, Routledge, London

Baumann, P. (1999) 'Democratising Development? Panchayati Raj Institutions in Watershed Development in India', in Farrington, J. et al (ed.), *Participatory Watershed Development: Challenges for the 21st Century*, Oxford University Press, New Delhi

Baviskar, A. (1995) *In the belly of the river: tribal conflicts over development in the Narmada Valley*, Oxford University Press

Baviskar, A. (2007) 'The Dream Machine: The Model Development Project and the Remaking of the State' in Baviskar, A. (ed.) *Waterscapes: The Cultural Politics of a Natural Resource*, Permanent Black, Delhi

Behar, A. (1999), 'Initiatives for Decentralisation of Governance in Madhya Pradesh', *Economic and Political Weekly*, November 6, www.epw.org.in

Behar, A. (2001) 'Madhya Pradesh: Gram Swaraj, Experiment in Direct Democracy', *Economic and Political Weekly*, Volume 36, no. 10, pp 823–826

Behar, A. (2003) 'Madhya Pradesh: Experiment with Direct Democracy: Time for Reappraisal', *Economic and Political Weekly*, May 17–23, www.epw.org.in

Beteille, A. (1996) 'Caste in Contemporary India', in Fuller, C. (ed.), *Caste Today*, Oxford University Press, Delhi

Bhagwati, J. N. (1982) 'Directly Unproductive Profit Seeking (DUP) Activities', *Journal of Political Economy*, Volume 90, no. 5 (Oct.), pp 988–1002

Bhagwati, J. N. (1991) *India in Transition: Freeing the Economy*, Clarendon Press, Oxford

Bharadwaj, K. (1985) 'A View on Commercialisation in Indian Agriculture and the Development of Capitalism', *Journal of Peasant Studies*, Volume 12, pp 25–47

Blair, H. (1996) 'Democracy, Equity and Common Property Resource Management in the Indian Sub Continent', *Development and Change*, Volume 27, no. 3, pp 475–497

Bloch, M. and Parry, J. (1989) 'Introduction: Money and the Morality of Exchange', in M. Bloch and J. Parry, *Money and the Morality of Exchange*, Cambridge University Press, Cambridge

Clague, C. (1997) 'The New Institutional Economics and Economic Development', in Clague, C. (ed.), *Institutions and Economic Development: Growth and Governance in Less Developed and Post-Socialist Countries*, The John Hopkins' University Press, Baltimore, Maryland

Chakravaraty-Kaul, M. (1996) *Common lands and customary law: Institutional change in North India over the past two centuries*, Oxford University Press, New Delhi

Chandhoke, N. (1995) *State and Civil Society: Explorations in Political Theory*, Sage Publications, New Delhi

Chandra, B. (1989) *India's struggle for independence: 1857–1947*, Penguin Books, India

Chatterjee, P. (1988) 'On Gramsci's Fundamental Mistake', *Economic and Political Weekly*, January 30 issue, pp PE 24–26

Chatterjee, P. (1994) 'Was there a hegemonic project' in Engels, D. and Marks, S. (eds), *Contesting colonial hegemony: State and society in Africa and India*, British Academic Press and the German Historical Institute, London and New York

Chatterjee, P. (1998) 'Development Planning and the Indian State', in Byres, T. (ed.), *State, Development Planning and Liberalisation in India*, Oxford University Press, Oxford

Chatterjee, P. (1999) 'The Nation and its Fragments: Colonial and postcolonial histories', in *The Partha Chatterjee Omnibus*, Oxford University Press, New Delhi

Chhotray, V. (2004) 'The negation of politics in participatory development programmes in Kurnool, Andhra Pradesh', *Development and Change*, Vol. 36, no. 2, pp 237–262

Chhotray, V. (2005) 'Who cares about participation? How a rhetorical state policy is practised incredulously', *Contemporary South Asia*, Volume 14 (4), pp 429–446

Chhotray, V. (2007) 'The "Anti-Politics Machine" in India: Depoliticisation through local institution building for participatory watershed development, *Journal of Development Studies*, Vol. 43, no. 6, pp 1037–1056

Chhotray, V. and Stoker, G. (2009) *Governance theory and practice: A cross-disciplinary approach*, Palgrave Macmillan, London

Chhotray, V. and Hulme, D. (2009) 'Contrasting visions for aid and governance in the 21st century: White House Millennium Challenge Account versus DFID's Drivers of Change', *World Development*, Volume 37, no. 1, pp 36–49

Cohen, S. (1985) *Visions of social control*, Polity Press, Cambridge

Colclough, C. and Manor, J. (1991) (eds) *States and Markets: Neoliberalism and the Development Policy Debate*, Clarendon Press, Oxford

Colletti, L. (1972) *From Rousseau to Lenin*, New Left Books, London

Cook, S. (1966) 'The obsolete "Anti-Market" mentality: A critique of the substantive approach to economic anthropology', *American Anthropologist*, Vol 68, no. 2, part 1, pp 323–345

Corbridge, S. (2007) 'The (im)possibility of development studies', *Economy and Society*, Volume 36, no. 1, pp 179–211

Corbridge, S. and Harriss, J. (2000) *Reinventing India: Liberalization, Hindu Nationalism and Popular Democracy*, Polity Press, Cambridge

Corbridge, S., Williams, G., Srivastava, M. and Veron, R. (2005) *Seeing the State: Governance and Governmentality in India*, Cambridge University Press, Cambridge

DFID, OIKOS and IIRR (2000) *Social and Institutional Issues in Watershed Management in India*, International Institute of Rural Reconstruction, Philippines

Dharia Committee (1995) *Report of the High Level Committee on Wastelands Development*, Government of India, New Delhi

Dirks, N. (1996) 'Recasting Tamil Society: The Politics of Caste and Race in Contemporary South India', in Fuller, C. (ed.), *Caste Today*, Oxford University Press, Delhi

Doornboos, M. (2000) *Institutionalising Development Policies and Resource Strategies in Eastern Africa and India: Developing Winners and Losers*, McMillan Press Ltd, London

Dube, S. C. (1968) 'Caste Dominance and Factionalism', *Contributions to Indian Sociology*, Volume 2, no, 2, pp 58–81

Dumont, L. (1970) *Homo hierarchicus: The Caste System and its Implications*, Translated by Sainsbury M., Weidenfeld and Nicolson, London

Dunn, J. (2000) *The Cunning of Unreason: Making Sense of Politics*, Harper Collins, London

Easterly, W. (2006) *The White Man's Burden: Why the West's efforts to aid the rest have done so much ill and so little good*, Penguin Press, New York

Escobar, A. (1999) 'Planning', Sachs, W. (ed.), *The Development's Dictionary: A Guide to Knowledge as Power*, Zed Books Limited, London and New York

Evans, P. (1996) 'Introduction: Development Strategies across the Public-Private Divide', *World Development*, Volume 24, no. 6, pp 1033–1077

Farrington, J., Turton, C. and James, A. J. (1999) *Participatory Watershed Development: Challenges for the 21st Century*, Oxford University Press, New Delhi

Ferguson, J. (1990) *The Anti-Politics Machine: "Development", Depoliticisation and Bureaucratic Power in Lesotho*, Cambridge University Press, Cambridge

Fine, B. (1999) 'The developmental state is dead – long live social capital?' *Development and Change*, Volume 30, pp 1–19

Fine, B. (2001) 'Neither the Washington nor the Post-Washington Consensus', in Fine, B., Lapavistas, C., Pincus, J. (eds), *Development Policy in the twenty-first century: Beyond the post-Washington Consensus*, Routledge, London and New York

Flyvbjerg, B. (2001) *Making Social Science Matter: Why Social Inquiry fails and how it can succeed again*, Cambridge University Press, Cambridge

Foucault, M. (1980) *Power/Knowledge: Selected Interviews and Other Writings*, Pantheon Books, New York

Fourcade-Gourinchas, M. and Babb, S. L. (2006) 'The rebirth of the liberal creed: Paths to neoliberalism in four countries', *American Journal of Sociology*, Volume 108, no. 3, pp 533–579

Frankel, F. (1978) *India's Political Economy 1947–1977, The Gradual Revolution*, Princeton University Press, Guildford

Frykenberg, R. E. (1965) *Guntur District, 1788–1848: A History of Local Influence and Central Authority in South India*, Clarendon Press, Oxford

Fuller, C. J. (1996) (ed.) *Caste Today*, Oxford University Press, Delhi

Fuller, C. J. and Harriss, J. (2001) 'For an Anthropology of the Indian State', in Fuller, C. J. and Benei, V. (eds), *The Everday State and Society in Modern India*, Hurst and Company, London

Goffman, E. (1997) 'The presentation of self in everyday life' in Lemert, C. and Branaman, A. (eds), *The Goffman Reader*, Blackwell, Oxford

Goodman, D. and Redclift, M. (1991) *Refashioning Nature: Food, Ecology and Culture*, Routledge, London

Government of India (1999) *Guidelines for District Rural Development Agencies*, Ministry of Rural Development, New Delhi

Government of India (2008) 'Common guidelines for watershed development projects', National Rainfed Area Authority, Ministry of Agriculture, Government of India, New Delhi

Government of Madhya Pradesh (1994) *Mission Guidelines for Watershed Development*, Rajiv Gandhi Mission, Bhopal

Gray, J. (2000) *The Two Faces of Liberalism*, Polity Press, Cambridge

Guha, R. (2007) *India after Gandhi: The history of the World's largest democracy*, Macmillan, London

Gupta, A. (1995) 'Blurred Boundaries: The Discourse of Corruption, the Culture of Politics and the Imagined State', *American Ethnologist*, Volume 22, no. 2, pp 375–402

Gupta, A. (1998) *Post Colonial Developments: Agriculture in the making of Modern India*, Duke University Press

Gupta, S. (2004) Nature of Elite Formation in the Hindi Heartland: A Comparative Assessment of Bihar and Madhya Pradesh. Conference on State Politics in India in the 1990s: Political Mobilisation and Political Competition, December

Gupta, S. (2005) 'Socio-economic base of political dynamics in Madhya Pradesh', *Economic and Political Weekly*, November 26, www.epw.nic.in

Habermas, J. (1975) *The Legitimation Crisis*, Translated by McCarthy, T., Beacon Press, Boston, Massachusetts

Hadiz, V. R. (2004) Decentralisation and Democracy in Indonesia: A Critique of Neo-Institutionalist Perspectives. *Development and Change*, Volume 35, no. 4, pp 697–718

Hansen, T. B. (1999) *The saffron wave: Democracy and Hindu Nationalism in modern India*, Princeton University Press, Chichester

Hansen, T. B. and Stepputat, F. (2001) (eds) *States of Imagination: Ethnographic explorations of the postcolonial state*, Duke University Press, Durham

Hardiman, D. (1982) '"The Indian Faction": A Political Theory Examined', in Guha, R. (ed.), *Subaltern Studies I*, Oxford University Press, Delhi

Harriss, J. (2001) *Depoliticising Development: The World Bank and Social Capital* (New Delhi: Leftword)

Harriss, J., Stokke, K. and Tornquist, O. (2004) *Politicising Democracy: The New Local Politics of Democratisation*. Palgrave Macmillan, Basingstoke

Hardin, G. (1968) 'The Tragedy of the Commons', *Nature*, as reprinted in Bell, G. D. (1970) (ed.), *The Environmental Handbook*, Friends of the Earth Books, New York

Heller, A. (1991) 'The concept of the political revisited', in Held, D. (ed.), *Political Theory Today*, Polity, Cambridge

Heller, P. (2001) 'Moving the State: The Politics of Democratic Decentralisation in Kerala, South Africa and Porto Alegre' in *Politics and Society*, Volume 29, no. 1, pp131–163

Hickey, S. (2008) 'The return of politics in development studies I: getting lost within the poverty agenda', *Progress in Development Studies 8*, Volume 4, pp 349–358

Hickey, S. (2010) 'The government of chronic poverty: From exclusion to citizenship?', *Journal of Development Studies*, Volume 46, no. 7, pp 1–17

Hickey, S. and Mohan, G. (2004) (eds) *Participation: From tyranny to transformation*, Zed Books, London

Hinchcliffe, F., Thompson, J., Pretty, J., Guijt, I. and Shah, P. (1999) (eds) '*The Impact of Participatory Watershed Management*', IT Publications, London

Hoffman, J. (1984) *The Gramscian Challenge: Coercion and Consent in Marxist Political Theory*, Blackwell Publishers, Oxford

Hulme, D. and Woodhouse, P. (2000) 'Governance and the Environment', in P. Woodhouse, H. Bernstein and D. Hulme, *African Enclosures?: The Social Dynamics of Wetlands in Drylands*, James Curry, Oxford

Isaac, B. (2005), 'Karl Polyani', in Carrier, J. G. (ed.) *A handbook of economic anthropology*, Edward Elgar, Cheltenham, UK

Isaac. T. M. and Frank, R. W. (2000) *Local Democracy and Development: People's Campaign for Decentralised Planning in Kerala*, Leftword, New Delhi

Jaffrelot, C. (1996) *The Hindu Nationalist Movement and Indian Politics, 1925 to the 1990s*, Hurst, London

Jaffrelot, C. (2003) *India's silent revolution: The rise of the lower castes in north India*, Hurst, London

Jain, L. C. (1985) *Grass without Roots: Rural Development under Government Auspices*, Sage Publications, London and New Delhi

Jenkins, R., Jayalakshmi, K., Khorakiwala, T., Reddy, G., Reddy, R., Singh, V. and Geotz, A. M., (2003) 'State Responsiveness to Poverty: A Comparative Study of Development Interventions in the Indian States of Andhra Pradesh and Madhya Pradesh' Working Paper, Overseas Development Institute, London

Jodha, N. S. (1986) 'Common property resources and rural poor in dry regions of India', *Economic and Political Weekly*, Volume 21, pp 1169–1181

Johnson, C. (2004) 'Uncommon Ground: The 'Poverty of History' in Common Property Discourse', *Development and Change*, Volume 35, no. 3, pp 407–433

Johnson, C., Deshingkar, P. and Start, D. (2005) 'Grounding the State: Devolution and Development in India's *Panchayats*', *Journal of Development Studies*, Volume 41, no. 6, pp 937–970

Kalpagam, U. (2000) 'Colonial governmentality and economy', *Economy and Society*, Volume 29, no. 3, pp 418–438

Kamat, S. (2002) *Development Hegemony: NGOs and the State in India*, Oxford University Press, New Delhi

Kaviraj, S. (1984) 'On the crisis of Political Institutions in India', *Contributions to Indian Sociology*, Volume 18, pp 223–43

Kaviraj, S. (1988) 'A Critique of the Passive Revolution', *Economic and Political Weekly*, Special Number, November, pp 2429–2444

Kaviraj, S. (1991) 'State, Society and Discourse in India', in Manor, J. (ed.), *Rethinking Third World Politics*, Longman, Harlow

Kaviraj, S. (1994) 'On the construction of colonial power: Structure, discourse, hegemony' in Engels, D. and Marks, S. (eds.), *Contesting colonial hegemony: State and society in Africa and India*, British Academic Press and the German Historical Institute, London and New York

Kaviraj, S. (1995) 'Democracy and Development in India', in Bagchi, A. K. (ed.), *Democracy and Development: Proceedings of the IEA Conference held in Barcelona, Spain*, Macmillan in association with the International Economic Association, Basingstoke

Kaviraj, S. (1996) 'Dilemmas of Democratic Development in India', in Leftwich, A., *Democracy and Development: Theory and Practice*, Polity Press, Oxford

Kaviraj, S. (1997) 'The Modern State in India', in Doornbos, M. and Kaviraj, S. (eds), *Dynamics of State Formation: Europe and India compared*, Sage, New Delhi

Kaviraj, S. (2001) 'In Search for Civil Society', in Kaviraj, S. and Khilnani, S. (eds), *Civil Society: History and Possibilities*, Cambridge University Press, Cambridge

Kerr, J. (2002) 'Watershed development, environmental services and poverty alleviation in India', *World Development*, Vol. 30, no. 8, pp 1387–1400

Kerr, J. and Sanghi, N. K. (1992) *Soil and Water Conservation in India's Semi-Arid Tropics*, Sustainable Agriculture Programme Gatekeeper Series SA 34, IIED, London

Kerr, J., Pangare, G. and Pangare, V. (2002) 'An evaluation of watershed projects in India', *Research Report* 127, International Food Policy Research Institute, Washington

Khilnani, S. (1998) *The idea of India*, Penguin Books

Kohli, A. (1989) *The state and poverty in India: The politics of reform*, Cambridge University Press

Kohli, A. (1990), *Democracy and Discontent: India's Growing Crisis of Governability*, Cambridge University Press, Cambridge

Kothari, U. (2001) 'Power, knowledge and social control', in Cooke, B. and Kothari, U. (eds) *Participation: The new tyranny?*, Zed Books, London

Kothari, U. (2005) (ed.) *A radical history of development studies: Ideas, institutions and individuals*, Zed Books, London

Krueger, A.O. (1974) 'The Political Economy of the Rent Seeking Society', *American Economic Review*, Volume 64, no. 3, pp 291–303

Kumar, S. and Corbridge, S. (2002) 'Programmed to Fail? Development Projects and the Politics of Participation', *Journal of Development Studies*, Volume 39, no. 2, pp 73–103

Kumar, V. (2007) 'Behind the BSP victory', *Economic and Political Weekly*, Volume 42, no. 24, pp 2237–2239

Kymlicka, W. (1990) 'Communitarianism: Liberal Individualism and State Neutrality', in W. Kymlicka, *Contemporary Political Philosophy*, Oxford University Press, Oxford

Lal, D. (1988) *Cultural Stability and Economic Stagnation: India c 1500 BC- AD 1980*, Clarendon Press, Oxford

LaRocque, B. (2006) 'Social movements in India: Poverty, power and politics, *Contemporary Sociology: A journal of reviews*, Volume 35, pp 522–523

Leach, M., Mearns, R. and Scoones, I. (1997) 'Challenges to community-based sustainable development: Dynamics, entitlements and institutions', *IDS Bulletin*, Volume 28, no. 4, pp 4–14

Leftwich, A. (1996) (ed.) *Democracy and Development: Theory and Practice*, Polity Press, Oxford

Leftwich, A. (2006) 'Drivers of Change: Refining the Analytical Framework', Department of Politics, University of York

Lekha, S. (1997) 'Selected Issues in Local Level Fiscal Decentralisation: A Comparative Study of International and Indian Experience', Unpublished M.Phil. Thesis, Centre for Development Studies, Thiruvananthapuram, India

Li, T. M. (2007) *The will to improve: Governmentality, politics and the practice of development*, Duke University Press, Durham

Long, N. and Long, A. (1992) (ed.) *Battlefields of knowledge: The interlocking of theory and practice in social research and development*, Routledge, London

Luce, E. (1996) *In spite of the Gods: The strange rise of modern India*, Little, Brown, London

Ludden, D. (1992) 'India's Development Regime', in Dirks, N. B. (ed.), *Colonialism and Culture*, The University of Michigan Press, Ann Arbor

Mackintosh, M. and Roy, R. (1999) (eds) *Economic Decentralisation and Public Management Reform*, Edward Elgar, UK

Manor, J. (2000) 'Democratic Decentralisation in Two Indian States: Past and Present', Unpublished mimeo, Livelihoods Options Project, Overseas Development Institute, London

Manor, J. (2002) Democratic Decentralisation in Two Indian States: Past and Present. *The Indian Journal of Political Science*, Volume 63, no. 1, pp 51–71

Manor, J. (2004) 'Explaining political trajectories in Andhra Pradesh', in Jenkins, R. (ed.), *Regional reflections: Comparing politics across India's states*, Oxford University Press, New Delhi

Manor, J. (2005) 'User Committees: A Potentially Damaging Second Wave of Decentralisation', in Ribot, J. C. and Larson, A. M. (eds) *Democratic Decentralisation through a Natural Resource Lens*, Routledge, London, pp 192–213

Marx, K. (1964) *Pre-capitalist economic formations*, International Publishers, New York

Marx, K. (1977) *Capital*, Volume I, Vintage Press, New York

Mathews, G. (1995) *Panchayati Raj: From Legislation to Movement*, Institute of Social Sciences, New Delhi

Mazzucato, V. and Niemeijer, D. (2000) 'The Cultural Economy of Soil and Water Conservation in a Changing Society: A Case Study in Eastern Burkina Faso', *Development and Change*, Volume 31, no. 4, pp 831–855

Mendelsohn, O. (2002) 'Caste and Class: Social Reality and Political Representations', in Shah, G. (ed.), *Caste and Democratic Politics in India*, Permanent Black, Delhi

Ministry of Rural Development (MORD) (1994) *Guidelines for Watershed Development*, Government of India, New Delhi

Ministry of Rural Development (MORD) *Guidelines for Watershed Development*, Government of India, New Delhi

Ministry of Rural Development (MORD) (2003) *Guidelines for Hariyali*, www.nic.in

Ministry of Rural Development (MORD) (2008) *Common guidelines for watershed development projects*, Government of India, http://dolr.nic.in/CommonGuidelines2008.pdf

Mitchell, T. (1991) 'The limits of the state: Beyond statist approaches and their critics', *American Political Science Review*, Volume 85, no. 1, pp 77–96

Mitchell, T. (1998) 'Fixing the economy', *Cultural Studies*, Volume 12, no. 1, pp 82–101

Mitchell, T. (1999) 'Society, economy and the state effect' in Steinmetz, G. (ed.) *State/Culture: State formation after the cultural turn*, Cornell University Press, Ithaca, NY

Mitchell, T. (2002) *Rule of experts: Egypt, techno-politics, modernity*, University of California Press, Berkeley

Mooij, J. (2003) 'Smart Governance? Politics in the Policy Process in Andhra Pradesh, India', Working Paper 228, Overseas Development Institute, London

Moore, D. (1999) '"Sail on: O Ship of State": Neo-liberalism, Globalisation and the Governance of Africa', in *Journal of Peasant Studies*, Volume 27, no. 1, pp 61–96

Mosse, D. (1994) 'Authority, Gender and Knowledge: Theoretical Reflections on the Practice of Participatory Rural Appraisal', *Development and Change*, Volume 26, no. 3, pp 497–525

Mosse, D. (1997) 'The Ideology and Politics of Community Participation: Tank Irrigation Development in Colonial and Contemporary Tamil Nadu', in Grillo, R. D. and Stirrat, R. L. (eds), *Discourses of Development: Anthropological Perspectives*, Berg Publishers, Oxford

Mosse, D. (2001) '"People's knowledge", participation and patronage: Operations and representations in rural development', in Cooke, B. and Kothari, U. (eds) *Participation: The new tyranny?*, Zed Books, London

Mosse, D. (2003) *The Rule of Water: Statecraft, Ecology and Collective Action in South India*, Oxford University Press, New Delhi

Mosse, D. (2004) Is Good Policy Unimplementable? Reflections on the Ethnography of Aid Policy and Practice, *Development and Change*, Volume 35, no. 4, pp 639–671

Mosse, D. and Lewis, D. (2006) 'Theoretical approaches to brokerage and translation in development' in Mosse, D. and Lewis, D. (ed.) *Development brokers and translators: The ethnography of aid and agencies*, Kumarian Press Inc., USA

Mueller, D.C. (1979) *Public Choice*, Cambridge University Press, Cambridge

Mukherji, P.N. (1978), 'Naxalbari movement and the peasant revolt in NorthBengal', in Rao, M. S. A (ed.), *Social Movements in India* I, Manohar Press, Delhi

Munck, R. (2005) 'Neoliberalism and Politics', in Saad-Filho, A. and Johnston, D. (eds), *Neoliberalism: A critical reader*, Pluto Press, London

Murray-Li, T. (1999) 'Compromising Power: Development, Culture and Rule in Indonesia', *Cultural Anthropology*, Volume 14, no. 3, pp 285–322

Nabli, M. and Nugent, J. B. (1989) 'The New Institutional Economics and its Applicability to Development', *World Development*, Volume 17, no. 9, pp 1333–1347

Naidu, N. and Ninan, S. (2000) *Plain Speaking*, Viking, New Delhi

Nandy, A., Trivedy, S. and Yagnick, A. (1995) (eds.) *Creating a nationality: the Ramjanmabumi movement and fear of the self*, Oxford University Press, New Delhi

Nigam, A. (2004), 'Caste Politics in India', *South Asian Journal*, April-June, issue 4

Nonneman, G. (1996) (ed.) *Political and Economic Liberalisation: Dynamics and Linkages in Comparative Perspective*, Lyenne Rienner Publishers Inc., Colorado and London

North, D. C. (1990) *Institutions, Institutional Change and Economic Performance*, Cambridge University Press, Cambridge

Olson, M. (1971) *The Logic of Collective Action: Public Goods and the Theory of Groups*, Harvard University Press

Osella, F. and Osella, C. (2001) 'The return of King Mahabali: The politics of morality in Kerala', in Fuller, C. J. and Benei, V. (eds), *The Everday State and Society in Modern India*, Hurst and Company, London

Ostrom, E. (1986) 'Common Property, Reciprocity and Community', *Journal of Economic Issues*, Volume 24, no. 2

Ostrom, E. (1990) *Governing the Commons: The Evolution of Institutions for Collective Action*, Cambridge University Press

Ostrom, E (1996) 'Crossing the Great Divide: Co production, Synergy and Development', *World Development*, Volume 24, no. 6, pp 1073–1087

Palshikar, S. (2004), 'Majoritarian middle ground', *Economic and Political Weekly*, December 18

Pant, P. (2004), 'India after elections', *South Asian Journal: Electoral Politics in South Asia*, Volume 5, July–September

Pateman, C. (1985) *The Problem of Political Obligation: A Critique of Liberal Theory*, Polity in Association with Blackwell, Cambridge

Pati, B. (2004) 'BJP's "stumbling blocks": The voter, pluralism and democracy', *Economic and Political Weekly*, May 22

Polyani, K. (1944) *The Great Transformation: the political and economic origins of our time*, Holt, Rinehart and Winston, New York

Polyani, K. (1957) 'The economy as instituted process', in Polyani, K., Arensberg, C. and Pearson, H. (eds), *Trade and Market in the early empires*, Free Press, Glencoe, Illinois

Poulantzas, N. (1973) *Political Power and Social Classes*, New Left Books, London

PRAI (1963) *Soil Conservation Programme in Village Sherpur Sarraiya (Etawah): A Case Study*, Planning Research and Action Research Publication no. 307, Lucknow

Prasad, A. (2002) 'Tribal survival and the land question', in Jha, P. K. (ed.), *Land Reforms in India: Issues of Equity in Rural Madhya Pradesh*, Sage, New Delhi

Pretty, J. N. (1995) 'Participatory Learning for Sustainable Agriculture', *World Development*, Volume 23, no. 8, pp 1247–1263

Pretty, J. N. and Shah, P. (1994) *Soil Conservation in the 20th Century: A History of Coercion and Control*, Rural History Centre Research Series no. 1, University of Reading, Reading

Putnam, R. (1993) *Making democracy work: Civic traditions in modern Italy*, Princeton University Press, Princeton

Putnam, R. (2000) *Bowling alone: The collapse and revival of American community*, Simon and Schuster, New York and London

Raghavulu, C. V. and Narayana, E. A. (1999) 'Reforms in *Panchayat Raj*: A Comparative Analysis of Andhra Pradesh, Karnataka and West Bengal', in Jha, S. N. and Mathur, P. C. (eds), *Decentralisation and Local Politics: Readings in Indian Government and Politics (2)*, Sage, London

Raj, S. L. and Choudhury, A. R. (1998) (eds) *Contemporary social movements in India: Achievements and hurdles*, Indian Social Institute, New Delhi

Rajaraman, I., Bohra, O. P, Renganathan, V. S. (1996) 'Augmentation of Panchayat Resources', *Economic and Political Weekly*, Volume 31, no. 18, pp 1071–1083

Rao, M. (1995) 'Whither India's Environment?', *Economic and Political Weekly*, April 1

Rao, M. (1997) 'Agricultural Development under State Planning', in T. Byres (ed.), *State, Development Planning and Liberalisation in India*, Oxford University Press, Oxford

Rao, M. S. A (1978) (ed.) *Social Movements in India* I, Manohar Press, Delhi

Rao, M. S. A (1979) (ed.) *Social Movements in India* II, Manohar Press, Delhi

Ray, R. (1999) *Fields of Protest: Women's movements in India*, University of Minnesota Press, Minneapolis

Ray, R. and Katzenstein, M.F. (2005) *Social movements in India: Poverty, power and politics*, Rowman and Littlefield Publishers, Oxford

Reddy, K. (2002) New Populism and Liberalisation: Regime Shift under Chandrababu Naidu in AP, *Economic and Political Weekly*, Volume 32, pp 871–883

Robertson, A. F. (1984) *People and the state: An anthropology of planned development*, Cambridge University Press, Cambridge

Robinson, M. (1988) *Local Politics: The law of the fishes*, Oxford University Press, Oxford

Rose, N. (1990) *Governing the Soul: The Shaping of the Private Soul*, Routledge, London and New York

Roseberry, W. (1989) *Anthropologies and Histories: Essays in Culture, History and Political Economy*, Rutgers University Press, New Brunswick and London

Roseberry, W. (1994) 'Hegemony and the Language of Contention', in Joseph, G. M. and Nugent, D. (1994) (eds), *Everyday Forms of State Formation: Revolution and the Negotiation of Rule in Mexico*, Duke University Press, Durham and London

Roseberry, W. (1997) 'Afterword', in Carrier, J. G. (ed.), *Meanings of the Market: The Free Market in Western Culture*, Berg, Oxford and New York

Rostow, W. (1990) *The Stages of Economic Growth: a Non-Communist Manifesto*. Cambridge, Cambridge University Press (3rd edition)

Roy, S. (1989) *Pricing, Planning and Politics*, Institute of Economic Affairs, London

Roy, D. (2002) 'Land reform, peoples' movements and protests', Jha, P. K. (ed.), *Land reforms in India: Issues of equity in rural Madhya Pradesh*, Sage Publications, New Delhi

Rudolph, S. and Rudolph, L. (1987) *In Pursuit of Lakshmi: The Political Economy of the Indian State*, University of Chicago Press, Chicago

Russell, R.V. (1916) *The Tribes and Castes of the Central Provinces of India*, Assisted by Hiralal, R. B., Published under the orders of the Central Provinces Administration, Macmillan and Co., London

Ruud, A.E. (2001) 'Talking dirty about politics: A view from a Bengali village', Fuller, C. J. and Benei, V. (eds), *The Everday State and Society in Modern India*, Hurst and Company, London

Saad-Filho, A. and Johnston, D. (2005) *Neoliberalism: A critical reader*, Pluto Press, London

Samuel, A., Joy, K. J., Paranjape, S., Peddi, S., Adagale, R., Deshpande, P. and Kulkarni, S. (2006) 'Watershed Development in Maharashtra: Present scenario and issues for restructuring the programme', Society for Promoting Participative Ecosystem Management (SOPPECOM), Forum for Watershed Research and Policy Dialogue, Pune

Sandel, M. (2001) 'The Procedural Republic', in Avineri, S. and De-Shalit, A. (eds), *Communitarianism and Individualism*, Oxford University Press, Oxford

Sangameswaran, P. (2008) 'Community formation, "ideal" villages and watershed development in Western India, *Journal of Development Studies*, Volume 44, no. 3, pp 384–408

Sarkar, S. (1989), *Modern India: 1885–1947*, Macmillan, Basingstoke

Saxena, N. C. (2001) 'Rehabilitating degraded lands', National Workshop on Watershed Area Development: Challenges and solutions, Lucknow 28–29 July 2001, http://upgov.up.nic.in/watershed/ncsaxena.htm

Schmitt, C. (1976) *The concept of the political*, translation, introduction and notes by George Schwab, Rutgers University Press, New Brunswick

Scott, J. C. (1985) *Weapons of the Weak: Everyday Forms of Peasant Resistance*, Yale University Press, New Haven

Scott, J. C. (1990) *Domination and the Arts of Resistance: Hidden Transcripts*, Yale University Press, New Haven

Seal, A. (1973) 'Imperialism and Nationalism in India', in Gallagher, J., Johnson, G. and Seal, A. (eds), *Locality, Province and Nation: Essays on Indian Politics 1870 to 1940*, Cambridge University Press, Cambridge

Self, P. (1993) *Government by the Market?: The Politics of Public Choice*, Macmillan, London

Shah, M. (1997) *Technical Advisory Committee report for the review of the Rajiv Gandhi Mission for Watershed Development*, Samaj Pragati Sahyog, Dewas, Madhya Pradesh

Shah, M. (2005) 'First you push them in, then you throw them out', *Economic and Political Weekly*, Volume 40, no. 47, www.epw.nic.in

Shah, M. (2006), 'Overhauling watershed programme: Towards reform', *Economic and Political Weekly*, Volume 45, no. 28, pp 2981–2984

Shah, M., Banerji, D., Vijayshankar, P. S., Ambasta, P. (1998) *India's Drylands: Tribal Societies and Development through Environmental Regeneration*, Oxford University Press, New Delhi

Shaheena, P. (1999) *A Comparison of the Recommendations of the State Finance Commission Reports*, Centre for Development Studies, Thiruvananthapuram.

Simmel, G. (1978) *The philosophy of money*, translated from the German by Tom Bottomore and David Frisby, Routledge and Kegan Paul, London

Sinha, S. (1999) '"Community" and the Legitimation of the Developmentalist State: A Preliminary Note on India's Community Development Programme', Preliminary Draft, Department of Development Studies, School of Oriental and African Studies, London

Sinha, S., Gururani, S. and Greenberg, B. (1998) 'New traditionalist discourse of Indian environmentalism', *Journal of Peasant Studies*, Volume 24, no. 3, pp 169–204

Sivaramakrishnan, K. (2000) 'State Sciences and Development Histories: Encoding Local Forestry Knowledge in Bengal', *Development and Change*, Volume 31, pp 61–89

Skaria, A. (1999) *Hybrid histories: Forests, frontiers and wilderness in Western India*, Oxford University Press, New Delhi

Smith, A. (1904) *An enquiry into the nature and causes of the wealth of nations*, Cannon, E. (ed.), 2 Volumes, Metheun, London

Srinivas, M. N. (1955) 'The Social System of a Mysore Village', in Marriott, M. (ed.), *Village India*, University of Chicago Press, Chicago

Srinivas, M. N. (1998) *Village, caste, gender, method: Essays in Indian social anthropology*, Oxford University Press, UK

Sridharan, E. (1993) 'Economic Liberalisation and India's Political Economy: Towards a Paradigm Synthesis', *Journal of Commonwealth and Comparative Politics*, Volume 31, no. 3, pp 1–31

Srinivasan, T. N. (1985) 'Neoclassical Political Economy, the State and Economic Development', *Asian Development Review*, Volume 3, no. 2, pp 38–58

Srinivasan, T. N. (1991), 'Reform of Industrial and Trade Policies', *Economic and Political Weekly*, 14 September, Volume 26, no. 37, pp 2143–2145

Srinivasulu, K. (2002) 'Caste, Class and Social Articulation in Andhra Pradesh: Mapping differential regional trajectories', Working Paper 179, ODI, London

Stoker, G. (2006) *Why Politics Matters*, Palgrave Macmillan, London

Sundar, N. (2000) 'Unpacking the "Joint" in Joint Forest Management', *Development and Change*, Volume 31, no. 1, pp 255–279

Suri, K. C. (2002) 'Democratic process and electoral politics in Andhra Pradesh', ODI Working paper 180, Overseas Development Institute, London

Taylor, M. (1987) *The Possibility of Cooperation*, Cambridge University Press, Cambridge

Taylor, M. (1989) 'Structure, Culture and Action in the Explanation of Social Change, *Politics and Society*, Volume 17, pp 115–162

Tideman, E.M. (1998) *Watershed Management: Guidelines for Indian Conditions*, Omega Scientific Publishers, New Delhi

Tordella, J. (2003) 'The Anti-Politics Machine Revisited: The Accommodation of Power and the Depoliticisation of Development and Relief in Rural India', Working paper series, No. 03–43, Destin, London School of Economics

Tornquist, O. and Tharakan, M. (1996) 'Democratisation and the Attempt to Renew the Radical Political Development Project', *Economic and Political Weekly*, July 27, pp 2041–2045

Toye, J. (1991) 'Is there a New Political Economy of Development?' in Colclough, C. and Manor, J. (eds), *States or Markets? Neoliberalism and the Development Policy Debate*, Clarendon Press, Oxford

Toye, J. (1993) 'The New Political Economy applied to India's Development', in Toye, J. (ed.), *Dilemmas of Development*, Blackwell, Oxford

Thompson, E. P. (1963) *The making of the English working class*, Gollancz, London

Turton, C. (2000) 'Enhancing Livelihoods through Participatory Watershed Development in India', Working Paper 131, Overseas Development Institute, London

Vaidyanathan, A. M. (1994), 'Performance of Indian Agriculture since Independence', in Basu, K. (ed.), *Agrarian Questions*, Oxford University Press, New Delhi

Vaidyanathan, A. M. (1999), *Water Resource Management: Irrigation and Irrigation Development in India*, Oxford University Press, New Delhi

Van der Veer, P. (1994) *Religious Nationalism: Hindus and Muslims in India*, University of California Press, Berkeley and Los Angeles

Veron, R., Williams, G., Corbridge, S. and Srivastava, M. (2006) 'Decentralised Corruption or Corrupt Decentralisation? Community Monitoring of Poverty Alleviation Schemes in Eastern India', *World Development*, Volume 34, no. 11, pp 1922–1941

Wade, R. (1990), *Governing the Market: Economic Theory and the Role of Government in East Asian Industrialisation*, Princeton University Press, Princeton, New Jersey

Wade, R. (1994) *Village Republics: Economic Conditions for Collective Action in South India*, Institute for Contemporary Studies, San Francisco

Washbrook, D. (1973) 'Country Politics: Madras 1880 to 1930, in Gallagher, J., Johnson, G. and Seal, A. (eds), *Locality, Province and Nation: Essays on Indian Politics 1870 to 1940*, Cambridge University Press, Cambridge

Weber, M. (1981) *General Economic History*, Tramsaction Books, New Brunswick, NJ

Webster, N. (1992) 'Panchayat Raj in West Bengal: Popular Participation for the People or the Party?', *Development and Change*, Volume 23, no. 4, pp 129–163

Williams, D. and Young, T. (1994) 'Governance, the World Bank and Liberal Theory', *Political Studies*, XLII, pp 84–100

Wood, G. (1985) 'The Politics of Development Policy Labelling', in *Development and Change*, Volume 16, no. 16, pp 347–373

Wood, G. (1999) 'Concepts and themes: Landscaping social development', DFID, London

Woodhouse, P., Bernstein, H. and Hulme, D. (2000) (eds) *African Enclosures? The Social Dynamics of Wetlands in Drylands*, James Curry, Oxford

World Bank (1997) *World Development Report: The State in a Changing World*, Oxford University Press

Yadav, Y. (2004) 'The elusive mandate of 2004', *Economic and Political Weekly*, December 18

List of Websites

http://www.ashanet.org/conferences/asha-12/T223.1.PDF
http://www.dolr.nic.in/fguidelines.htm
http://www.fao.org/docrep/x5669e/x5669e06.htm#approachesmethods%20used%20 for%20people's%20participation
http://www.goodnewsindia.com/Pages/content/inspirational/paniPanchayat.htm
www.samprag.org
http://upgov.up.nic.in/watershed/ncsaxena.htm

INDEX

Abrams, Phil xxxv, xl
actor-network theory, for development
projects xxiii, xxvi
actors and agencies, for depoliticization
project xxi–xxiv
AICRPDA *see* All-India Coordinated
Research Project for Dryland
Agriculture (AICRPDA)
Akali Dal 38
All-India Coordinated Research Project for
Dryland Agriculture (AICRPDA) 56
All India Coordination Committee of
Communist Revolutionaries 46
Andhra Pradesh, politics in 86;
administrative arrangements for WSD
programmes 94–5; dalit movement
97; depoliticization of Kurnool WSD
programme 106–9, 121–3, 132–4;
factionalism in Rayalseema region
99; NTR's 'welfarist/populist' agenda
87; OBC mobilization 97; peasant
castes, domination of 95; regional
dimensions of dominance in 95–105;
secessionist movements in Telangana
region 98–9; *see also* Lilpauram
village; Malligundu village; Naidu,
Chandrababu
Andhra Pradesh Farmers Management of
Irrigation Systems Act 129
anti-politics 205–6; association with
development xviii; beingness of
25–6; dark side of 16–23; and
depoliticization 1–5; history of
5–16; and Indian state xxv–xxvii;
politics within xvii–xxi;; thrust of
development, significance 196–9

*The Anti-Politics Machine: "Development,"
Depoliticisation and Bureaucratic Power in
Lesotho* (Ferguson) 1
anti-tribal coalition xxxix
Ashok Mehta Committee (1978) xxxi
'autonomous' economy, construction of
6–7; 'disembedded' economy 7–10;
economy as field of intervention
10–13; factors influencing
6; rationality, planning and
development for 13–16
autonomous individuals 155

Baba Amte Centre 150, 190
Backward Caste group xxxviii–xxxix
Bagli village 112, 113
Bahujan Samaj Party (BSP) 40, 98
Balwantrai Mehta Committee (1957) xxx
Bardhan, Pranab 32
Baviskar, A. 78, 103–4, 109, 112, 142, 164
'benami' land, forcible occupation of 46
Bharatiya Janata Party (BJP) 40–5, 89, 100,
139
Bharti, Uma 101
Bhave, Vinoba 47
'Bhoodan' (voluntary land redistribution)
movement 47
Bhopal Declaration 101
biotic production 61
BJP *see* Bharatiya Janata Party (BJP)
Bomireddypalli village 121
British India: notions of modernity
and statehood in xxxiv; principle
of 'colonial difference' 27; village
panchayats in xxx
BSP *see* Bahujan Samaj Party (BSP)

Canadian International Development
  Agency (CIDA) 2
CAPART *see* Council for Advancement
  of Rural Action and Peoples'
  Technology (CAPART)
capitalism: defined 8; development of 8–9
capitalist development: 'rational' strategy
  of 32; state-initiated 33
CDP *see* Community Development
  Programme (CDP)
Central Research Institute for Dryland
  Agriculture (CRIDA) 56
Central Soil and Water Conservation
  Research and Training Institute
  (CSWRTI) 56
centralized economic planning xxxii
CH Hanumantha Rao Committee 63
Charitable Trusts Act, 1950 114
Chatterjee, P. xxxv, 14–16, 24, 27–9, 31
Chhatra Yuwa Sangharsha Vahinee 47
Chief Minister's Empowerment of Youth
  Programme 168
CIDA *see* Canadian International
  Development Agency (CIDA)
CMP *see* Community Mobilization
  Programme (CMP)
collective action, economic and social
  conditions for 5
'colonial difference', principle of 27
colonial rule, and nature of rationality
  26–9
colonization of Egypt 11–12
Communist Party of India (Marxist)
  (CPI-M) xxxi, 38, 46
community-based organizations xxviii
Community Development Programme
  (CDP) xxx, xxv, 35
community-level institutions 4
community-management xxx
Community Mobilization Programme
  (CMP) 165
Congress party *see* Indian National
  Congress
consensual communities 155
consent, in WSD participatory practice
  203–4; Malligundu village 172–8;
  NGO's use of 182–90; *see also*
  Kurnool WSD programme

constitutional amendment bill, for
  panchayat reform xxxii
Council for Advancement of Rural Action
  and Peoples' Technology (CAPART)
  114, 149; guidelines 80
CPI (Marxist-Leninist) 46
CPI-M *see* Communist Party of India
  (Marxist) (CPI-M)
CRIDA *see* Central Research Institute for
  Dryland Agriculture (CRIDA)
CSWRTI *see* Central Soil and Water
  Conservation Research and Training
  Institute (CSWRTI)

dalit politics 97; Bhopal Declaration 101
dalits: exploitation by high caste politicians
  40; political mobilization of 39; *see
  also* Scheduled Castes (SC)
DDP *see* Desert Development Programme
  (DDP)
DDRC *see* District Development and
  Review Committee (DDRC)
decentralization policies 196, 199–201;
  actors and agencies xxi–xxiv;
  communitarian arguments for xxix; for
  development xviii; factors influencing
  xvi; history of xxix–xxxiv; Naidu,
  Chandrababu 86–9; New Political
  Economy (NPE) view of xxvii;
  Singh, Digvijay 89–92; and State
  xxvii–xxix; for structural reform and
  political mobilization xxxi; watershed
  development (WSD), in India xxiii,
  51–2, 65–8; *see also* depoliticization
decision-making xvi; community-based
  xxxvii
degraded lands 61
'deinstitutionalization' of Indian politics 37
democratic politics, expansion of xvi
Department of Land Resources (DoLR) 64
Department of Women and Child Welfare
  (DWCRA) 168
*Depoliticising Development: The World Bank and
  Social Capital* (Harriss) 2
depoliticization 51–2, 65–8, 196, 199–201,
  204–5; of Dewas WSD programme
  109–15; of Kurnool WSD
  programme 106–9, 121–3, 132–4

Desert Development Programme (DDP) 63
Development Hegemony: NGOs and the State in India (Kamat) 2
development planning 25
DFO *see* Divisional Forest Officer (DFO)
Dharia Committee xxxiv, 61–3
Directive Principles of State Policy xxx
dirigisme syndrome 34
'disembedded' economy 7–10
District Development and Review Committee (DDRC) 88
District Planning Committee Act, 1995 90
District Planning Committees (DPCs) 88, 90
District Rural Development Agency (DRDA) 66, 88, 92, 93, 110, 142, 180
District Watershed Advisory Committee (DWAC) 67, 93, 107, 110
Divisional Forest Officer (DFO) 130
DMK *see* Dravida Munnetra Kazhagam (DMK)
DoLR *see* Department of Land Resources (DoLR)
dominance politics 86; atrocities against *dalits* and backward castes 97; caste-based mobilization against Brahmin domination 95; landed gentry of Telangana region 95–6; in Madhya Pradesh 99–105; of Rajputs and Khatis in Kishangarh village 135–8; regional dimensions 95–105; secessionist movements in Telangana region 98–9
donor-driven development project xvii
DPCs *see* District Planning Committees (DPCs)
Dravida Munnetra Kazhagam (DMK) 38
DRDA *see* District Rural Development Agency (DRDA)
dryland areas 55–6
Dube, S. C. 123
Dumont, L. 123
Dunn, John xviii, 18, 19, 22, 24
DWAC *see* District Watershed Advisory Committee (DWAC)
DWCRA *see* Department of Women and Child Welfare (DWCRA)

East Asian developmental states 4
Egypt, colonization of 11–12
electoral politics, impact on development in India 25
Employment Assurance Scheme (EAS) 64
Enlightenment in Europe 27
Enron project 44
'entry-point' activities (EPAs) 169
erosion-prone lands, protection of 61
Eswaran Committee 77

faction-villages 109
farmhouses 61
Ferguson, James xvii, 1, 18, 195; *The Anti-Politics Machine: "Development," Depoliticisation and Bureaucratic Power in Lesotho* 1; ideas on depoliticization 3
Fine, Ben 4
Foucault, Michel xix, 1, 10, 72–3

Gandhi, Indira 37, 38; declaration of national emergency 47; repression of Naxalites 46
Gandhi, Mahatma 39
Gandhi, Rajiv 41
Gaur, Babu Lal 101
ghaat-neeche xxxviii–xxxix, 104–5, 111–17, 112, 121, 142, 144, 150, 156, 182, 189, 193, 194, 200
ghaat-upar xxxviii, 104, 110–11, 115, 200
Government of India Act (1935) xxx
gram swaraj 91, 92
'gramdan' movement 47
grassroots NGO xxiv
The Great Transformation (Polyani) 7
Green Revolution 37, 54–6, 97
Gupta, A. 101–2

Hansen, T. B. xxvi, 28, 35–6, 43–4
Hardiman, D. 99
Hardin, G. 71
Hariyali guidelines 81
Harriss, John 2
Hindu deshmukhs 96
Hindu Mahasabha xxx
Hindu nationalism, rise of 41–5
Hoffman, J. 156

ICAR *see* Indian Council for Agricultural Research (ICAR)
ICRISAT *see* International Crop Research Centre for the Semi-Arid Tropics (ICRISAT)
India: bureaucratic functioning in 28; colonial rule and nature of rationality 26–9; decolonization and nation-building 14; development planning and politics 25; Directive Principles of State Policy xxx; history of decentralization policies xxix–xxxiv; National Planning Committee 15; panchayat reform policies xxxiii; as rent seeking society 34; state-society relationships in xxxiv–xxxvii
Indian Council for Agricultural Research (ICAR) 56
Indian Councils Act (1861) xxx
Indian democracy 34–6; pluralization of politics and rise of lower castes 37–41; radical and confrontationist politics 45–8; rise of Hindu nationalism and 41–5
Indian Easements Act (1882) 185
Indian National Congress xxx, 32, 38, 89, 96, 97, 100
Indian politics, communalization of 41
Integrated Watershed Development Project (IWDP) 56
International Crop Research Centre for the Semi-Arid Tropics (ICRISAT) 56
International Women's Year 47
interventionism, syndrome of 34
intra-organizational dynamics, concept of xxiv
IWDP *see* Integrated Watershed Development Project (IWDP)

Jaffrelot, C. 38, 42
Janmabhoomi fund 87
Janmabhoomi initiative 85, 87–8, 175
Jawahar Gram Samriddhi Yojana (JGSY) 64
Joint Forestry Management (JFM) xxxiii, 65
Joshi, Kailash 104

Kamat, Sangeeta 2
Kamma community 86, 95–7, 99, 116, 200
Kant, Immanuel 156
Kapu community 38, 95–7
Kaviraj, Sudipta 26, 28, 48
KDRSO *see* Kurnool District Rural Service Organization (KDRSO)
Kerr, J. 75
Keynes, John Maynard 12
Khan, Mahbub 143, 145–6, 184–5
Khan, Majid 190
Kishangarh village 111, 134–42; agriculture in 137; of caste-based polarization and crime 136–7; denial of consent and project expedience in 178–82; dominance of Rajputs and Khatis 135–8; formation of watershed committees 140–2; panchayat politics in 138–40; Rajiv Gandhi Watershed Mission 134–5; water resources 137
Kumarappa, J. C. 15
Kurnool District Rural Service Organization (KDRSO) 108, 112
Kurnool WSD programme: allocation of project funds 161; calculations of cost and consent 161–3; collective decision-making in 163; consensual community, role of 159–66; depoliticization 106–9, 121–3, 132–4; individual consent and contribution 163–4; itemized protocol of participation 163–4; minor irrigation (MI) 161–2; paperworks 164–5; practice of securing sammati-patrams 166–7; project action plan 160–1; project transactions 165–6

Lachappakunta 127
Lal, Mungeri 101
land reform policies 32
Land Use Survey 60, 61
Left Democratic Front (LDF) xxxi
Leftwich, A. 17, 18
Lilpauram village 108–9; agriculture in 124–5; backward castes 122; caste relations in 123–4; KWO's project initiation rituals in 166–72;

landownership 124–5; panchayats
128–30; Reddy 'domination' 124–6,
128–9, 132–3, 166; SC households
125–6; sources of water 125; WSD
action plan 160
L'kotalla village 121
local institutions, in WSD programmes
77–82, 201–2
Locke, John 156
lower castes: political mobilization of 40;
reservations for educational seats and
governmental jobs 39; rise of 37–41

MacIntyre, Alasdair xxvii
macroeconomics, micro-foundations of 5
Madhya Pradesh, politics in 86;
administrative arrangements for
WSD programmes 92–4; Bhopal
Declaration 101; depoliticization of
Dewas WSD programme 109–15;
Dewas district, dimensions of
dominance in 104–5; domination of
upper castes (Brahmins, Rajputs and
Banias) 99–100; Kishangarh village
134–42; OBC mobilization 101–2;
regional dimensions of dominance in
99–105; tribal dispossession of forests
102–3
Madhya Pradesh Panchayat Raj Act,
1997 90
Mahajan Commission 100
Malligundu village 108–9, 121; Boya–
Reddy hostility 131; caste relations
126; dialectics of consent for WSD
programme 172–8; economic
deprivation and suffering in 127; land
ownership 126–7; panchayats 130–2;
Reddy domination within village
127–8, 130–1; WSD action plan 160
Mandal Commission 39, 40, 41
Mandal Commission Report 100–1
Manor, J. 78, 90, 99
Maoist movement 46–7
market-capitalist economy 7
market society 7
Marx, Karl 8–10, 14, 20, 156
Mazumdar, Charu 46
Meghapalli village 144

micro-watersheds 72
Millennium Development Goals 5
milli-watersheds 110
Ministry of Environment and Forests
(MoEF) 64
Ministry of Rural Areas and
Employment 63
Ministry of Rural Development (MORD)
52, 63–4, 63–6, 65, 66–7, 69, 73, 80,
81, 107, 188
Mitchell, Timothy xxxv, 12, 24
Montague Chelmsford Reforms (1919) xxx
MORD see Ministry of Rural Development
(MORD)
Morley–Minto Reforms (1909) xxx
Mosse, David xviii, 73, 166, 182
MP Land Revenue Code (1950) 113
Muralidhar Rao Commission Report 97
Murray-Li, Tanya 155
Muslim 'jagirdars' 95
Muslim League xxx
Muslim Women's Bill (1986) 41

Nag, Kartar Singh 148–9, 190
Naidu, Chandra Mohan 130–1
Naidu, Chandrababu xxxiii, xxxviii, 85,
98; attitude towards bureaucracy
89; decentralization policies
86–9; governance reforms 85;
Janmabhoomi initiative 85, 87–8;
pro-panchayat steps 88
National Democratic Alliance 45
National Front government 39
National Planning Committee 15
National Wastelands Board 62
National Watershed Development
Programme for Rainfed Areas
(NWDPRA) 56, 58, 64
nationalist movement 35
Naxalbari and Peasant Struggle Assistance
Committee (NKSSS) 46
Naxalbari peasant uprising 46, 47
Neelpura village 110, 113–15, 183;
Bhimpura–Neelpura panchayat
148–9, 187; leadership and
domination in 143–5; pattern of land
ownership 143; watershed committee
145–8; watershed project in 142–3

new institutional economics (NIE) 4
new institutionalism (NI) theory 71–2
New Political Economy (NPE) xxvii, 33, 70, 72
newly independent state, concept of 30–4
NIE *see* new institutional economics (NIE)
NKSSS *see* Naxalbari and Peasant Struggle Assistance Committee (NKSSS)
North, Douglass 4
NPE *see* New Political Economy (NPE)
NWDPRA *see* National Watershed Development Programme for Rainfed Areas (NWDPRA)
OBC *see* Other Backward Classes (OBC)
Olson, M. 71
Ostrom, Elinor xxviii, 22, 71
Other Backward Classes (OBC) 100; intensified democratic revolution 39; political mobilization of 86, 97, 116; reservations for educational seats and governmental jobs 39; upper-class caste dominance 102

Panchayat Act, 2001 91
Panchayat Raj Institutions (PRIs) xxx–xxxii
panchayats xxiii
Parthasarathy Committee 77, 80
participatory irrigation management (PIM) 129
participatory rural appraisal (PRA) exercises 67
participatory watershed projects 60, 67–8
passive revolution 31–2
Patel, Akshay 138–9
Patwa, Sunderlal 104
peasant castes of Andhra, domination of 95–6
peasant mobilization 37, 46
PIA *see* Project Implementing Agency (PIA)
PIM *see* participatory irrigation management (PIM)
planning commission xxv, 25, 48
Planning Committee xxv
politico-social organizations 43
Politics (Aristotle) 17
politics in India, pluralization of 37–41
Polyani, Karl xix, 7–14

Post-Washington Consensus (PWC) xxviii, xxxiii, 4
poverty, depoliticisation of 2
Poverty Reduction Strategy Papers (PRSPs) 5
Prabhari Mantri 91
Prasad, A. 102
PRIs *see* Panchayat Raj Institutions (PRIs)
'Prisoner's Dilemma', concept of 21–2
private corporations xxviii
productivist shift, in Indian agriculture 55
Progressive Organization of Women 47
Project Implementing Agency (PIA) xxxvii, xxxix, 66–8, 81, 107–8, 121–2, 142
PRSPs *see* Poverty Reduction Strategy Papers (PRSPs)
public capital 32
Public Law 480 55
Purogami Stree Sangathana 47
Putnam, Robert 2
PWC *see* Post-Washington Consensus (PWC)

quota politics 39

radical confrontations 45–8
radical political economy, concepts of 5
radical student movements 47
rainfed agriculture 56
Rajiv Gandhi Technology Missions 89–90
Rajiv Gandhi Watershed Mission 109, 114
Ram, Kanshi 40, 97, 98
Ram, Raja 139
'ramjanmabhoomi' issue 41
Rao, N. T. Rama (NTR) 86–7, 96; populist schemes 98
Rashtriya Swayamsevak Sangh (RSS) 41
rational consensus 156
Rayalseema Development Trust (RDT) 108
Rayalseema region 99, 130
RDT *see* Rayalseema Development Trust (RDT)
Reddy, Gangadhar 129, 133
Reddy, Harekrishna 128, 130
Reddy, K. Brahmanana 96
Reddy, Mohan 128
Reddy, N. Sanjeeva 96

Reddy, Narayan 121
Reddy, Satya 128–9, 131, 167–8
Reddy, Sriram 174
Reddy caste 96
Republican Party of India (RPI) 39
Roseberry, W. 157
Roy, D. 102
RPI *see* Republican Party of India (RPI)
RSS *see* Rashtriya Swayamsevak Sangh (RSS)
rural development project 2
rural livelihoods programme xvi
Rural Works Programme 58, 63

Samaj Pragati Sahyog (SPS) 80, 112–15, 143–50; consent and project implementation of WSD programme 182–90
Samajwadi Party 40, 98
Sangh Parivar 43, 44
Sardaan, Oliver de xxii
Sarkar, S. 103
Sarkaria Commission (1983–1988) xxxii
sarpanch raj 91
'Sarvodaya' movement 47
Savarkar, Veer 45
Saxena, N. C. 74
Scheduled Castes (SC) 38–40, 66, 95
Schmitt, Carl 21
Scott, James 157
self-deception, concept of 16
Self Help Groups (SHGs) 173
Seventh Plan document of the Government of India (GOI) 56
Shah Bano Case 41
Shiv Sena 44
Simple, Moral, Accountable, Responsive and Transparent government (SMART government) 89
Singh, Arjun 100–1
Singh, Charan 37, 39
Singh, Digvijay xxxiii, 85, 101, 115, 144–6; decentralization policies 89–92; governance reforms 85; panchayat raj system 90, 91; Rajiv Gandhi Technology Missions 89–90
Singh, Lakhan 144
Singh, V. P. 39

Smith, Adam 7
social capital 2
social justice, depoliticisation of 2
soil and water conservation (SWC) works 52–4, 62–3, 74
soil conservation projects xvi
Sombart, Werner 9
Srinivas, M. N. 123
state-market-society relationships xxviii
state socialism 7
state-society relationships in India xxxiv–xxxvii
State Watershed Programme Implementation and Review Committee (SWPIRC) 65–6
Stree Mukti Sanghatana 47
SWC *see* soil and water conservation (SWC) works

Taylor, Charles xxvii
Taylor, Michael xxviii, 71
Telangana, peasant insurrection in 46
Telugu Desam Party (TDP) xxxiii, 38, 85, 96–7
temple renovation rituals 42
Third World nations 55
Tonk-Khurd tehsil 110–11

United Front government 46
United Progressive Alliance 45
universal egoism, concept of 17
universalization 155–6

Vakil, Jawahar Lal 139
Van Suraksha Samiti (VSS) 129
Varma, Suren 110
Veldurthi mandal 129
VHP *see* Vishwa Hindu Parishad (VHP)
village panchayats xxx, xxxi, 67, 119, 123, 128, 129, 131, 132, 134, 138, 144
village self-government xxv, xxx
village wastelands 62
Vishwa Hindu Parishad (VHP) 41
Vision 2020 document 89
VSS *see* Van Suraksha Samiti (VSS)

Washington Consensus xxviii, 3, 4
WASSAN 108

water conservation projects xvi, 113, 144
Water Users' Association (WUA) 129–30
watershed development (WSD), in India:
annual expenditure 64; bureaucratic
responses to 60–5; community-
based participation, issues in 69–73;
consent and community in 157–9;
decentralization and depoliticization
of 51–2, 65–8, 105–15; Dharia
Committee's recommendations
61–3; dissonance between liberals
and communitarians 70–1; equity
issues 74–7; guidelines 65–8;
Hanumantha Rao Committee
recommendations 63; New
Agricultural Strategy (NAS) 54–5,
54–6; non-elected village watershed
committee (WC) 65; panchayat
vs. watershed committee 78–9; as
political promotion for winning
elections 105–6; and poverty
reduction 74–5; problem of
dedicated local institutions 77–82;
resource ownership and property

rights, issue of 75; sexual division of
labour in participation 76; soil and
water conservation (SWC) works
52–4, 62; through water harvesting
57–60; wage allocation, issue of
76–7; 'watershed plus' scheme 63
Watershed Development Fund (WDF) 68,
162
watershed development projects xvi, xxxiii;
state policies for decentralized and
participatory xxi, xxiii
Watershed Development Team (WDT)
66–8, 94
Wilcox, Wayne 100
World Bank xxviii, xxix, 2, 4, 5, 56, 58–9
World Hindu Council see Vishwa Hindu
Parishad (VHP)

Yadav, Subhash 100

Zilla Panchayat (ZP) 66–7, 88, 91, 110,
115
Zilla Parishad 88, 96
Zilla Sarkar 90, 91, 93, 110

Lightning Source UK Ltd.
Milton Keynes UK
UKOW050736160312

189073UK00001B/55/P